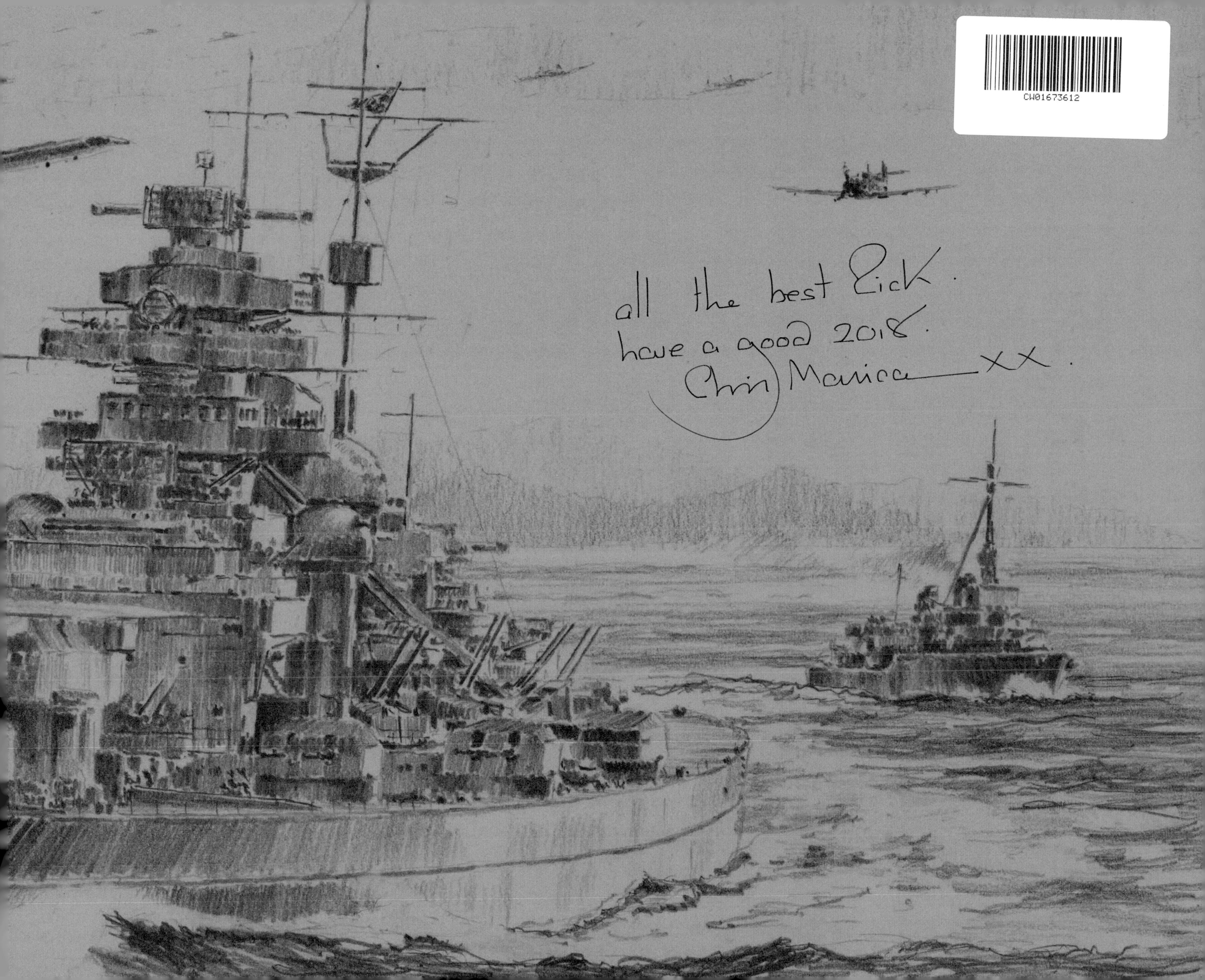
all the best Rick.
have a good 2018.
Chris Marica xx.

WINGS OF WAR

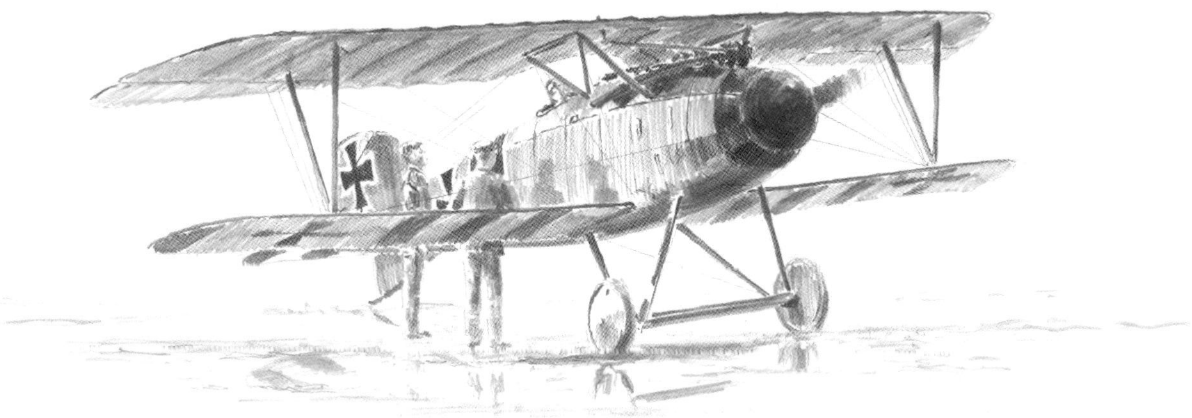

THE AVIATION AND MILITARY ART OF

ANTHONY SAUNDERS

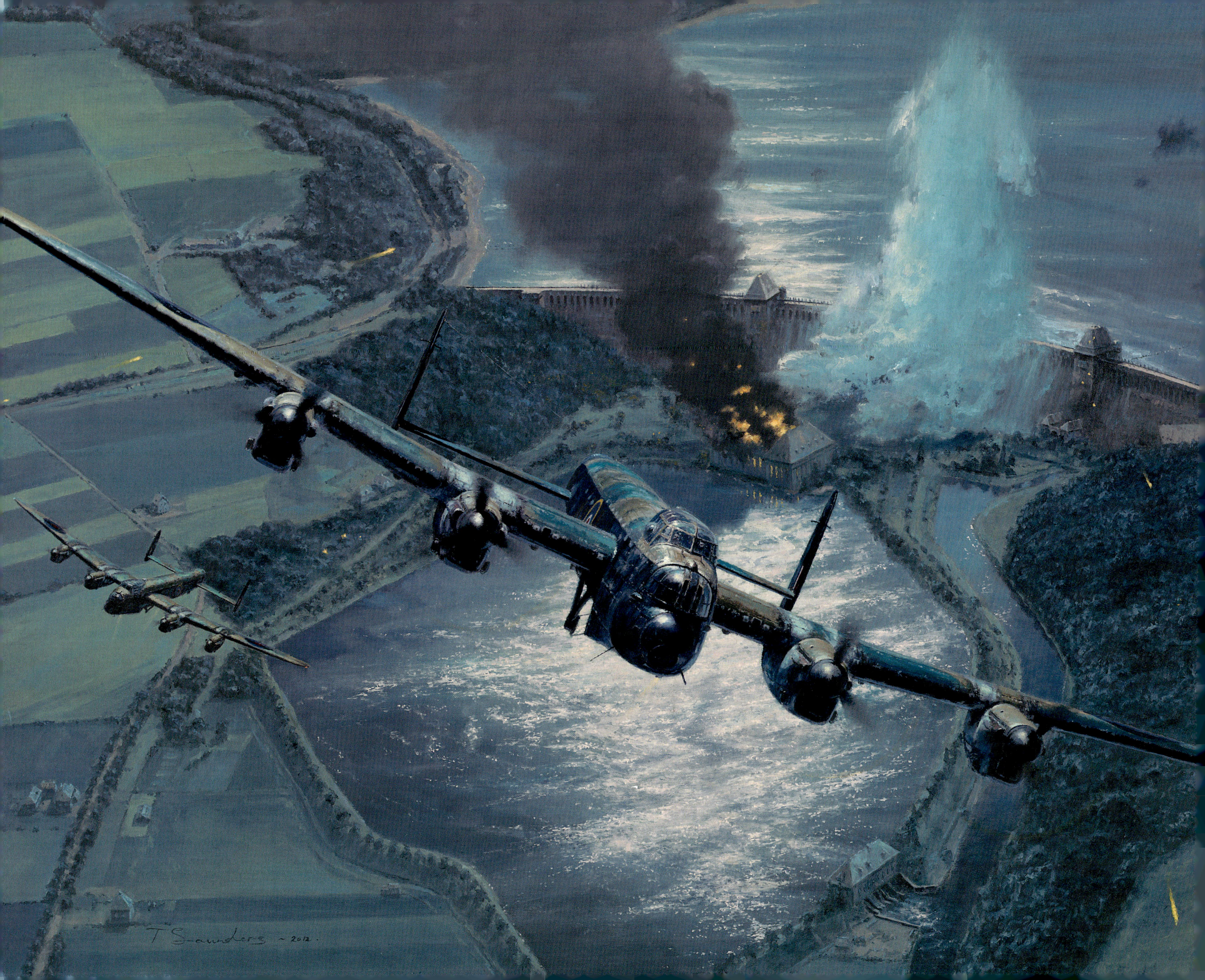
T Saunders - 2012

WINGS OF WAR

THE AVIATION AND MILITARY ART OF ANTHONY SAUNDERS

FOREWORD BY

Squadron Leader George 'Johnny' Johnson DFM

GRIFFON INTERNATIONAL

WINGS OF WAR
THE AVIATION AND MILITARY ART OF ANTHONY SAUNDERS

Many of the images featured in this book have been reproduced as limited edition prints by the Military Gallery.

www.militarygallery.com

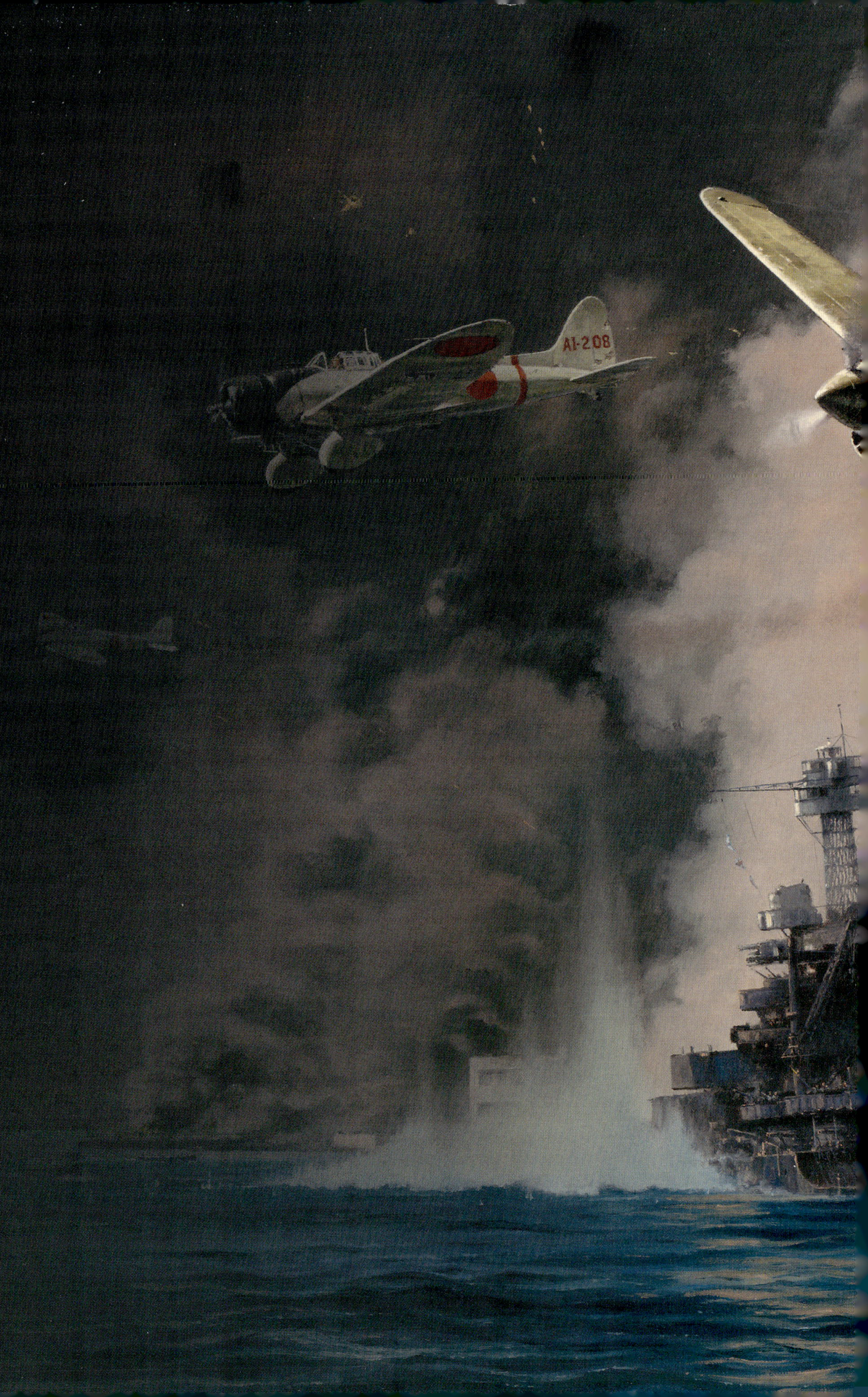

ISBN 978-0-9549970-6-9
A GRIFFON INTERNATIONAL BOOK

First published in the United Kingdom in 2016 by Griffon International Limited,
2 Station Approach, Wendover, Buckinghamshire, HP22 6BN

A catalogue record for this book is available from the British Library.

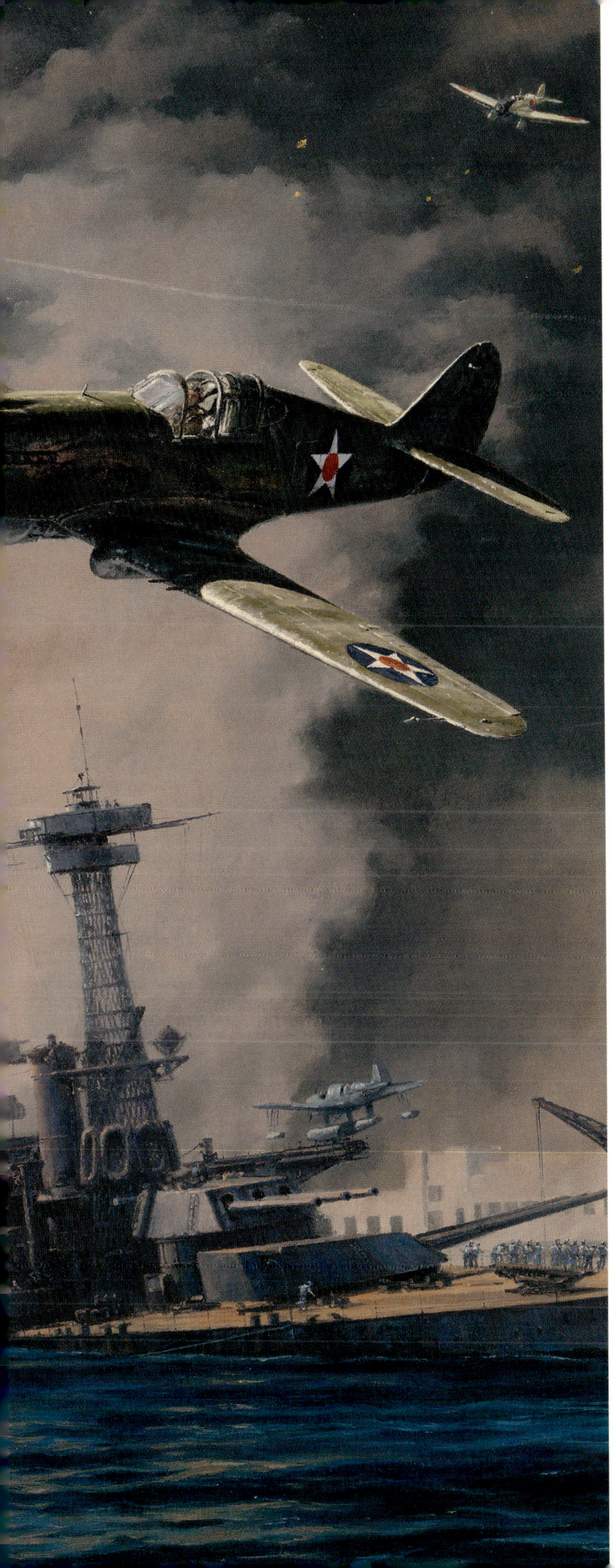

CONTENTS

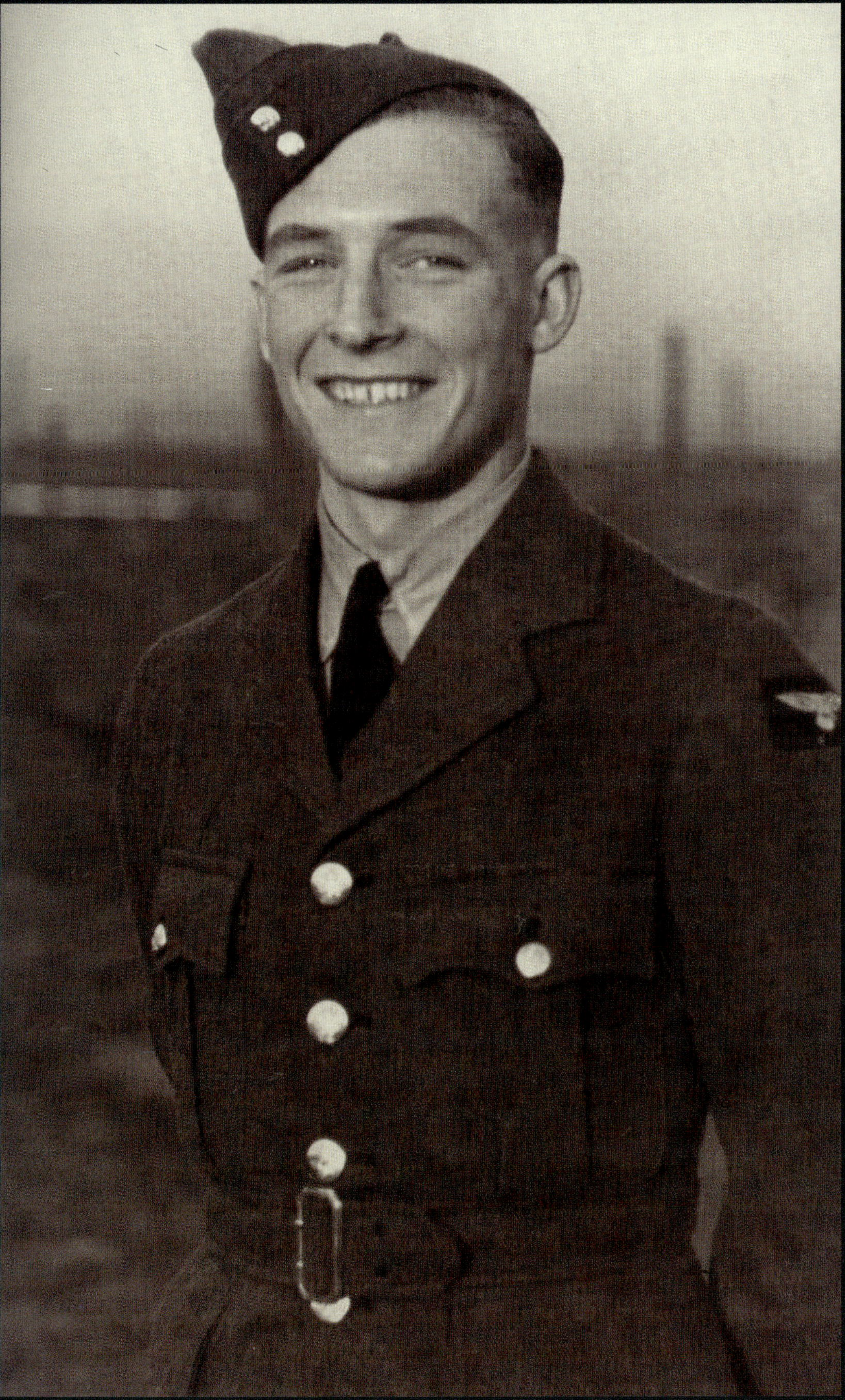

Johnny as a new recruit aged 19

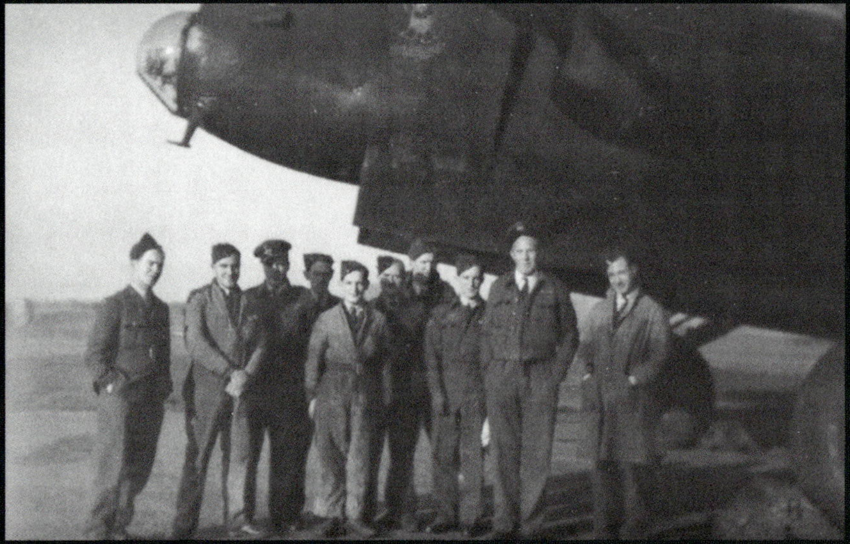

The Q-Queenie crew and ground crew, April 1943

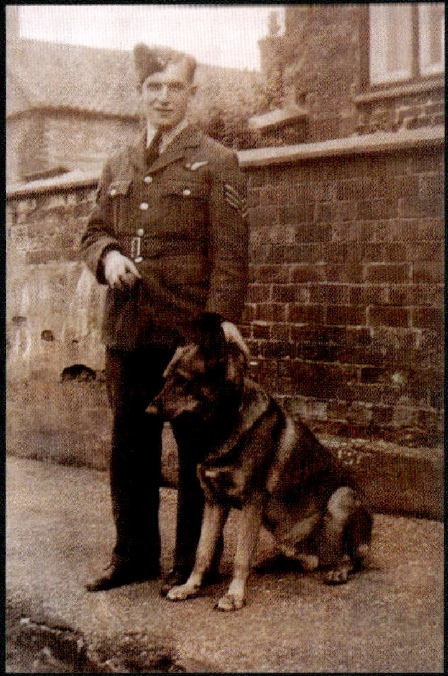

Johnny as a newly promoted Sergeant, spring 1942

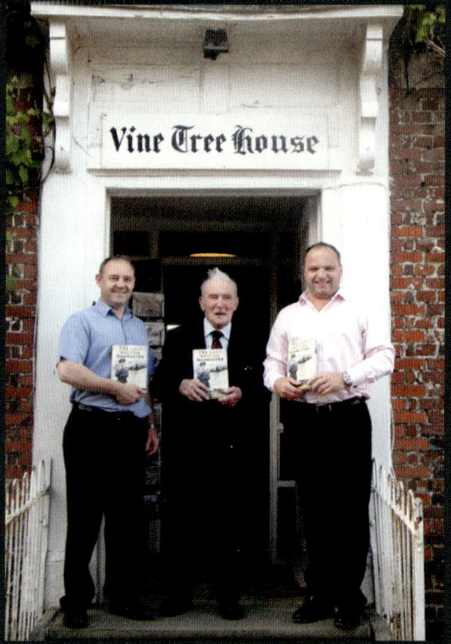

Johnny with Rick Taylor and Colin Hudson at Aces High Gallery, Wendover, for the launch of Johnny's book 'The Last British Dambuster'

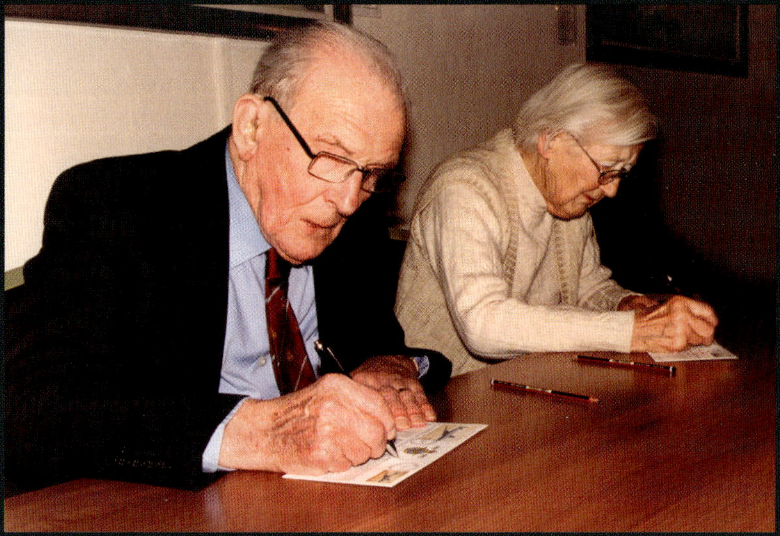

Photo: Mike Jowett

Johnny with Dr Mary Stopes-Roe, the daughter of Sir Barnes Wallis who invented the Bouncing Bomb, signing at an Aces High event

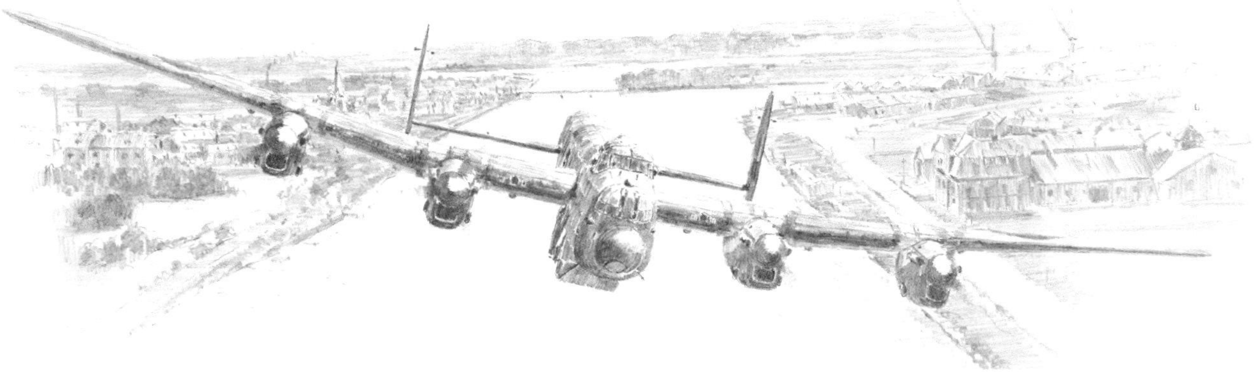

FOREWORD

by

Squadron Leader George 'Johnny' Johnson DFM

'Some are born great, some achieve greatness by their endeavours and some have greatness thrust upon them' so said Malvolio in Shakespeare's *Twelfth Night*. I would like to paraphrase the third part of that quotation by substituting the word 'greatness' with 'honour'. In that form the phrase signifies my feelings at being asked to write this Foreword to Anthony Saunders' wonderful book *Wings of War*. It is indeed an honour and a privilege.

At this stage I would like to stress the accuracy and attention to detail which is so much a pattern of Anthony's work. It reminds me of the great Robert Taylor. In his work, and also in Anthony's, you can see exactly what is happening just by looking at the picture. There is simply no need for written words; the story is there on canvas for all to see.

I hope that readers will accept that my main interests are in his many portrayals of The Dams Raid. In his painting *En-Route* it is the individual nature of the operation and the low flying that are clearly visible, whilst in *Dambusters* you can feel the excitement and satisfaction of the crew at the success of their operation. Similarly, he depicts the same feelings of the crew in *The Breach* as well as also showing damage to the other parts of the Dam and the German defences. I think *Final Briefing* beautifully captures the importance of crew co-operation in which each member carries out his duties to the best of his ability to ensure the ultimate success of the operation, and the companionship they have for each other. *Pathway to the Ruhr* is one of my particular favourites, a striking painting in which Anthony brings home the fact that it was a relative few who took part in the raid and he perfectly captures the feeling of loneliness that most of us felt.

There is one further painting that, in my eyes, stands out. It is *Strike on Berlin*. Berlin was very heavily defended and Anthony's graphic portrayal leaves no doubt in the observer's mind not only of the damage inflicted by that particular raid but by the immense bravery of those who took part.

I appreciate that this is just a brief appreciation of Anthony's work, but it is only the foreword. Of one thing I am sure and that is every reader will thoroughly enjoy this wonderful book.

Thank you Anthony for all your great work and may I wish you continued success in all your endeavours.

G.L. (Johnny) Johnson, D.F.M

G.L. (JOHNNY) JOHNSON

'Johnny' Johnson is the last surviving RAF veteran of the Dambuster Raid. On 16 May 1943 'Johnny' took off from RAF Scampton as Bomb-Aimer with American Joe McCarthy's crew in Lancaster AJ-T tasked with attacking and destroying the Sorpe Dam.

But things weren't that simple: their Lancaster was one of the reserve aircraft and therefore hadn't been fitted with the twin Aldis spotlights needed for accurately gauging their height. Nevertheless, after several dummy runs, 'Johnny' successfully released their bomb bang on target, scoring a direct hit. The dam, however, survived.

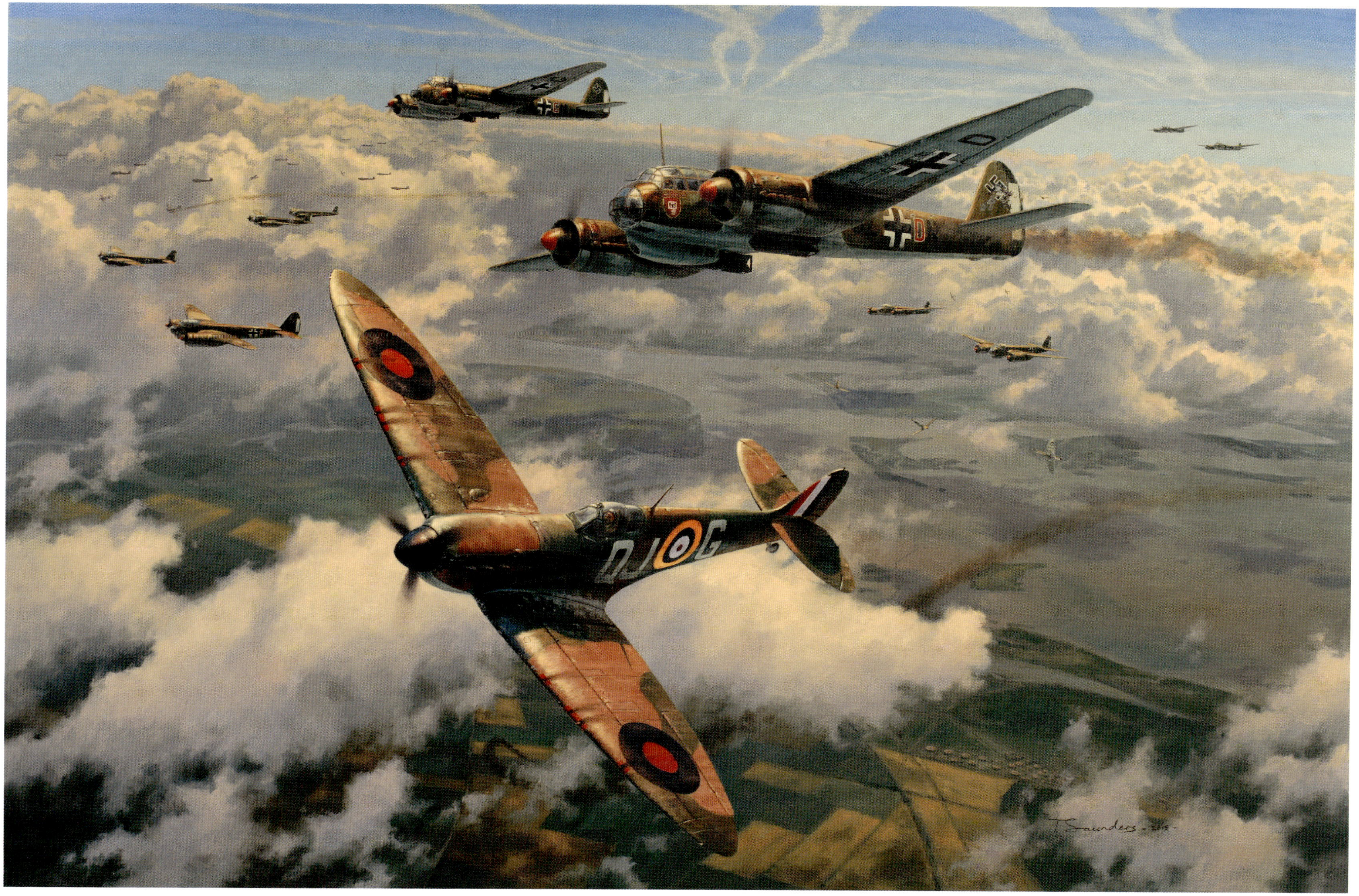

DECISIVE BLOW

IN THE COLLECTION OF MR ALAIN MARDLE

ANTHONY SAUNDERS

I've always loved aeroplanes, they seem to have been part of my life from the very beginning. One of the earliest things I can ever remember involved a plane but perhaps that has a lot to do with the fact that it was such a strange-looking one, an Armstrong Whitworth Argosy car transporter! All I remember is not the holiday in France that followed, but the huge excitement of seeing our Rover car being lifted on a large ramp through big, open doors in the nose of this strange-looking aircraft.

It was a couple of years later, aged five, when I first saw – and heard – Concorde fly low over our house and from then on I was hooked. I believe this was one of Concorde's earliest test flights and although the memory can play tricks, I'm sure it was only a few hundred feet in the air. I especially remember the deafening thunder of Concorde's engines – the noise alone was enough to enthuse any little boy.

I was born in Chelmsford in 1964 and as a child I was always drawing, I loved it. Recently I unearthed one of my first school reports. It had been packed away and hidden for years, and reading through it brought back memories of Sister Rosario, the strict Irish nun who had written it and who taught me at St Theresa's Roman Catholic Primary School. In her eyes I could do no right and would never amount to much, but her words brought a smile to my face as I read all I excelled in was art. It was a harsh, but I fear in hindsight, accurate observation. Even now, many years later, that report brought it all back especially the happy hours I'd spent in class drawing Spitfires whilst the other children stood behind my chair to watch.

It must have been around that time that my older brother, Paul, introduced me to the magical world of painting with oils. He'd just got a 'teach yourself oil painting' kit for his birthday, and I can still remember that first smell of turpentine. At that time he was the artistic one in the family, brilliant at drawing and making models, which was something else he introduced me to. We used to pin the completed models to our bedroom ceiling and engage in mock dogfights – I've never found out what our parents thought about all those pin holes!

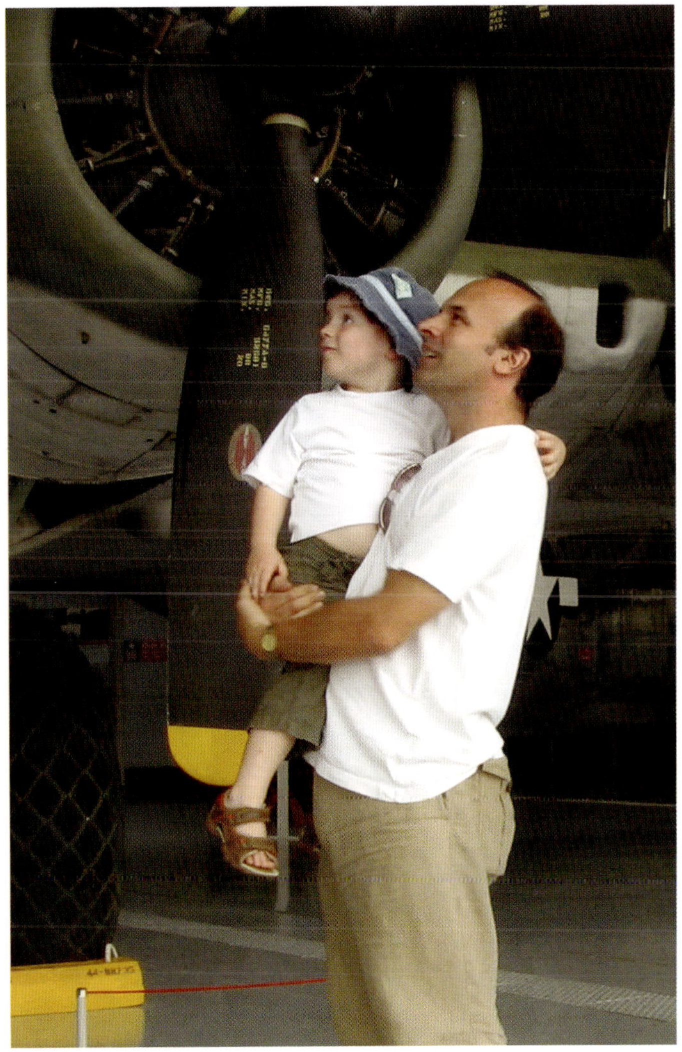

Many of those early models were made by Airfix, and at the time I was seriously impressed by the art on the front of the boxes. I've since learnt that many of them were painted by Roy Cross, a gifted artist who would later, like my favourite maritime painter John Stobart, produce some of the finest maritime paintings you'll ever see.

Whenever I'm asked what made me start painting aircraft in earnest, I never hesitate. It was Robert Taylor, or more specifically his first book, *The Air Combat Paintings of Robert Taylor*. In my early twenties I'd regularly walk into Colchester town centre from my parents' house and on the way I'd pass a little book shop which had all sorts of books displayed in the window. Nothing ever inspired me enough to venture inside until, one day, this wonderful-looking book appeared. I went straight in and asked if I could have a look. I remember that it was fairly expensive, but it took only a quick turn of the pages to know I just had to have it. Robert's book was inspirational. I still have it, and from the moment I read it all I wanted to do, one day, was become a professional artist. That was the dream at any rate.

Despite Sister Rosario's dire predictions, I learnt enough at school to go into engineering when I left, and served a four-year apprenticeship at the Colchester Lathe Company. I must have had some hidden talent because in 1986, I surprised everyone, including myself, by being named their 'Apprentice of the Year'. But it was later, after I had joined Anglian Water as a project engineer that I eventually decided to create a small publishing company of my own, producing limited edition prints of my aviation paintings in my spare time.

Looking back, I must either have had great self-belief or been extremely foolhardy because, after publishing the grand total of just four prints, I decided to go the

When I started publishing my own aviation prints and began to get better known, I received this unusual commission from my then employers at Anglian Water. As you can see it was a huge mural of the Red Arrows used to advertise the Clacton Air Show. Measuring 10 feet high and 50 feet long it won me far more acclaim than the day job – even the director wrote to thank me.

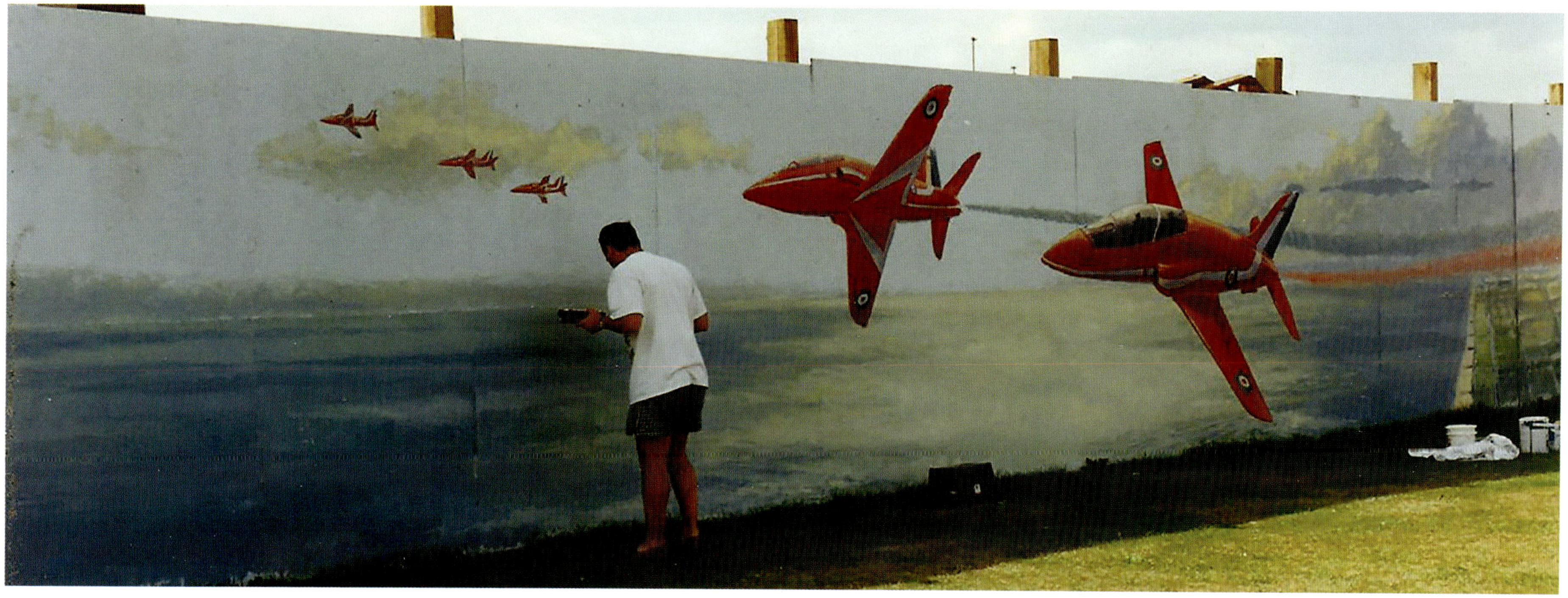

Taken at the opening of the 2005 Guild of Aviation Artists exhibition in the prestigious Mall Galleries in London – Amelia and Bernadette cast a critical eye over my work. I'm an associate member of the Guild and used to regularly exhibit in their annual exhibitions, as well as those of the Royal Society of Marine Artists.

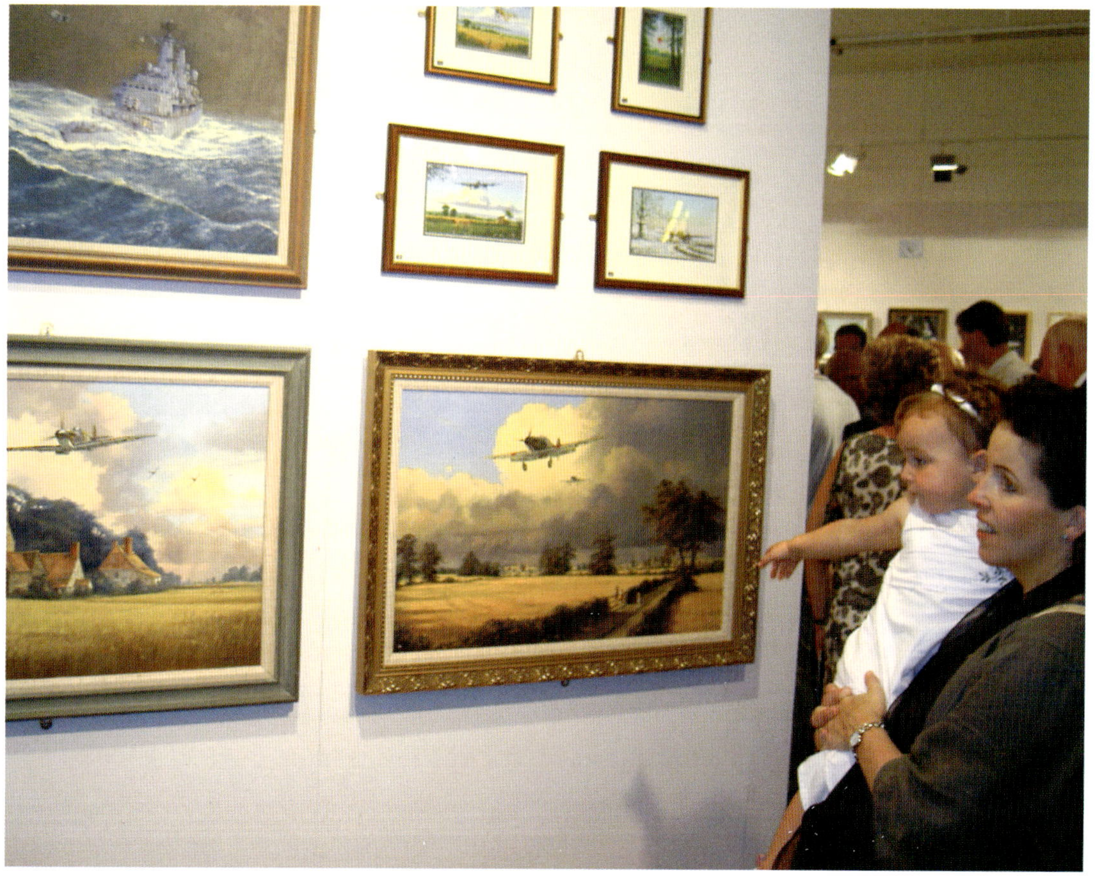

whole hog and advertise one of them in the Sunday Mail. You can imagine the cost, it set me back a lot of money, which I did get back – just. But what the whole operation taught me most was that trying to pursue three careers at the same time – project engineer, artist and self-publisher – was a step too far.

Although my own publishing efforts came to an abrupt end, I was lucky enough to find a publisher for some of my work and, in 2002, was asked to paint naval and maritime paintings on a full-time basis. It was a tough call to make. I'd only been married for a couple of years, having met my wonderful wife Bernadette on a blind date organised by my cousin Cheryl! I'd proposed to Bernadette in Castell'Arquato, a beautiful medieval hilltop village in Italy, the same village, incidentally, that would appear in one of my paintings – *Roam at Will*. She must have been carried away by the place because she actually agreed and said yes. And now here I was, two years later, suggesting that I give up my full-time job with Anglian Water to become a professional artist. I know a lot of wives might have baulked at the loss of security, especially as we were planning on having a family, but Bernadette was incredibly supportive and backed me all the way. I took the plunge and have never looked back.

Working from my studio at home, it has been a wonderful experience to watch our two children growing up and I consider myself very lucky that Amelia, our daughter who was born in 2002 and James who followed three years later, are so close at hand.

Working as a naval artist was great and even though I often managed to sneak in an aeroplane whenever I could, they weren't aviation paintings. That was my true passion, and what I'd always dreamt of was to be an aviation artist. Then in 2008 the unbelievable happened and my dream came true – I was invited to join the Military Gallery, the same company so closely associated with my favourite aviation artist, Robert Taylor.

It started with a Dambuster painting that I'd just completed and which I'd sent to Rick Taylor and Colin Hudson, who run the Military Gallery, as a purely speculative shot in the dark – he who dares and all that, but it worked! They asked me to paint another Dambuster painting, perhaps to see if the first hadn't been a lucky one off. When I duly supplied the painting I was stunned when they then asked if I'd like to join them.

To be working for the same company as Robert Taylor, whom I have so avidly followed and admired for so many years is a great honour. I can honestly say that I have fulfilled my ambition.

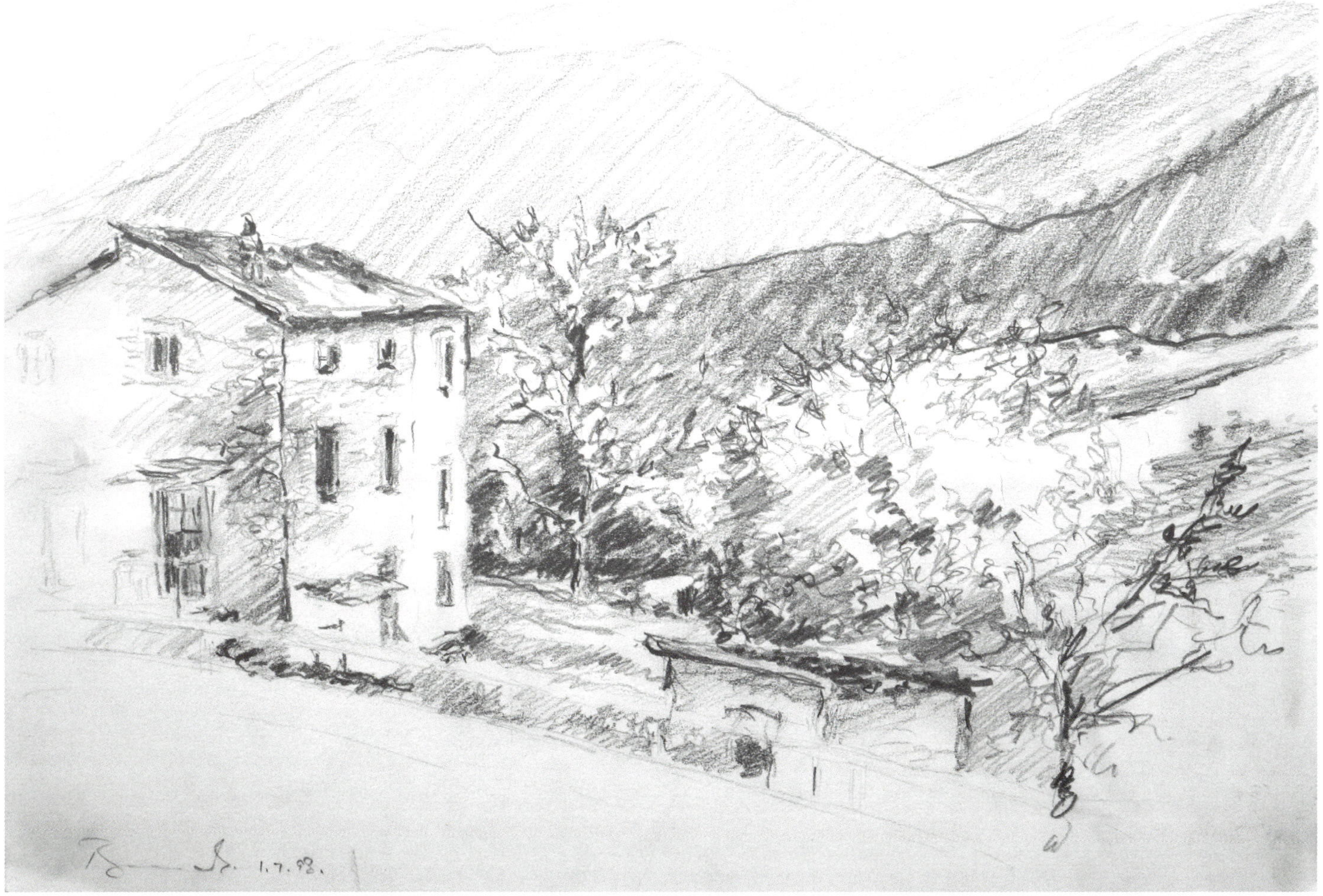

The family house nestled in the Apennine Mountains in Northern Italy

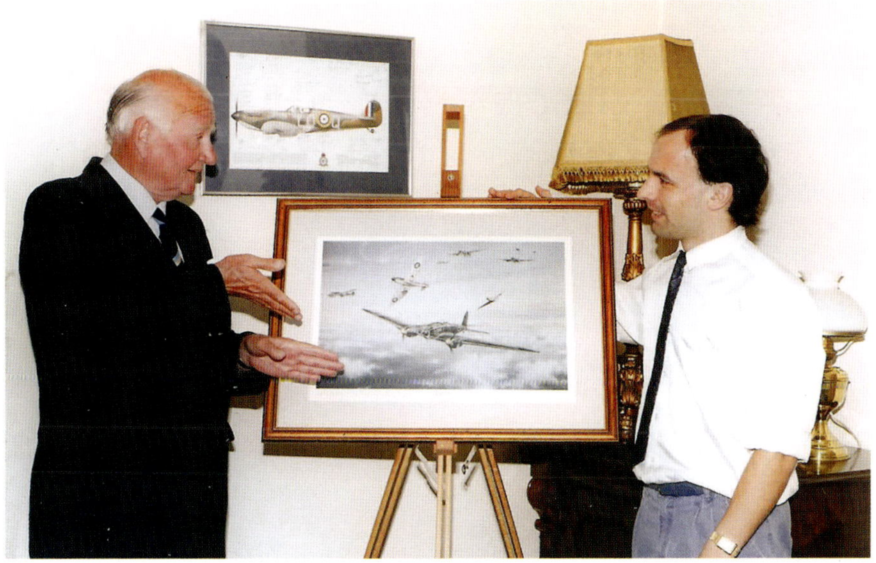

The famous Spitfire Ace 'Sandy' Johnstone chats about his encounter with a Heinkel 111 and an Me109 over Portsmouth in 1940. He, along with two other Battle of Britain veterans, had just signed 'Gauntlet', one of my first self-published prints. I had to travel the length and breadth of the country to get the signings done, which was an exciting exercise, and it gave me a good understanding of the process, and hard work, involved in getting a print on the market.

This was the first oil painting I ever attempted - Warwick Castle portrayed in a classical Victorian style! Other than going to life classes for a couple of years I've never had any 'formal' art training, and the canvas took me nearly a year to complete, but taught me some of the techniques I needed to learn about painting with oils.

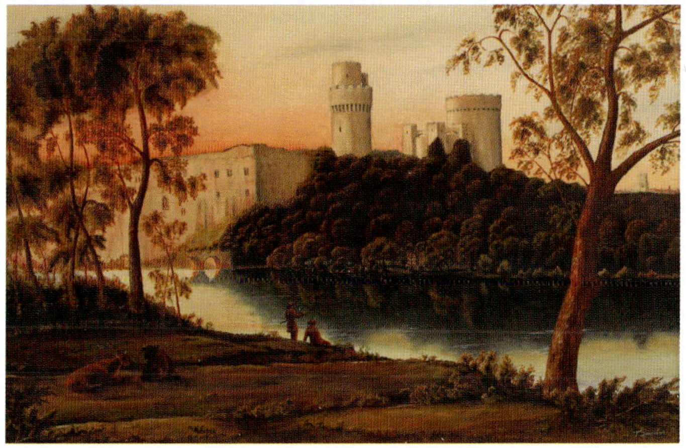

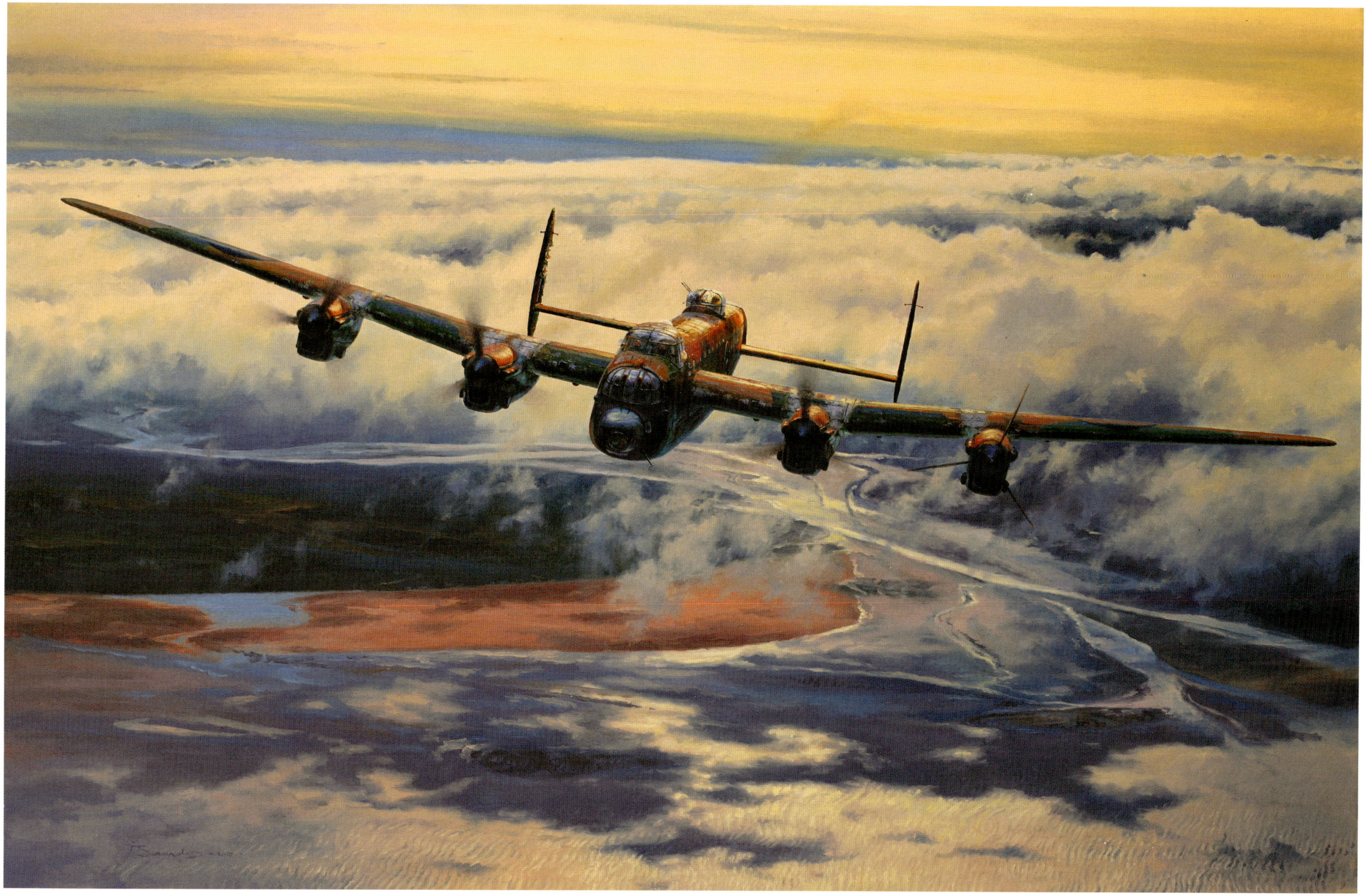

BACK FROM THE BIG CITY IN THE COLLECTION OF MR DAVID JEPHSON

THE PAINTINGS

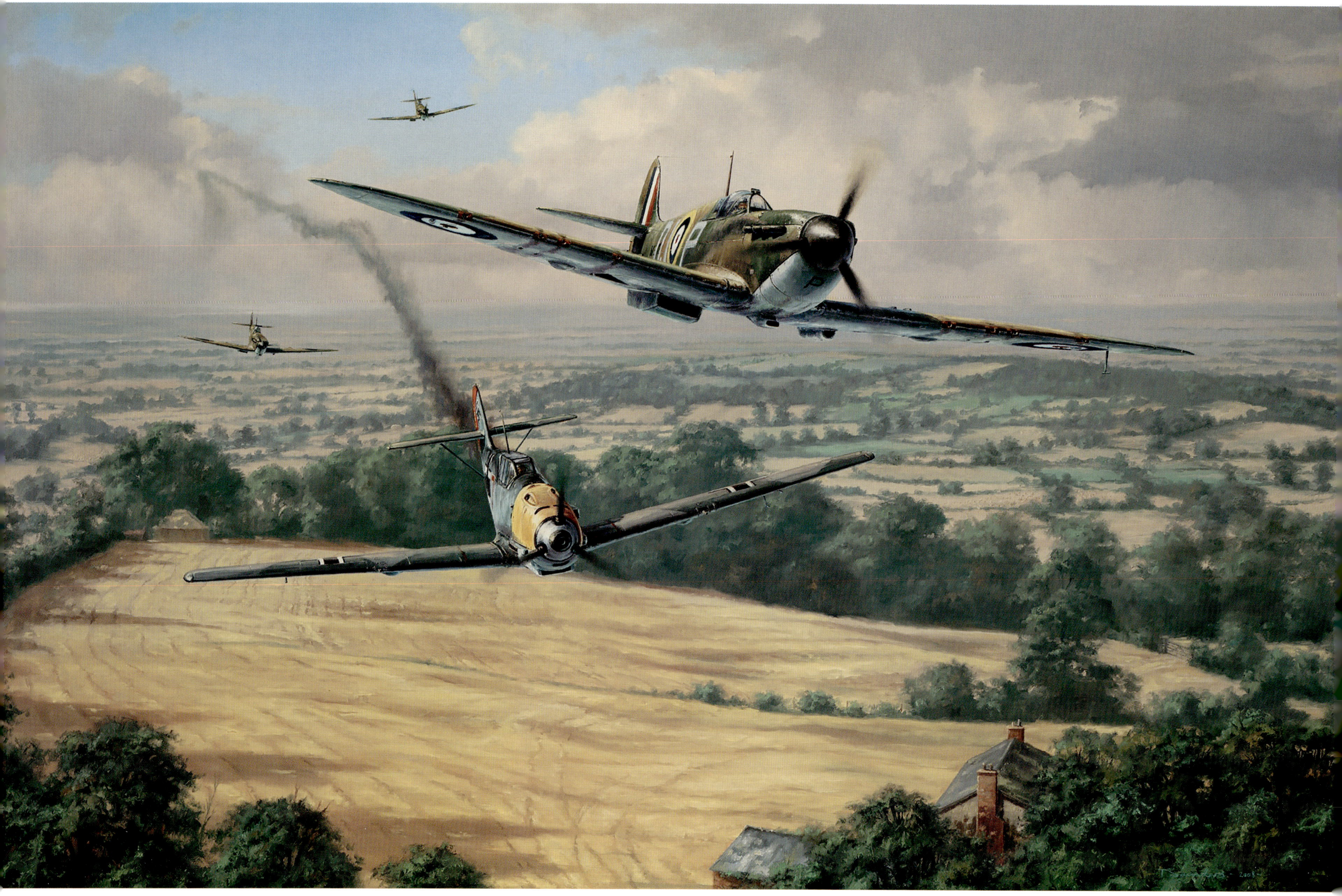

HIGH SUMMER IN THE COLLECTION OF MR & MRS P SHIPP

HIGH SUMMER

After joining the Military Gallery in 2008 my first commission was for two paintings featuring the Battle of Britain. One was to be a representation of the battle from an RAF point of view – prints of which would be signed by three Spitfire pilots who had fought in the Battle of Britain – and the other was to be a Luftwaffe subject, likewise signed by German veterans. I obviously wanted to make both paintings something special, I always do but especially as these were the first with my new publisher, but when you realise Robert Taylor is your new stable mate – well, let's just say it concentrates the mind!

The Battle of Britain has been depicted by aviation artists many times, and it's often difficult to come up with a composition, however unintentionally, that hasn't been tried by someone else in the past. In a way it's like composing a piece of music where a melody comes from your subconscious that you think is original, but you can't be quite sure that it's something you've heard somewhere before. It's the same with painting; perhaps the composition in my mind is from something I've seen in the past but forgotten about, till now. Unlike the vast array of music on offer, however, there haven't been so many Battle of Britain prints published that I don't know by now what most of them look like, but knowing what's out there with collectors is something to at least be aware of.

I sometimes find that leafing through books can trigger an idea for a painting, at other times ideas just come out of the blue at any time – maybe whilst taking the children to the park, or driving through the countryside, or perhaps watching a film. For *High Summer* the idea definitely came from a book, a tatty old thing that I'd bought in an antiquated book shop in Saffron Walden. Printed in black and white, and published just before the war, in 1937, it was called *The Country Life Picture Book of Britain*, and in it was a perfect photograph of exactly the type of landscape I was looking for. It's one of several similar books depicting the countryside of pre-war Britain and, when in need of

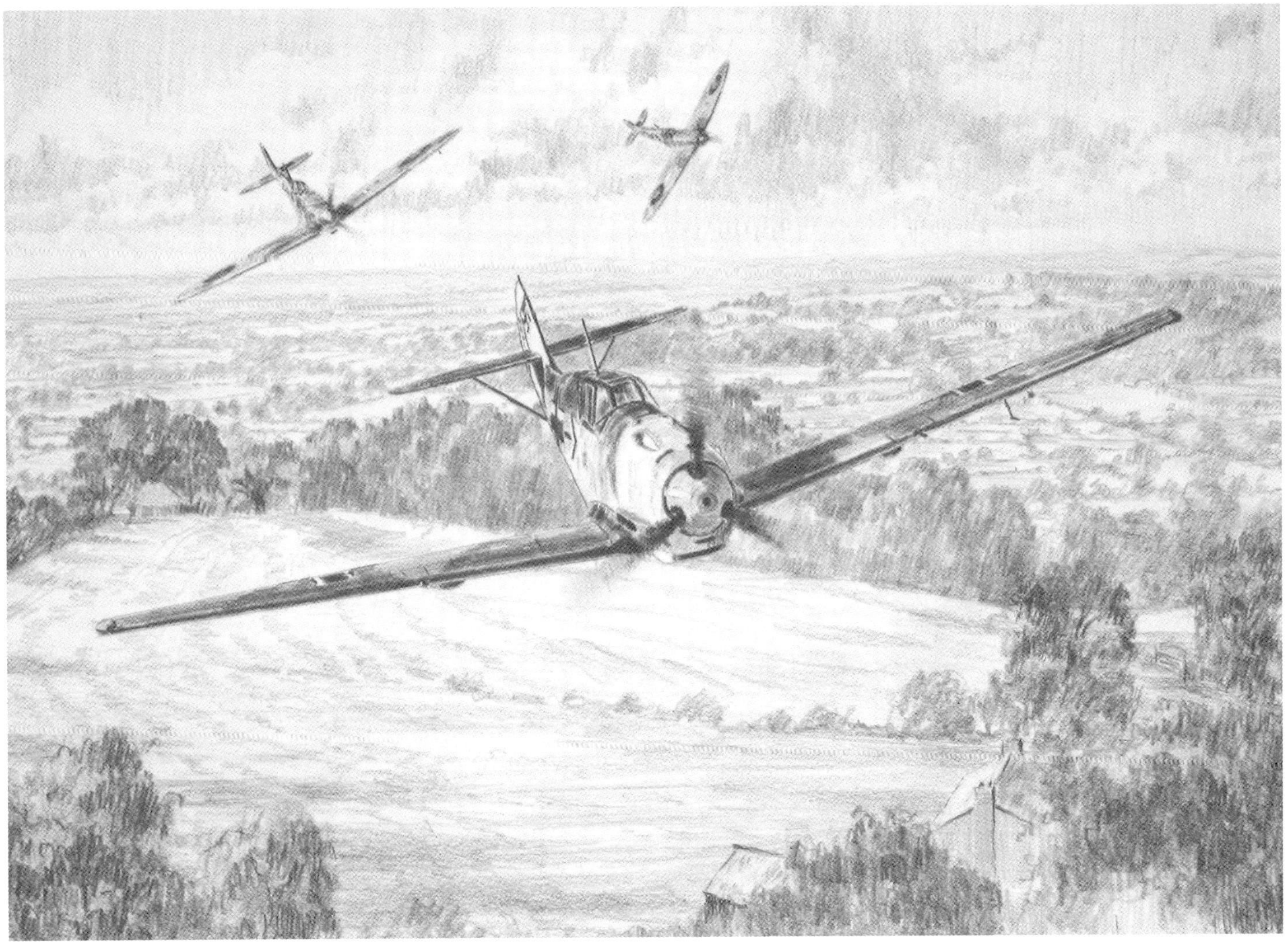

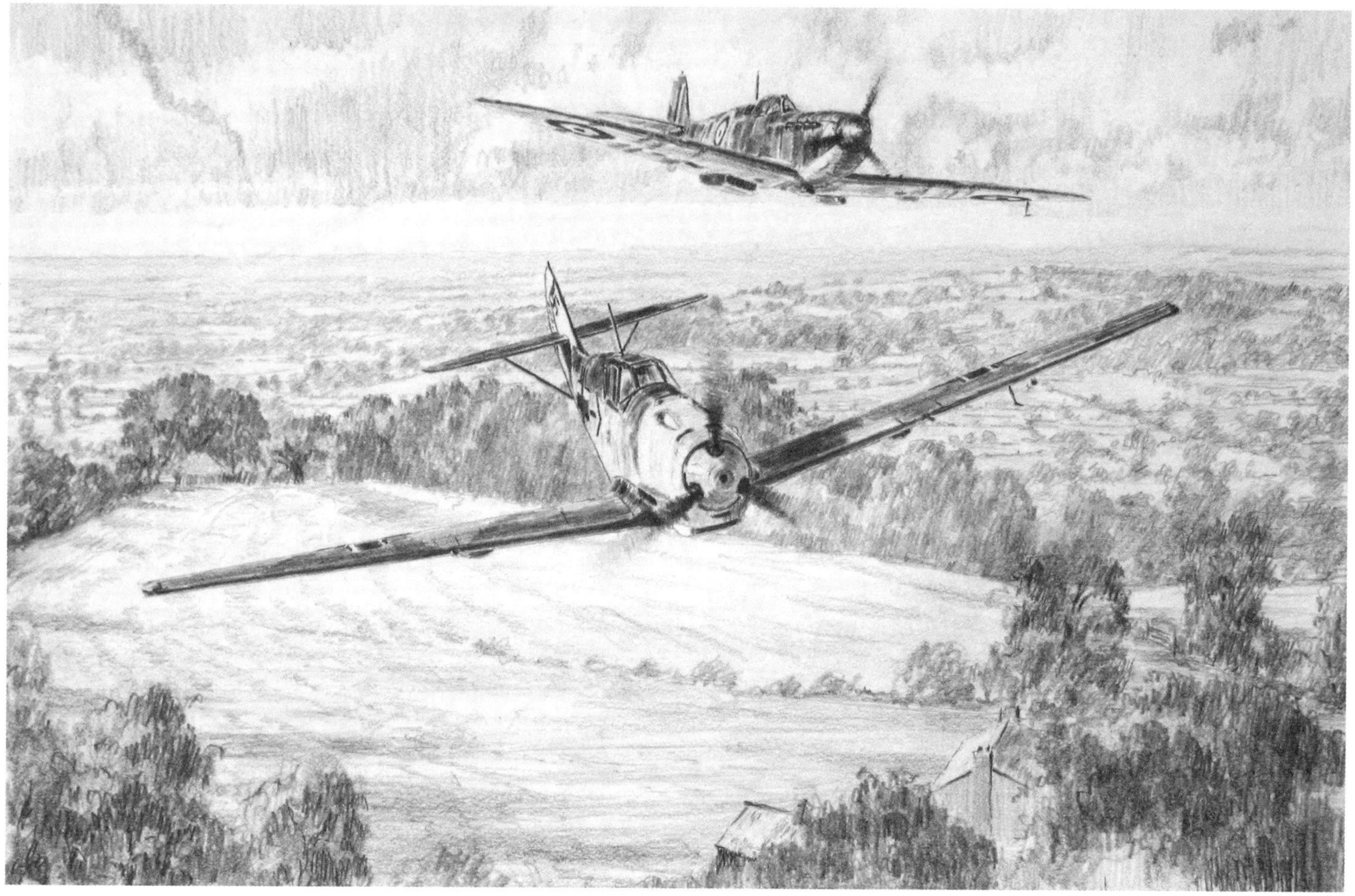

inspiration, a glance through any of them is often worth the effort. I think it's vital to have such books at hand, not just for moments of inspiration when looking for a composition, but for historical accuracy too.

The British countryside has changed a lot since the war, especially in England. Some things are more individually obvious than others, for instance the almost total disappearance of the distinctive Elm tree, but there has also been a more general change to the landscape through deforestation and the huge reduction in the number of hedgerows. As farming has got more intensive, economies of scale and increasing mechanisation has seen hedges ripped out to make way for ever bigger fields to grow more crops. Although it's a process that started during the war as Britain strove for self-sufficiency the pace of change increased rapidly in the sixties and continues today.

I knew that I wanted to depict some kind of low-level duel and, using the new-found photo, I produced an initial couple of rough drawings – above and on previous page – but couldn't quite get the effect I was looking for. Originally my idea was to have the Messerschmitt as the main aircraft with the Spitfire on its tail, but eventually, after a lot of juggling around and countless thumbnail sketches, it was the Spitfire that took main stage. Which wasn't a bad thing because it was, after all, the victor in this particular duel.

The eventual drawing I used for the painting – on the right – was also quite rough, but I had spent so long working on the composition, that I almost knew it backwards and it was quite easy to make a start. Luckily the painting itself went smoothly, the only minor problem was making the distant stretch of coastline look very far away – the colours for distant objects have to be quite muted compared to those in the foreground but just how muted to make them, when all you have is a small black and white photo in a book, is down to experience.

I sometimes get a little suspicious when things go too easily but really I should be grateful because there have been times, on other paintings, when things have gone really wrong. Thankfully they're rare but there have been occasions when I've had to spend many worrying hours painting and repainting parts of a picture until they look right.

I know it might sound odd but something I've found with painting Battle of Britain subjects is that it helps if you paint them in the summer months when the light is quite different from the winter months. I know this isn't always possible, but when it is, just being able to look out of the studio at the colours of the clouds against the sky, or to walk down a country lane between fields of ripening corn, can be a great help.

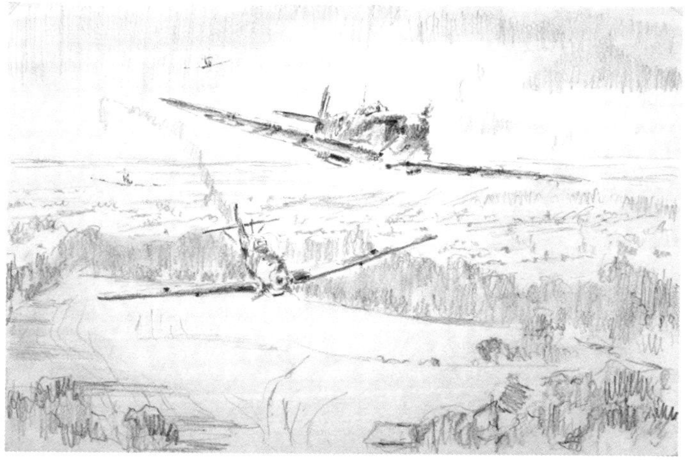

HOMEWARD BOUND

'As England, despite her hopeless military situation, still shows no sign of willingness to come to terms, I have decided to prepare, and if necessary to carry out, a landing operation against her. The aim of this operation is to eliminate the English motherland as a base from which war against Germany can be continued and if necessary, to occupy the country completely.'

The Battle of Britain had already begun but with these few succinct words, from the Führer's Directive No.16 dated 16th July 1940, Hitler made clear his future ambitions for Britain. But for his invasion to succeed his Luftwaffe would have to control the skies over the Channel, and what had started out at the beginning of July with light bombing raids by the Luftwaffe, mainly against shipping in the English Channel, very quickly escalated into one of the most important air battles ever fought. And for Britain it was a battle for survival.

I started painting *Homeward Bound* immediately after I'd finished *High Summer*. The new painting, the second of the Battle of Britain pair that I was now working on, was to be seen from a Luftwaffe perspective. I decided not to make this an action scene, partly as a deliberate contrast to *High Summer*, but also to avoid sensitivities because prints of the painting were going to be signed by Luftwaffe veterans.

By the summer of 1940 the Luftwaffe was the most powerful and professional air force in the world. It had brushed aside opposition in Poland, France and Belgium with ease and its pilots were bubbling over with confidence, as was their leader, Reichmarschall Hermann Goering. But Goering had fooled himself – he was over-confident. Underestimating the resolve of the opposition and over-optimistic with what the Luftwaffe could achieve, he assured Hitler that victory over the RAF would take only a few days. By the beginning of August, however, little progress had been made.

An increasingly impatient Hitler demanded the Luftwaffe 'overpower the English Air Force with all the forces at its command, in the shortest possible time' and the thrust of their attack would now be directed to the RAF airfields of southern England, and the radar sites on the south coast. It almost worked.

By the beginning of September the situation for Fighter Command was growing increasingly grim, with the loss of pilots and aircraft as well as damage to airfields reaching unsustainable levels. The Luftwaffe, however, was also suffering. Goering's over-confidence was telling.

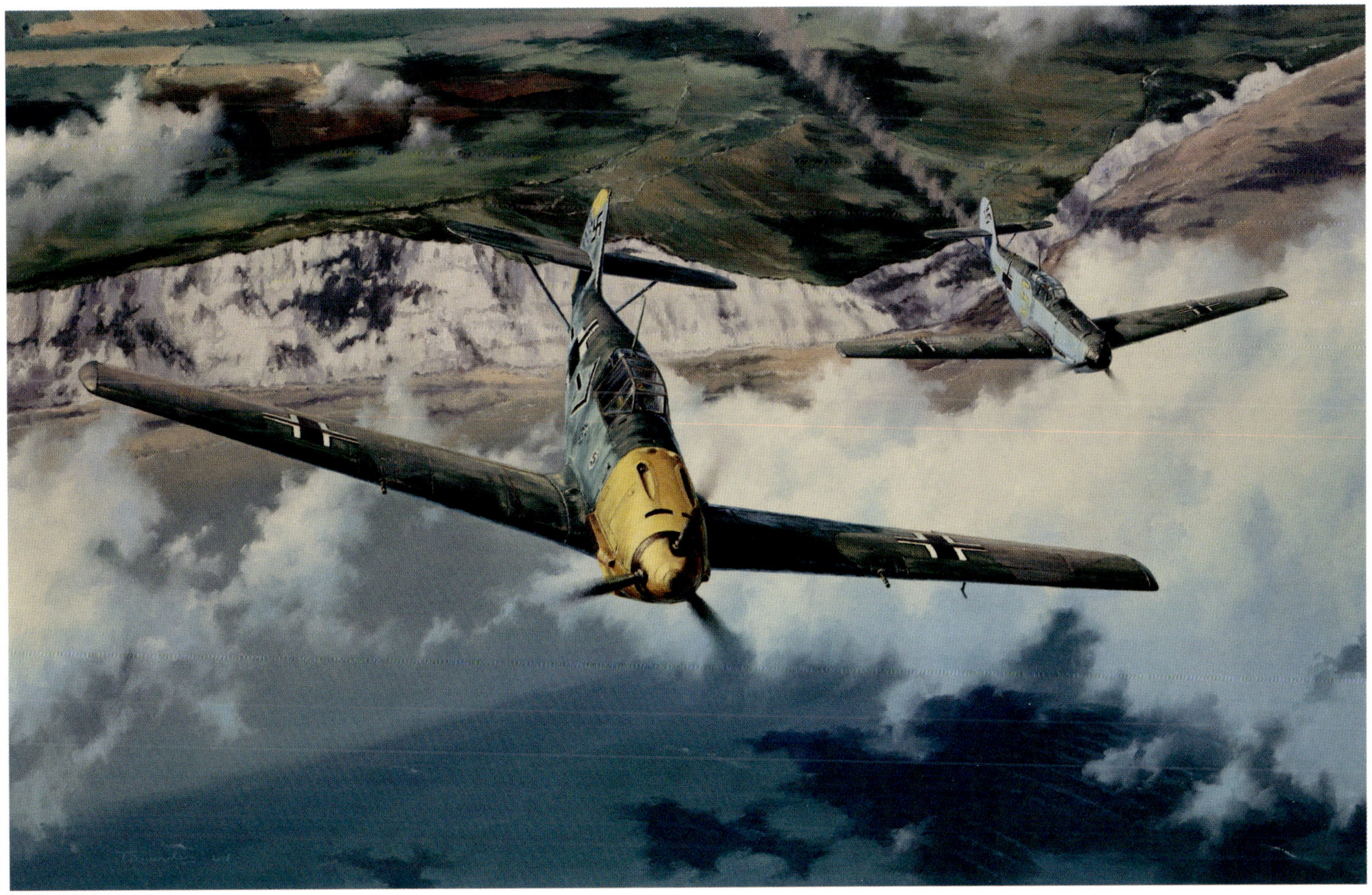

HOMEWARD BOUND

IN THE COLLECTION OF MR R NELLA

It was a small twist of fate that turned the battle in Britain's favour when, on the night of 24/25 August, a formation of German bombers mistook their target and dropped their bombs on London. It was a mistake, and against Hitler's orders. In retaliation, Bomber Command attacked Berlin the following night. Hitler was enraged. Encouraged by Goering into believing Fighter Command was broken, he ordered the Luftwaffe to switch their attack away from the airfields on to London. The British capital was to be pounded into submission.

His decision was fatal. Fighter Command might have been up against the ropes but it hadn't been knocked out. It now had the few days breathing space it needed to regroup. Within a few days the airfields had been repaired, replacement pilots rushed in and, with fighting now over London, other squadrons based to the north of the capital could join the battle.

By mid-September Fighter Command had regained its composure and strength and was able to repel the heavy Luftwaffe raids across southern England and London. Whilst German intelligence estimated that the British had only two or three hundred fighters left, the Luftwaffe crews were instead encountering ever-increasing numbers of Spitfires and Hurricanes. German morale was suffering.

Although the Luftwaffe and RAF were roughly equal in strength, the enemy faced one major disadvantage. Unlike his RAF counterpart who, when shot down (if uninjured) could return to his squadron the same day, a Luftwaffe pilot in the same situation could only look forward to an indefinite stay in a POW camp. It was a choice often made, especially as the results inflicted by the .303 calibre machine guns that equipped both the Spitfire and the Hurricane at the time, were just as likely to damage your plane as rip it apart.

I thought the dilemma of whether to bale out and risk almost certain captivity or try to make it back across the Channel to the safety of France would make a good painting and, with prints being signed by German pilots, would be one that they would be happy to sign.

In *Homeward Bound* the pilot from JG26 has chosen the more difficult option of trying to make it home. And I deliberately made the outcome ambiguous. With around 2,000ft between him and the cold English Channel below he will probably make it home – just – especially if his engine doesn't deteriorate further. Of course having his Squadron Commander, the legendary Adolf Galland, as escort can only increase his chances further.

The background, by the way, was partly inspired by a fantastic, if brief, scene in the film, *The Battle of Britain*. The shot only lasts for a few frames so I guess you'd be hard pressed to find it, especially with the changes I'd made so that the composition would work better, but if you ever want an excuse to watch that great film again…?

After completing a painting and before I deliver it to my publishers, I always like to hold on to it for a week or so, just to double-check it for any minor omissions or errors that I can spot. And with this one I was glad I did, because the first thing I realised is that I'd painted the damaged plane with the later style E-4 canopy. In fact it had the earlier style and I should have known better. This was particularly annoying as the canopy is one of the more tricky things to paint.

The second thing I found after studying a photograph of Adolf Galland's Me109 that I hadn't seen before. To my horror I noticed that his aircraft didn't have the engine-mounted machine gun which fired through the propeller hub!

This, thank goodness, was a much easier amendment to make, but it did teach me a very valuable lesson – never completely trust someone else's colour profiles. Now, whenever I use them, I always try and find at least one wartime photo of the aircraft in question in order to double-check their accuracy.

In case you're wondering, for me the Me109 will always be an Me109 not a Bf109. I know that, to be correct, it should be a Bf109 as originally designated by the German War Ministry after *Bayrische Flugzeugwerke*, the company that originally built it. Only when Willy Messerschmitt, who'd been the chief designer, took control of the company and gave it his name, did the designation of new models thereafter become *Me* not *Bf*. But when I was a child I built models called Me109s and the name has stuck and, when I've spoken to veterans, especially from the RAF, they have always referred to the German fighter as an Me109. So, at the very least, I feel I'm in good company!

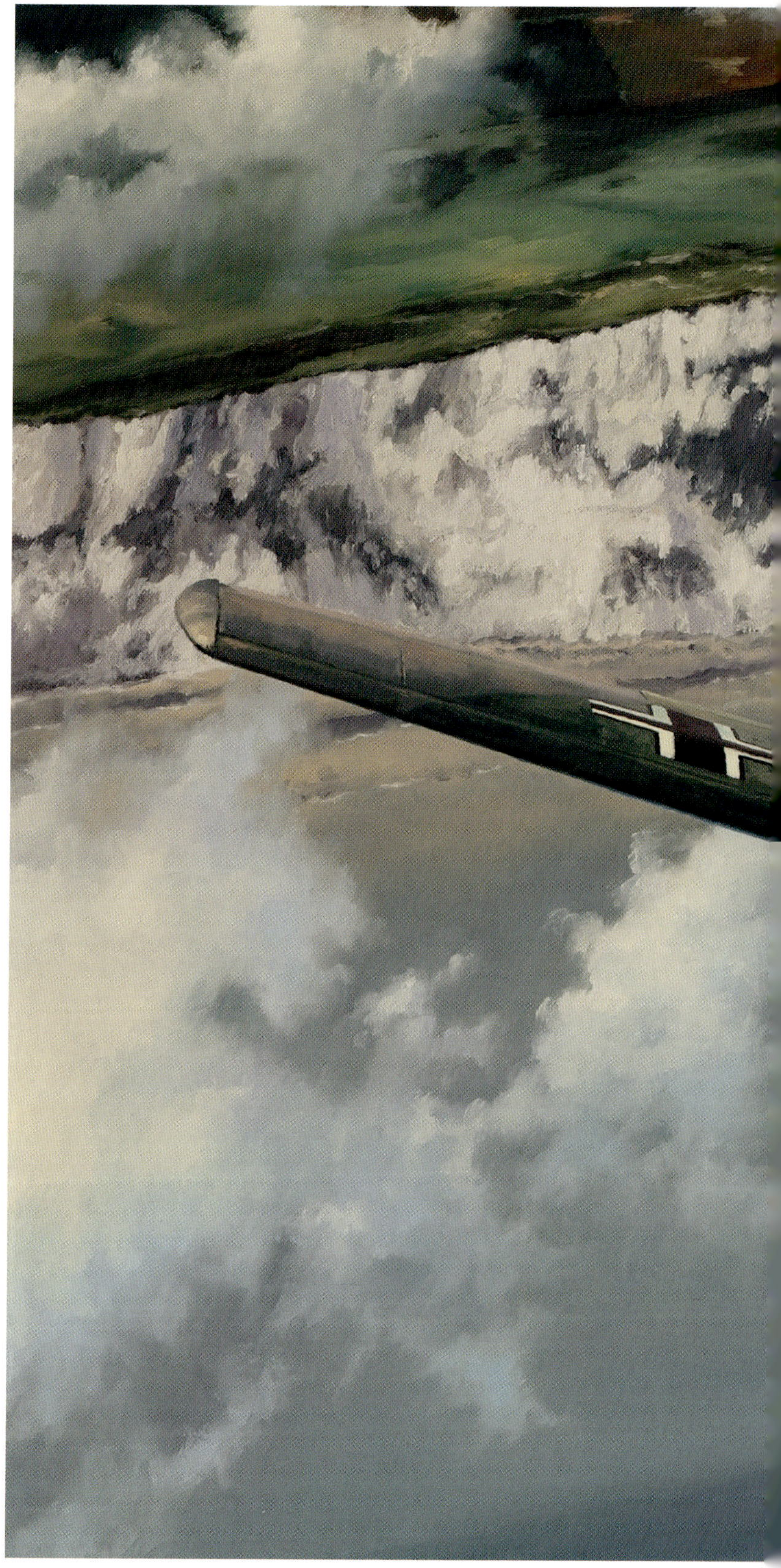

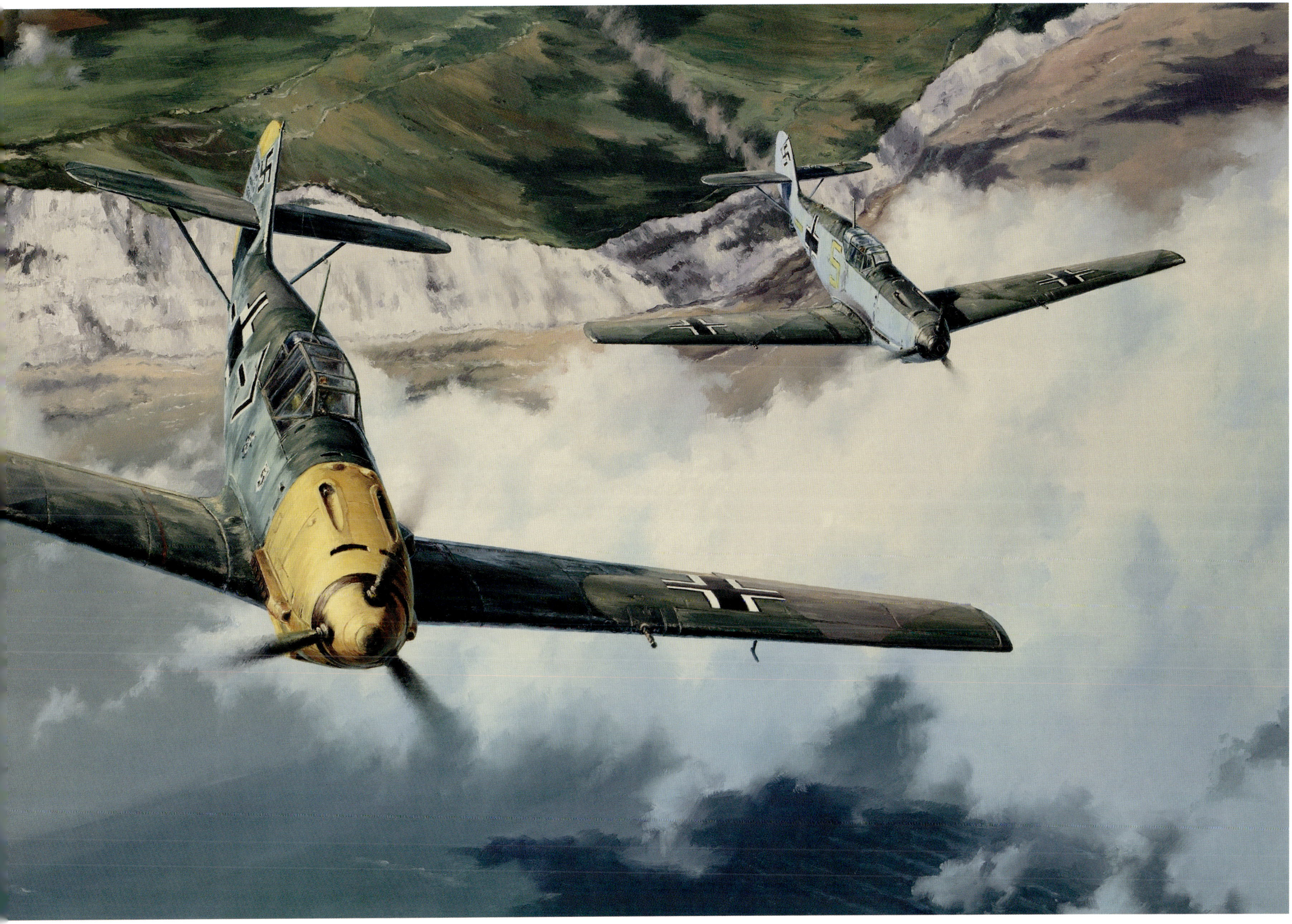

THUNDER IN THE ARDENNES

Strictly known as the Ardennes Counter-offensive, the Germans' last-ditch major effort to halt the Allied advance from the west in its tracks is better known by the name given to it by the press – The Battle of the Bulge.

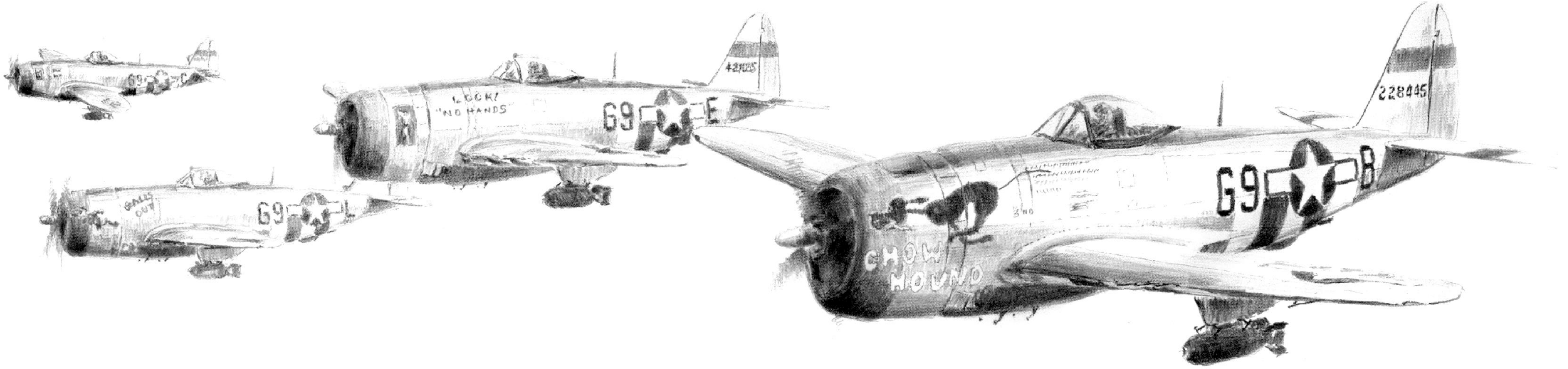

As the Allies pressed ever closer to the German border Hitler, ignoring the advice of his generals, gambled everything on a plan he was convinced would hurl the enemy back to the sea. Assembling three armies with little detection, Hitler threw the dice and, on 16 December 1944, launched his attack in the one place the Allies least expected – the wooded hills of the Ardennes.

This section of the front line was thinly held by the American Army, whose only strategic reserve were the 82nd and 101st Airborne Divisions encamped near Reims, over a hundred miles away. Exhausted by the hard-fought, but ultimately fruitless attempt to cross the Rhine at Arnhem during Operation *Market Garden*, the two airborne divisions had been sent to Reims to rest and recuperate. But they never got the chance.

Sergeant William Dunfee, a squad leader in the 505th Parachute Infantry Regiment, 82nd Airborne Division, later wrote about his surprise call back into action: 'We were quite comfortable and would have been content to sit out the rest of the war there. The night of 17/18 December 1944, sometime after lights out, we were awakened out of a doze by Lieutenant Vande Vegt, Executive Officer of 'I' Company. We thought he was either drunk or had lost his mind. He was sounding off about how the Germans had broken through, and we were to move out before daylight. By the time we were fully awake, we realized he was neither drunk, nor kidding.'

The 82nd Airborne were hastily loaded into trucks and driven to the small town of Werbomont in Belgium, on the northern shoulder of the Bulge. It was cold, wet and miserable and from here they began a month of even more bitter fighting. After two weeks, however, they had managed to secure and hold crucial positions, and helped defeat of elements from three SS Panzer divisions until, on 3 January 1945, following the first heavy snowfall of the winter, they finally went on the offensive. Despite terrible casualties and freezing winter conditions they would drive the Germans steadily back towards the Siegfried Line and the German border.

Yet had it not been for the overwhelming superiority of Allied air power the story might have had a very different ending. Hitler had carefully chosen the time and circumstances under which his great offensive would be launched but, for the first time in the war, Germany was embarking on a major offensive without the assurance of air superiority. By now Hitler had all but lost confidence in the Luftwaffe's capabilities and forbade the opening of the attack until there was a forecast of poor weather that he knew would keep the Allied planes firmly on the ground. In mid-December he got his chance. With most aircraft grounded by fog, mist and snow the German panzers struck hard and fast, and the American lines began to buckle. But, as the veil of cloud and fog finally lifted, the Allied air forces hit back with a vengeance.

For *Thunder in the Ardennes* I wanted to show both the air and ground forces as they push their way through the Ardennes, having gone on the offensive. Showing both these elements together in one painting, however, was going to need some careful planning. Surprisingly, it was the 1970 film *Patton* that provided the initial inspiration and gave me a rough idea of the look I was after.

The film culminates with the Battle of the Bulge, and one brief scene shows a column of tanks and armoured vehicles of Patton's US Third Army moving through a snow-covered landscape as they advance to relieve the airborne troops besieged, but still holding, Bastogne. I later found out that this particular scene was actually filmed in Spain, not that it mattered!

Having got the idea of a heavy armoured column moving through the settled snow, the next thing was to think about the aerial element that would accompany it. My first thoughts had been to portray P-38 Lightnings of the 474th Fighter Group, which I knew had been involved in the Ardennes fighting that winter, but I quickly discovered that the wide wingspan of the P-38

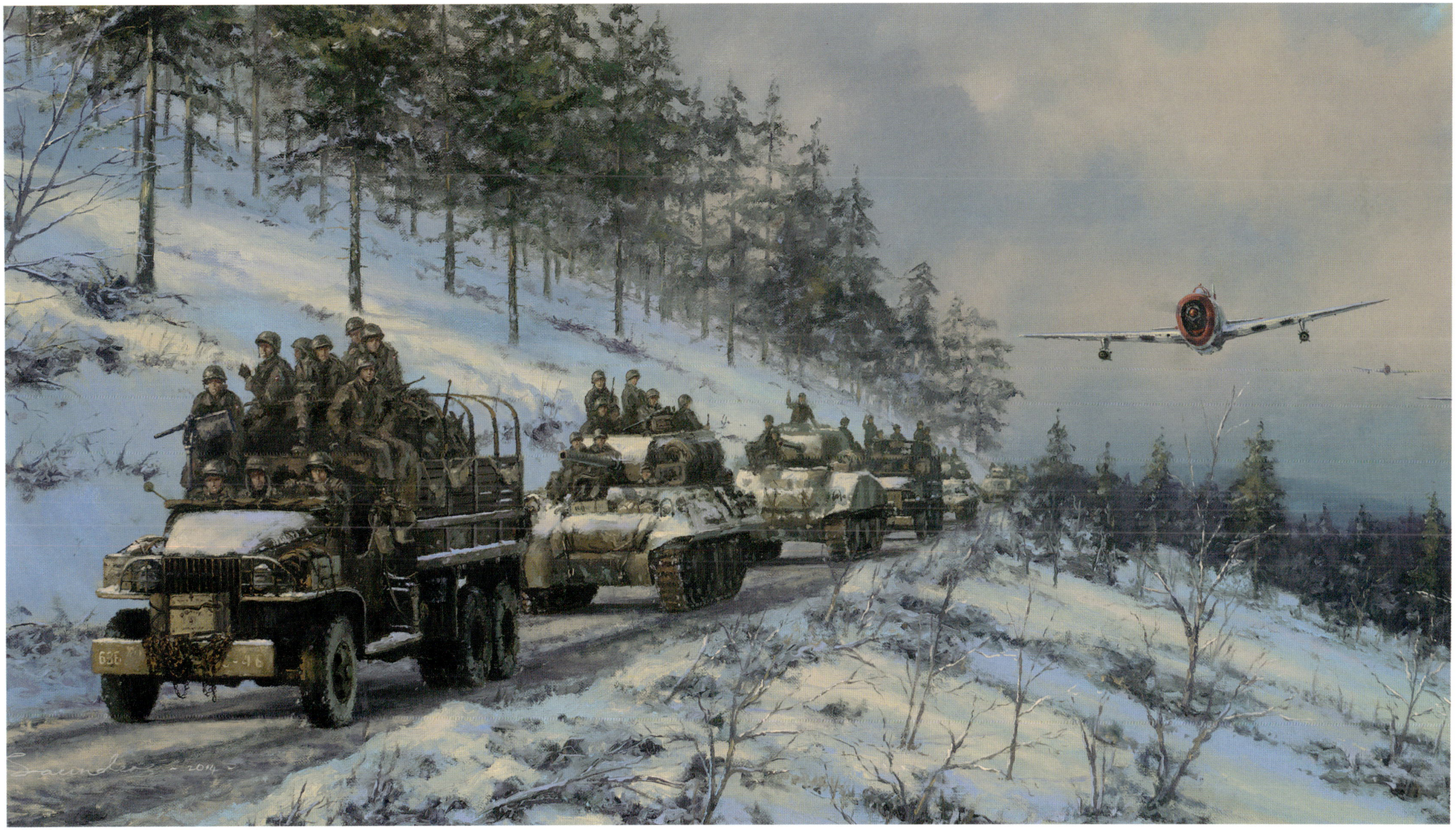

was not going to work very well in the restricted space available on the canvas. Instead I opted for the rugged P-47 Thunderbolt, which I guess should have been the more obvious choice from the outset as it played such a pivotal role in the battle.

After much research, the P-47 unit I opted for was the 405th Fighter Group, one of those assigned to provide close air support to Patton's advancing Third Army. The 405th Fighter Group were known as the 'Thunder Monsters', and for those German troops on the ground unlucky enough to have been caught by them on their retreat back towards the Siegfried Line, it must have seemed a particularly apt nickname.

Many of these P-47s carried some pretty extravagant nose art, and none more so than that of Major Robert Blackburn, Commanding Officer of the 509th Fighter Squadron. His aircraft was adorned with a huge sprinting dog that he'd named *Chow Hound*. I thought this would be a great-looking aircraft to paint and the fact that it still carried invasion stripes on its under-wing surfaces was an added bonus. In the painting Major Blackburn is seen leading a flight of eight aircraft on 26 January 1945, on a patrol to attack enemy armoured vehicles. En-route they give a rousing reception for the men of the 82nd Airborne Division and the 740th Tank Battalion to which they were attached.

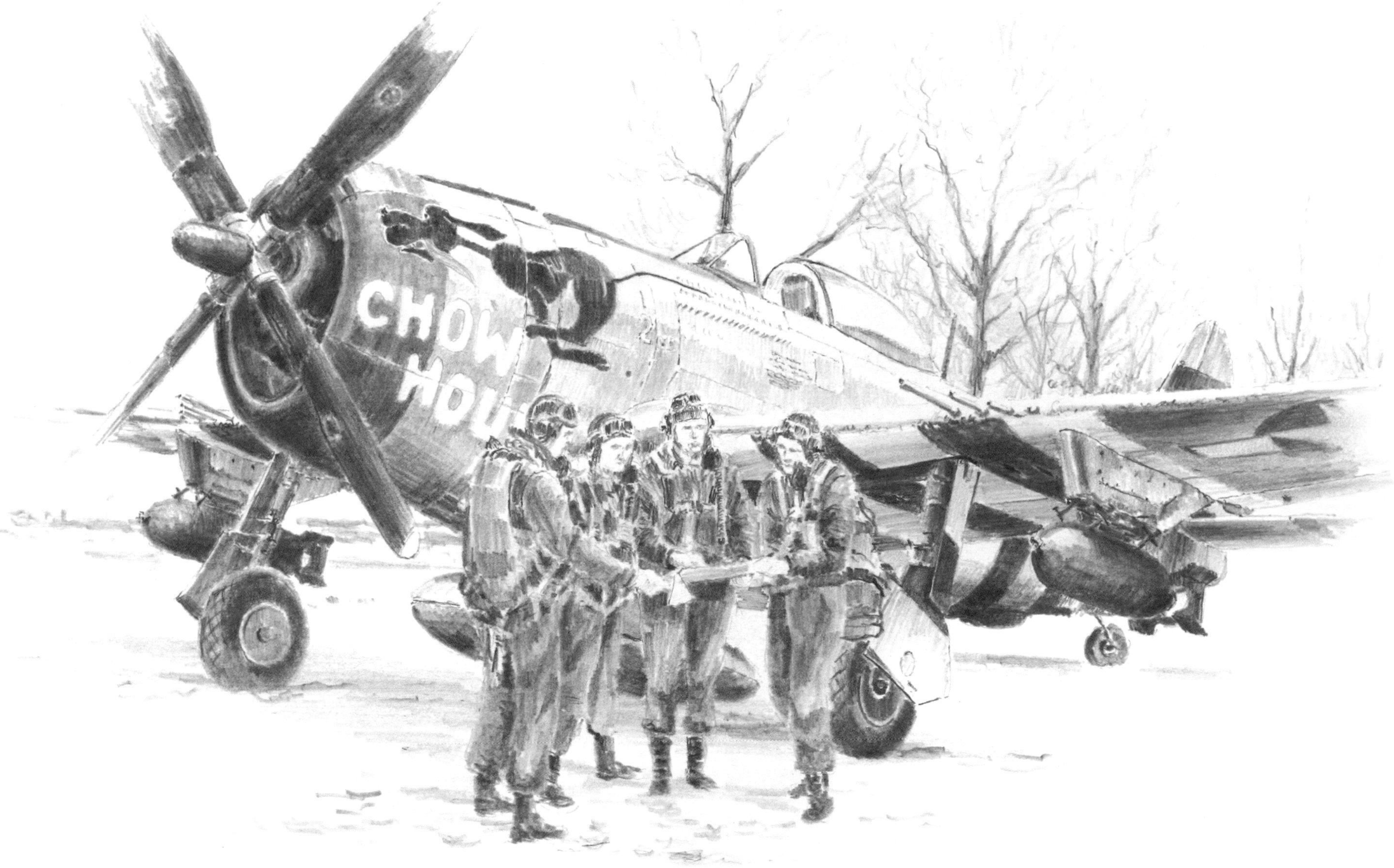

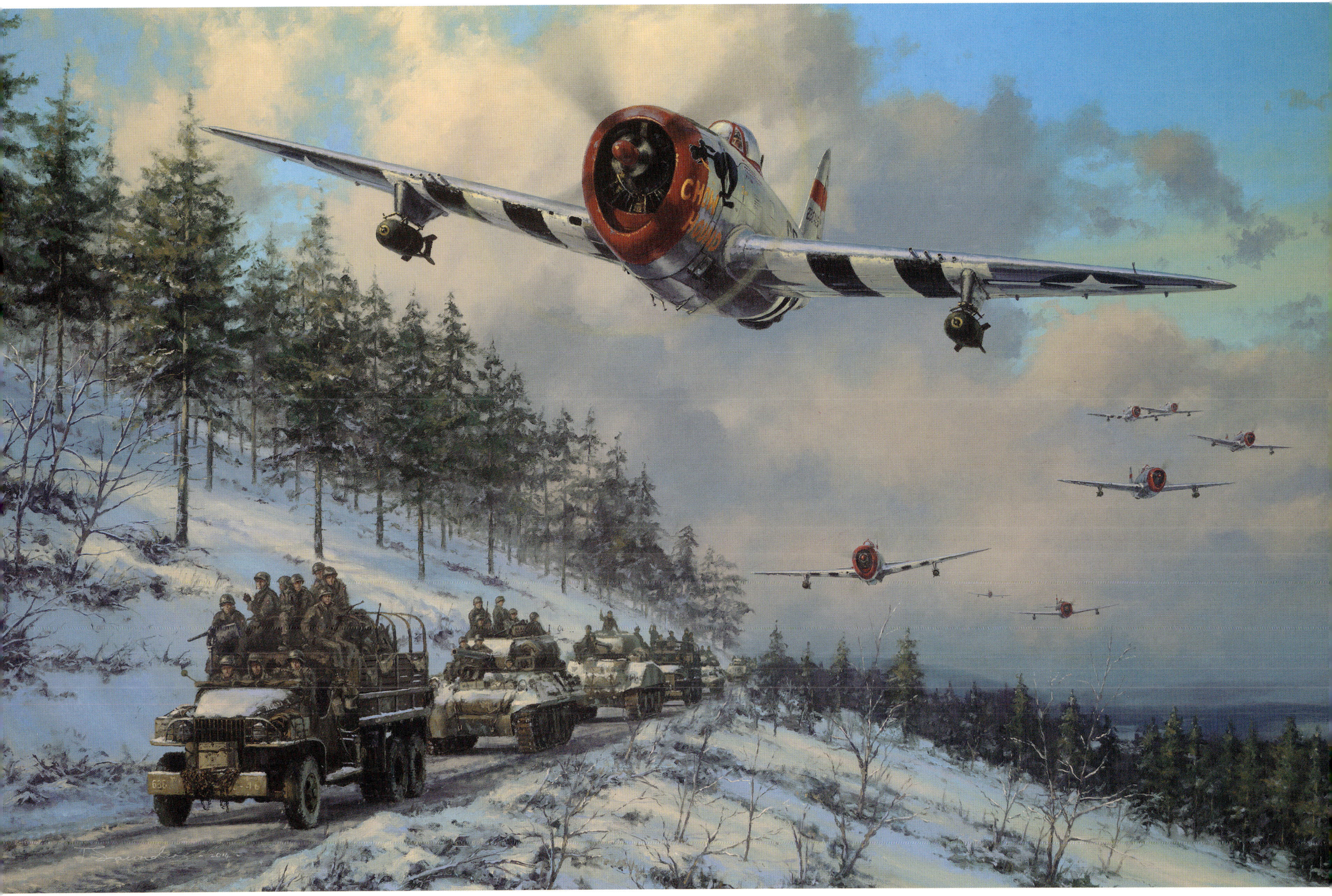

THUNDER IN THE ARDENNES IN THE COLLECTION OF BILL WARD FINE ART SERVICES

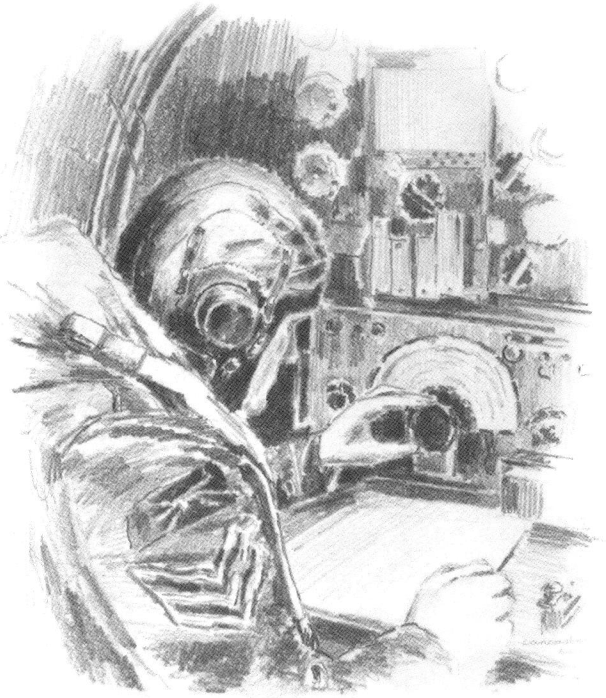

THE AUGSBURG RAID

I'm surprised that the Augsburg Raid hasn't been depicted more often. It has all the elements that an aviation artist looks for in a subject – audacity, skill and a lot of courage – a low-level daylight raid deep into enemy territory.

On 17 April 1942 the RAF sent a force of twelve Lancasters to attack the M.A.N diesel engine factory at Augsburg in Southern Bavaria. Led by Squadron Leader John Nettleton, the first wave of six aircraft came from 44 Squadron, the second wave consisted of six Lancasters from 97 Squadron. They were led by 23 year old Squadron Leader John Sherwood DFC and for all of them the round trip would involve flying more than a thousand miles, further, by far, than any mission to date.

At this time the Augsburg factory not only made engines for the tanks and trucks of Hitler's army, but also the big marine diesels used by the Kriegsmarine, especially those that powered the U-boats. Germany had taken great steps to safeguard its main U-boat bases, the ones in occupied France that covered the Atlantic: at St Nazaire, Lorient, Brest, La Pallice and Bordeaux, huge, fortified bomb-proof pens had been constructed which, by the spring of 1942, were covered by reinforced concrete and granite roofs over 26 feet thick. Despite determined efforts no bomb in the RAF's existing arsenal could penetrate them and, for the moment, Bomber Command's main effort against the U-boats was to hit the construction yards, and factories that supplied them.

Soon after taking his position as Commander-in-Chief of RAF Bomber Command, Air Marshal Arthur 'Bomber' Harris wanted to lay on a 'special show', something that would also put the new four-engined Lancaster bomber through its paces. The Lancaster was designed to fly high, at night and individually but to avoid detection, for this mission, they would have to fly low, hedge-hopping at only 50 feet and in formation. The diesel engine factory at Augsburg would be a baptism of fire both for Harris and the Lancaster.

To research this subject I found a great book written by Jack Currie DFC, simply called *The Augsburg Raid*. Although not on the raid himself, he had flown with 44 Squadron and was able to gain first-hand accounts from some of the survivors. On YouTube I also found a very useful documentary he made about the raid in 1989 for BBC Leeds. I'm not sure if it was ever broadcast nationwide, but on YouTube it's now available for everyone to view and I think I must have watched it at least a dozen times.

At one point Jack Currie stands on one of the factory roof tops and describes in detail how the Lancasters came in. When the film was made there were still parts of the factory that had changed very little from the day of the raid and a few of the factory's imposing brick chimneys were still standing. They served as a graphic reminder of just how low the bombers came in: they either had to fly between the chimneys or hop over them. It was these dramatic moments that I wanted to portray.

The Lancasters had all approached the target from the south-east with the sun just setting on their left. Rather than have the setting sun in the picture I decided on a viewpoint that placed it behind the viewer. This way I could show the pastel shades and shadows on the Lancaster's fuselage.

Despite diversionary tactics, Nettleton had lost four of his six Lancasters to enemy fighters as they crossed France. Nevertheless he and the remaining bomber pressed on to the target whilst Sherwood's six aircraft, still unscathed, followed on ten minutes behind. It was this second section that I wanted to portray in the attack, for two reasons: The first was that being the second wave to go they had to fly through the smoke and fires left by the first attack and, with the defences now fully alerted, there was a barrage of flak through which Sherwood's formation must fly. It would make for a more dramatic painting.

The second reason was that the description of Sherwood's plight had sparked my imagination. Soon after dropping his bomb load Sherwood's aircraft, *K-King*, was hit by flak. In the documentary Ernest Rodley, pilot of *F-Freddie* and flying to Sherwood's port side, describes how he could clearly see flames within the aircraft through its dorsal windows. He asked his tail gunner to keep an eye on the stricken plane. Shortly afterwards the gunner reported back that Sherwood's aircraft had hit the ground and gone up like 'a flaming chrysanthemum!'

Everyone who saw the cataclysmic crash believed no-one could have possibly survived and that all the crew had perished. When the next of kin were informed, Sherwood's wife had quietly told the informing officer that she was sure her husband was alive. She was right.

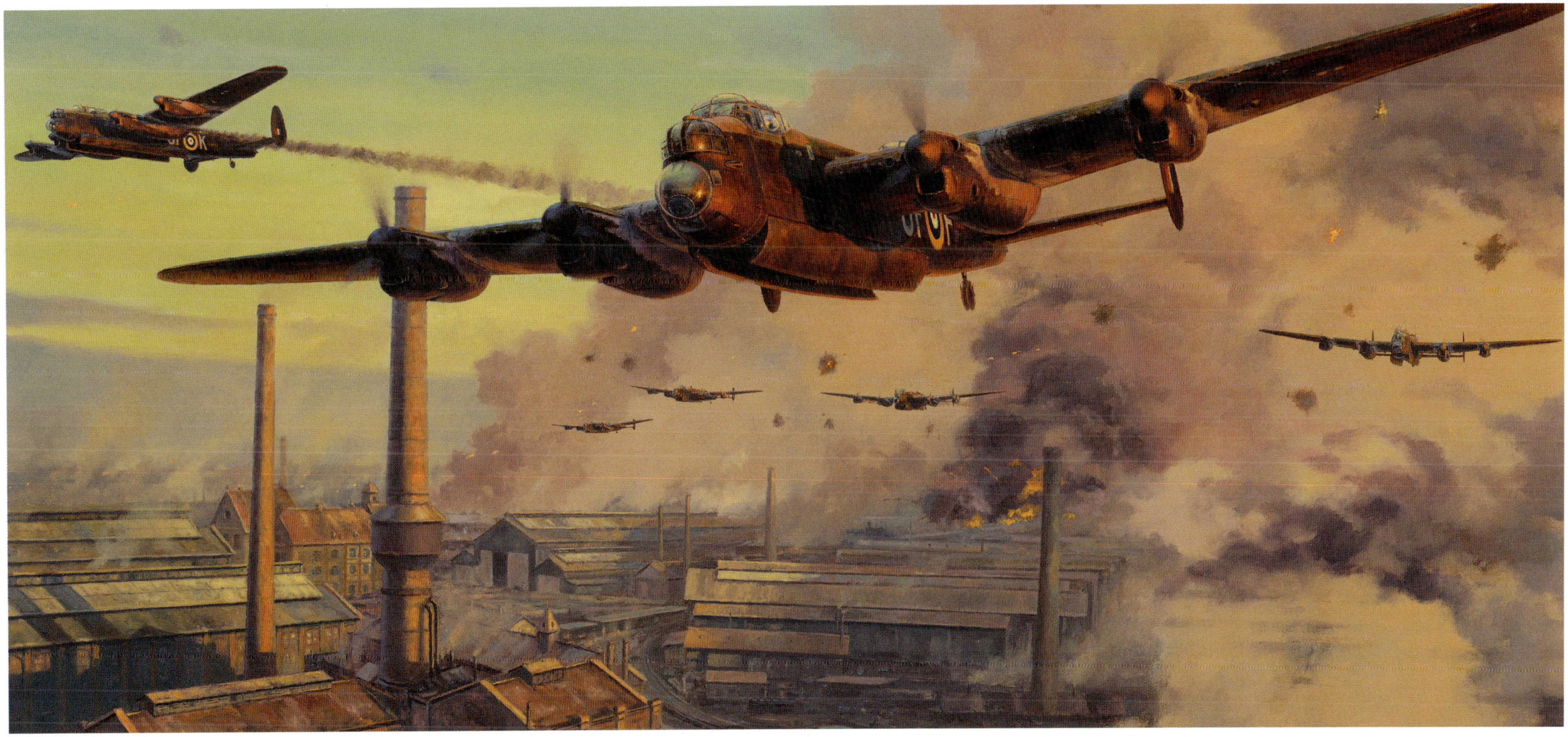

When the flaming Lancaster had come down in woods near the target, Sherwood, still strapped to his seat, was catapulted out of the cockpit, his fall broken by trees. He was the sole survivor.

John Nettleton was awarded the VC for his actions. Sherwood was also recommended for what was thought to be a posthumous VC. This was endorsed by 'Bomber' Harris but, and no-one is quite sure why, he was eventually only awarded the DSO. Sherwood's wife, however, was unfazed at what many thought an injustice. She was, it was reported, much happier with a living DSO than a dead VC.

In recent years the Augsburg raid has been somewhat undervalued, described by some as a heroic failure. Out of the twelve aircraft that had set out, only five returned and 37 aircrew had lost their lives; 12 more had been taken prisoner. Perhaps these are some of the reasons the raid is seldom portrayed. In Germany, however, the raid was seen as a stark warning that the bombers could get through. They would be back and, as with the Dambuster raid a year later, the Augsburg mission was full of heroism and self-sacrifice that showed a beleaguered Britain that all was not lost. The effect on morale was immeasurable.

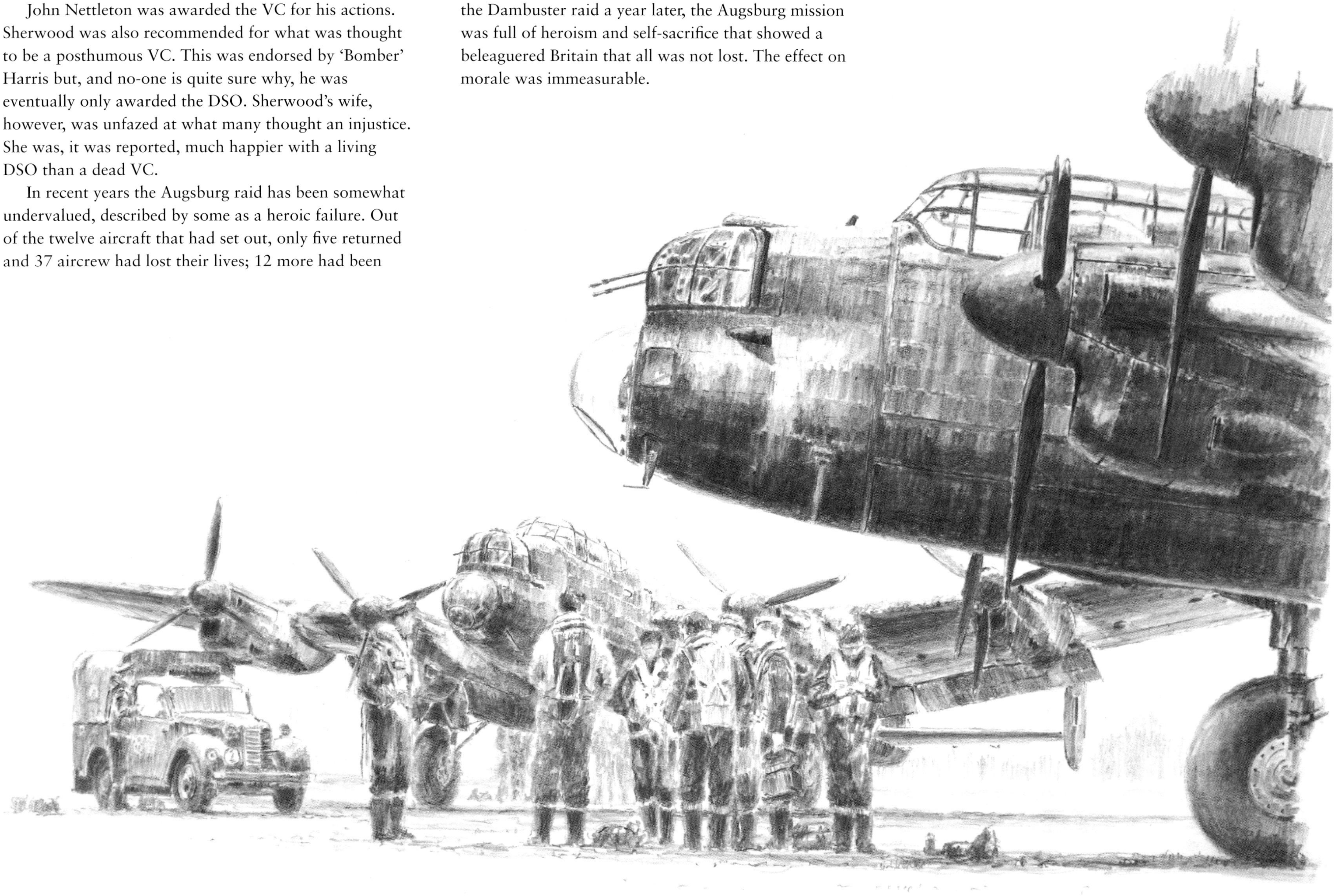

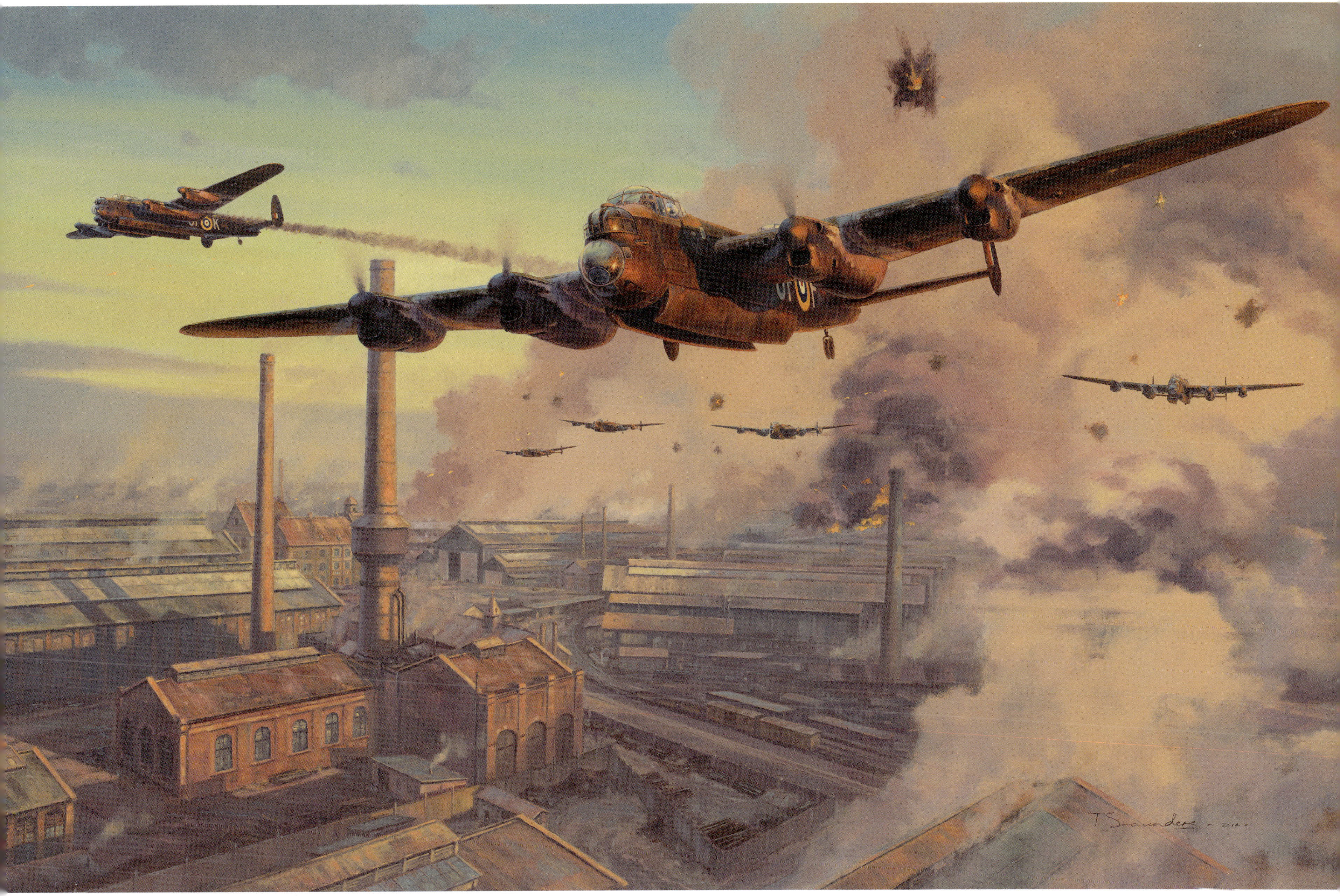

THE AUGSBURG RAID IN THE COLLECTION OF MR & MRS D. GREEN

DAY OF INFAMY

On the morning of 7 December 1941 a warm breeze was blowing gently over Pearl Harbor. As the US Pacific Fleet mustered itself for another restful Sunday the peace was suddenly shattered: they were under an unprovoked attack from hundreds of Japanese aircraft. In the words of President Franklin Roosevelt that morning was 'a date that will live in infamy.'

Just over a year earlier, on 11 November 1940, the Royal Navy had launched an audacious attack on Mussolini's Italian battle fleet lying at anchor within the heavily protected harbour at Taranto in the heel of southern Italy. A small force of 21 obsolescent Fairey Swordfish torpedo-bombers, launched from the aircraft carrier HMS *Illustrious*, had managed to cripple three battleships, three cruisers and a destroyer in a daring low-level raid over the shallow waters of the harbour. Only two aircraft had been lost yet the balance of naval power in the Mediterranean had been altered at a stroke.

Those in command of the Imperial Japanese Navy paid close attention to the events at Taranto and quickly dispatched a senior naval attaché to the Italian port to analyse the effect of the attack. The British had achieved a stunning success through the combination of complete tactical surprise and the ability to solve what was thought to be the long-standing problem of effectively dropping torpedoes in a shallow anchorage. The conclusion was obvious: if a handful of out-dated bi-planes could wreak such damage, imagine what a massed attack by the Japanese Navy's ultra modern aircraft could achieve. Secret plans for launching a similar surprise attack to knockout the American Pacific fleet at Pearl Harbor were set in motion, a strategy that culminated on that fateful Sunday morning in December.

Events on the small Hawaiian island of Oahu began at 07.49 hours when the first Japanese aircraft of the First Wave attack were spotted. As they crossed Waimea Bay observers assumed they were nothing more than part of a military exercise until, a few minutes later, what sounded like thunder was heard coming from the nearby Wheeler Army Airfield, followed by the sight of black acrid smoke billowing into the sky. This was no exercise, it was unprovoked war.

As Wheeler Field came under attack, several formations of Japanese aircraft peeled away and headed south, straight for the main naval base at Pearl Harbor. Here they found the battleships of the US Pacific Fleet peacefully at anchor, all but one neatly moored in a row, and all completely unprepared for action.

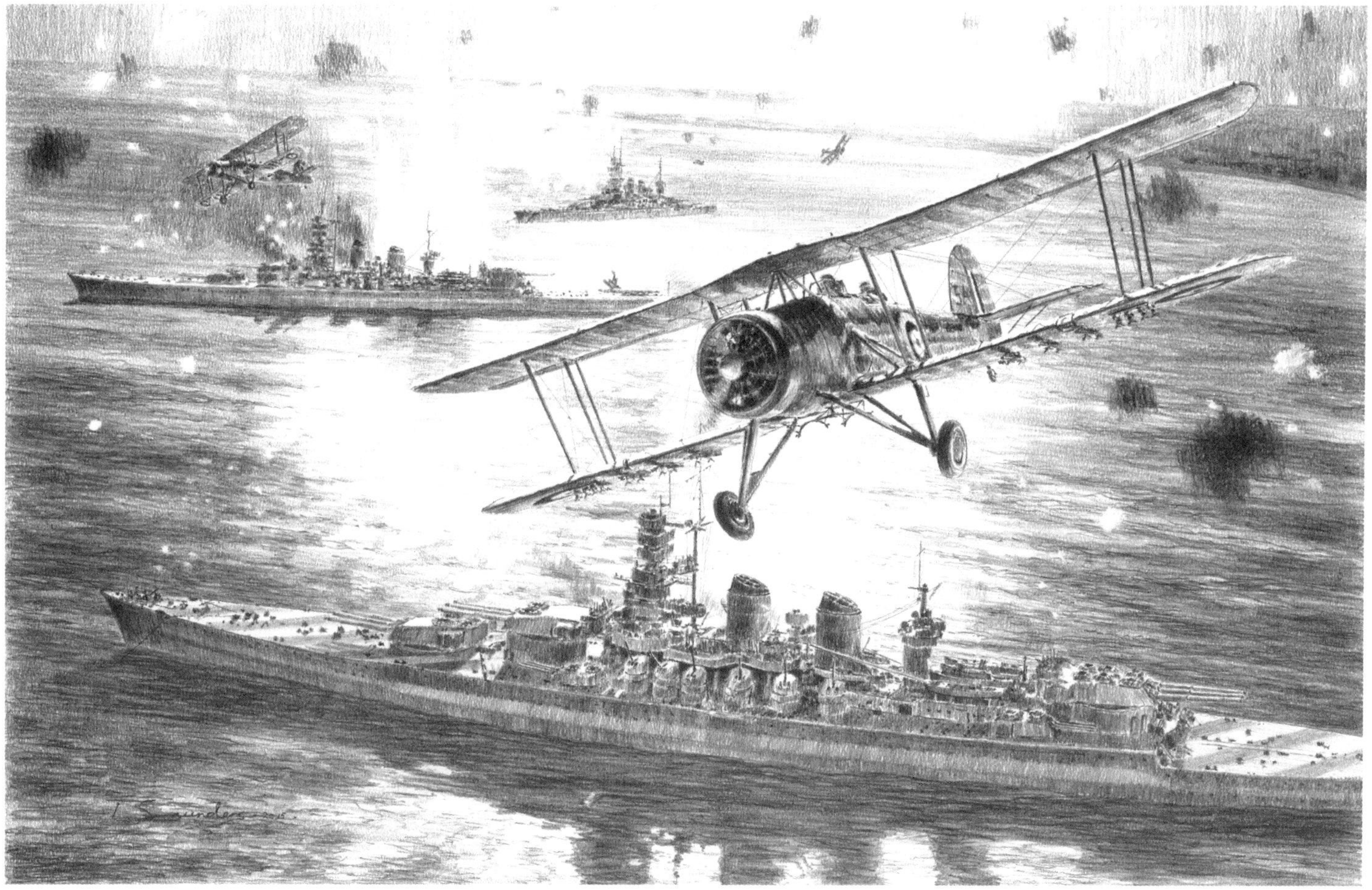

THE BATTLE OF TARANTO

11 November 1940

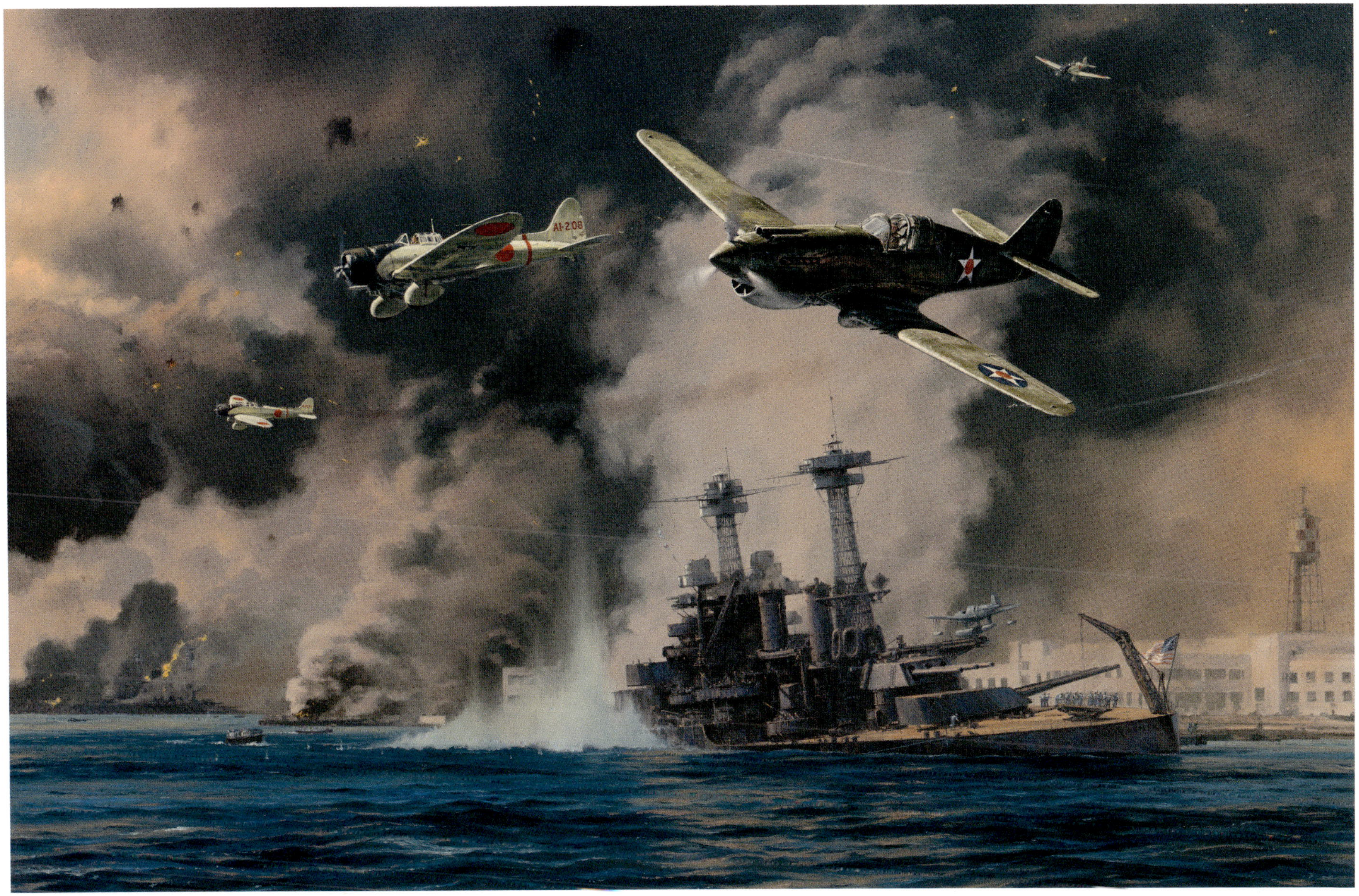

DAY OF INFAMY

IN THE COLLECTION OF
MR EUGENE EISENBERG

The Japanese attack lasted just under two hours and the effects were devastating: 18 ships, including all eight battleships, had been either sunk or damaged, over 180 aircraft destroyed on the ground and more than 2,400 Americans lay dead. But despite the carnage there was a faint glimmer of hope. The Japanese had missed one of their primary targets – the American carriers that happened to be at sea. They had also failed to destroy much of the dockyard whose facilities would soon be back in action repairing and salvaging the damaged vessels. In the end these omissions would prove costly; their attack had dragged the United States into the war but they had failed to deliver the knockout blow they hoped for. Instead they had galvanised the strongest economy on earth into action on a path that eventually would take it, and its allies, to victory.

I had painted the attack on Pearl Harbor some years before but as the 70th Anniversary commemorations drew close I felt I'd like to portray it again but this time try to include something of the American response, which although tiny, included a valiant effort by the handful of fighter pilots who managed to get airborne.

For this painting, *Day of Infamy*, I thought I'd go straight to the centre of the main action with the attack on Battleship Row, which lay just off the south-east shore of Ford Island. It was here that seven of the eight battleships were moored whilst a little further on, moored on its own and an easy target for the Aichi D-3A Val dive bombers, lay the USS *California*. Like many of the battleships around her the *California* had been

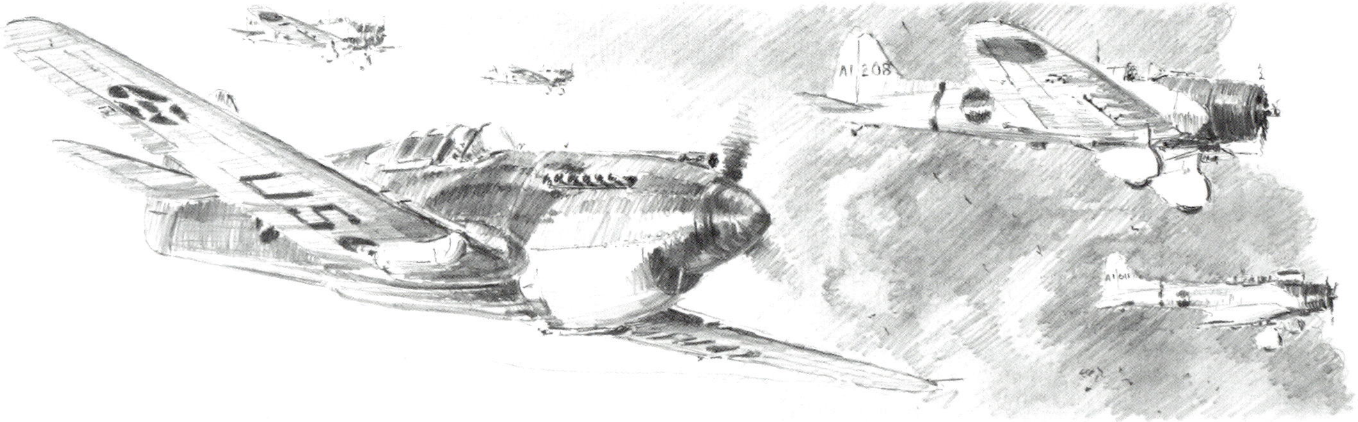

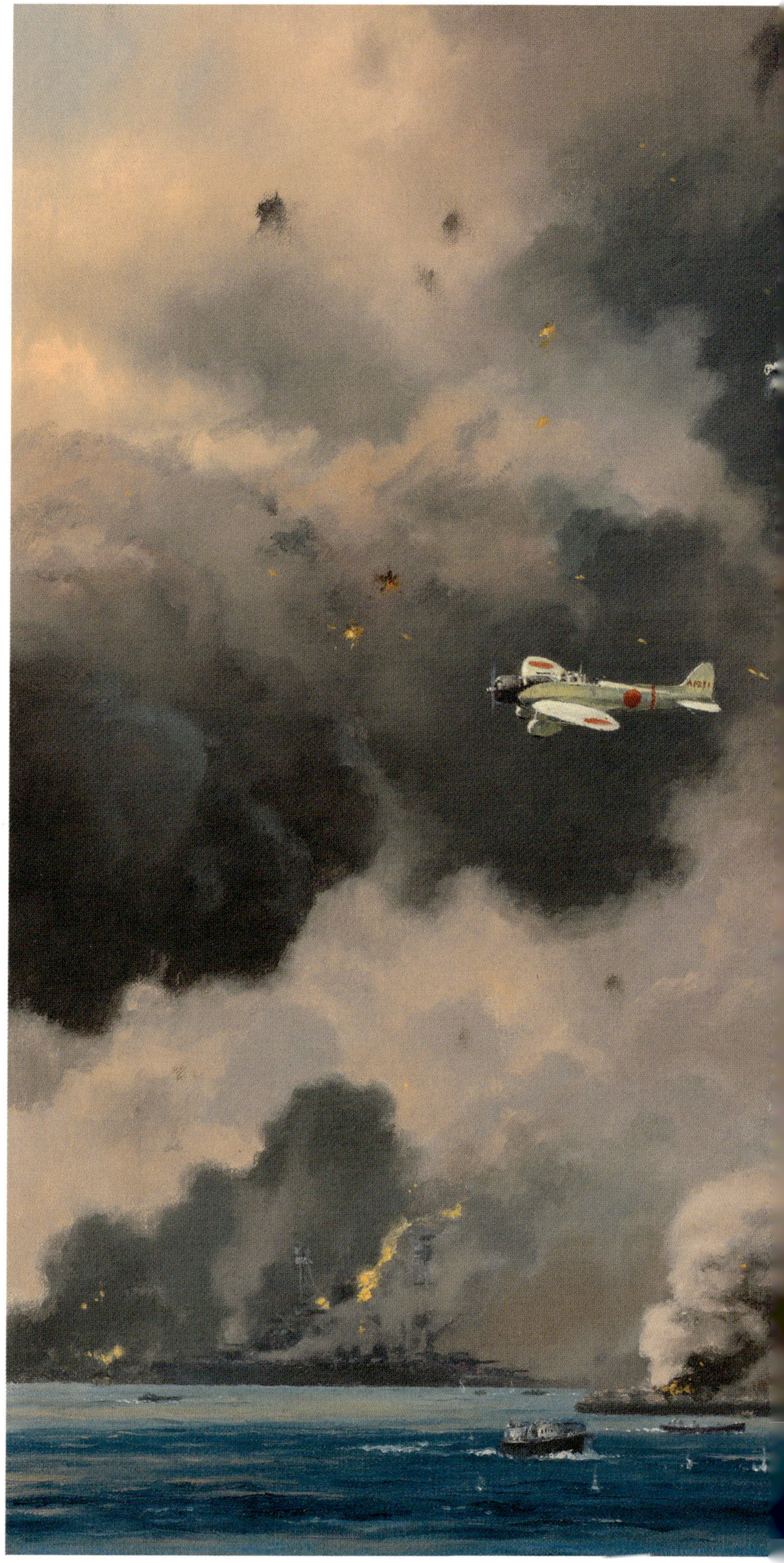

intended for use in the First World War. Building had begun in 1916 but, as she hadn't been launched until November 1919, she was too late to play a part in it. Her appearance had changed little in the intervening years.

From an artistic view point I suppose some might argue that an old grey battleship might not be the prettiest thing to portray in an oil painting, but maybe because I see things with an engineer's eye, as well as an artist's, I would disagree. For me, the *California* was a beautiful ship and, above all else, I wanted her distinctive and very dramatic lattice-work 'cage' masts to stand out in the painting. They were painted white and, catching the bright morning light, must have looked like homing-beacons for the Japanese pilots.

The *California*, as with most of the other damaged battleships, and those that were raised after sinking, underwent a complete modernisation after the attack to re-emerge as an almost unrecognisable modern battleship. One of the first things that disappeared were the two cage masts!

It was relatively easy to make sure the view of the *California* was historically accurate as there are quite a few photos of the ship taken that morning, many of which I could use for reference. I was therefore more than happy with detailing the *California* and with her position. The Val dive bombers, too, were relatively easy to place at the scene; the ones shown are from the Japanese carrier *Akagi* which formed part of the Second Wave attack. The main problem, however, was where and how to portray the American P-40 Warhawk.

I knew that only a handful of American fighters had got into the air, and most of these had been busy fighting off the attacks at the airfields well to the north. None of the books in my collection, however, could help me out with the question of whether any P-40s got into action over Pearl Harbor itself so, as a last hope, I contacted aviation guru Mark Copeland in the States for advice. Initially he wasn't sure either but, after discussing the matter with some friends and experts, the consensus of opinion was that in all the confusion a P-40 could well have chased one of the Japanese attackers down over Battleship Row.

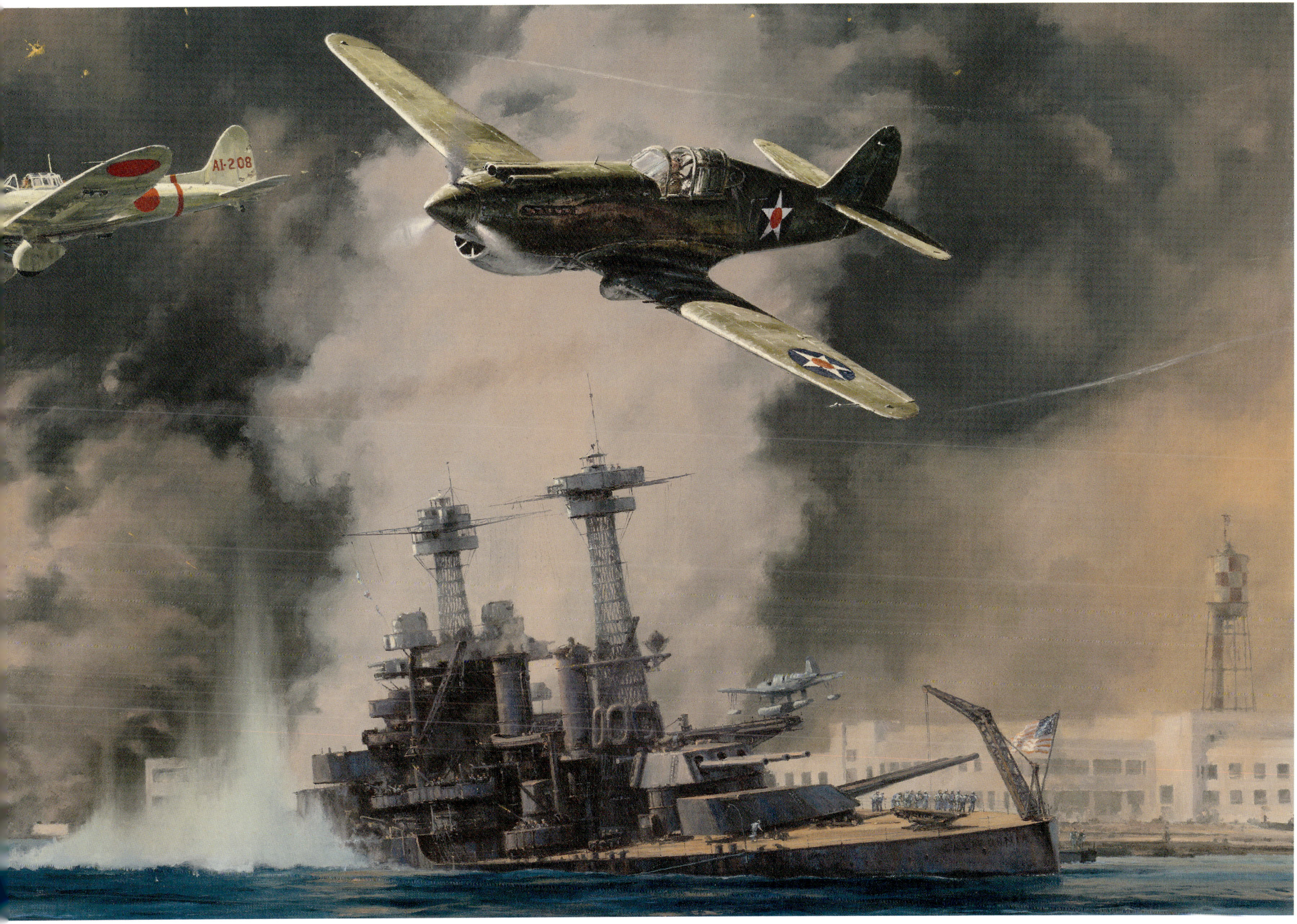
AI-208

PATHWAY TO THE RUHR

My wife Bernadette comes from a small village called Mayobridge in County Down, which is just north of the border in Northern Ireland. Every year we make the 12-hour car journey to visit her family and it was on one of these trips, a few years ago, that the concept for this painting was pretty much handed to me on a plate.

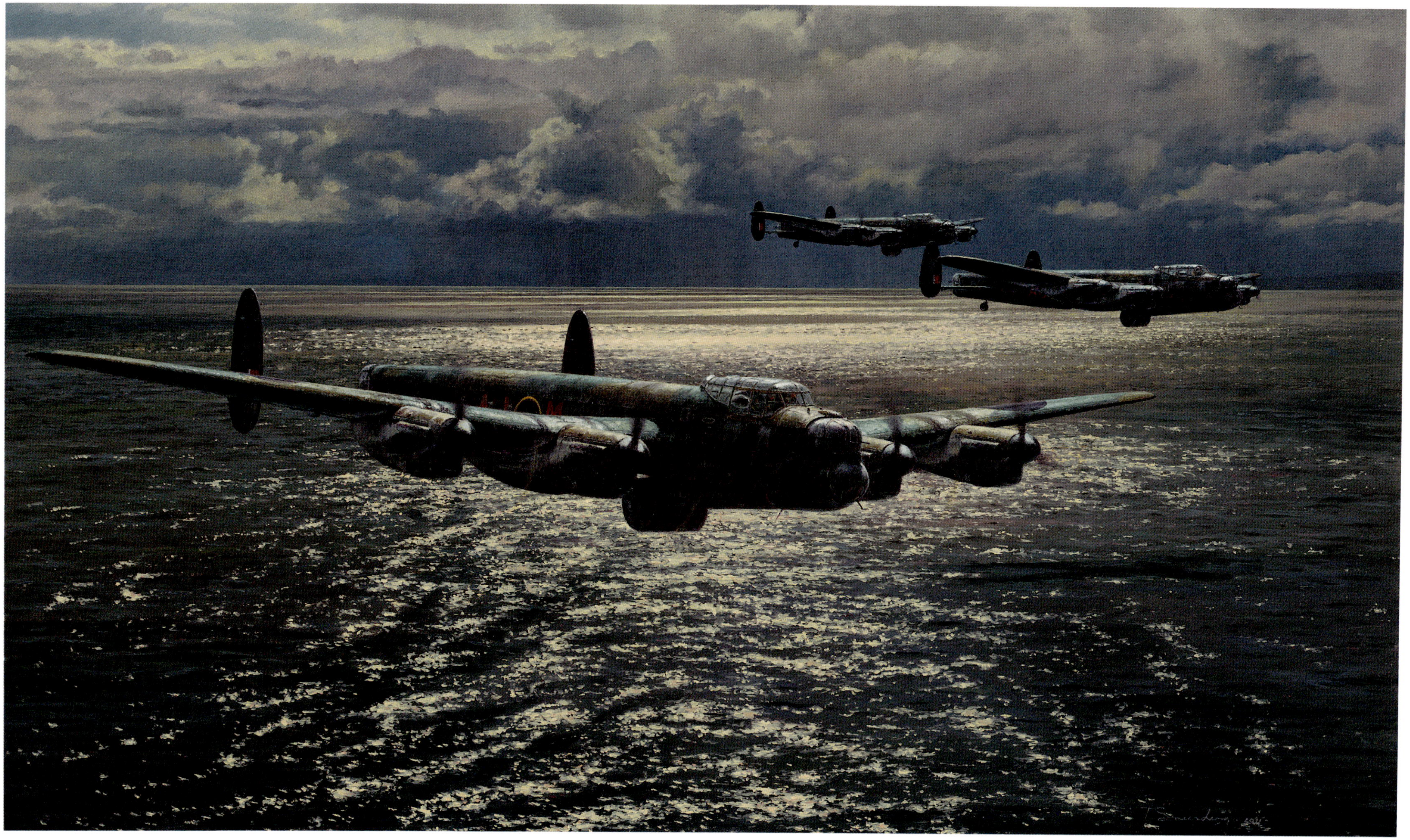

PATHWAY TO THE RUHR IN THE COLLECTION OF MR & MRS C HOARE

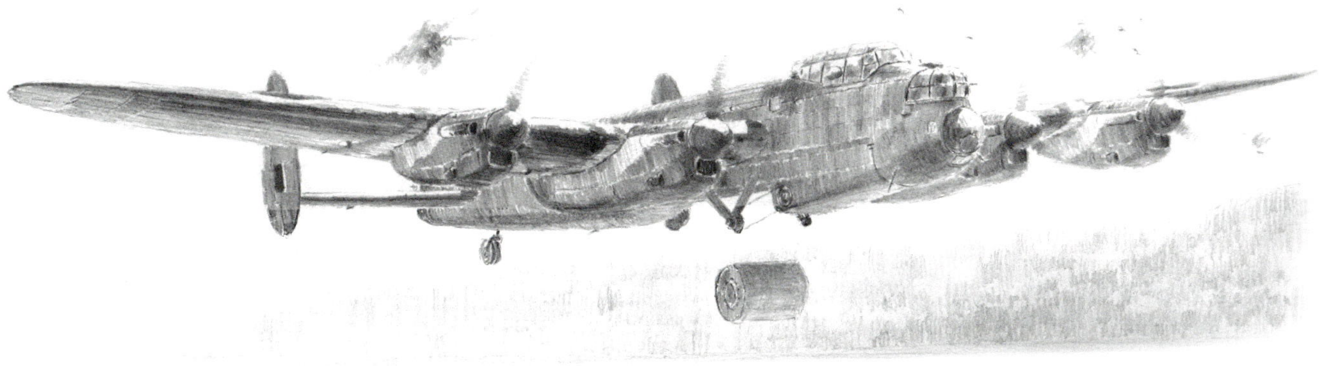

The company that operates the ferry service from Stranraer to Belfast promotes the voyage as 'the best ferry experience on the Irish Sea', and I think they're right. As soon as we arrive on board the first thing my children usually do, once they are safely out of the car, is to dash up the five or six flights of stairs to the forward end of the main deck to try and secure us a good window seat, because the views from up here are spectacular.

On this particular day, as the ship raced across the Irish Sea at an impressive 40 knots, there was a lot of thick broken cloud around which was casting some wonderful shadows on the surface of the water. As my children played, I happily snapped away with my trusty Canon Powershot S80, a brilliant little digital camera that I pretty much take everywhere I go. Today, however, it wasn't the family on the receiving end but the wonderful sea and cloudscape that was slowly unfolding in front of our eyes.

I took dozens of photos at varying exposures, using up megapixels as if they were going out of fashion, and when I eventually sat down and reviewed the images there was one that instantly stood out as the perfect backdrop for a painting that I'd been thinking about for some time.

The photo was under-exposed – probably the reason that it was so evocative and moody – but under-exposed or not, it was ideal for the purpose I had in mind: a stand-in for the North Sea as Guy Gibson had described it on the night of 16/17 May 1943. In his book *Enemy Coast Ahead* he describes the waves 'slopping by a few feet below with monotonous regularity' and how 'the moon dancing in those waves had become almost a hypnotising crystal'. I'd long wanted to portray his formation of Lancasters as they made their way across the North Sea on their way to attack the mighty dams of the Ruhr valley and the photo in front of me matched his words exactly.

That night Gibson, and the other pilots of the specially-formed 617 Squadron, had flown their aircraft very low across the sea to avoid detection by enemy radar. In fact one of them, Lancaster *AJ-H* flown by F/O Geoff Rice on the second wave, had flown so low that at one point his aircraft had skimmed the top of the sea. The impact had ripped his bomb away and left a gaping hole in the underside of the fuselage full of water. Only by quick-thinking and a dose of good luck did he keep his Lancaster flying, albeit he was forced to abort the mission. It was incredible to think that the Dambuster crews had flown at about the same height as we were now sitting on our monster ferry. I was confident that from where I had taken the photo was, more or less, the correct angle and height, and the recession of the cloud shadows on the sea into the far distance gave the

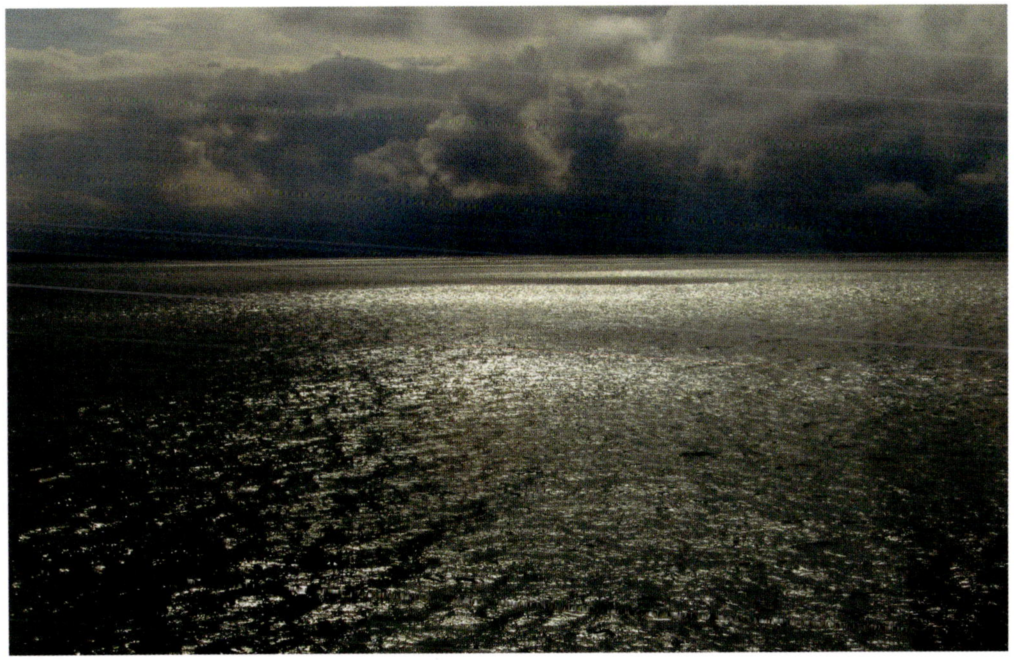

The original under-exposed shot of what became the North Sea in May 1943.

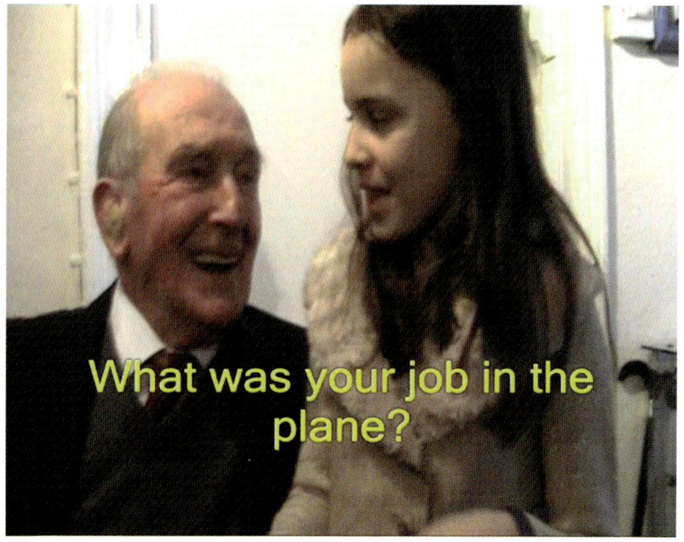

Rookie interviewer Amelia asks 'Johnny' Johnson the obvious question...

composition a great feeling of perspective. I was happy to leave it almost exactly as I had captured it.

Once we got home from Ireland I started to plan out the final composition. The children were still on half term which was a good thing because working on compositions needs a lower level of concentration than painting! Although under-exposed, the photo still didn't quite pass for a moonlit night but, after a bit of editing on the computer that simply involved reducing the brightness and increasing the contrast in equal measure, the image was pretty much perfect for what I needed.

All I had to do now was correctly create and insert Gibson's group of three Lancasters into the loose 'Vic' formation that they were flying in as they approached the Dutch coast. Luckily I have three model Lancasters all of the same scale. Only one was actually of the modified Dambuster variety that had been specially adapted to carry the bouncing bomb but, at this stage of proceedings, that didn't matter because all I was doing now was working out at which angle the three aircraft worked best together.

It didn't take more than a few days and then I was able to start painting which, for me, was wonderful, as the process of working out a composition usually takes several weeks. As I need at least another four, five or sometimes six weeks to actually complete the process of applying paint to canvas, this one was finished relatively quickly.

When painting, an artist needs to be able to add something more than a faithful reproduction of a photograph, however good it is. The human eye is amazingly subtle and can, in nature, pick out and distinguish many sophisticated colour tones that are difficult to capture in a photo, especially in shaded areas where the camera is rarely able to compensate for the delicate contrasts between bright and dark in the same way that the human brain can.

And there will always be a few other changes needed, either to make a composition more balanced or perhaps to make the subject stand out more, or a combination of both.

I was particularly pleased with how this painting turned out and was sad to see it go but I guess that's the same for all professional artists when a painting is sold. This one, however, did leave me with something – a memory I shall never forget: it gave me the opportunity to meet 'Johnny' Johnson, the last surviving British Dambuster. 'Johnny' was the bomb aimer in *AJ-T*, one of the Lancasters that attacked the Sorpe Dam, and the occasion happened at a signing event held by Aces High Gallery in Wendover shortly after the painting had been released as a limited edition print.

Johnny was one of the veterans signing the print and I was lucky enough not only to meet him but to have a long and really interesting chat as well. He told me how much he liked the print and how he had had a copy framed to hang in one of his rooms – I thought this the highest commendation possible! He was also great fun

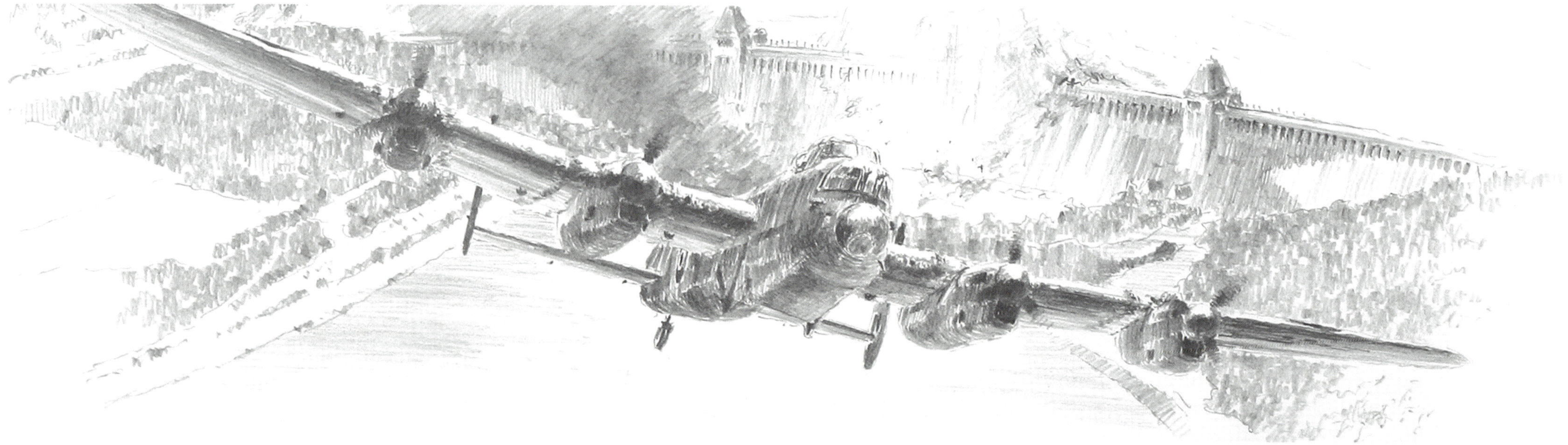

and the perfect gentleman to my daughter Amelia, who was then 11 years old. She had asked if she could come to the event as well, because she was studying the Second World War at school, and Johnny kindly agreed to her request for an interview with her video camera so that she could give a presentation to her class.

Johnny gave a wonderful interview – I certainly learnt some things that I hadn't known before – and I later heard that the video presentation had gone down very well with her class!

DAMBUSTERS

The painting on the right is simply called Dambusters *and I'm very fond of it, mainly because it's the one that got me noticed by the Military Gallery.*

My original intention had been to enter it at the Guild of Aviation Artists' Annual Exhibition which takes place at the prestigious Mall Galleries near Admiralty Arch in London, but I was so pleased with the finished result that I decided instead to include it as part of a portfolio of work that I sent to the Military Gallery. I'm glad I did because, luckily, they not only liked it but asked me if I could produce another, on the same subject, to make a pair. The second painting was called *En-Route*.

I'd painted the Möhne Dam a few years ago and was therefore keen to have a go at the other dam that 617 Squadron managed to breach that night – the Eder Dam. This was a far more difficult target to hit than the Möhne, lying in a deep valley surrounded on all sides by high, imposing hills. But this inaccessibility also proved a great advantage to the attacking Lancaster crews as the Germans thought it unnecessary to protect the dam with anti-aircraft batteries.

Recently the pilot of a small twin-engined aircraft carried out an experiment for a television programme: he approached the dam using the same flight path as the RAF pilots did, except that due to modern flight restrictions around the dam, the pilot was restricted to a minimum height of 500 ft. It was also carried out during daylight hours. Even so, the experienced pilot concluded that to attack the dam at 60ft, and at night in a heavily-laden, large four-engined bomber, as the Dambuster crews did, must have been almost impossible.

And, as if this weren't enough, there were also two other problems those amazing pilots had to deal with at the Eder Dam – that night a mist had unexpectedly developed over the valley and time was running short. If the Lancaster crews were going to get back and cross the enemy coast by dawn, they would have to move fast.

For this painting I wanted to show the actual breach and the devastating effect of the escaping torrent of water which I thought would be a novel portrayal of events. But to include the attacking Lancaster in the foreground meant using a bit of artistic licence with the timings. Once the *Upkeep* mine was dropped it had to bounce five times before finally coming to rest at the top of the dam wall; it would then sink 30ft at which level the hydro-static fuses were set to explode. I roughly estimated that this part of the process would take about 30 seconds. I then had to add on time for the actual explosion and the subsequent breach so the attacking Lancaster would probably have been at least a mile down the valley.

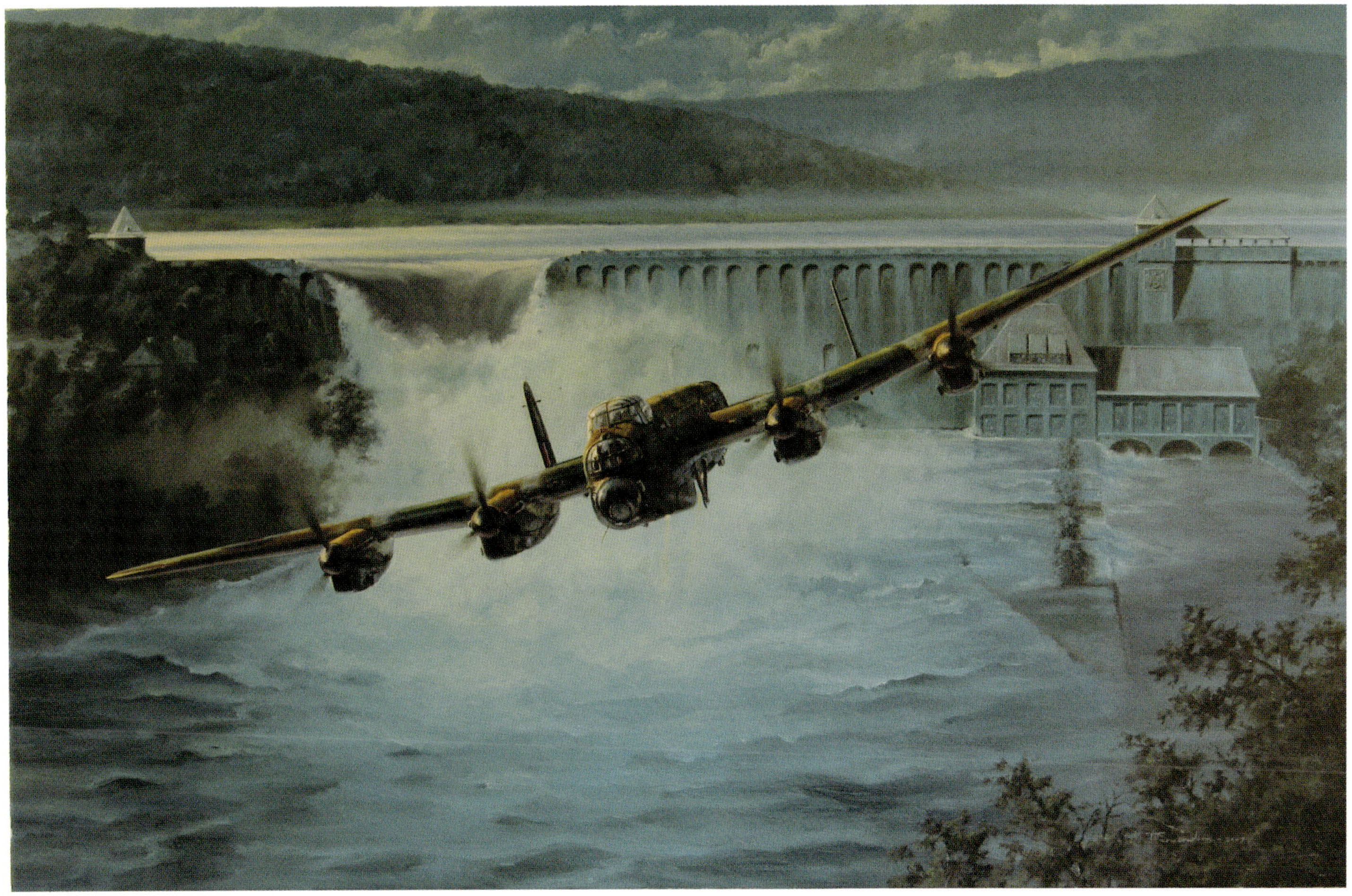

DAMBUSTERS IN THE COLLECTION OF SIR PETER JACKSON

A WELCOME RETURN

During the Second World War the US Eighth Air Force was based across a large swathe of central east England that ran, in the main, from Essex in the south, through East Anglia, the Fens and Cambridgeshire into the heart of Northamptonshire. It was the largest air unit ever committed to battle. Today many of their former bases are but ghosts and one was closer to home than I thought.

My daughter Amelia must have been three years old when I took her to her first-ever swimming lesson. The location was Kimbolton School and, weather and traffic permitting, the journey across country by car from home takes under half an hour. After turning off the main A41 on to the small country lane that leads down through broad open fields into Kimbolton village, I noticed a grey granite memorial erected by the side of the road. It stood in front of a small, isolated industrial estate and, curiosity gaining the upper hand, I slowed to a stop.

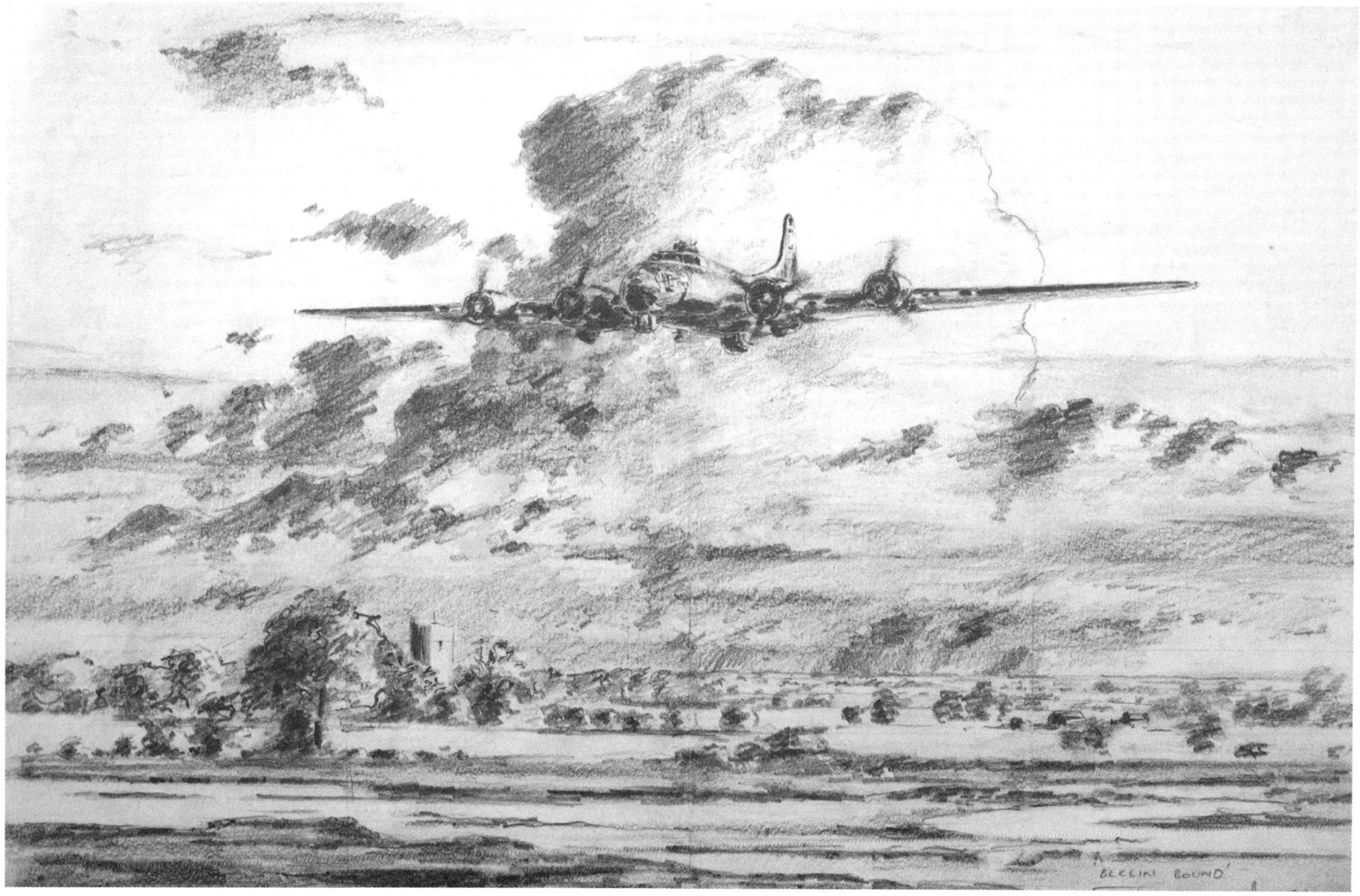

Three badges and the profile of a B-17 were carved into the stone and inscribed below them were the words:

SITE OF UNITED STATES ARMY AIR FORCE STATION
KIMBOLTON AIRFIELD
20TH MAY 1943 TO 4TH JULY 1945

The remaining text described the site as the one-time home to the 379th Bombardment Group (Heavy), a unit of the mighty Eighth Air Force that had flown 330 combat missions from here in the B-17s to destroy targets in Germany and Occupied Europe during World War II, and finished with IN MEMORY OF THOSE WHO SERVED.

Looking around, however, there was little to suggest that any part of the surrounding countryside had once been an airfield, and one of considerable importance. Nothing was immediately visible from the car except for a small pile of concrete rubble in the adjacent field. We were now running late but, as we resumed our journey, I made a silent pledge to re-visit and explore the place when time allowed. I would also find out a bit more about the 379th Bombardment Group and the airfield that I'd just discovered.

The 379th turned out to have an inspirational record: they flew more combat sorties than any other Bomb Group in the Eighth Air Force, they had the distinction of dropping the highest tonnage of bombs of any Bomb Group operating from Britain during the Second World War and, from the date of their arrival in May 1943, they attained the lowest rate of aborted missions of any

Group. These impressive feats were made all the more sobering by the fact that so little physical evidence of their existence at Kimbolton remained on the ground.

Reading through Roger Freeman's impressive *Mighty Eighth War Manual* I found a plan of the airfield complex, officially known as *Station 117,* which hopefully might help to identify any traces of its existence. Unfortunately my second and subsequent visits proved little more informative than the first but, using the plan, I was at least able to work out which way each of the three runways originally ran.

During the war the site had possessed maintenance hangars, a control tower, ammunition and fuel dumps, administration buildings and barrack blocks capable of accommodating hundreds of men. All long gone along with runways and perimeter track. The only hard-standing that survives intact is a tiny figure-of-eight portion – part of a dispersal area on the extreme east side of the site – and now used as a karting track. It brought a smile to my face to see that the kart club incorporates the 'Triangle K' tail symbol used by the 379th into their flag.

Apart from the little track, however, there's not much evidence, apart from the rubble I'd originally seen, to suggest that this was a bustling airfield whose main runway once stretched 2,000 yards across the rather bleak neighbouring field.

Now the place is eerily quiet. After several hours of trudging up and down public footpaths across the muddy fields all I ever found was a single dilapidated building hidden away amongst a lonely stand of trees and surrounded by brambles. Empty but for some sparrows, nature seemed to be winning a long battle with the remaining fabric and the roof looked highly unstable, kept up more by willpower than brick walls. My look inside, hoping to find at least some trace of the previous occupants, was therefore brief!

There was nothing left, of course, but the slow, decaying air of the place started me thinking about the men who might once have thought of this building as home. Probably there were a few who had spent a final hour under this now crumbling roof, setting out one morning on a raid never to return. But many more must have stumbled exhausted in through the gap where the door once stood, glad to have made it back in one piece. Another mission completed, another day closer to the end of their tour.

In its own way it was a very moving place and I felt sure that the story of the men who flew from here, and

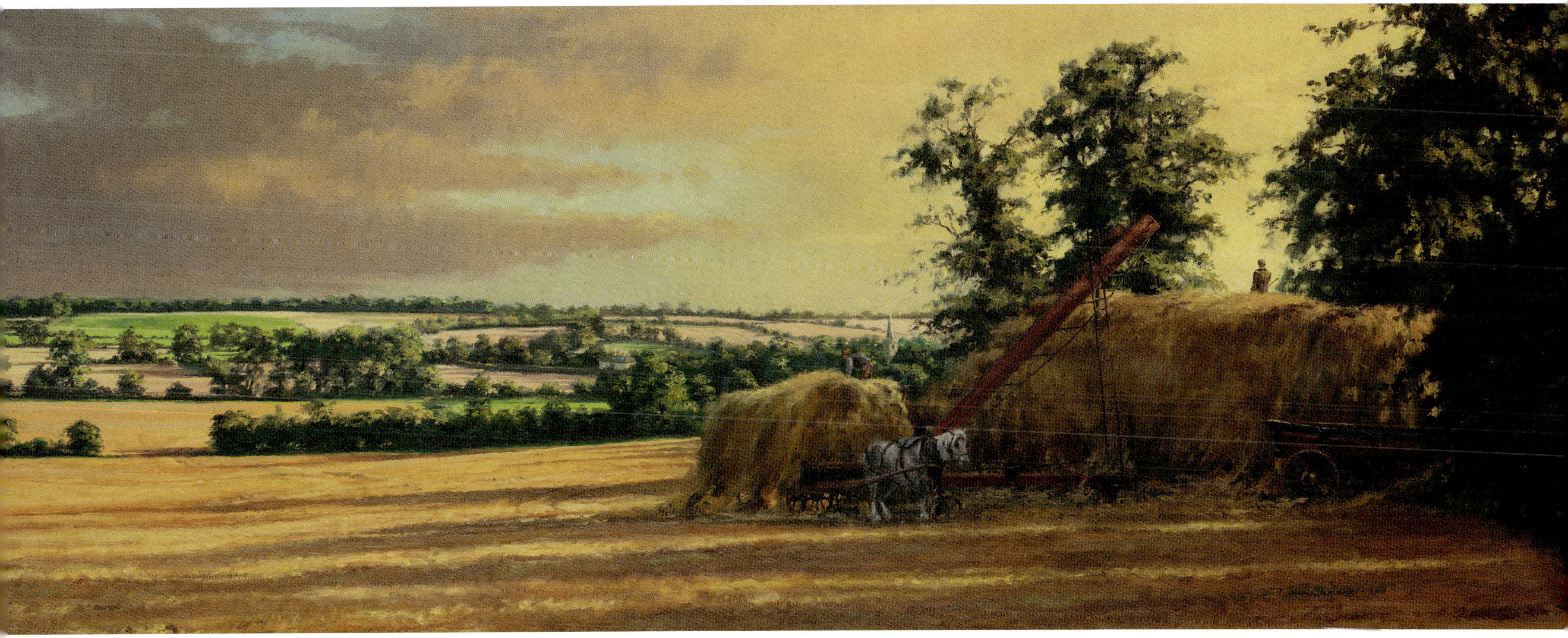

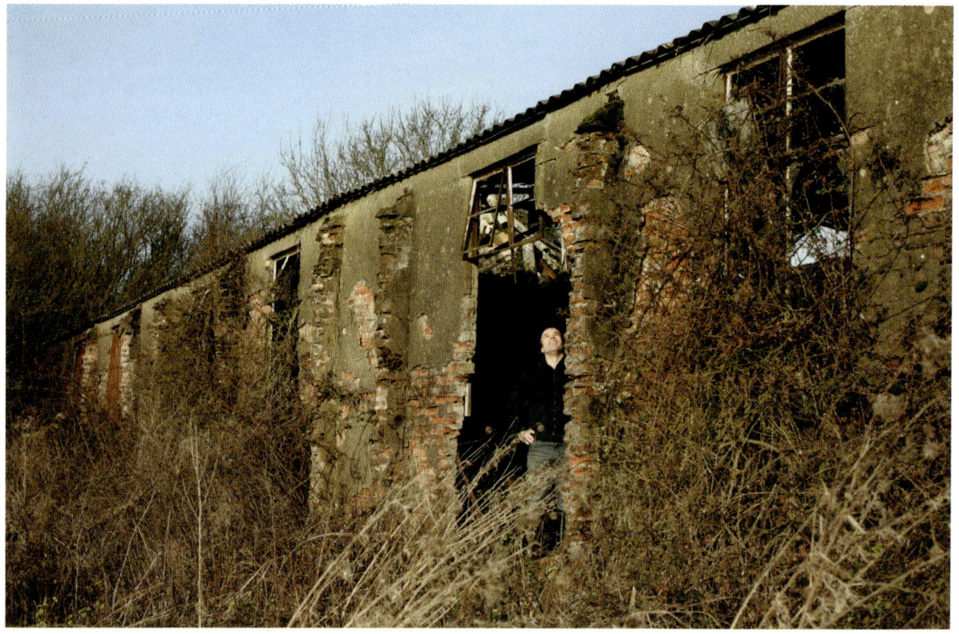

This crumbling old brick building was the only remnant I could find of what was once a busy airbase

the welcome relief they must have felt on a safe return, could be turned into a good painting. Anyway it was a great subject to tackle.

I managed to find an almost perfect spot from which to view the approach to the main runway from where I could imagine the tired B-17 pilots holding their aircraft steady and throttling back for final touchdown at the end of a long day. In the distance the steeple of nearby Tilbrook village church was just showing across the sloping valley but the foreground was a bit uninteresting. If the painting was going to work this area would need some attention.

Firstly I added some trees. In my research I had come across a photograph taken at Kimbolton in 1943 and it clearly shows trees on the perimeter that are no longer there. In all likelihood these were probably elms, amongst some of the twenty million or so in England that have been lost to Dutch elm disease – one of the most serious tree diseases in the world – since the war. Adding a few back in wouldn't be stretching artistic licence beyond the realms of possibility.

I also included some farm hands unloading a horse-drawn cart piled high with straw, and building a rick. The horse was probably well used to the thunder of engines but, nevertheless, it is being firmly held by one of the men just in case it bolts.

The only thing left now was to find a good source of reference for a B-17 that was stationed at Kimbolton, and preferably one with a notable pedigree. Although I do nearly all my own research, Rick Taylor at the Military Gallery put me in touch with Mark Copeland in the States. Mark is a leading authority on the Eighth Air Force and kindly supplied some amazing photographs of a 379th Bomb Group Flying Fortress called *Ol' Gappy*. She was a veteran of the 524th Bomb Squadron and during her combat service notched up 157 combat missions. They don't come much more distinguished than that.

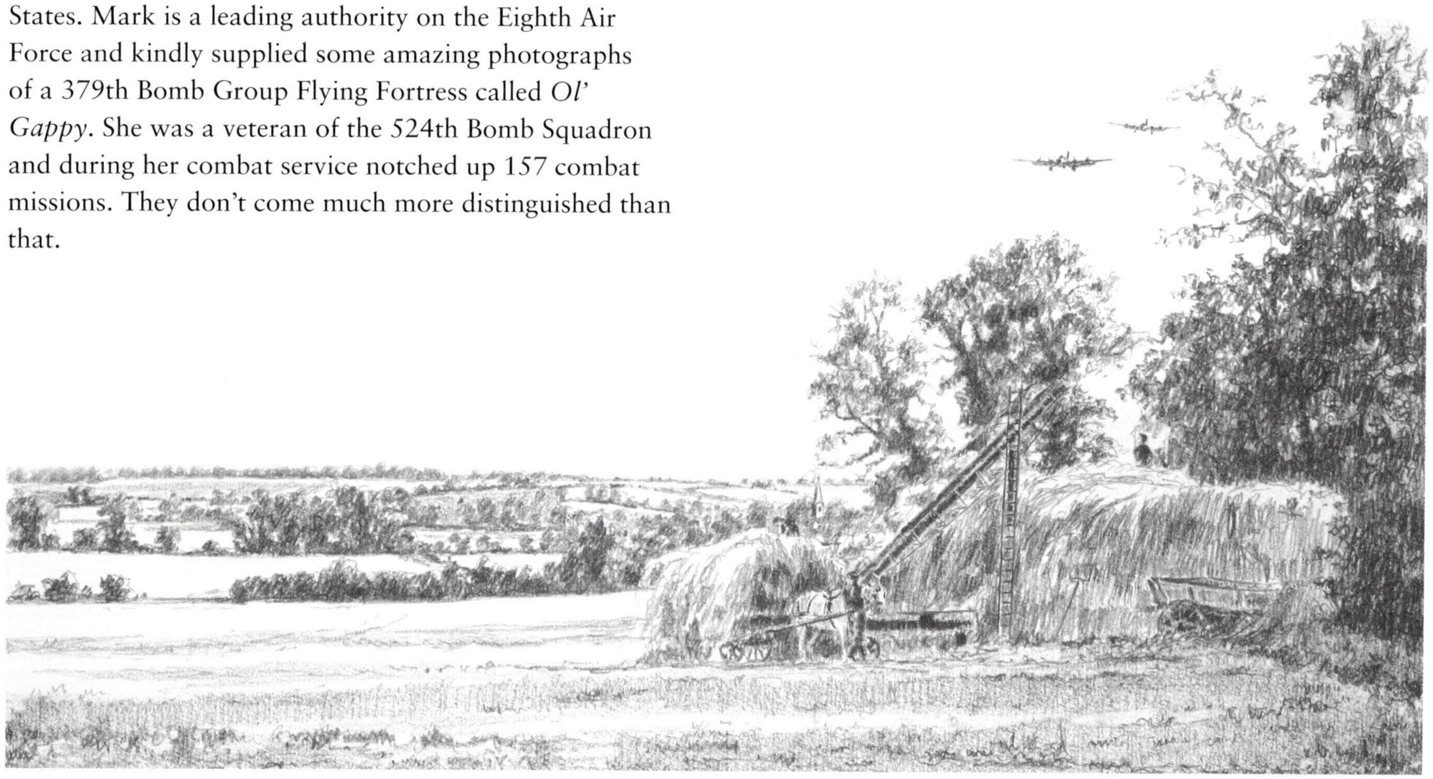

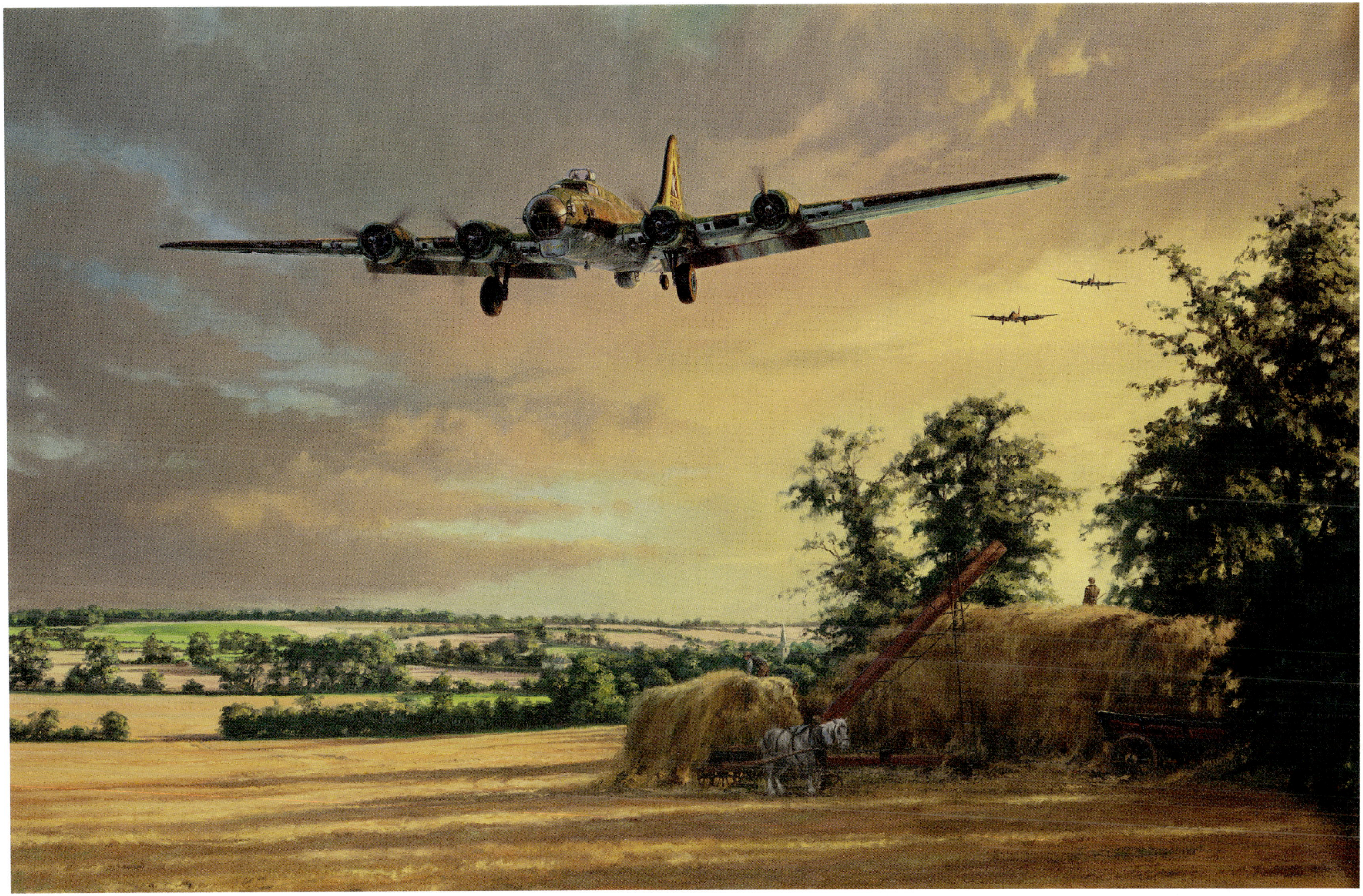

A WELCOME RETURN IN THE COLLECTION OF MR & MRS P. SHIPP

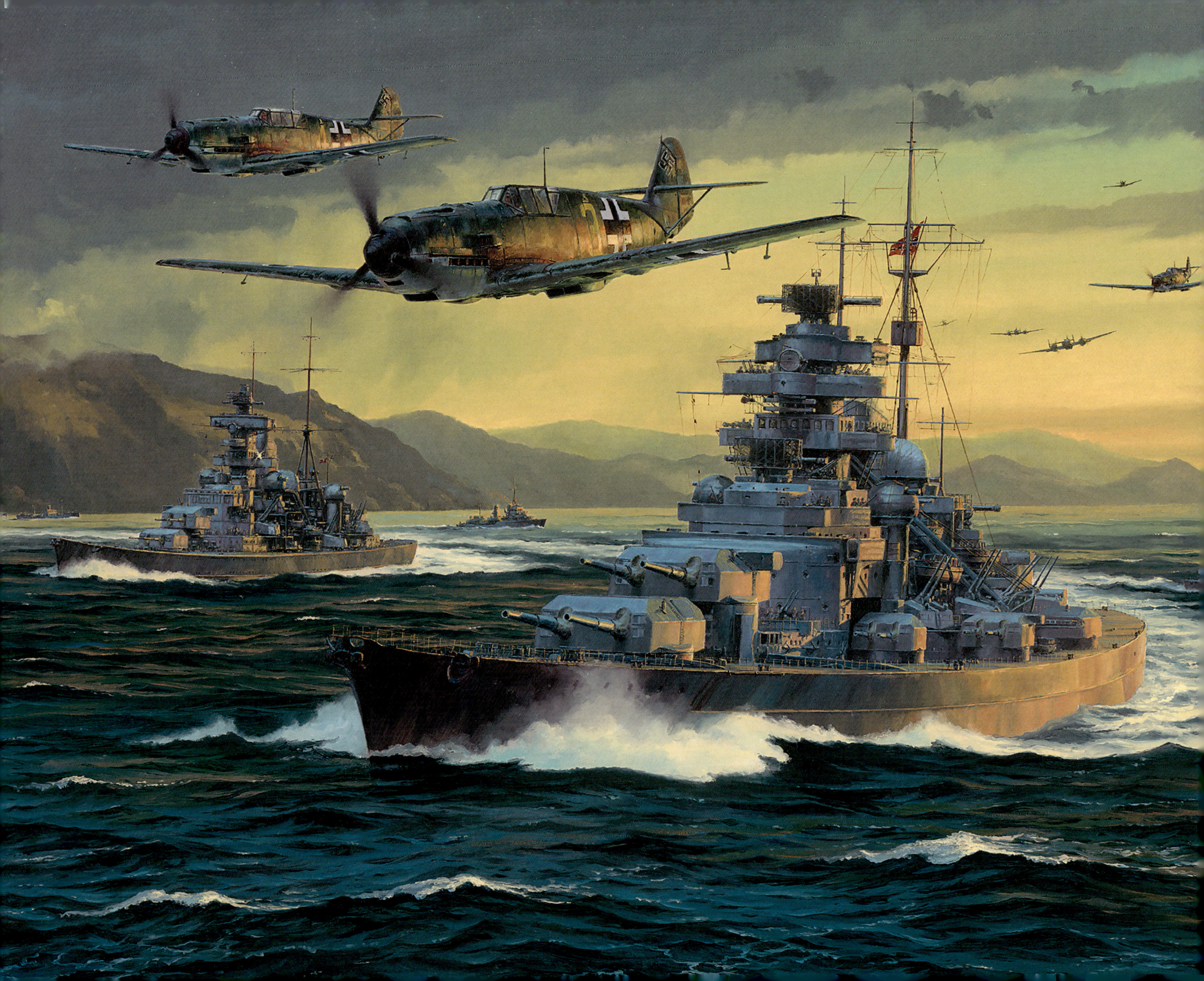

BREAKOUT

The clash between Hitler's largest battleship and the battlecruiser Hood – 'Pride of the Royal Navy' – became known as the Battle of the Denmark Strait. Fought on Saturday 24 May 1941, it was a brief, one-sided affair that ended in disaster for the Hood but, a few days later, the British Home Fleet would exact revenge.

The story of the duel between *Bismarck* and *Hood* is one that has enthralled me, and I suspect many others, since childhood. They were two of the most beautiful-looking ships of their kind and, many years later, I still have a clear memory of the day when, together with a friend, we re-enacted our own, small-scale, version of what happened when the two ships fought each other. Ours, however, differed greatly from reality.

In readiness for the big event I'd spent days making models of both ships from Airfix kits before we officially 'launched' them in a pond in his parents' garden, ready for battle, our catapults standing in for the massive 15-inch guns that both ships carried. Just as with the real event our version was over quickly, but it had a twist – this time it was *Bismarck* that succumbed and was quickly obliterated. The *Hood*, of course, survived without a scratch.

Strange to think that amidst all the excitement of *Hood's* great 'victory' I've no recollection of being annoyed that one of my models had just been completely smashed to smithereens and was beyond repair. It must have taken me a week to build, and cost a lot of pocket money!

On 24 May 1941, in company with the Royal Navy's latest battleship *Prince of Wales*, HMS *Hood* was flying the flag of Vice-Admiral Lancelot Holland, a gunnery expert who, as he steamed at full-speed towards *Bismarck* and her escort, the battlecruiser *Prinz Eugen*, was only too aware of his ship's main weakness – the deck armour was only three inches thick, highly vulnerable to long-range plunging fire. The ageing flagship, launched in 1918, had been due for a major refit to rectify the problem but the outbreak of war had forced the Admiralty to keep her in service.

With this in mind Holland tried to close the distance between himself and *Bismarck* as quickly as possible so that the trajectory of *Bismarck*'s shells would be flatter and less likely to drop vertically on to *Hood's* inadequately armoured deck. But it wasn't to be.

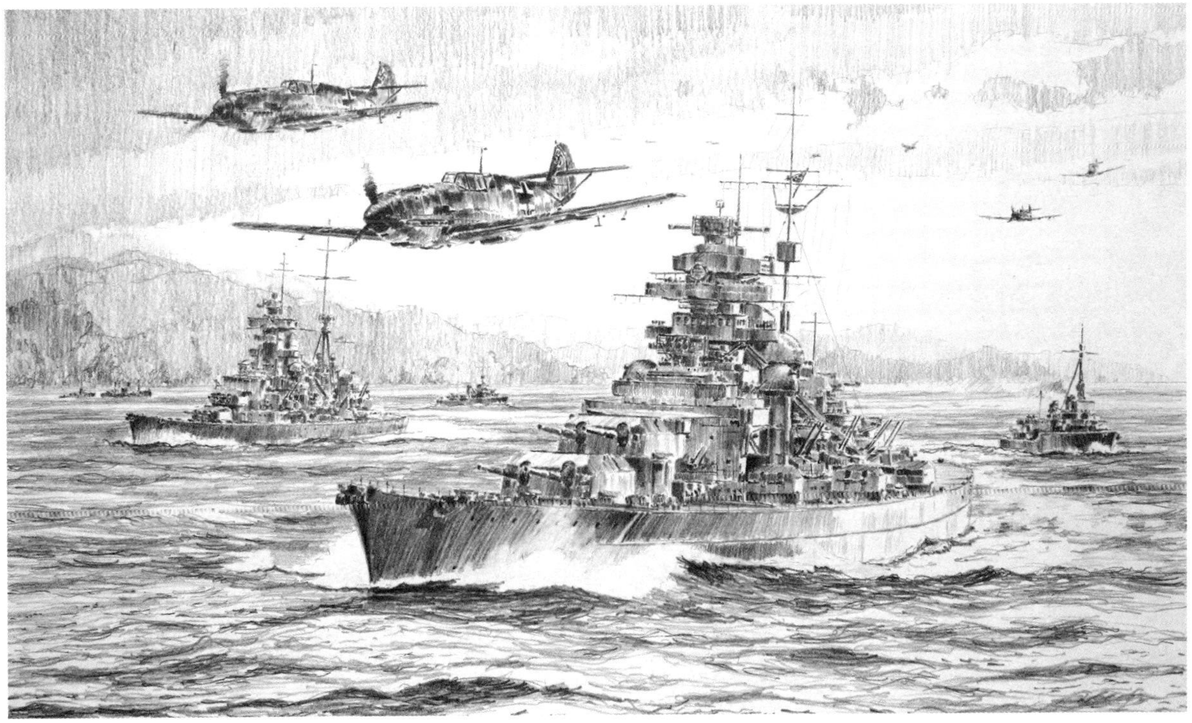

Although *Prince of Wales* struck *Bismarck* first, it was the German battleship who hit *Hood* with its third salvo – a shell penetrating near one of the after 4 inch gun mountings, starting a serious fire which spread to the ammunition lockers, the exploding shells causing havoc. After nearly ten minutes in action *Hood* had yet to hit her target. Then disaster struck. With both German ships targeting the British flagship, a single 15 inch armour-piercing shell from *Bismarck's* fifth salvo now hit the *Hood* amidships and detonated in one of the ship's main magazines. Onlookers could only watch dumbstruck as a pillar of flame erupted into the sky followed by the sound of thunder as a massive explosion ripped through the ship, breaking her in two. As her bow reared up and slid back into the sea the forward turrets were seen to fire off one last salvo: the *Hood* had delivered her final act of defiance.

Within three minutes the 'pride of the Navy' had disappeared beneath the waves, taking with her 1,418 men. There were only three survivors. The mighty *Hood*, symbol of British sea power, was a bitter loss that the Royal Navy vowed to avenge at all costs, and they did. Three days later it was *Bismarck* that lay at the bottom of the ocean.

A week earlier *Bismarck* had lain quietly at anchor alongside *Prinz Eugen* in Korsfjord, south of Bergen in Norway. During their brief stay both ships had their distinctive striped camouflage hastily painted over in Sea Grey, and the *Prinz Eugen* had refuelled. *Bismarck*, however, did not. It would later prove to be a costly mistake, but for now Admiral Günther Lütjens, commanding the battlegroup, was more concerned with breaking out to the open sea undetected.

As evening drew near on 21 May 1941, the two ships slipped anchor and crept out of the fjord, but Lütjens was unaware that his movements were known to the Royal Navy. Not only had the flotilla been photographed earlier that day by a photoreconnaissance Spitfire from Coastal Command, but his departure had been spotted by the Norwegian Resistance who immediately relayed the information to London.

I've always wanted to paint *Bismarck*. Whatever the ills of Nazi Germany there is no denying she was a beautiful-looking ship and, displacing 41,700 tons, was then probably the most powerful battleship in the world. As she entered the North Sea on that ill-fated voyage, just as the sun was setting, she must have appeared indestructible. Surrounded by her escort of destroyers and other support vessels, a force of around 40 twin and single-engine fighters of Luftflotte 5, including Me109s from JG/77 and Me110s of ZG/76, arrived overhead from their bases further south at Stavanger. They were to provide air cover to the maximum limit of their range and I thought the moment of the arrival would make a great setting.

Before I could start work, the first thing I needed to do was to find and build models of the German ships, not just the *Bismarck* and *Prinz Eugen*, but the destroyers as well. In the composition I had in mind they would all be partially side-lit, set against the stark light of the setting sun in the west. I therefore needed to see how this lighting would fall on the superstructure of each ship, and where the shadows for things such as the 105mm anti-aircraft guns would be cast. I love looking into small details like this that bring life to a painting, and the only way to discover them is to have a really good, accurate model, and for the minutest details, to be able to lay your hands on as many reference books, journals and photographs as you can find.

It had been a long time since I had built that first model of the *Bismarck*, but I can safely say that the model I used this time was itself a work of art, far larger, much more detailed and vastly superior to the one we destroyed in the pond. If this one gets damaged I really will be upset!

EISMEER PATROL

Sister ship to the Bismarck, *and every bit as deadly, the* Tirpitz *was a fearsome warship. Deployed in the fjords of occupied Norway, her mere presence caused havoc amongst Allied surface ships. This was never more evident than with the story of the Allied convoy* PQ17.

The Arctic may be the smallest of the world's five great oceans but in the summer of 1942 it was probably the most deadly because when Britain and America had agreed to send aid to Russia the previous year, it was the only viable route. Initially the Allied convoys got through to the two ice-free ports of Murmansk and Archangel with relatively few losses but, once the German High Command realised that one Allied merchant ship sunk could easily save the lives of thousands of German soldiers on the Russian front, it started to increase the number of heavy warships, U-boats and planes stationed in Norway to counter the convoys.

PQ17 was the largest Arctic convoy ever assembled. When the 35 mainly British and American merchant ships left the coast of Iceland, on 27 June 1942, bound

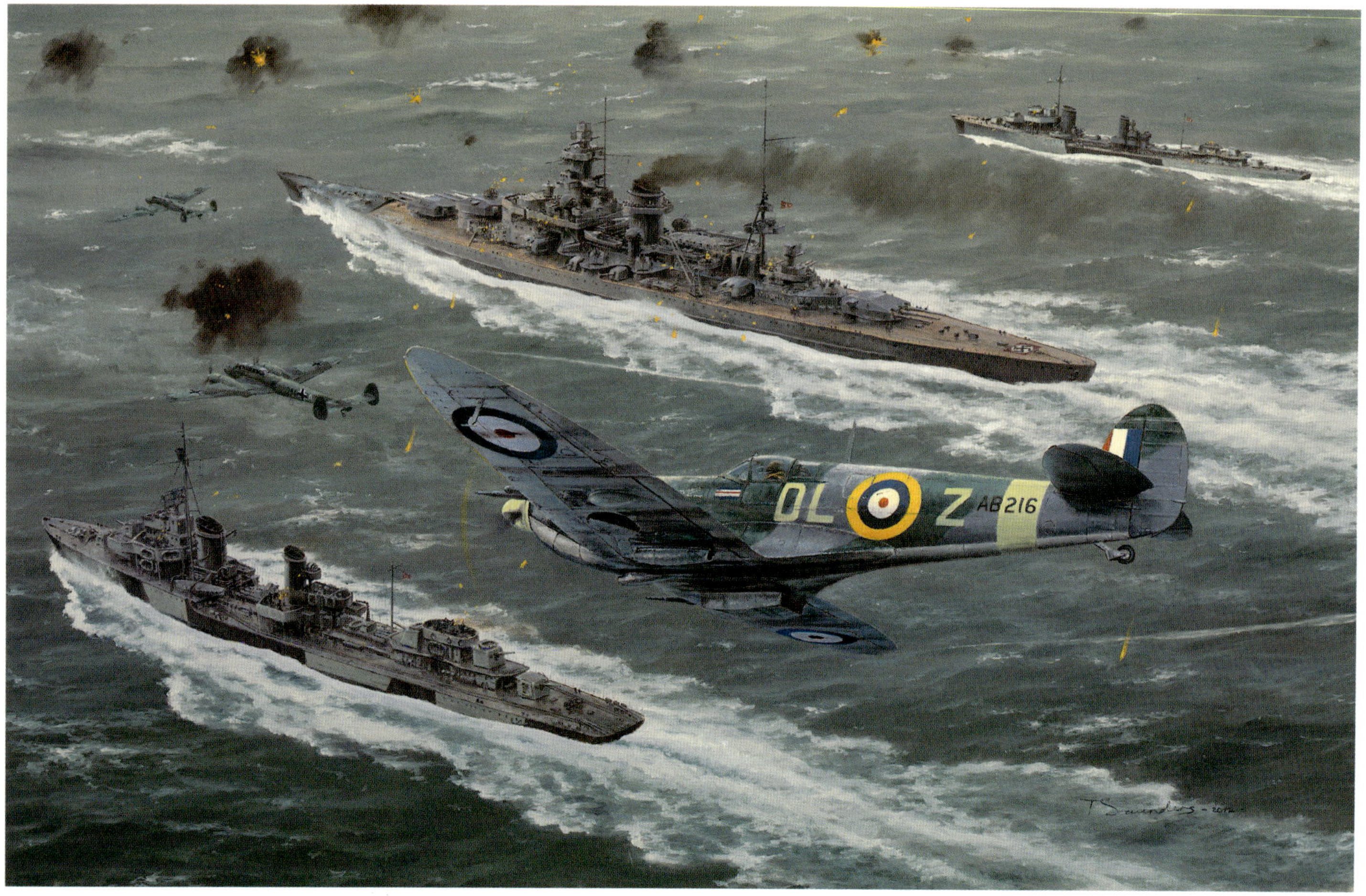

CONVOY PATROL –
THE CHANNEL DASH

IN THE COLLECTION OF MR JULIAN PARKER

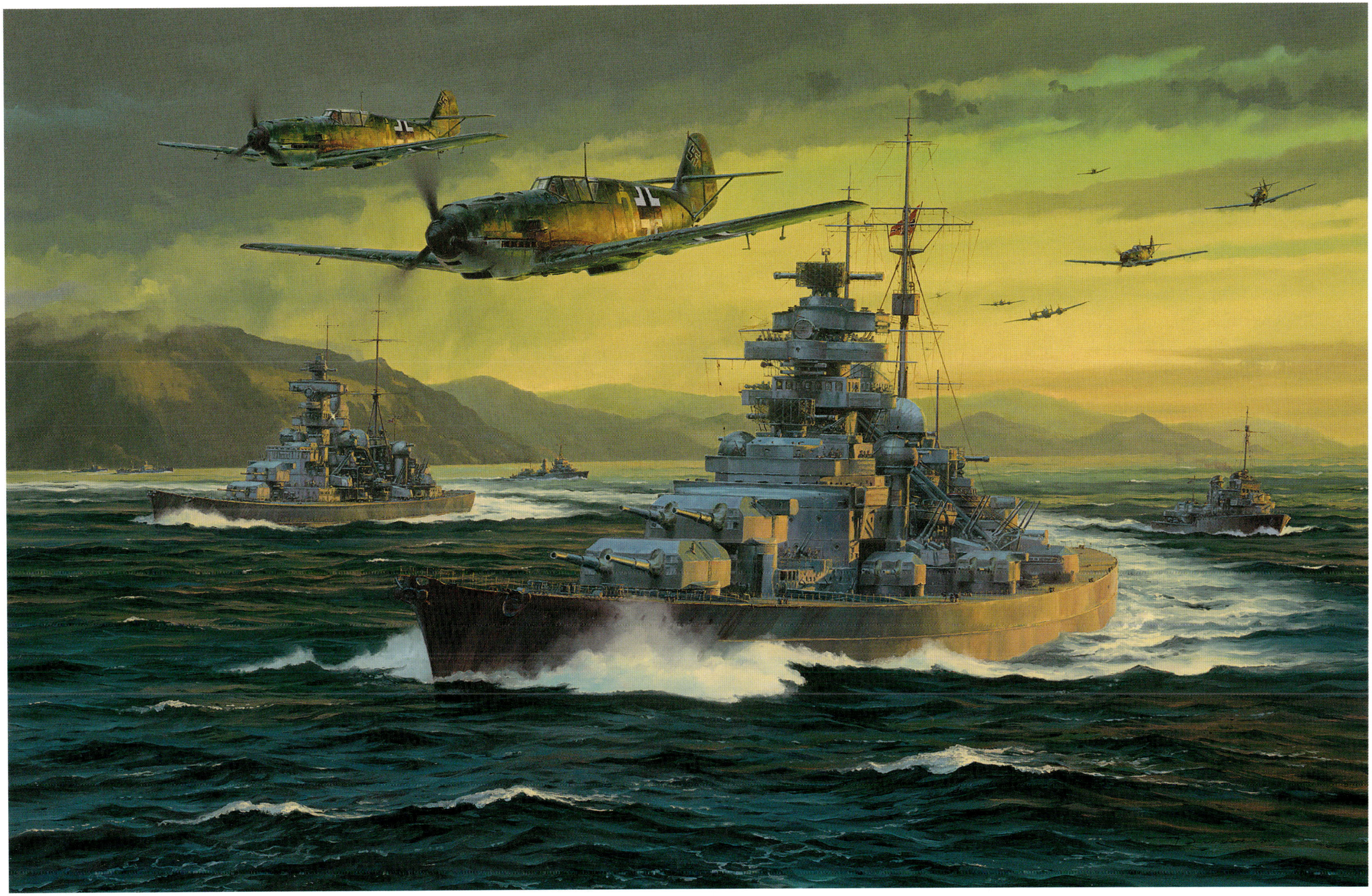

BREAKOUT PRIVATE COLLECTION

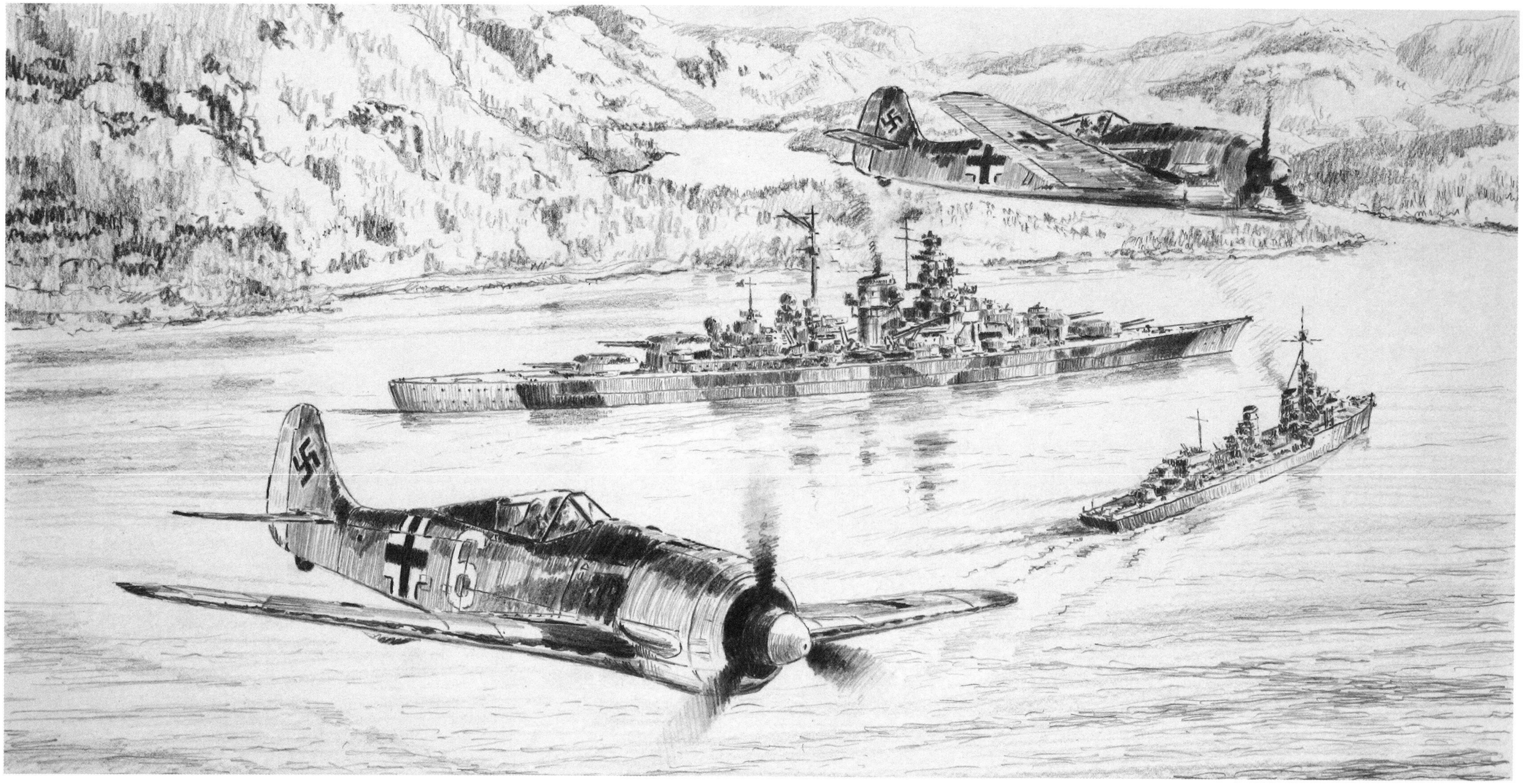

for Archangel, they were escorted by no less than 26 Allied warships.

To start with things looked good for the convoy, and although several merchant ships were lost to Luftwaffe attacks, the close escorts managed to thwart most of the German attacks.

But on the evening of 4 July, following Swedish intelligence that a large force of German surface ships had left their base in Norway, including the most feared ship of them all – the *Tirpitz* – the Admiralty issued the order for the convoy escort ships to withdraw, believing they were no match for the German battleship. The convoy was now alone and still 800 miles from its destination. A few minutes later another order was issued – this time ordering the convoy to 'scatter'. If the *Tirpitz* and her escorts were on the loose then, in the constant daylight of the Arctic summer, the merchant ships would have nowhere to hide.

PQ17 was later described by Churchill as 'one of the most melancholy naval episodes of the entire war'. Two-thirds of the convoy were eventually lost to German air and U-boat attacks, but ironically on this occasion, the much-feared *Tirpitz* never even left its base.

But the threat of her presence had been enough. The Royal Navy was now forced to keep much of the Home Fleet in readiness to contain her, and the RAF would devote a series of large-scale raids to try and sink the German battleship.

In *Eismeer Patrol*, Fw190s of IV./JG5 provide aerial protection on the morning of 11 March 1943 as the *Tirpitz* prepares to leave her temporary base in southern Norway, heading for Bogenfjord near Narvik in the north, in order to try and escape the increasingly persistent raids by the RAF. She would, however, also be closer to her intended prey – the Arctic convoys.

Tirpitz was eventually sunk in November 1944 by British Lancaster bombers from 9 and 617 Squadrons equipped with 12,000-pound 'Tallboy' bombs.

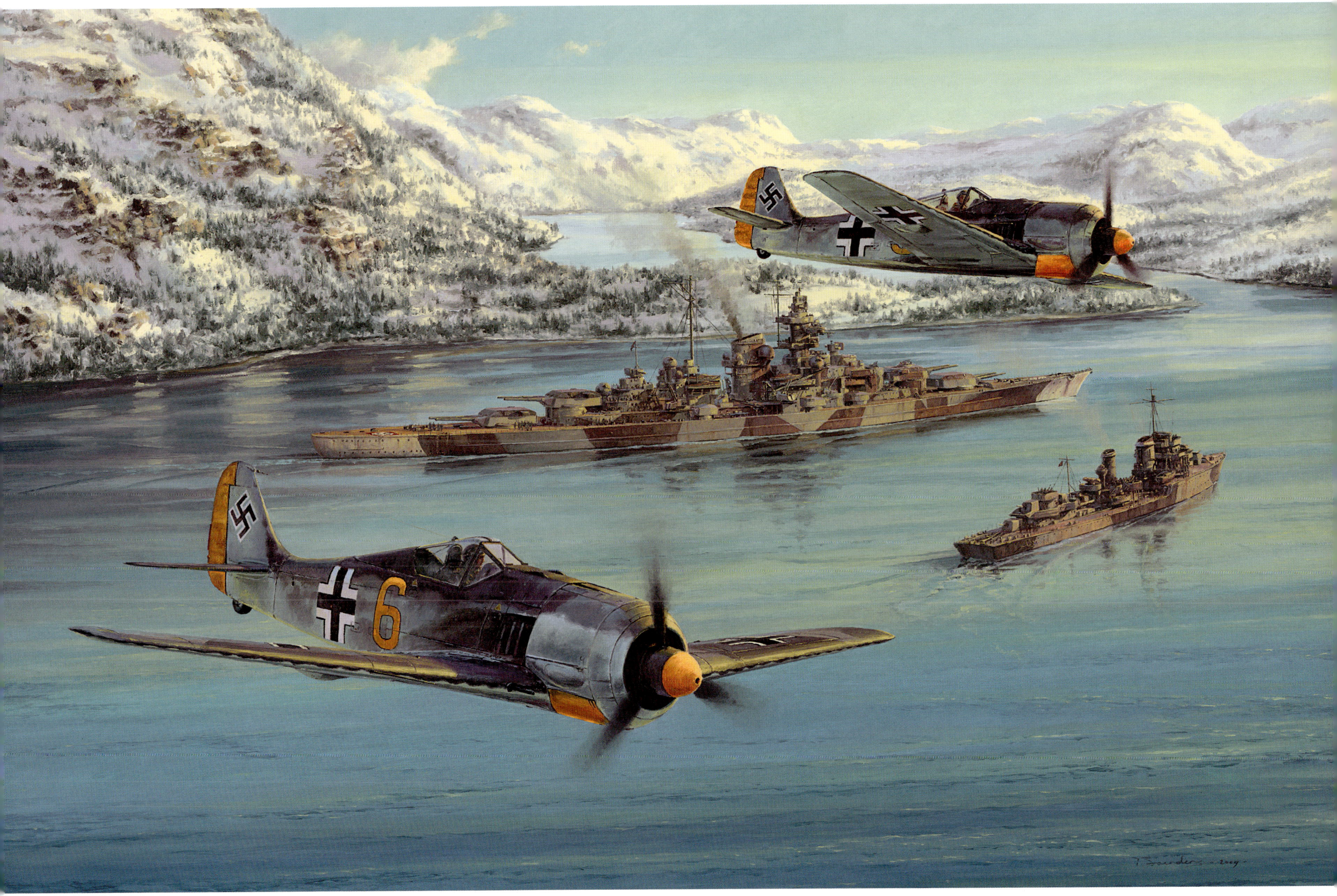

EISMEER PATROL IN THE COLLECTION OF MR TERRY BROWN

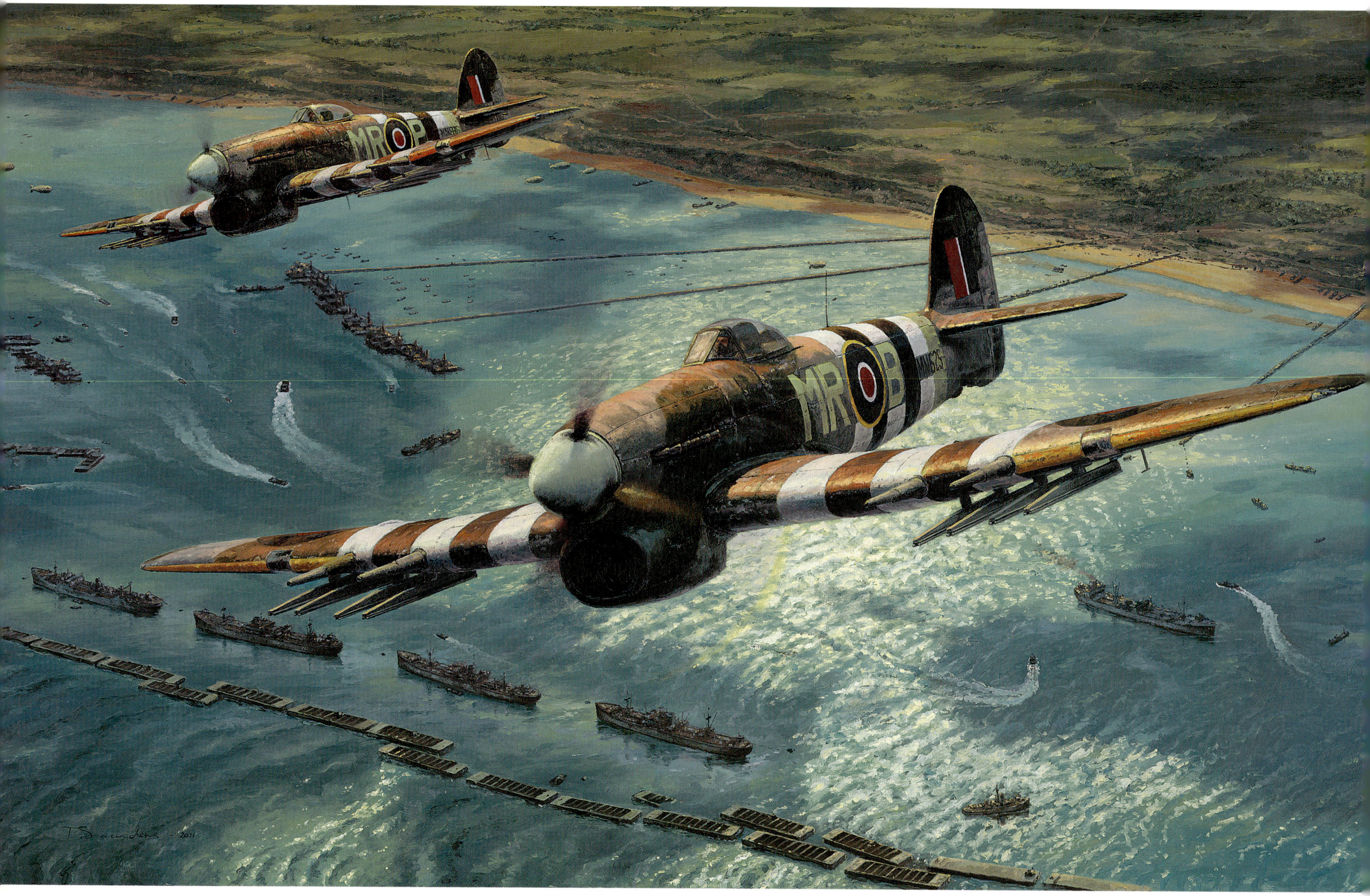

RETURN OF THE HUNTERS IN THE COLLECTION OF MR MARK BROWN

RETURN OF THE HUNTERS

Originally designed as a fighter to replace the Hawker Hurricane, the Typhoon suffered from many teething problems until it was discovered that its ruggedness and fire power made it the ideal ground attack aircraft – a quality put to devastating effect on D-Day and the battle for Normandy.

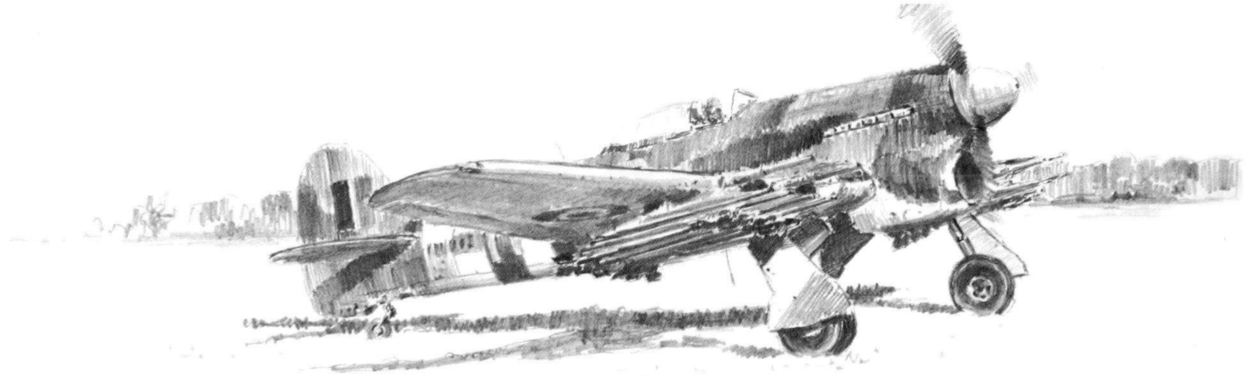

By June 1944 the tide of war had turned in favour of the Allies and much had happened since the dark days of 1940, when Britain stood alone against the seemingly invincible might of Germany. The Battle of Britain had caused Hitler to postpone his invasion of the British Isles and the following year his attack on the Soviet Union, although initially successful, had propelled that powerful country into the Allied camp. And then, at the end of 1941, the Japanese attack on the United States Pacific Fleet at Pearl Harbor had drawn the most powerful economy in the world into the fight against the Axis powers.

There would, however, be long, hard-fought battles before even a glimmer of victory began to show. But, slowly, the tide did turn. At El Alamein the British 8th Army started an advance that would result in the Germans being pushed out of north Africa. At Stalingrad the Red Army annihilated the German 6th Army. In the North Atlantic the U-boat menace had all but been defeated whilst in the Mediterranean a series of amphibious operations had, by the summer of 1944, brought the Allies almost to the gates of Rome.

In the Far East, too, the war was turning. The Japanese had finally been held in Burma and were being driven back in New Guinea and the Pacific islands.

In Britain, meanwhile, the Allied bombing offensive was pounding the enemy by day and night as a build-up of men and equipment from across the Atlantic grew ever stronger. But there was one inescapable fact: Germany would have to be beaten on mainland Europe and to do that the Allies would need to invade. The planning would take time and a huge amount of resources but, on 6 June 1944, after nearly five years of war, the Allies launched the greatest amphibious operation in history – Operation *Overlord*.

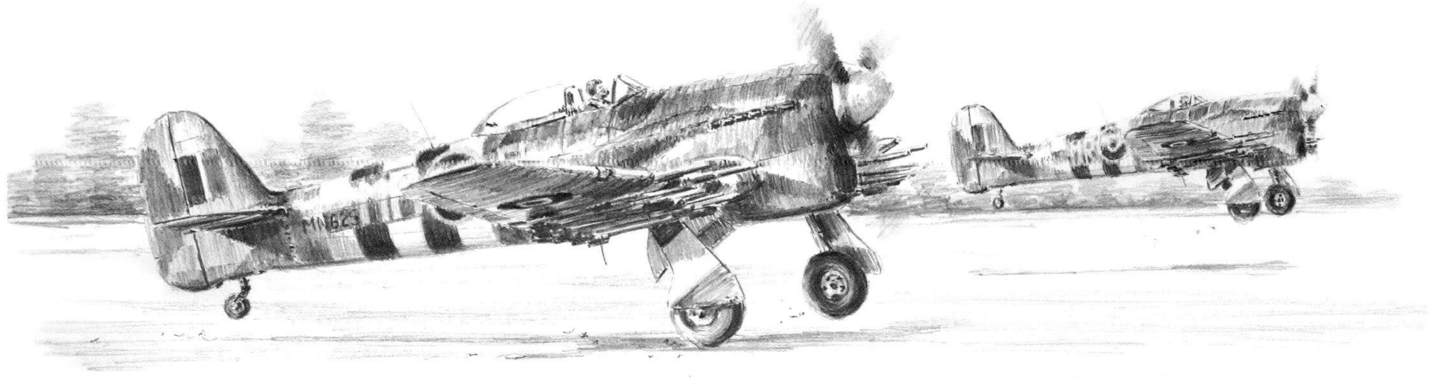

Allied air supremacy over the Channel and landing beaches would be crucial to the success of the operation and one aircraft now came into its own – the Hawker Typhoon. The Typhoon had had a troubled development with many design problems associated with its large and powerful Sabre engine, as well as structural weaknesses near the tail section. In some instances the tail had sheared off completely with disastrous consequences. But the ever-resourceful designers at Hawker had overcome these problems and by D-Day twenty front-line RAF squadrons were equipped with Typhoons. Eighteen of these squadrons were assigned to the 2nd Tactical Air Force, a component of the Allied Expeditionary Air Force providing air support for the invasion of Europe.

The Typhoons' first task before the invasion was to attack the German coastal radar chain. Heavily defended, these sites often required repeat attacks, which resulted in high losses, but the anti-radar campaign was so successful that during the landings the German defenders were blinded by large gaps in their radar coverage.

Once the troops were ashore and advancing out of the beach areas, the Typhoons provided extremely effective tactical support. The Normandy countryside was perfect for defensive tank warfare with the many small fields and deep hedgerows providing plenty of cover for the enemy tanks and heavy weapons. A system known as the Visual Control Post or 'cab rank' was devised whereby advancing troops could call in Typhoons, usually equipped with rockets, and, with the use of gridded maps and special coloured smoke markers laid down by the ground forces with mortars, the Typhoons could make pin-point attacks where they were most urgently needed.

The German tanks, particularly the Tiger tank with its 88mm gun, often outclassed the Allied Sherman tank except in numbers, and even though the Sherman had a similar fire power to many German tanks it often came off worse in a one-on-one battle because the cast steel armour of the Sherman lacked the toughness of the rolled steel plate used by the Germans. This, coupled with its high profile, gave the Sherman a serious tendency to burst into flames when hit by armour-piercing shells. British tank crews ironically called it a 'brew-up'. Luckily the rocket-firing Typhoons of the 2nd TAF more than made up for any Allied shortfall in tank quality.

In *Return of the Hunters* I've portrayed two Typhoons of 245 Squadron homeward bound after attacking German positions in Normandy. In contrast to the usual view of showing them in action I decided to include one of the two massive 'Mulberry' artificial harbours that had been constructed. Each the size of Dover harbour, in a remarkable feat of logistics, it had taken just seven days to assemble!

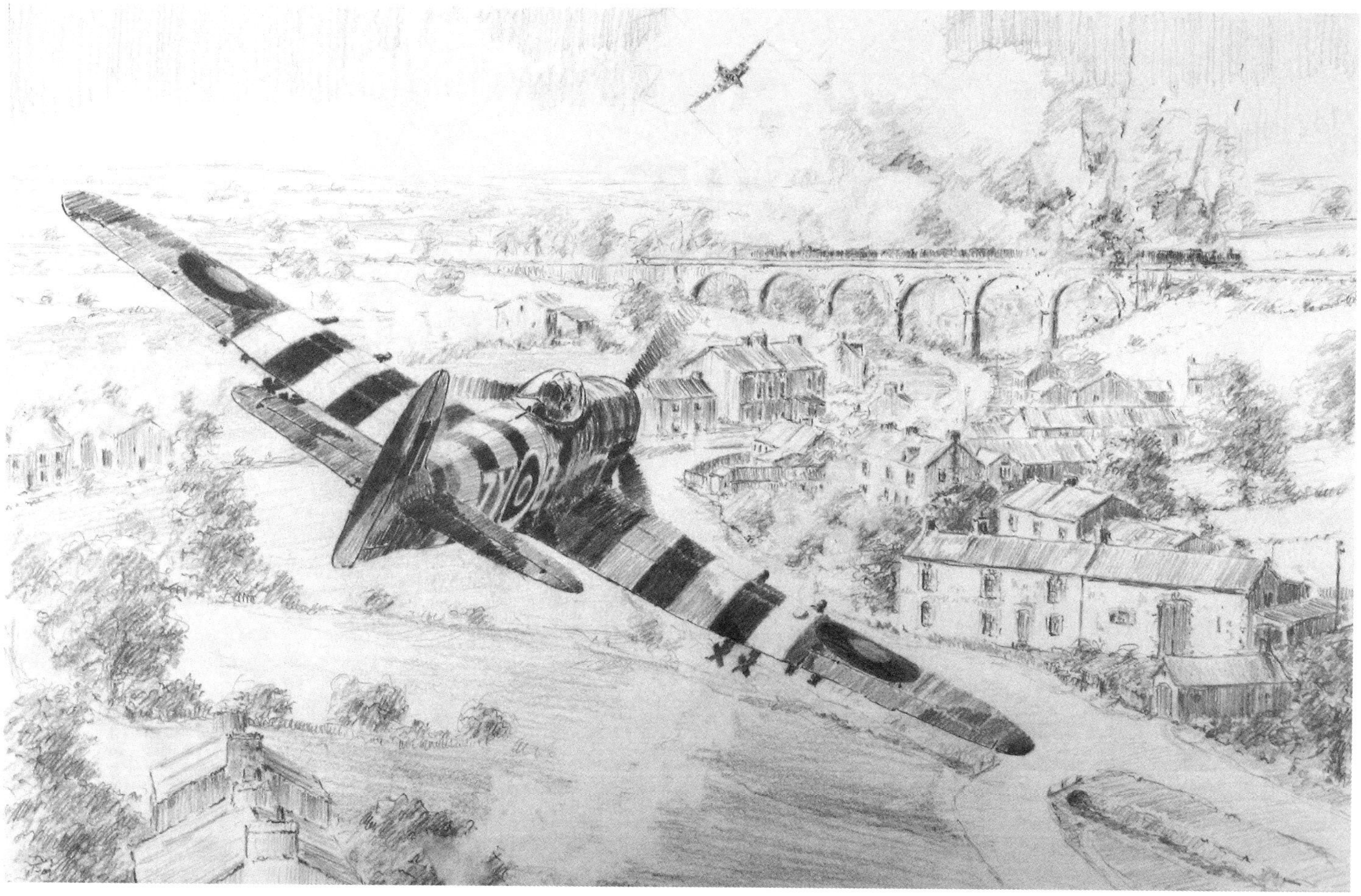

BRIDGE BUSTERS

Produced in more numbers than any other American fighter, Republic's P-47 Thunderbolt became the workhorse of the USAAF but, lacking the sleek lines of the Spitfire or P-51 Mustang, it had to earn the appreciation of the men that flew it.

When the first P-47s arrived in England many fighter pilots just shook their heads in amazement – 'It's too big' some said, 'and too heavy', whilst 'you could take a shower in there' was a common remark. And it was certainly big: 36 ft long and nearly 15ft high, it's said that a Spitfire could park under its wing. Fully loaded it weighed in at over 6 tons, making it the largest and heaviest fighter powered by a single piston engine, yet it didn't take long for the Thunderbolt to earn a reputation equal to its massive proportions.

Pioneering the technique of daylight bomber escort, the 'Jug', as many called it, was largely responsible for establishing initial Allied air superiority over Germany. It was only when replaced in this role by the P-51 Mustang, however, that it found its true forte, that of the fighter-bomber – a role in which it would excel, particularly during D-Day and the subsequent battle for Normandy.

The Overlord invasion saw the greatest concentration of striking air power ever witnessed, with over 12,000 Allied combat aircraft involved. Whilst the heavy and medium bombers targeted coastal guns, marshalling yards and military stores, it fell to the fighter-bombers, such as the P-47 and the Hawker Typhoon, to attack the tactical targets. It was here in Normandy that both aircraft would earn their legendary status as the most

My original working drawing for Bridge Busters with a Typhoon

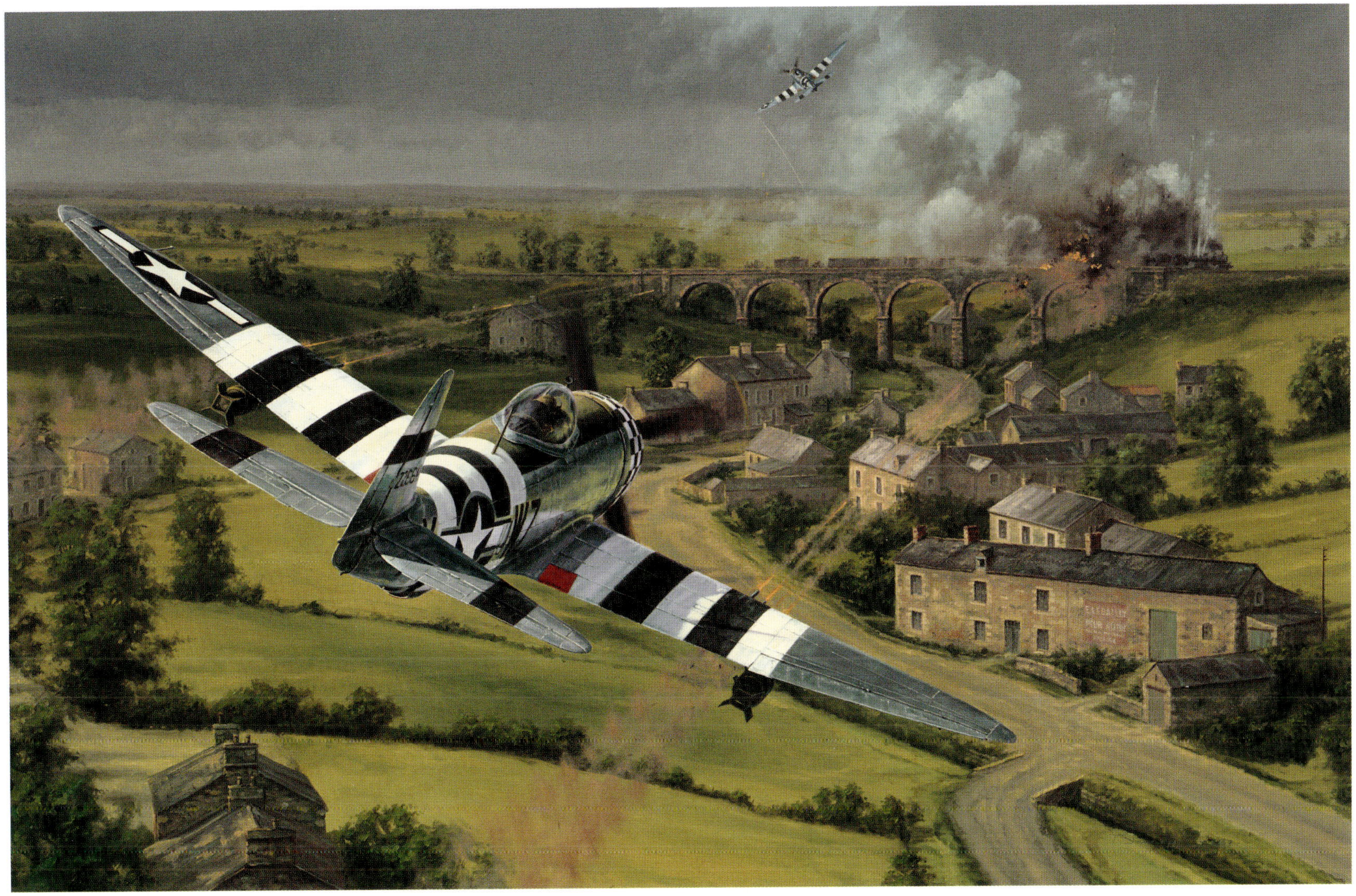

BRIDGE BUSTERS

PRIVATE COLLECTION

devastating ground attack aircraft of World War II, extremely adept at destroying Wehrmacht columns and supply lines whether by cannon fire, rockets or bombs.

The cost of inflicting such devastating fire-power on the enemy, however, was high. On 10 June 1944, the 78th Fighter Group lost 10 pilots, mainly from ground fire but, had it not been for the P-47, the toll might have been higher because it could take more punishment than most. Its huge 2,000 horsepower radial engine could sometimes take several hits and still get its pilot safely home, albeit with the aircraft covered in oil. These qualities are probably what inspired Hub Zemke, the legendary commander of the 56th Fighter Group, to write, 'If you wanted to impress a girl back home you'd fly a P-51. If you wanted to get back to that girl, you'd fly a P-47'.

When I first started working on *Bridge Busters* I'd intended the main aircraft to be a Hawker Typhoon that was sweeping low over a small French village, targeting a German supply train that the pilot had spotted crossing the viaduct nearby. But there was something about the Typhoon's long rounded wings that, from this particular angle, didn't quite look or feel right. It was only when I considered the P-47's smaller elliptical wing, with its more pronounced dihedral angle, that it dawned on me that using a P-47 might, in this case, work much better.

As much as I've always loved the rugged Typhoon, once I had started painting the P-47 I knew I had made the right choice as it had some great visual qualities that helped it stand out against the green fields of the landscape below. Both, of course, had the dramatic black-and-white D-Day stripes but the P-47s of the 78th Fighter Group had the addition of that famous black-and-white checker around the engine cowling. But, more importantly, the American P-47s, unlike the dark earth brown and olive green camouflage of the RAF Typhoons, had a shiny bare metal finish which was great for imbuing with some subtle daylight tones.

NIGHT HUNTERS

On 26 July 1944, the first official report of an encounter with an Me262 was submitted by a Mosquito crew from 544 Squadron. Flight Lieutenant A E Wall and his navigator had taken off from their base at Benson, Oxfordshire, on a sortie to Munich. At 29,000ft over the target area a twin-engined aircraft was sighted by the navigator; and it was closing fast….

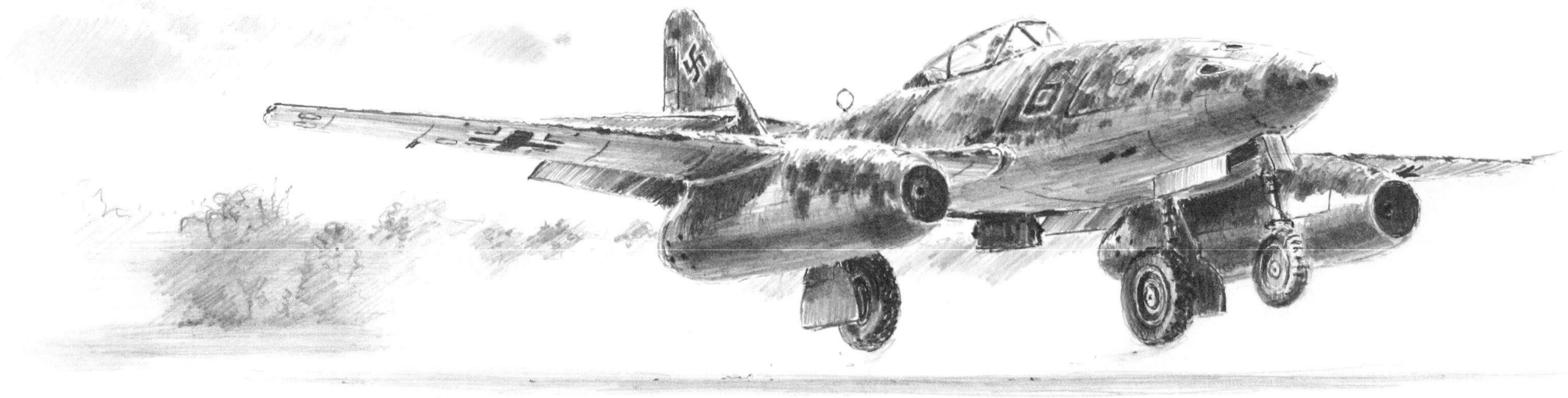

Wall immediately opened up the throttles to escape. At that altitude the Mosquito was capable of out-running any enemy fighter, but the two men were horrified to find the German interceptor easily overtaking them, and without opening fire. The German pilot, Leutnant Alfred Schreiber, was obviously enjoying the moment – to be able to smoothly cruise past the illusive Mosquito was a triumph, but the Mosquito crew were in no mood for games. Realising their new adversary was jet-powered they broke hard to starboard.

The Me262, however, was quickly on their tail and opened fire as the Mosquito once again broke away. But it wasn't over. Using every trick and manoeuvre in the book, Flight Lieutenant Wall evaded five more attacks until he could finally dive into cloud cover and safety.

The arrival of the Me262 jet was a big shock to the RAF Mosquito crews who, up till then, had enjoyed relative immunity and few losses from conventional German fighters as they swept over Berlin and the big German cities. From now on, however, they would have to be a lot more wary, and *Night Hunters* was a painting that would feature another encounter between the two aircraft involving elite units from the opposing sides.

10./NJG11 had been formed by Oberleutnant Kurt Welter, a skilled night-fighter Ace who had honed his skills flying supercharged Me109Gs with JG300, the *Wilde Sau.* He was one of the few Me109 pilots to achieve a night victory over the Mosquito which had long been a thorn in the Germans' side. He wanted more, and at the beginning of 1945 he got his chance when he was appointed to command 10./NJG11, a new unit set up specifically to counter raids carried out by Mosquitos of the RAF's Light Night Striking Force on the big German cities, especially Berlin. What had started out as nuisance raids by the RAF had, by the end of 1944, developed into far more sustained and damaging attacks.

To do the job 10./NJG11 was given a handful of the revolutionary new Me262 jet fighters. A few of these were the two seater, radar-equipped variant adapted for night-fighting, but most were just standard day fighters whose pilots had to rely on skill and contact with their ground control stations to seek out the night-time intruders. Welter soon added to his tally of Mosquitos and probably became the highest scoring Me262 pilot of the war, with over 20 victories to his name.

However, few pilots were as proficient as Welter and flying such an advanced aircraft was a difficult enough task by day – flying it by night would take the very best pilots the Luftwaffe had. And by 1945 such pilots had become a rarity.

Welter hand-picked the pilots for his new squadron, one of whom was Leutnant Jorg Czypionka, a 23-year-old, highly experienced night-fighter pilot who, like Welter, had previously flown Me109s with JG300. It was with this unit, whilst pursuing a Mosquito over Berlin, that Czypionka nearly met with death. Even though the Mosquito was coned by as many as 30 searchlights, Czypionka could only catch his fast adversary by pushing his Me109 way over its safety limits. When he finally did get in range, however, the Mosquito escaped the searchlights but, before he could throttle back, the Me109's engine exploded, covering the windscreen with a thick layer of oil. Czypionka was forced to bale out, only to encounter a small group of irate civilians on the ground who he now had to convince he wasn't an Allied airman before eventually making it back to base.

In March 1945 when Welter asked Jorg Czypionka if he would like to join his elite new squadron, Czypionka jumped at the chance. Not just because it was a golden opportunity to fly the world's first operational jet fighter but also because it meant that he'd be posted further west to Burg, near Magdeburg. By this stage in the war things were starting to fall apart around Berlin as the Russians pushed ever closer and fuel shortages had become so acute that, one by one, whole Luftwaffe units began to disappear. The jets, however, were given just enough precious fuel to continue flying right to the end.

Night Hunters was to feature one of 10./NJG11's few remaining jets – I'd chosen that of Jorg Czypionka – engaging a powerful force of fast, high-flying Mosquitos approaching Berlin. The Mosquitos are from 139 (Jamaica) Squadron, part of Bomber Command's crack Pathfinder Force. During my research I was lucky enough to be able to speak to Jorg Czypionka. He now lives in the United States, and to call him I had to wait up until it was early morning in the UK, but it was well worth the wait. I believe he is now the last surviving Me262 night-fighter pilot and to be able to talk with him, and ask the many questions I had in order to make my painting as authentic as possible, was an opportunity I shall never forget.

One of the things he explained was how he would sometimes follow the Mosquito contrails, trying to work his way above them before making his attack. He also said what great respect he had for both the Mosquito – which he called a 'most beautiful aircraft' – and the formidable crews who flew them. They were, of course, some of the most experienced airmen in Bomber Command and even with the potent new jet fighter at

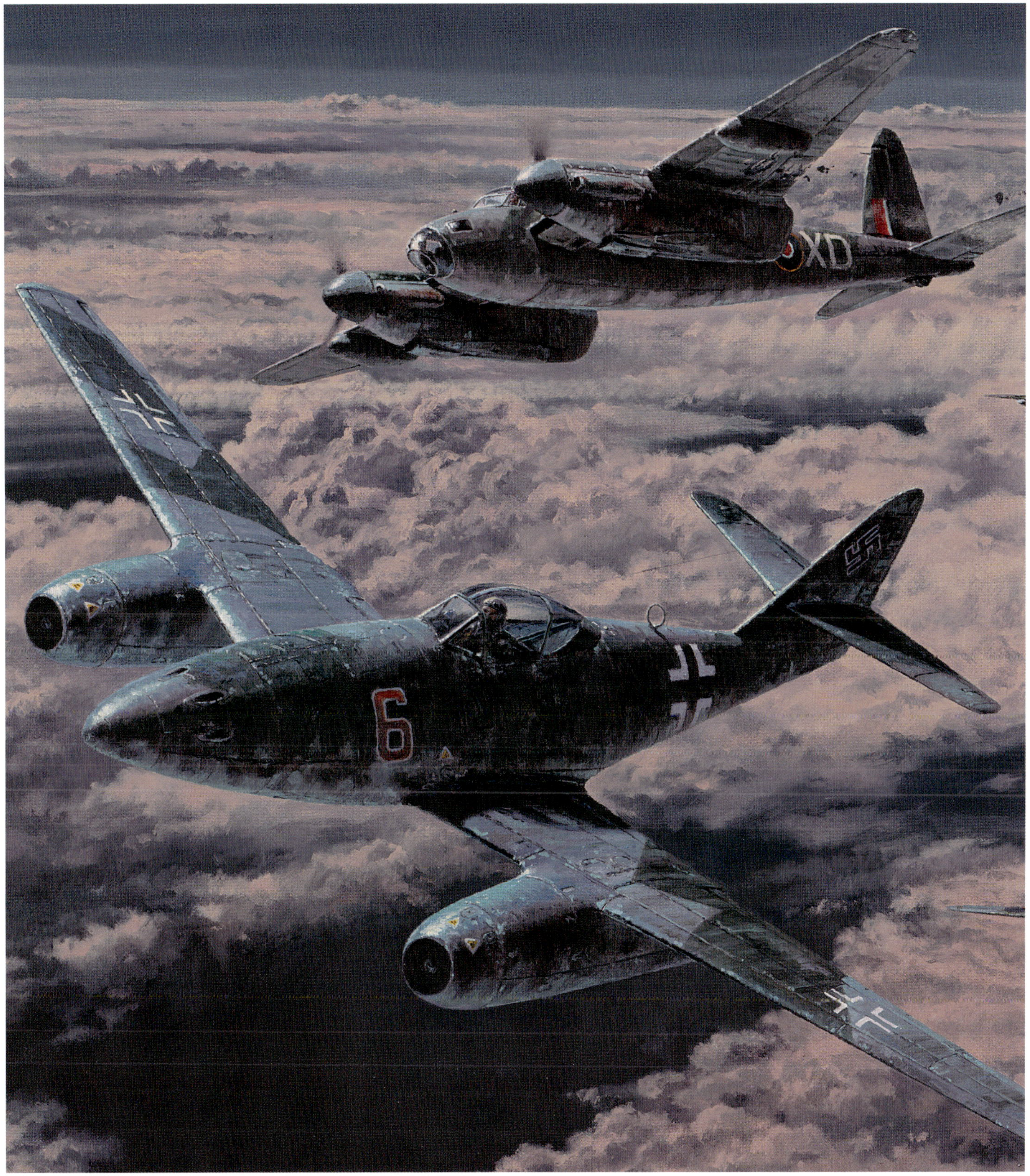

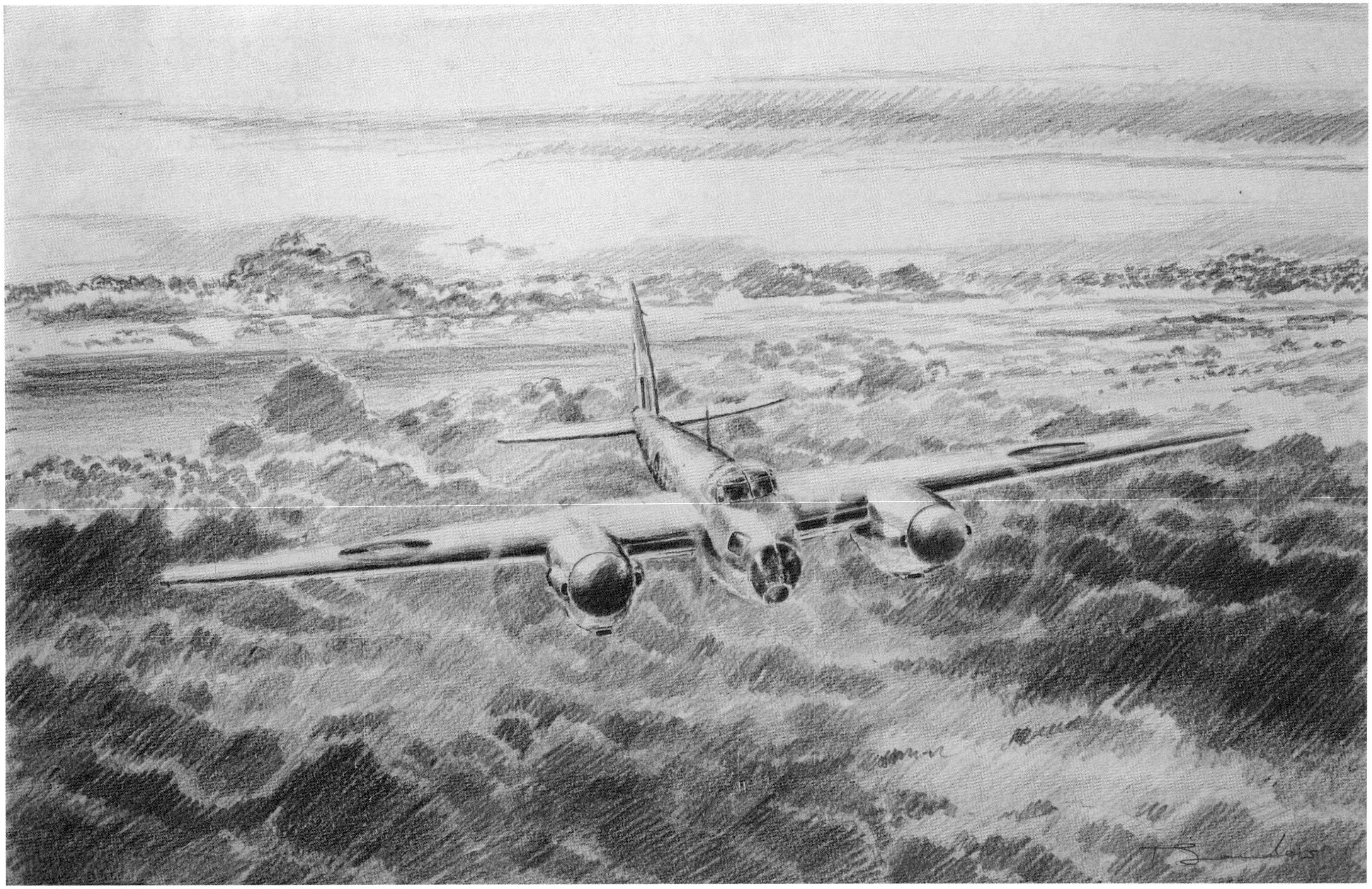

his disposal, it was no easy matter to bring one down. Nevertheless Jorg Czypionka did achieve two confirmed victories over Mosquitos in the last weeks of the war.

He also described how those last few days of the war were such difficult and desperate times for all the German forces but told me that he was lucky, he had an ace up his sleeve. Rather than destroy their precious jet fighters, the whole squadron flew them instead to Schleswig-Jagel, the last remaining operational night-fighter airfield near the Danish border, where they awaited the arrival of the western Allies. It turned out to be a shrewd decision. As he was the only pilot to speak any English, when the British did arrive, Jorg was the one they turned to for help in evaluating the Me262. In return for his help he was allowed to return straight home without having to go through a long, uncertain stay in a relocation camp.

Not that long ago Jorg got to speak with the navigator of one of the Mosquitos he had shot down; he had last seen the RAF airman hanging from the wing of his stricken aircraft! When the navigator was told that it had been a jet that had shot him down he was surprised – he hadn't thought the Me262 flew at night. Jorg Czypionka, however, is living proof that they most certainly did – and with devastating effect!

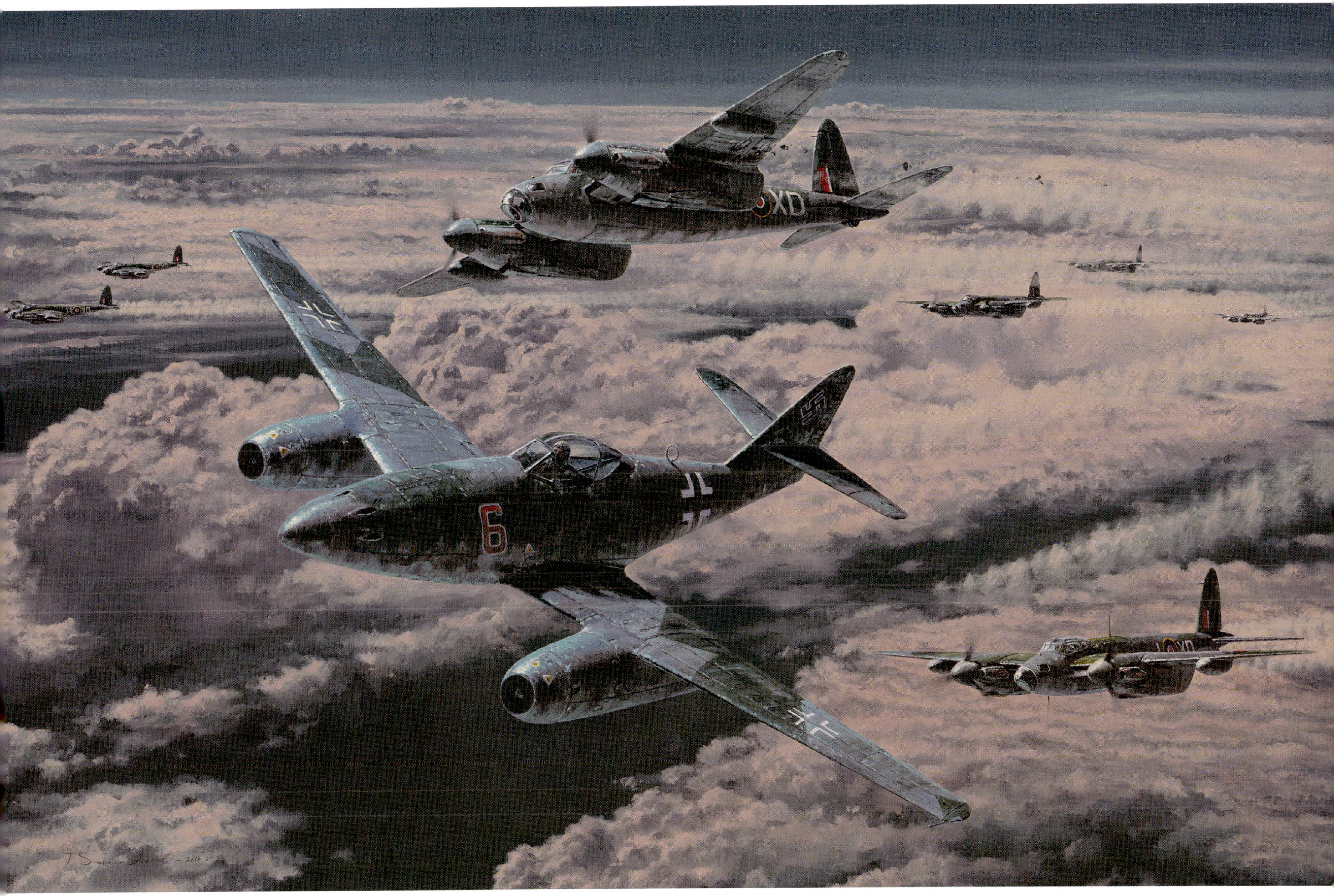

NIGHT HUNTERS IN THE COLLECTION OF MR MARK BROWN

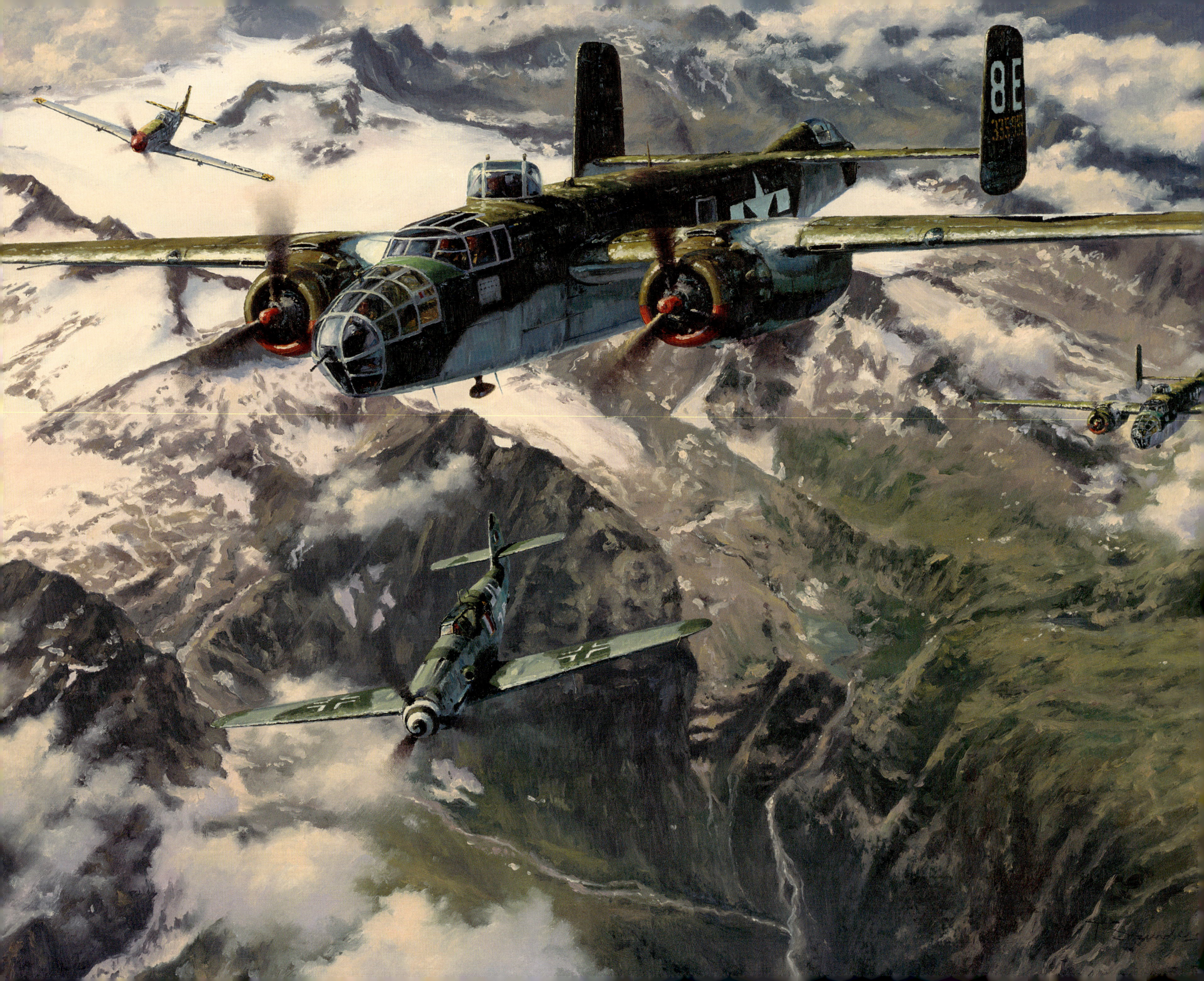
8E

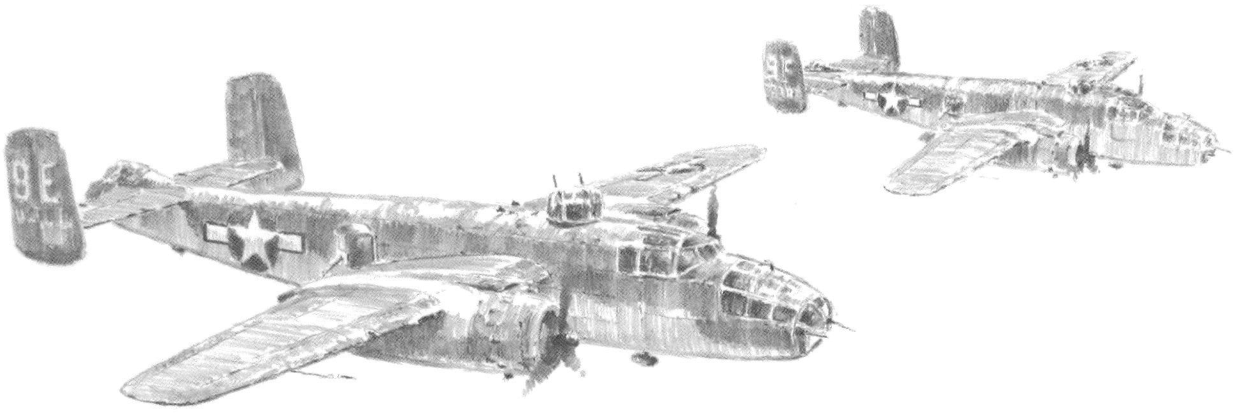

BATTLE OF THE BRENNER

Up until a few years ago Ryanair flew into the small airport at Ghedi, situated at the foot of the Alps in northern Italy. It's about 10 miles south of Brescia and whenever we went to Italy, this was our airport of choice as it's only about an hour's drive away from our family house in Castell'Arquato.

Ghedi is really more of an airfield, in the middle of nowhere, which is probably one of the reasons I liked it so much. But as the aircraft makes its final descent, it almost literally skims the top off some of the taller peaks of the Brenner Pass. It's quite a ride and perhaps not for the faint-hearted. But the views are breathtaking!

Ghedi was one of the many airfields in northern Italy that were used by the Luftwaffe and their Italian allies during the war and, as our plane taxied, you could make out some of the derelict war-time buildings that still lie around the perimeter. I knew the whole of this area had been bitterly contested towards the end of the war but little more than that. It got me thinking about what happened in this relatively unknown theatre, and was how my painting *Battle of the Brenner* was inspired. Little did I realise how difficult it would be to find the information I was looking for.

Although from time to time I'm only too glad to get help from others when researching for a painting – my publishers at the Military Gallery, for example, have many contacts and are always willing to help – in general I do it all myself. Mainly because I love it. The whole process of researching back into history is almost as fulfilling as the actual painting.

Over the years I seem to have amassed a collection of several hundred books and my studio is covered with them. Books are everywhere: they lie stacked in piles of varying sizes on the studio floor and our dining room has now begun to resemble a small library. Then there are books stored in large plastic packing cases up in the loft, ready to be delved into whenever the moment calls.

For me books are key. In my early days as an aviation artist I would spend hours scouring the local library or searching through bookshops but could rarely find the specialised type of information I needed. The collections were almost always limited to more generalised books.

Of course using the internet for research can be quick, easy and good up to a point, but it's still difficult to find the fine details I'm looking for; things such as first-hand accounts, rare photographs from private collections, little-known units and the in-depth writing found in specialist books on which authors have spent years of investigation.

Having said that, without the internet I wouldn't have been able to discover a fraction of the titles that I have. Now, when starting a project, almost the first thing I do is a quick scan on the computer. Without fail I normally manage to find, and subsequently purchase, books devoted to some of the most obscure wartime aviation subjects.

Painting *Battle of the Brenner*, however, was a big exception! On this occasion there seemed to be relatively few books on offer covering the air war in Italy, and fewer still concerning the medium bomber units of the US Twelfth Air Force that flew here. But what I did find was a first class website called *57thbombwing.com* that had all the detail I required. I was amazed to find the declassified squadron mission reports for specific days including crew lists, their aircraft and even the formation they flew in. I spent many hours sifting through all this information; even after I'd found what I was looking for I still continued delving. It was just so incredibly interesting to scrutinize history in such detail. I highly recommend the site.

When planning a battle scene I often begin by focusing on which aircraft and units I'd like to portray, and then ploughing through the archives to see if my imaginings ever happened. But with this subject I was a bit more constrained because, by the time the Allies had reached this northern part of Italy, the Luftwaffe had retreated. Fighter operations had been left in the hands of the ANR, or *Aeronáutica Nationale Republicana.*

The ANR was what remained of the Italian fascist air force, the units that remained loyal to Mussolini after the Italian king and government of Marshal Badoglio had surrendered to the Allies in September 1943. Although supplied with the latest Me109s from their German partners, the ANR were always in short supply of everything else that makes a fighter aircraft effective: spare parts and fuel. Heavily outnumbered, one thing this ramshackle group of pilots did have was courage. Battling against one of the most powerful air forces ever assembled they continued fighting right up to the bitter end, even when it was obvious that their cause was lost.

Captain Hugo Drago of the ANR was one of these desperate men. On 19 April 1945, he and eighteen other Me109s took off for what would be their final stand. They found the B-25 Mitchells of the 488th Bomb Squadron, 340th Bomb Group just after the Americans had completed a bombing run on the Ora rail bridge in the Brenner Pass. As the bombers made a wide turn onto their return route the ANR 109s seized their chance, attacking what they thought was an unescorted force. The Italian pilots, however, were in for a nasty surprise. Almost immediately two flights of P-51 Mustangs from the 325th Fighter Group, the *Checkertails*, appeared on the scene and threw the Italian attack into chaos.

In the ensuing mêlée the Italians lost five planes and several more were damaged, they were the *Checkertails'* final victories of the war. The Americans were jubilant: they had suffered no losses, and knew that the war was almost at an end.

In *Battle of the Brenner* I've shown Captain Drago as he doggedly tries to outrun the nearest P-51. Although he was one of the survivors of the battle, even he must have been despondent as he led what was left of his tattered and badly mauled fighters back to Ghedi airfield. In the air the ANR pilots knew they were beaten but now, on the ground, they had another foe to face. Partisans had surrounded the airfield, and they were in no mood for forgiveness.

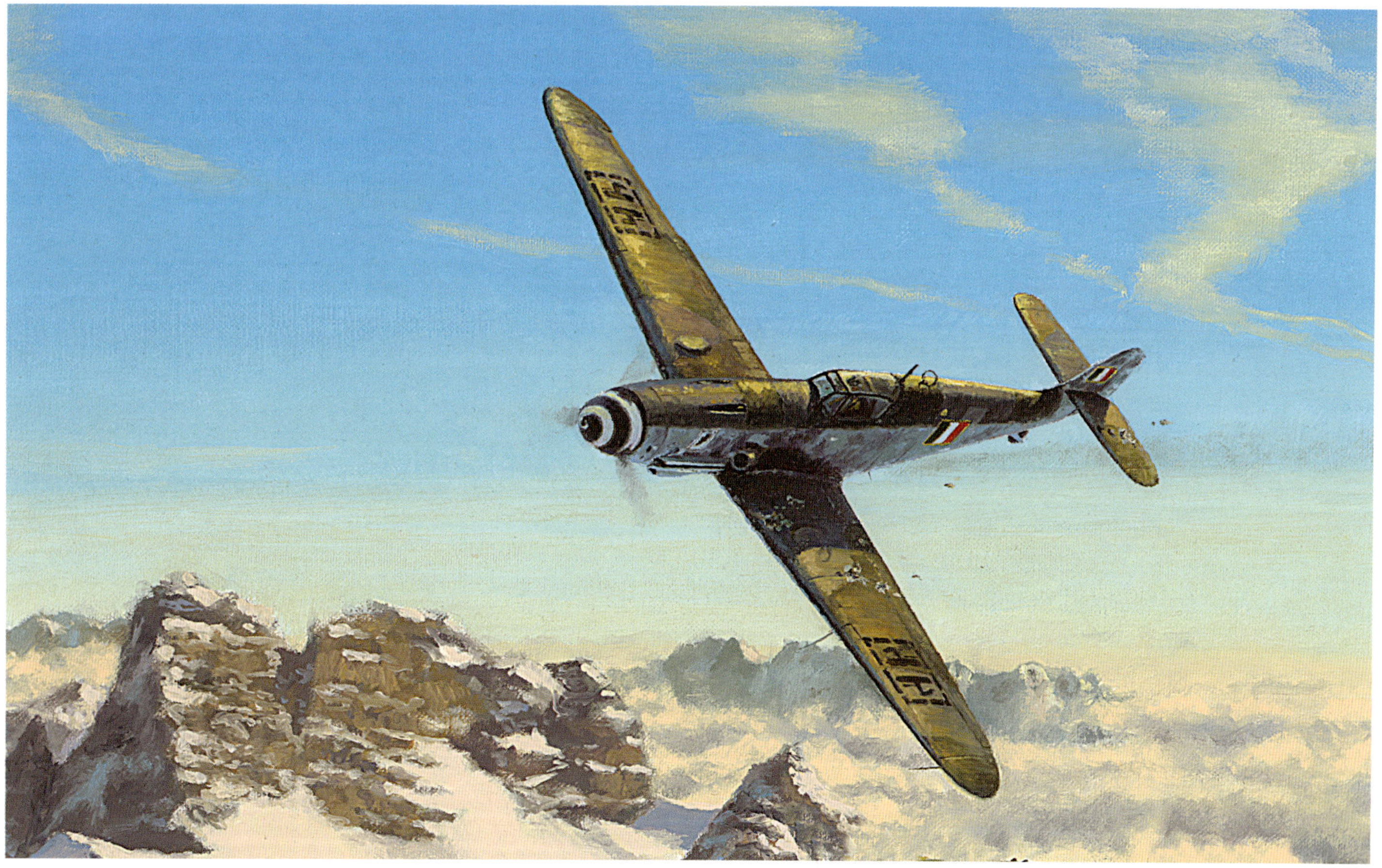

A detail from my painting Deadly Pass showing the Italian Me109 G10.

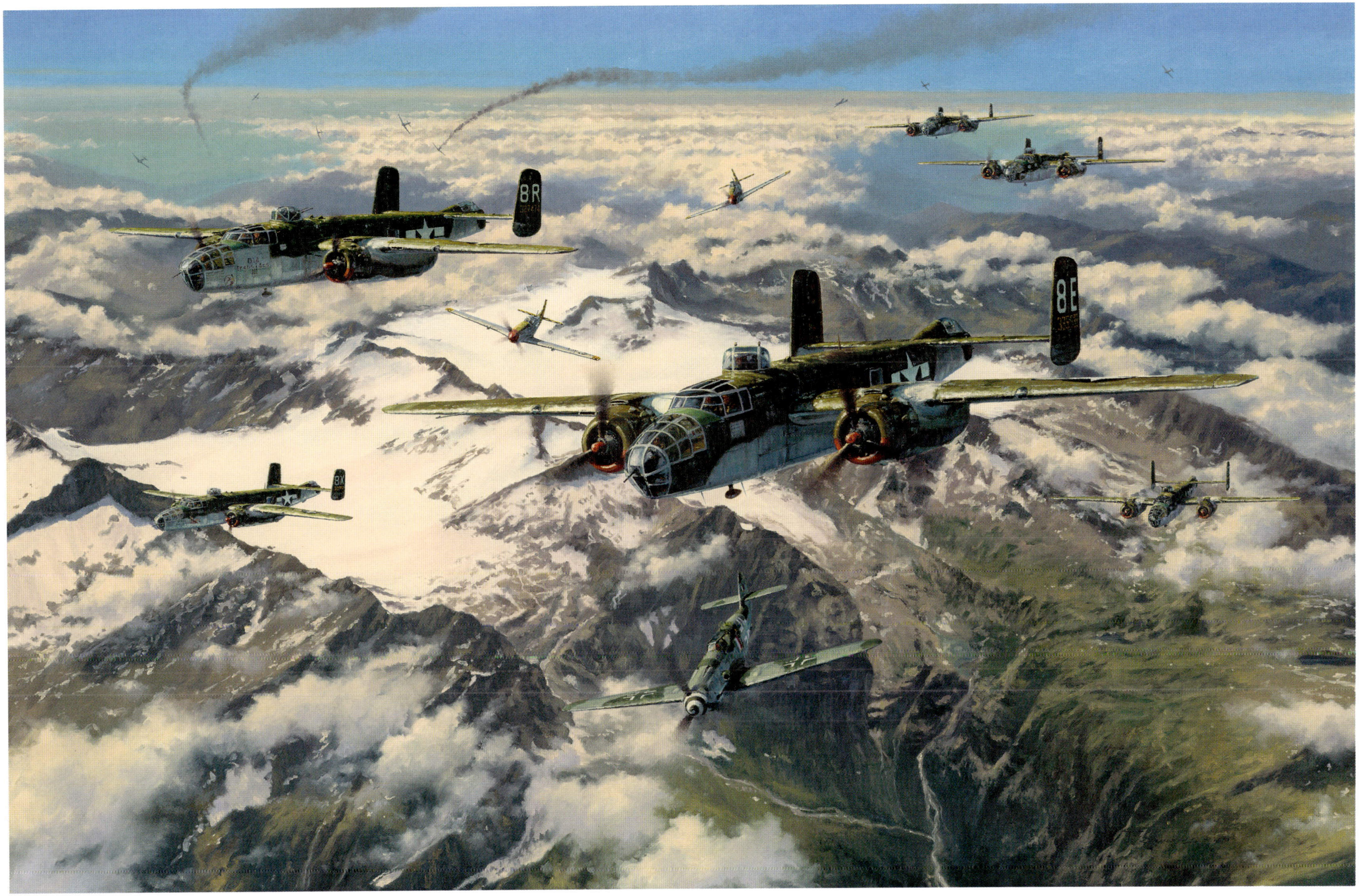

BATTLE OF THE BRENNER IN THE COLLECTION OF MR MICHAEL BURR

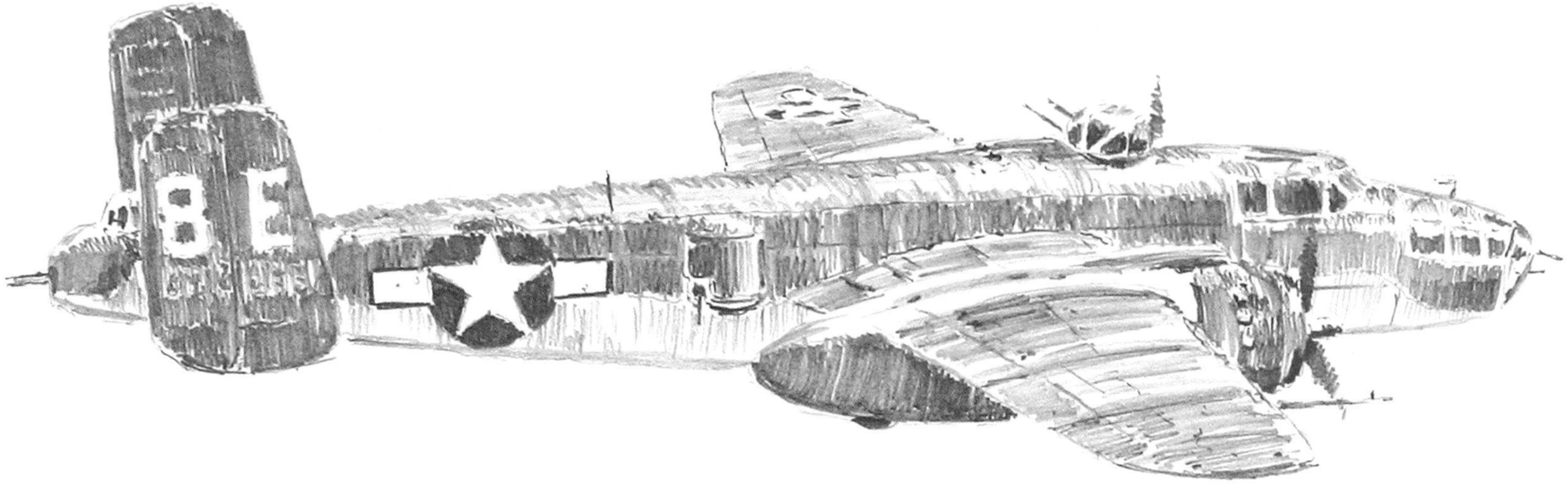

DEADLY PASS

I was surprised, but really pleased, to later receive a commission from an American collector who wanted me to paint a scene of an Italian Macchi C.205 Greyhound fighter from the ANR attacking a B-25 Mitchell from the 321st Bomb Group.

The surprise came because, as I mentioned before, this theatre in northern Italy is generally not well-known but, as it's one of my favourites, I was very much looking forward to painting it. There was a problem, however.

I knew from previous research that if the painting was to be accurate, by the period of the war when the B-25s started crossing the Alps, the very few Macchi fighters that remained in ANR hands had all but disappeared from combat. They'd been replaced by German Me109s. It was a pity because I'd dearly love to paint the sleek little Italian fighter that Test Pilot Captain Eric 'Winkle' Brown described as 'one of the finest aircraft I ever flew'. Reluctantly I would have to contact the collector and let him know.

Luckily the client agreed; he was more concerned with historical accuracy than whether the fighter was a Macchi or a Me109. What he did want to see, however, were ANR markings on the wings. These were the black 'fasces' – symbolic bundles of sticks, inspired by the ones carried in ancient Imperial Rome to exercise authority and adopted by the fascists of Mussolini's Italy.

A few days of research ploughing through some books I came up with a perfect scenario: on 14 March 1945, 2nd Lieutenant Charles Eddy flying a P-47 of the 350th Fighter Group had reported engaging in a head-on attack with a Me109 of the ANR. This was in close proximity to the B-25 bombers of the 321st Bomb Group whose route to their target that day, the Vipiteno rail bridge, took them over the Alta Badia, a beautiful range of mountains in the Dolomite region of the Italian Alps.

Major Adriano Visconti was the Italian pilot in the head-on encounter. Although a seasoned Ace and CO of *1 GruppoCaccia*, on this occasion his luck ran out. Visconti had taken several hits from Eddy's P-47 and had been forced to bale out at low altitude over the snow-covered mountains. Wounded, he somehow managed to make the journey back to base on foot. It must have been quite an ordeal but he didn't have much of a chance to tell the story because only a few weeks later, after being assured of his men's safety, he surrendered to partisans only to be shot in the back.

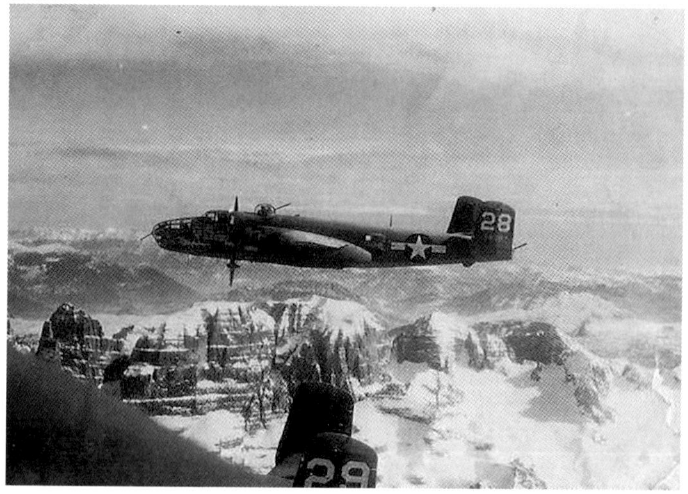

A B-25 Mitchell of the 321st Bomb Group over the same range of mountains depicted in Deadly Pass

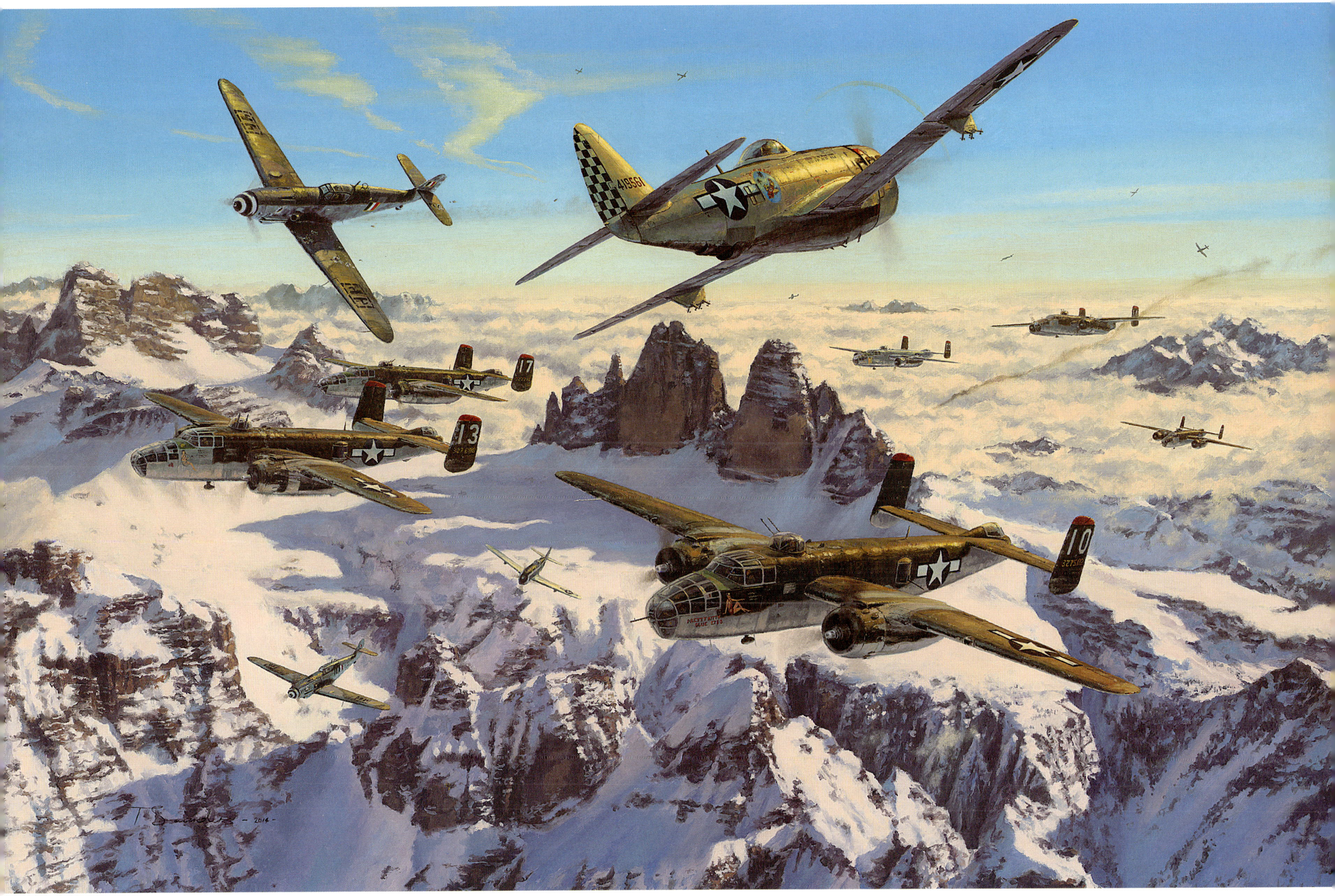

DEADLY PASS IN THE COLLECTION OF BILL WARD FINE ART SERVICES

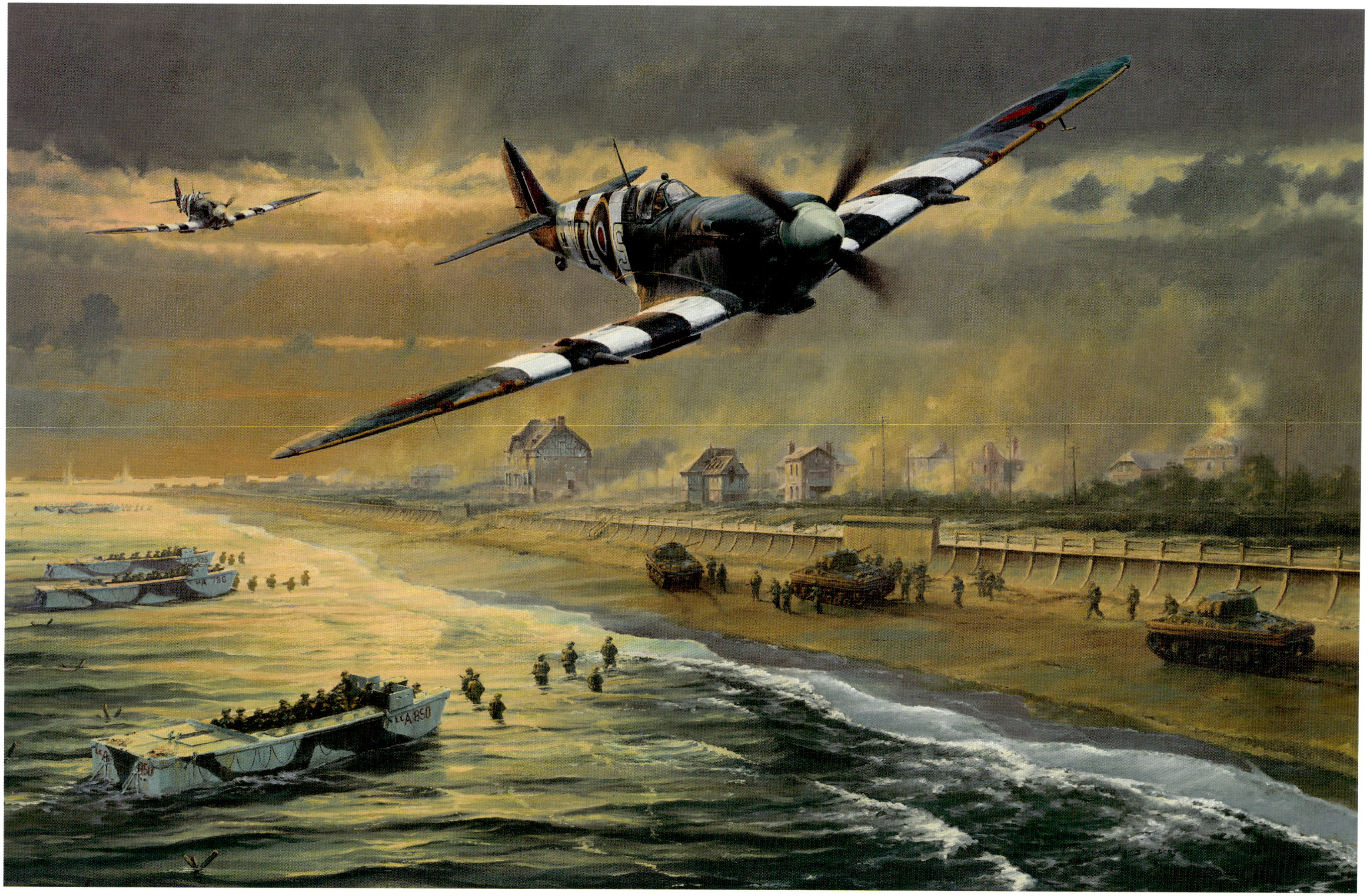

JUNO BEACH PRIVATE COLLECTION

JUNO BEACH

Untried in battle, on 6 June 1944 it fell to the 14,000 men of the 3rd Canadian Infantry Division to assault one of the most dangerous places on earth – the five-and-a-half mile strip of beach in Normandy called Juno.

Juno Beach lay between *Gold Beach* to the west and *Sword Beach* to the east. The Canadians were to attack *Juno* in two sectors: the 7th Brigade would land either side of the little harbour at Courseulles-sur-Mer, and east of there the 8th Brigade would attack between Bernières-sur-Mer and St.Aubin-sur-Mer. Both brigades formed part of the 3rd Canadian Infantry Division.

But the Canadians faced a difficulty: just offshore there was a reef that had to be covered by the rising tide before any landing craft could cross it. H-Hour on *Juno* was therefore later than on *Gold* and *Sword*, which gave the German defences plenty of time to prepare a rough reception for the untried Canadians. But it got worse.

The original H-Hour for the two sectors – 07.35 hours for the 7th Brigade and 07.45 hours for the 8th – had to be delayed by ten minutes due to the bad weather. Although seemingly minor, this delay had serious consequences – the higher tide now meant that the landing craft would have to touch down amongst the beach obstacles instead of short of them. The combination of the rough sea, choppy swell, the beach obstacles and concentrated firepower from an enemy on high alert made an unpleasant prospect for the crews manning the landing craft, but they were not daunted. In the words of Admiral Vian, Commander of the Eastern Task Force: 'Their spirit and seamanship alike rose to meet the greatness of the hour and they pressed forward and ashore, over or through mined obstacles in high heart and resolution; there was no faltering'. For the sodden and often sea-sick troops crammed inside, however, this was only the beginning.

I could visualise a great scene in my head before I started painting *Juno Beach*, but whether it would work was another question. I needed to establish two things: did the sun ever break through the cloud cover at any time during the first landings, and did the Spitfires I wanted to show ever fly really low over the beachhead? My instinctive reaction to both those questions was probably not.

Most of the photos taken during those first few hours seem to show pretty leaden skies, and most written accounts back that up. As to whether Spitfires, or any other Allied aircraft for that matter, ever got right in close to the beaches when there was so much shell fire around seemed extremely doubtful: I'd read that the covering fighters were given strict orders not to fly below a few thousand feet for fear of friendly fire. Navy gun crews, expecting attacks from the Luftwaffe, were more likely to fire first and ask questions later – despite the large black and white invasion stripes painted on all Allied aircraft specifically to prevent this from happening. An artist has to exercise licence at times but, on the other hand, with something as well-known and as well documented as D-Day, to try and do so would not only be an obvious mistake but could so easily attract serious criticism.

Ploughing through dozens of books trying to find the answers to such obscure questions can be frustrating but, after considerable searching, I found the answers to both in a great book called *D-Day, Juno Beach: Canada's 24 Hours of Destiny* by Lance Goddard. Firstly there was an excellent photograph taken early that morning that clearly showed a fleeting view of the sun breaking through a chink of thick cloud. And secondly, on the subject of the Spitfires, the book contained the following first-hand account written by Jim Parks of the Royal Winnipeg Rifles: 'We saw on the way in two Spitfires going along and strafing the beach. Somebody said one got hit further on by one of our own – got hit by our own shells'.

The quote certainly bore out the dangers of friendly fire but, more importantly, by pure luck it confirmed exactly the scenario I was thinking of. It was tempting to put several more Spitfires into the picture, to the right of the main one, but I resisted. After all, it had taken long enough to find the real story, so why embellish it?

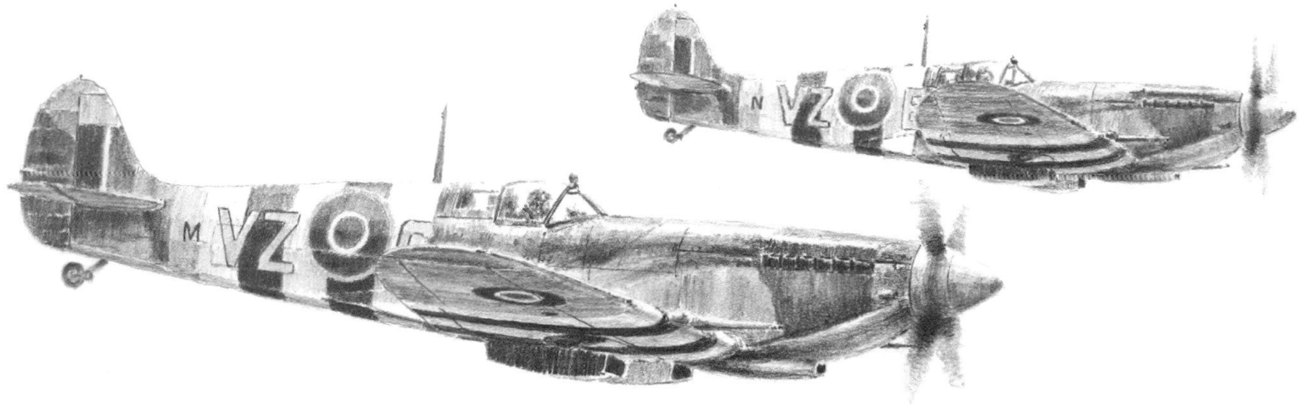

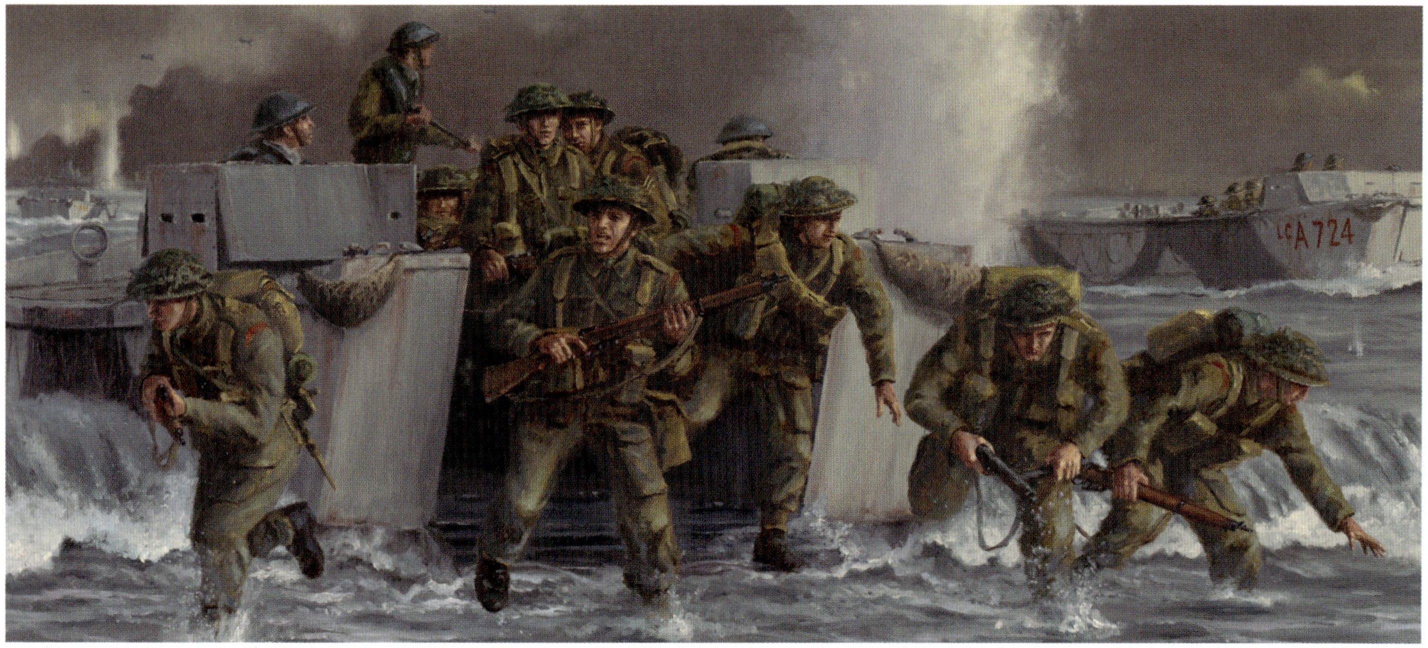

SWORD BEACH

IN THE COLLECTION OF MISS ELIZABETH GRAHAM

This is a detail taken from another of my D-Day paintings, this time depicting troops of the Royal Norfolk Regiment as they storm ashore with the first wave attacking the left flank of Sword Beach at 07.24 hours on D-Day.

Apart from this I wanted to show a significant landmark in the painting, something that could be easily recognised as part of *Juno Beach* and associated with the Canadians.

The large half-timbered house on the seafront at Bernières-sur-Mer, and the little railway station next door fitted the bill perfectly. The house, still standing, was cleared of enemy troops within twenty minutes of the first landing craft touching down, captured by men of the Queen's Own Rifles. It's thought to have been the first house in France to have been liberated by the amphibious forces on D-Day. Now called 'Canada House', many Canadians view it as one of the most famous buildings in their history.

Although the railway line, which once ran inland to Caen, is long gone, the station house also still survives – today it's a tourist office, along with many of the others in the painting. Not that long ago, during the opening of an Aces High exhibition held at the Utah Beach D-Day Museum, a very nice man approached me with a copy of a *Juno Beach* print in his hand. He'd just bought it and, after much kind but embarrassing praise, he pointed out that his house is next to the one on fire to the right of the painting. I was amazed, but also secretly delighted to think that after so many years had passed one of my prints had found a home in such a memorable place.

DAWNBREAKERS

The painting on the right is called Dawnbreakers. *It, too, has a link to* Juno Beach *and came with the rare opportunity to paint two very different aircraft, from two separate air forces, that would not normally be seen flying together. It was a chance not to be missed.*

Dawn broke unusually early for the P-51 pilots of the 359th Fighter Group on 6 June 1944. Surprised to be woken in the early hours, they soon learnt that in a few hours' time amphibious landings were going to start on the beaches of Normandy. The long-awaited invasion had begun and at 02.42 hours the 359th Fighter Group took to the air, tasked with engaging the enemy fighters that were soon expected.

It quickly became clear, however, that the Luftwaffe were not going to make an appearance and the American fighters were given a second mission – to escort the Allied heavy bombers hitting targets along the Normandy coast. Both the RAF, and their USAAF counterparts, were to attack and destroy the large German gun batteries that overlooked the invasion beaches and dominated the approaches. It was therefore American fighters that were now assigned to escort 23 RAF Halifax bombers from 76 Squadron that would try and obliterate a battery located at Mont Fleury, near Ver-sur-Mer, whose 122mm guns covered not only *Gold Beach* to its front but *Juno* as well.

Painting American P-51s in company with British Halifaxes was an exciting prospect and the only major difficulty I could foresee was how to deal successfully with the bad weather because low cloud covered much of the area. And dealing with the foul weather wasn't just a problem for me; it had caused all sorts of problems during the invasion itself, both in the air and at sea.

Wing Commander 'Hank' Iveson, leading 76 Squadron that morning, was forced to carry out his attack from just beneath the cloud base because, save for a few gaps, the cloud cover he encountered was thick and unyielding. Most of the other Halifax crews followed his example. This left them exposed and highly vulnerable to anti-aircraft fire but, if they were going to hit the battery with precision – which they did – they had no other choice. Once they had dropped their bombs, however, they quickly climbed back to relative safety above the clouds.

With so many aircraft in view I had to go to great lengths to get the trajectory of each plane just right and, for the landscape below, I found a terrific oblique aerial photo of *Gold Beach*, taken on D-Day, which showed some great detail. On the left there was a large inverted 'V' just inland from the beach, which turned out to be a massive anti-tank trench system, and the Mont Fleury battery was clearly visible on the higher ground behind it. The photo, however, had been taken much later in the morning, after the cloud had largely dispersed. Unfortunately by the time I'd painted back in the thick cloud that had so hindered the heavy bombers earlier, nearly all of this fantastic detail had to be covered over!

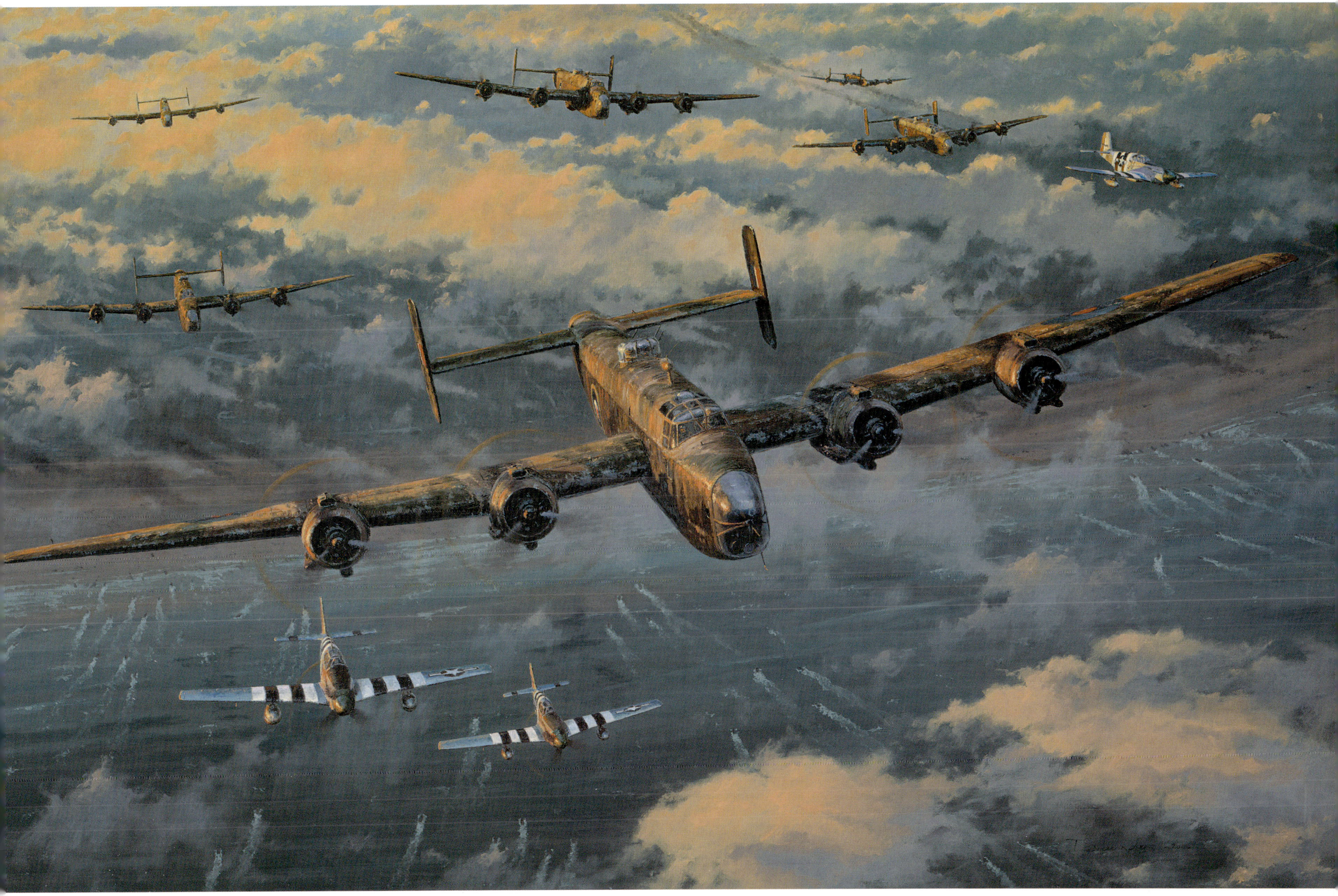

DAWNBREAKERS IN THE COLLECTION OF MR RICHARD HORN

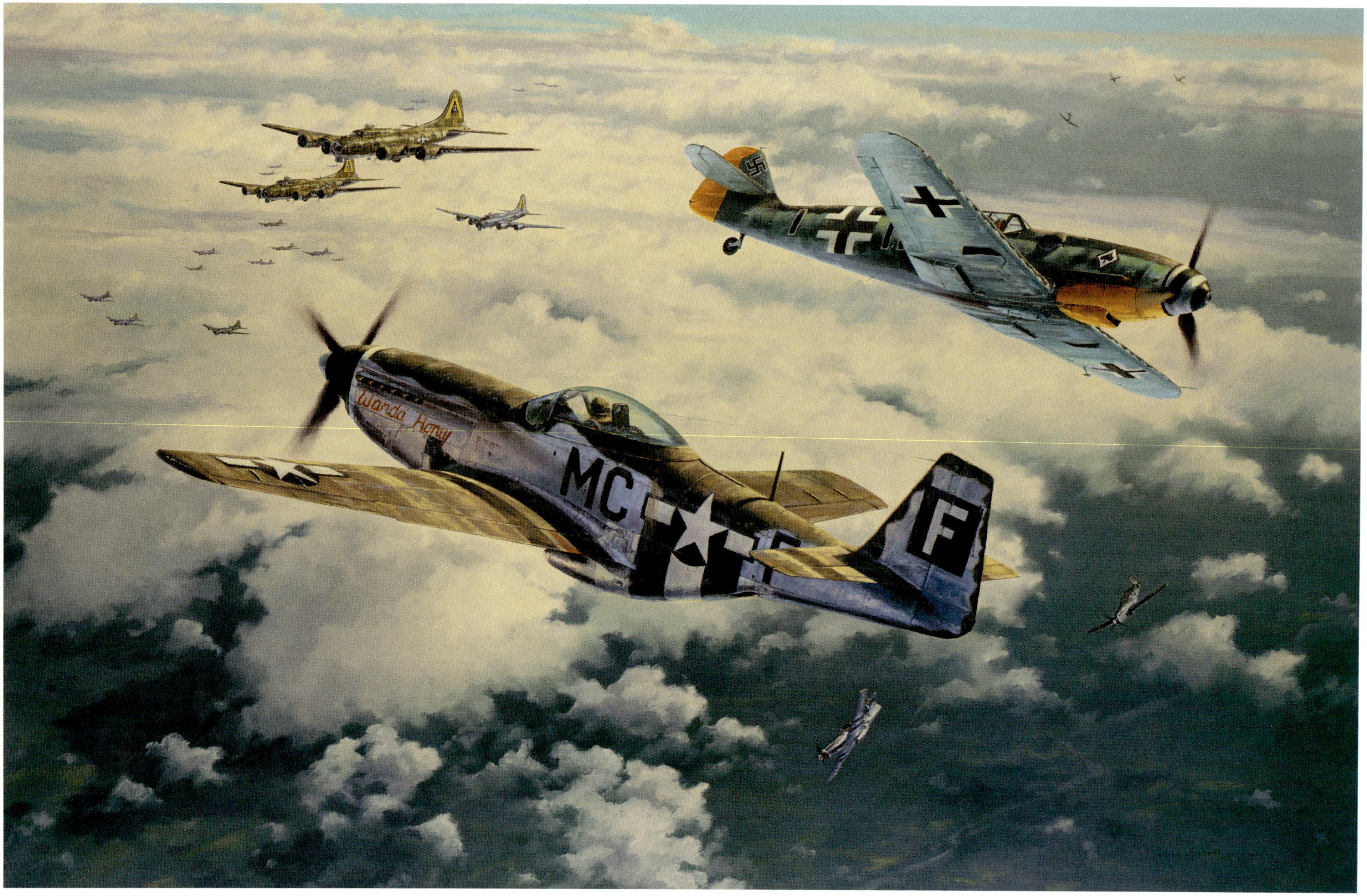

CLASH OF EAGLES IN THE COLLECTION OF MR MICHAEL BURR

CLASH OF EAGLES

The Eighth Air Force bomber crews had a saying: 'anywhere but Meresburg'. It was for good reason because, by late 1944, Meresburg was the most heavily-defended target in Germany.

Clash of Eagles was a painting commissioned by my publishers at The Military Gallery and features the P-51 Mustang. The painting was one of a pair alongside *A Welcome Return* which portrayed *Ol' Gappy*, a B-17 from the 397th Bomb Group, returning to Kimbolton after a mission in September 1944. Limited edition prints of both paintings were to be published as a portfolio in tribute to the bomber and fighter units that made up the Mighty Eighth.

To link the two paintings together I had the idea to include *Ol' Gappy* in *Clash of Eagles*, and depict her taking part in the raid from which she is seen returning in *A Welcome Return*. Rather than show the Flying Fortress up close – this was, after all, to be a painting of a P-51 – I decided to view *Ol' Gappy* in the middle distance and concentrate full attention on one of the fiercely- fought encounters the escorting P-51s had with German fighters on one particular mission. The date was 11 September 1944 and the raid in question was to Meresburg, a town 60 miles west of Leipzig.

It was here at the chemical complex of Leuna, three miles south of Meresburg, that *IG Farbenindustrie* had built one of the largest synthetic oil plants in the world. Derived from lignite, the brown coal found in abundance nearby, the fuel manufactured at Leuna supplied 10% of the Reich's output. Covering over three square miles, and comprising over 250 buildings, the site also produced a large variety of other chemicals, including half the ammonium nitrate used in German explosives, and deuterium oxide, more commonly known as 'heavy water', essential for the Nazis' secret atomic programme. *IG Farbenindustrie* itself held another dark secret: part of the company manufactured Zyklon B, used in the gas chambers of Auschwitz-Birkenau and the other extermination camps.

So vital was the Meresburg-Leuna plant to the German war effort that Hitler ordered it be given the strongest protection possible. By the second half of 1944 it was defended by more anti-aircraft guns than the whole of Berlin, the most fearsome of which was the 125mm flak gun whose exploding shells could bring down an aircraft a hundred yards away.

Roger Freeman, in his book *The Mighty Eighth*, describes Meresburg as 'synonymous with flak to crews in late 1944; it was what Schweinfurt had been to their predecessors in the autumn of 1943, for it became the most heavily-defended place in Hitler's crumbling empire'.

One of the squadrons protecting the *Ol' Gappy* and the other B-17s on the 11 September raid was the 79th Fighter Squadron, part of the 20th Fighter Group based at Kings Cliffe. From an artistic point of view this unit had great-looking P-51 Mustangs, often with a wavy olive drab upper fuselage and bare metal lower. At this point in the war they were still adorned with D-Day

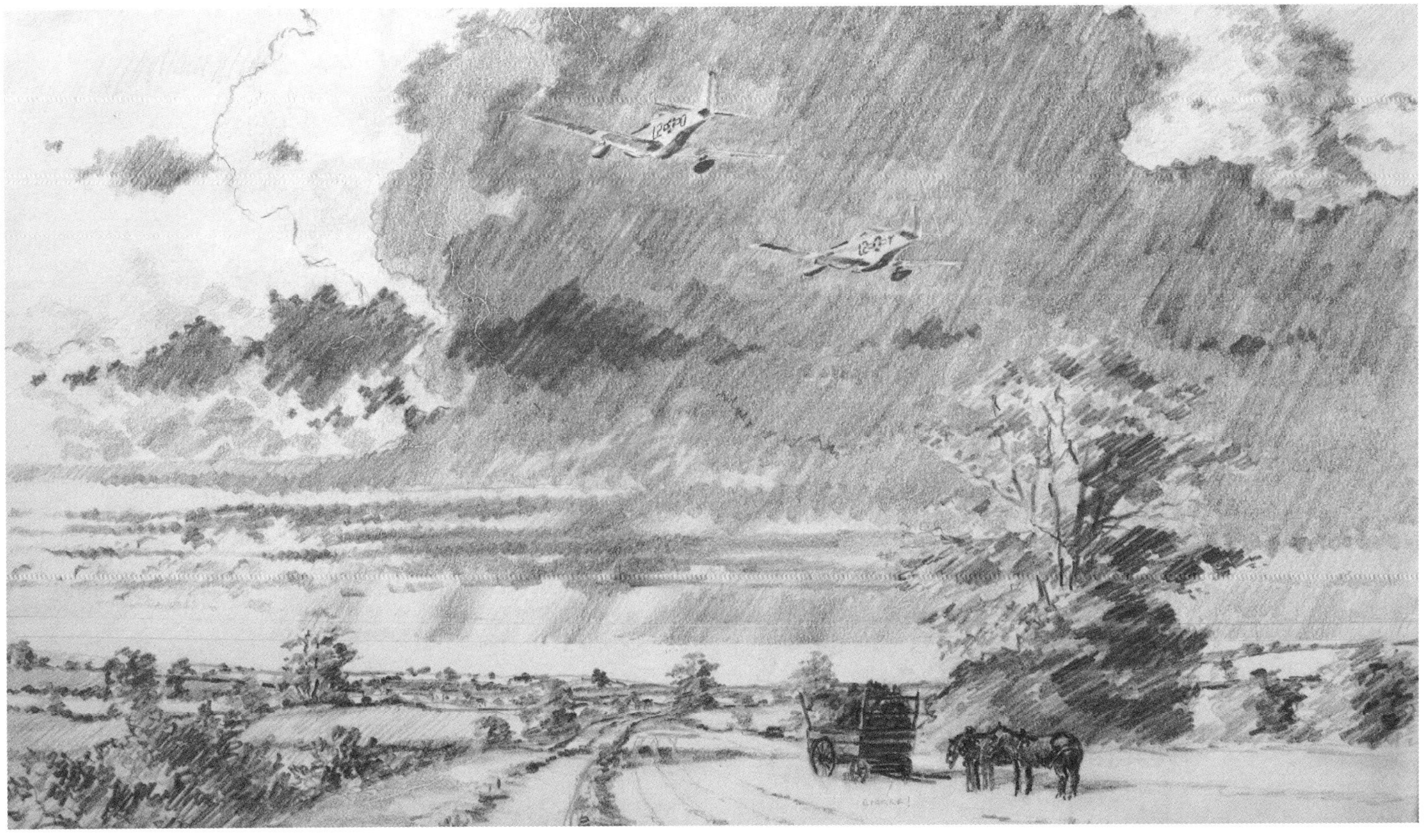

stripes, albeit only on the lower surfaces, and I had good photographic reference for First Lieutenant Robert E. Campbell's *Wanda Honey*, a P-51 that was flying escort duty over Meresburg that day. Finding who his adversary might have been was not quite so easy but I eventually found out that one of the airfields tasked with defending the Meresburg area was at Bad Lippspringe. So I decided to feature one of the Me109s of 8./JG53 that were based there.

The limited edition prints were going to be signed by both a P-51 pilot and a Me109 pilot, and my only brief was that neither adversary should look like the outright victor. With this in mind the first thing I did was to try and come up with a suitable composition.

I could picture in my mind a scenario that I thought would work well and, by playing around with models of the two aircraft, could check if it actually worked. In this particular instance I mounted both models on special stands. When I say special stands what I actually mean is old coat hangers – the steel wire variety – which are mounted on wooden bases! I've drilled a small 3mm hole in the bottom of all my models so that they can be mounted in this way. I can then view them from a distance and walk round them, trying to find the best possible angle. In this case it was also to give me a good idea of the perspective which, as the two planes were going to be passing within a few feet of each other, was something that had to be right.

Finally I found the angle that I was happiest with and could start thinking about the B-17s in the background. Although I wanted to clearly show that the nearest one was *Ol' Gappy*, I didn't want the bombers so close that they overpowered the painting. With this type of composition it's all too easy to get carried away. When you've put in a lot of research it's understandable that you want to get it all in, but the end result could end up as something resembling a 1970s style wallpaper!

For me the only answer is to retain a critical eye at all stages of the painting and keep asking yourself 'is the composition feasible, or realistic?' Of course you nearly always need some degree of artistic licence but the key is to discover how much you can, or can't get away with.

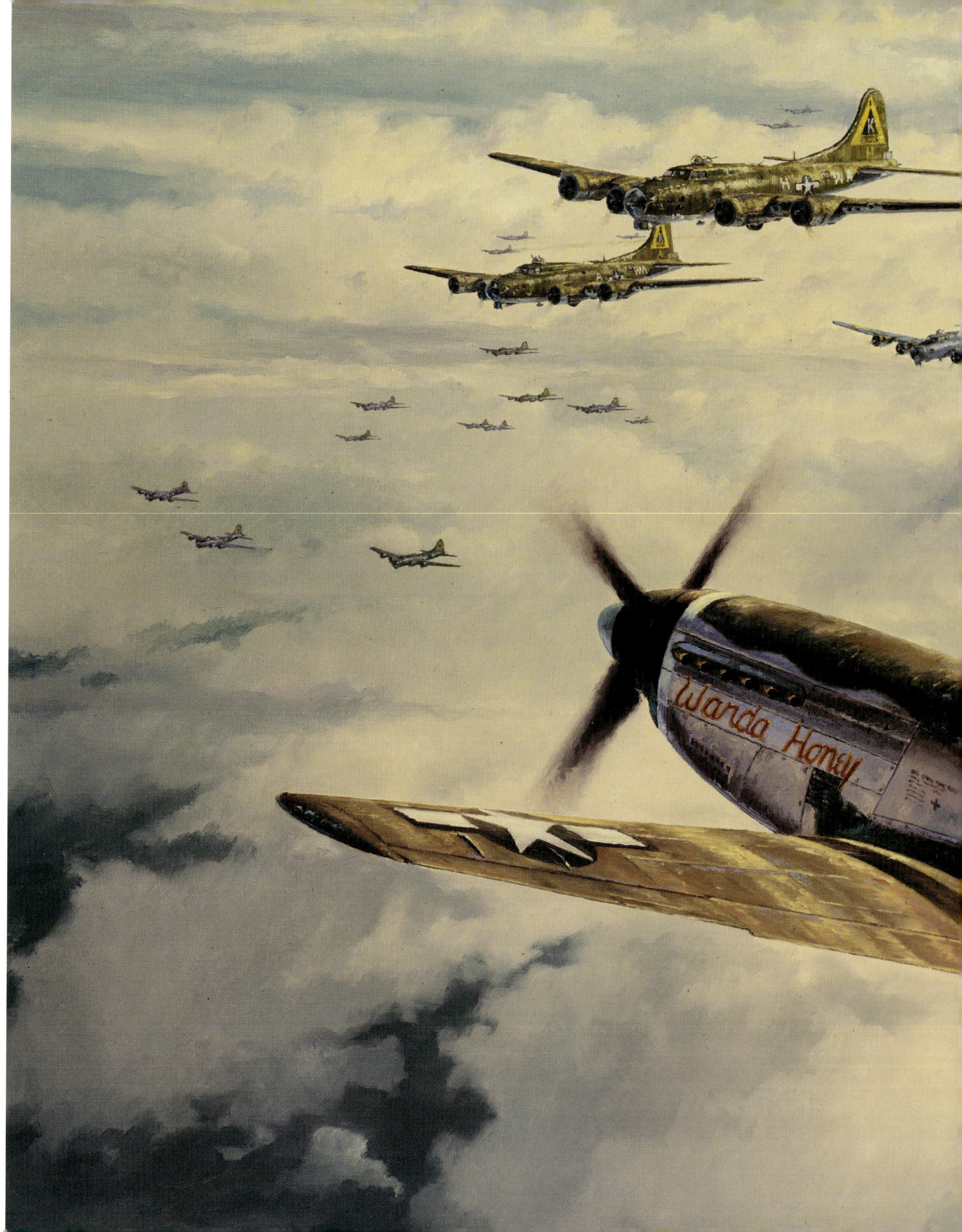

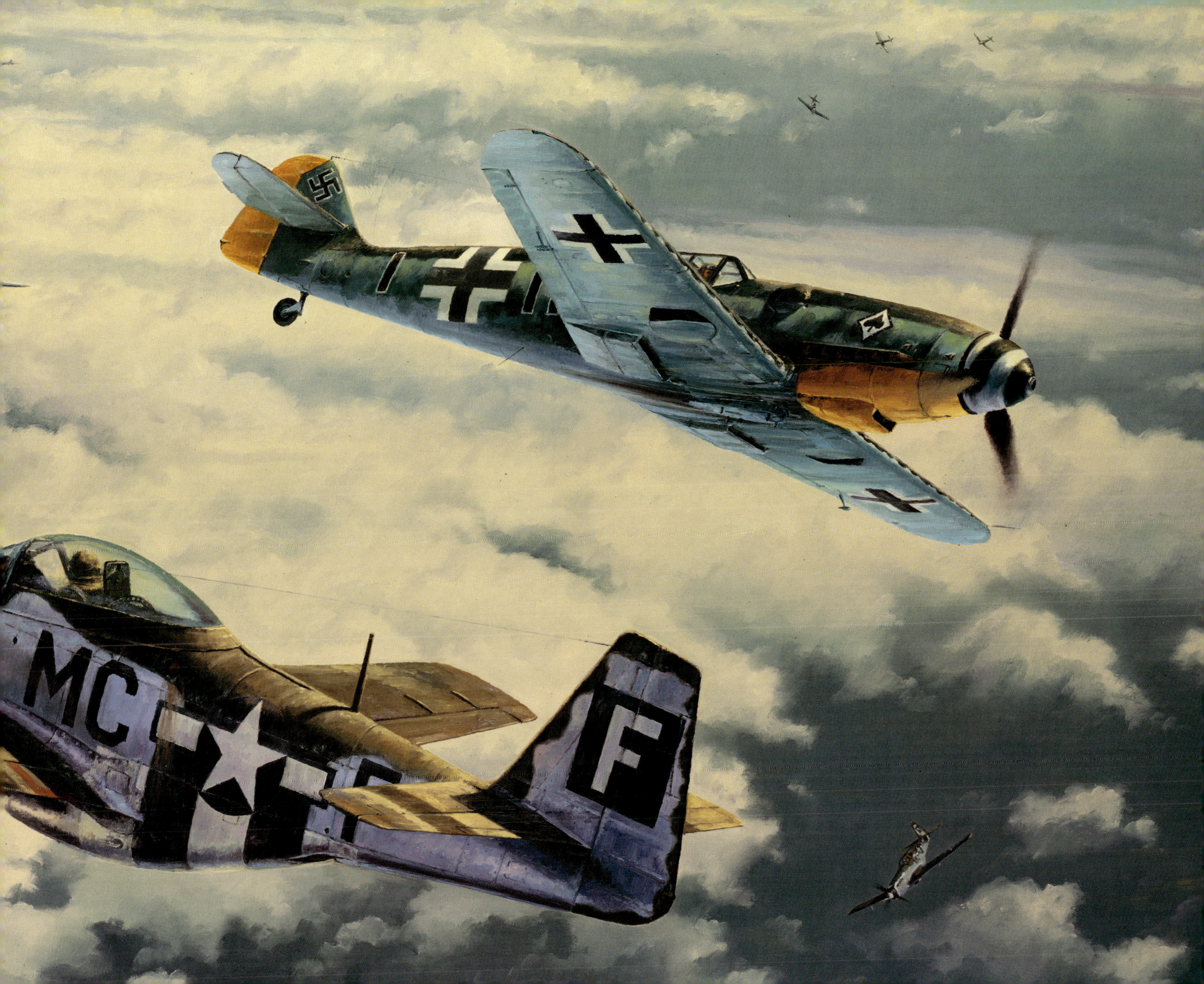

BERLIN BOAR FIGHT

The problem with painting a Lancaster at night is fairly obvious: there's very little light. Whilst the dark might be considered a friend for a bomber crew, it isn't for an artist. So when I started thinking about portraying a Lancaster at night over Berlin the first problem was how to light it.

The painting was inspired by a wonderful book I was reading called *The Berlin Raids*. It's written by military historian Martin Middlebrook and meticulously describes how, between August 1943 and March 1944, Bomber Command's night-time assault on Berlin became 'the longest and most sustained bombing offensive of the war'. In a series of nineteen major raids involving more than 10,000 aircraft sorties, the RAF dropped over 30,000 tons of bombs on Berlin. The author has not only gone to great lengths to interview or correspond with several hundred RAF bomber crew who took part in these raids, but also with some of the Luftwaffe night-fighter crews they fought against, and the people who lived in Berlin at the time. It's a great read and I highly recommend it to anyone remotely interested in the subject.

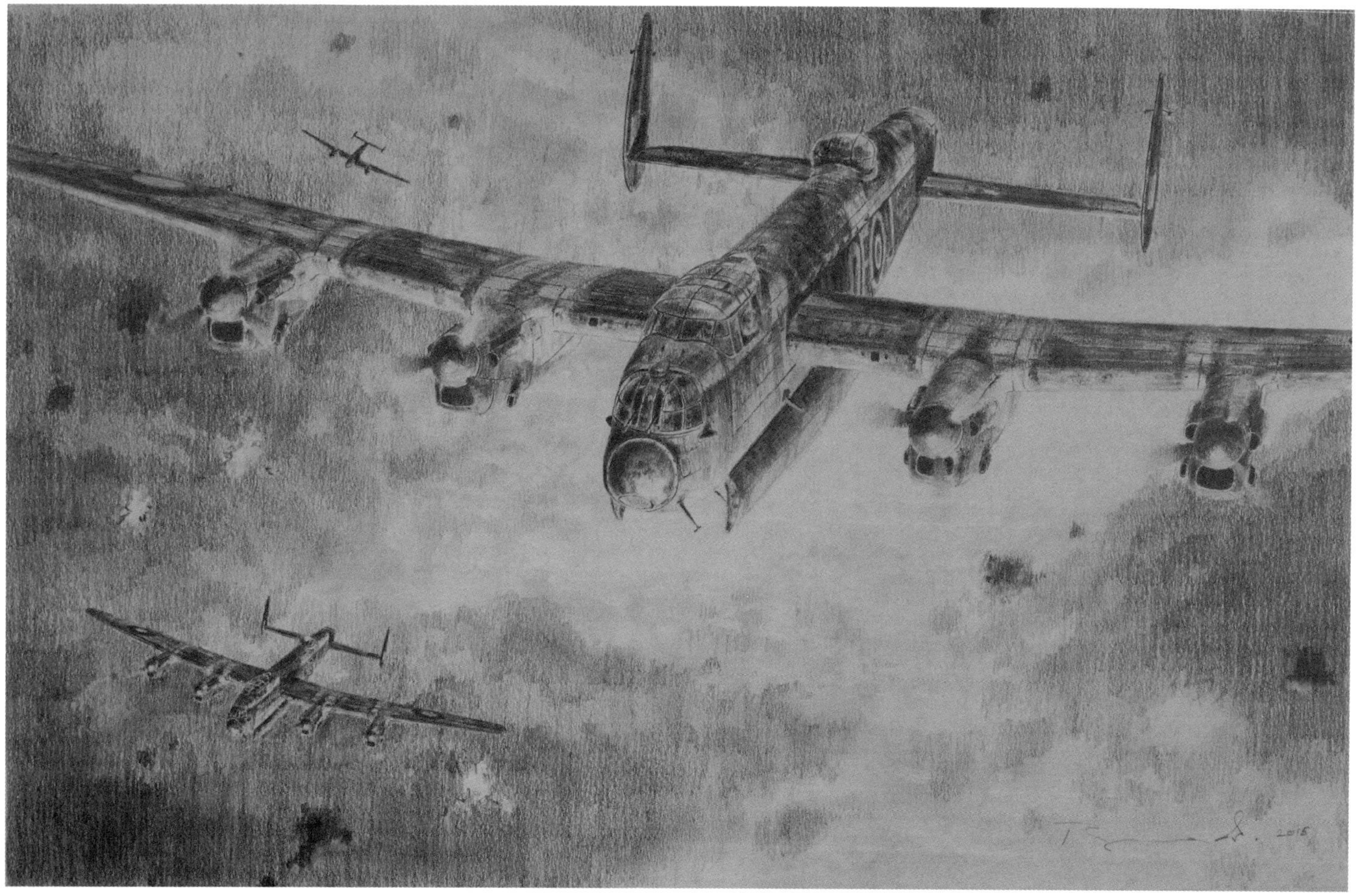

One of the things that stuck in my mind was how the bombers waited for the darkest, moonless nights to carry out their raids – and the innovative, often successful, tactics the German night-fighters used in response. Several of the bomber veterans described how on approaching Berlin they encountered something called the 'fighter flare'. It was a phrase I'd never heard of before but, reading on, I discovered that I./KG7 – a special Luftwaffe unit based just over a hundred miles north of Berlin – was given the task of using their high-flying Ju88s for the sole purpose of tracking the bomber stream on its way to the target area whilst releasing strings of bright white parachute flares as they went.

The bomber crews grudgingly admired 'the speed at which the flares were organized' and 'the blinding candle-power' that illuminated the whole area. I was particularly struck by two first-hand descriptions of what it was like to be lit up for all to see: 'It was like coming out of a dark lane into a brightly lit street', reported one, whilst another said that 'it was like running naked through a busy railway station, hoping no one would see you!' Although rather comical, it vividly made the point, as far as I was concerned, that there could be moments of intense light that I could justifiably incorporate into my painting.

I also wanted to include the RAF's own red and green marker flares going down. I have a rare picture taken from a bomber over Pforzheim in 1945, which showed all these elements. It also shows heavy bursts of flak and the distinctive way these were lit up by the flares.

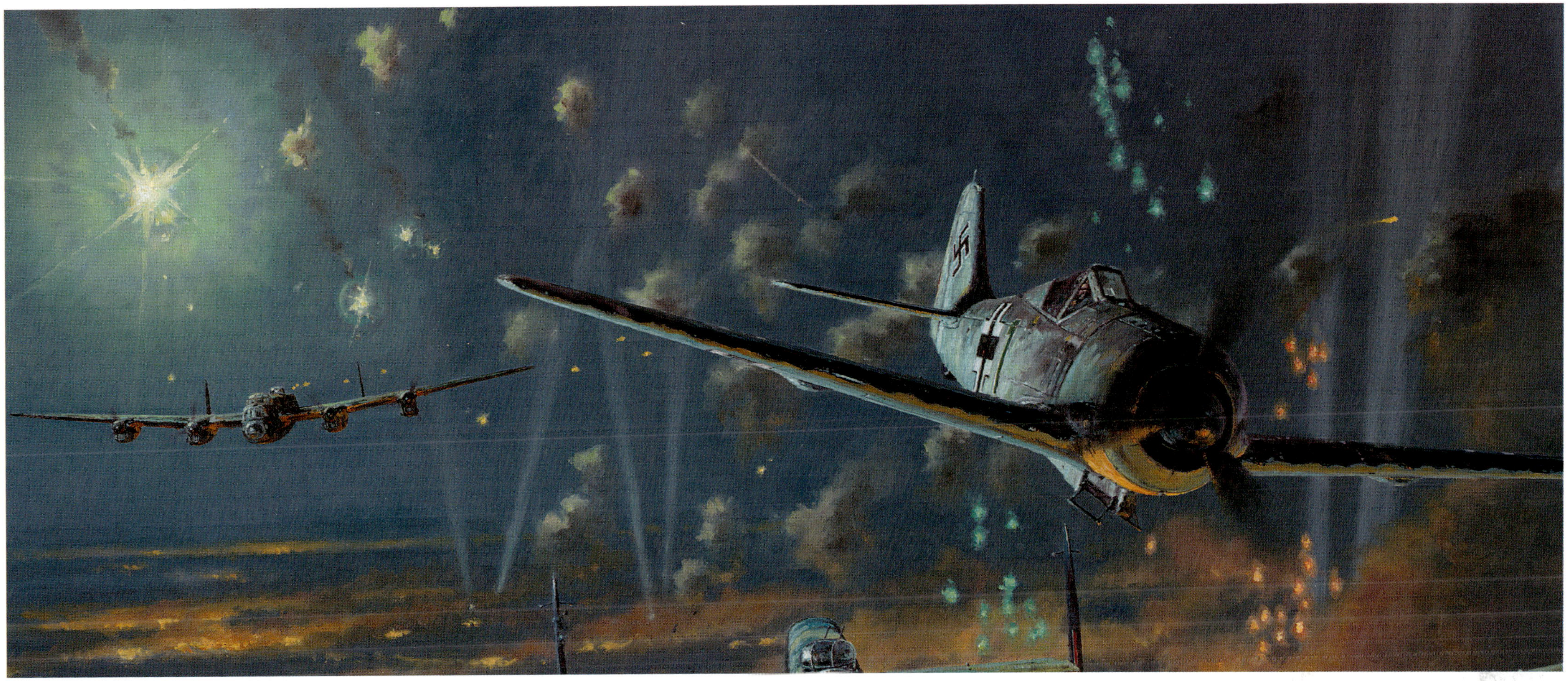

Nevertheless this was still going to be a tricky one to get right.

I think most artists use models to some extent because if you're going to produce an image that's truly unique there's no other way. I wouldn't describe myself as the best model maker in the world but, having built them on and off since I was about nine, I'm fairly competent and my Lancaster model is one of my better efforts. For the main Lancaster in the painting it was important to get the light and the angle of the wings right so I now spent a long time with the model, studying the effect that various light sources would have on the aircraft by using warm light from below, and cold light from above.

I also wanted to develop a low sheen on the airframe. War-time Lancasters were initially painted with something called Lamp Black using pigments that reflected very little light. Although truly black and completely matt it was found to be unstable and chipped off far too easily. It was quickly replaced with a more durable, but slightly less matt, black. If you look at old wartime photographs the paint applied to most aircraft was not completely matt, but neither were they the pristine high-gloss that many air show variants are painted in today. It might sound a bit weird but I originally got the low sheen effect I was looking for by rubbing a thin coating of butter over the model. It had the right effect, despite wearing off quite quickly, but butter wasn't the most pleasant medium to use – especially on a hot summer's day. I've since developed another 'potion' that's more pleasant to use, doesn't wear off so easily and still has the right effect.

Happy with the lighting on the Lancaster, the next step was to portray the night-fighter foe. I had in mind an Fw190 from JG300 flown by Hajo Herrmann, the founder of JG300 and instigator of the highly successful *Wilde Sau* tactics of free-roaming Fw190 night-fighters. Incidentally he was also the originator of I./KG7, the Ju88 flare-dropping unit.

Wilde Sau loosely translates to wild boar in English and, if you think of a wild boar, you understand how the tactics of JG300 worked – lone beasts allowed to freely roam and rely on their own initiative. The Luftwaffe also, by contrast, developed *Zahme Sau*, or tame sow, units that hunted in pre-determined areas away from the city.

Exposed to the same flak barrage over the target as the approaching bomber stream, the *Wilde Sau* pilots would seek out any unfortunate prey who happened to be illuminated by a flare, coned by a searchlight or silhouetted by the fires raging on the ground below. If the bomber crew was very observant they might just spot the fast-approaching fighter and get out of danger, making sudden and wild movements known as cork-screwing. But, with guns having a greater range than a Lancaster's or Halifax's .303 machine guns, an experienced *Wilde*

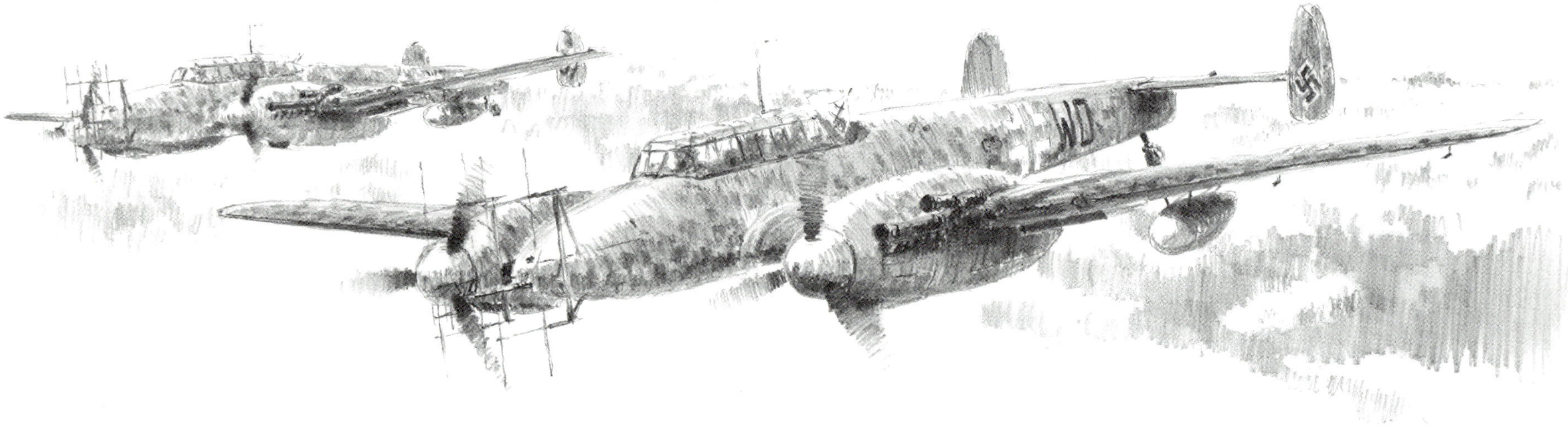

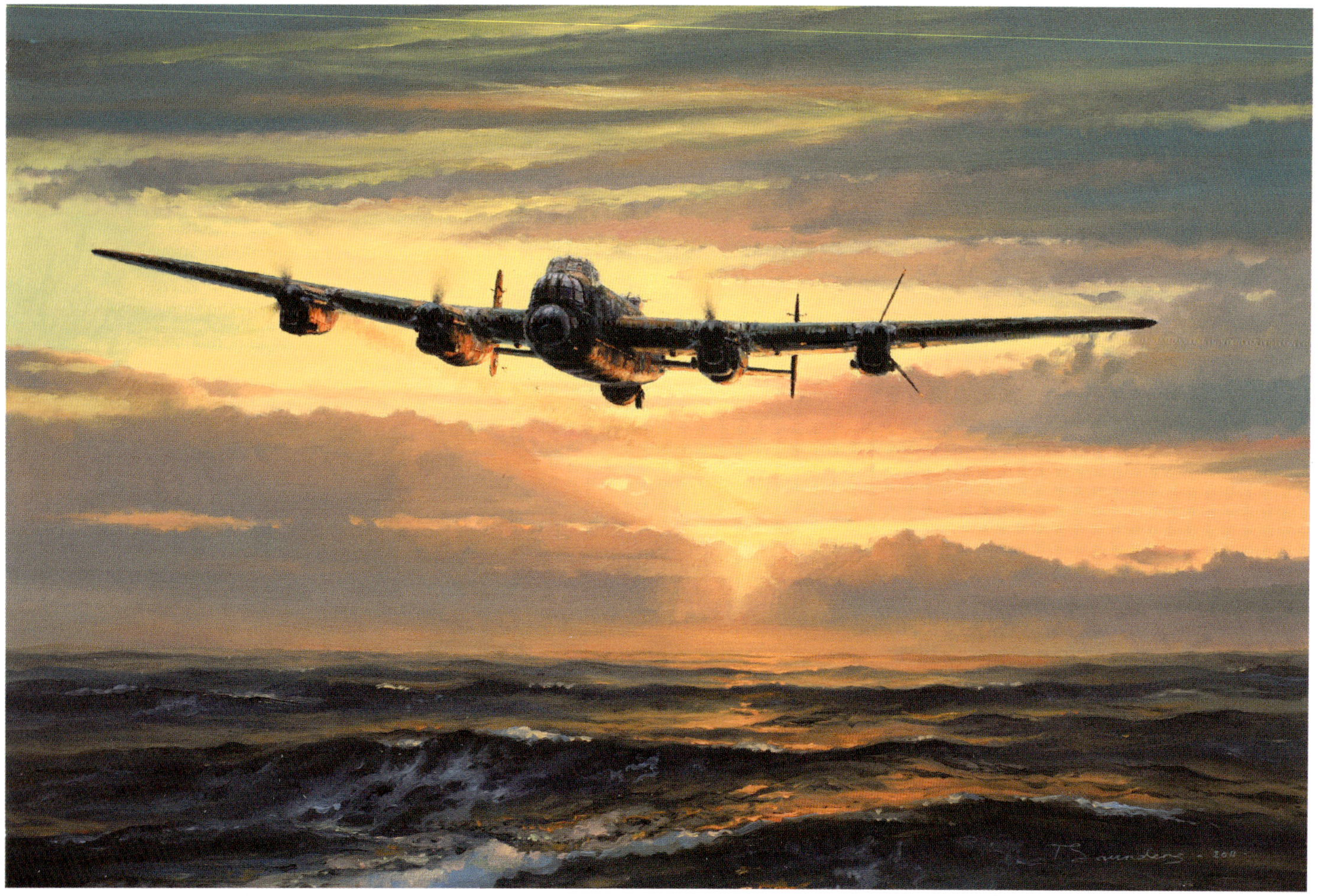

Sau pilot could pick off his victim whilst still out of range. Although some particularly skilled gunners did shoot enemy fighters down, it was all too often the bomber that was unfortunate.

I always try to find original wartime photos, rather than later colour profiles, and I found an excellent one of Hajo Herrmann's Fw190 'Green 1' in a book called *Jagdgeschwader Wilde 300 Sau* by Jean-Yves Lorant and Richard Goyat. This huge brick of a book also has a complete victory list for JG300, from which I could see that he shot down a Lancaster over Berlin on the night of 23/24 August 1943, the night that marked the beginning of what became to be known as the Battle of Berlin.

I cross-referenced my findings with Hajo Hermann's own autobiography, *Eagles Wings*, and although the Lancaster in the painting may or may not be the one that succumbed to his attack, at least I knew the clash was possible.

THE STRAGGLER

PRIVATE COLLECTION

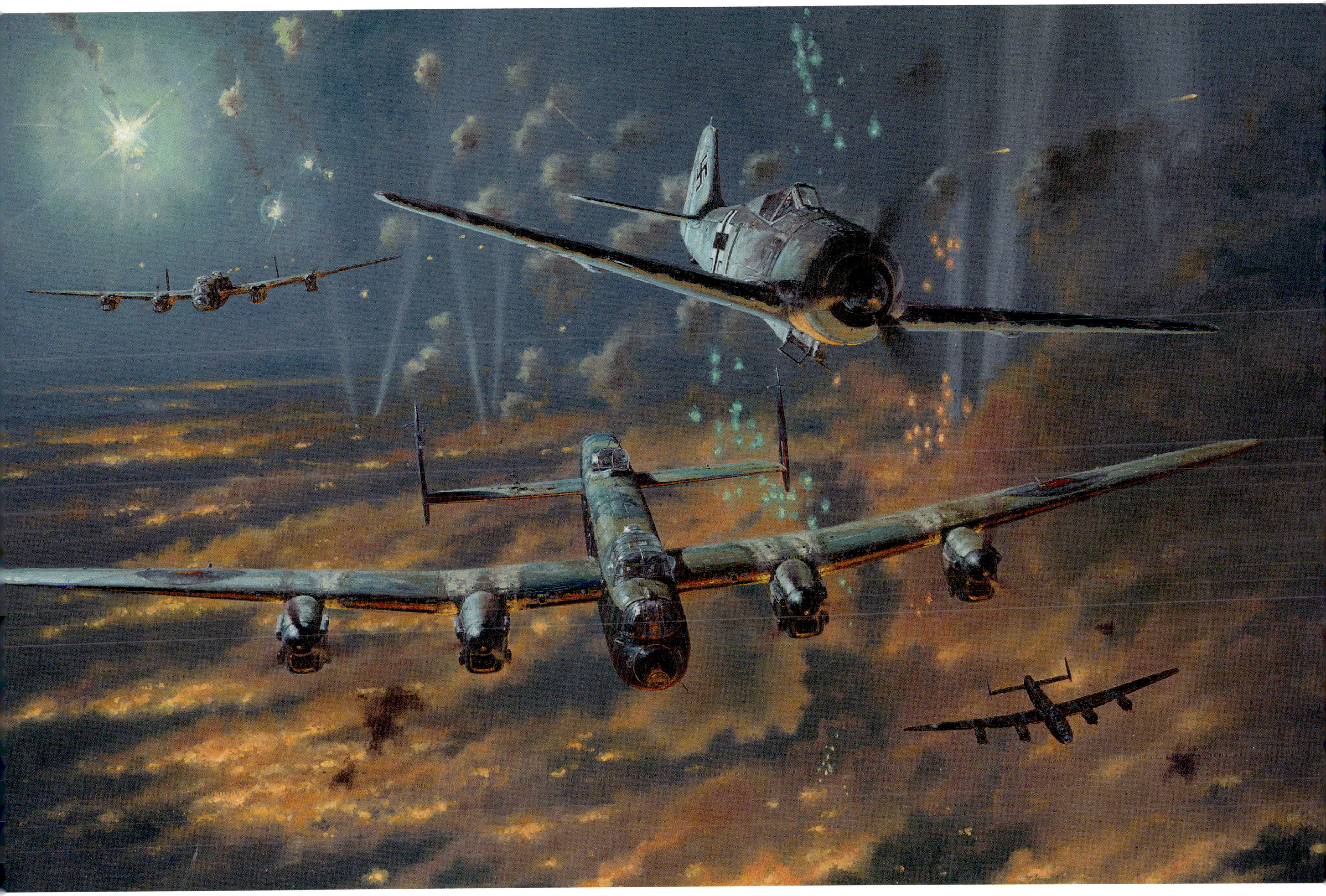

BERLIN BOAR FIGHT IN THE COLLECTION OF MR DAVID JOHNSON

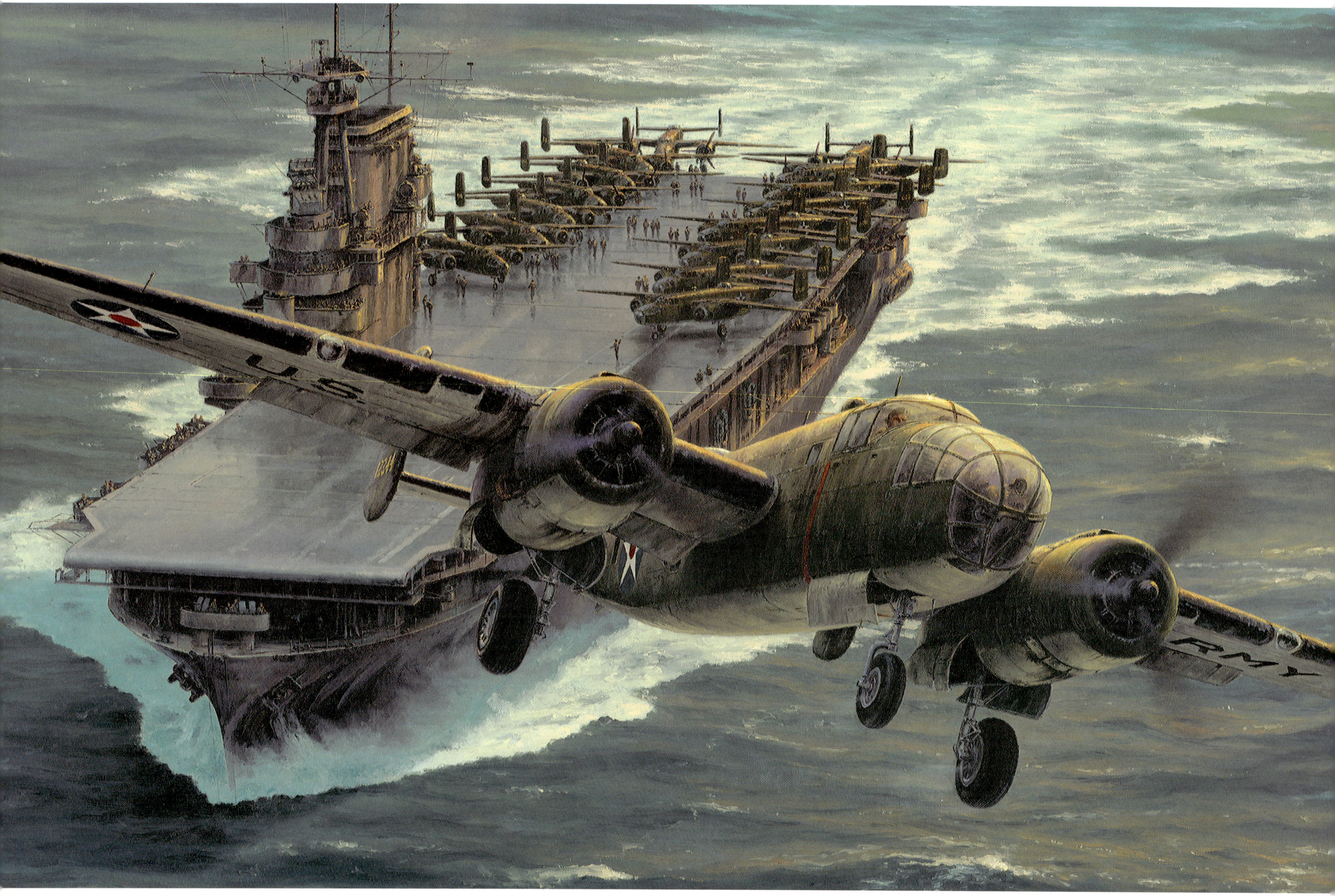
U.S.
RMY

DESTINATION TOKYO

Following the unprovoked Japanese attack on Pearl Harbor, President Roosevelt knew America had to hit back quickly, and hard. He tasked his senior military commanders to come up with a plan. Their answer was an audacious raid that would strike at the very heart of the Japanese empire – their capital, Tokyo.

For the first time in American history the plan called upon the Army and Navy to join forces: B-25 Mitchell medium bombers of the Army Air Force were to launch from the US Navy's newest aircraft carrier, the USS *Hornet*, and the mission plan called for three objectives. Firstly, to bomb the industrial centres of Tokyo and the surrounding area with specific targets being pinpointed to slow production of materials for the Japanese war effort. Secondly, to strike a psychological blow to a nation that had, up until then, been immune to the effects of war and, thirdly, and perhaps most important of all, to boost the morale of the American people.

All that remained for General 'Hap' Arnold, head of the US Army Air Forces, was to pick the right man to lead this all-important mission. He knew that whoever he chose would not only have to be a great commander and tactician, but someone well respected by his men – someone who would lead by example. The officer he selected was Lieutenant Colonel James H Doolittle.

Several weeks of testing the B-25 on dry land showed that with a light bomb load and a head wind, a short take-off equivalent to the length of the *Hornet's* deck was just possible, but an airfield was on dry, flat ground. To attempt it from the heaving deck of an aircraft carrier would require an unprecedented leap of faith, especially for Doolittle who would lead by example and be the first to go. Already famed for his pioneering derring-do, if anyone could succeed, he could.

At 08.20 hours on the blustery morning of 18 April 1942 it was Doolittle's Mitchell that was the first to power towards the pitching bow of the carrier just 150 yards away. With full flaps and throttle he timed his run to perfection and, with an audible gasp of relief from the onlookers, lifted slowly from the *Hornet's* spray-swept deck. One by one the 15 remaining bombers followed and proceeded in single file at almost wave-top level to their assigned targets.

All of them knew they were riding a one-way ticket. There would be no return. They had just managed to take off but landing a B-25 back on the carrier was an impossibility so, after successfully dropping their bombs on target, they headed east across the sea towards the Chinese mainland where recovery bases supposedly awaited them. But, as their fuel ran low and the weather deteriorated, many crews had no choice but to bail out over the mainland or crash-land along the coast. With the help of Chinese civilians most of them eventually made it safely back home and went on to fly combat missions again.

For the painting I was certain that the scenario I wanted to depict was the pivotal moment when Doolittle's Mitchell left the *Hornet's* deck. I knew this viewpoint had been done before by other artists but, with such a famous and often told moment, this was going to be inevitable. Something else that I was keen to include in some detail were the rest of the B-25s ranged along the carrier's afterdeck but, if I were going to show Doolittle's aircraft large in the painting heading away from the carrier, how could I insert all the others with anything like the detail I wanted? The answer lay in optics.

To get the angle I was looking for I built a 1/700 scale model of the *Hornet*, complete with 15 miniature B-25s placed on the flight deck behind the island in the configuration they had been in prior to take-off that morning. The model aircraft included with the kit were very basic, no more than little moulded pieces of plastic, but they did give me a good idea of what the carrier would have looked like with that many planes bunched so closely together. All of them were neatly parked in a 'herringbone' fashion along either side of the deck, apart from the last two at the back. These were facing straight-on to the deck with their tailplanes precariously hanging over the stern of the carrier which meant that I was able to nicely highlight both against the large milky wake left by the carrier as she steamed at full speed into the wind.

I normally photograph models using a 50mm or 55mm lens on my Canon 5D digital SLR camera. This is the lens that most closely replicates objects in the same way as the human eye. However, I photographed this model using an 80mm lens which has the effect of slightly

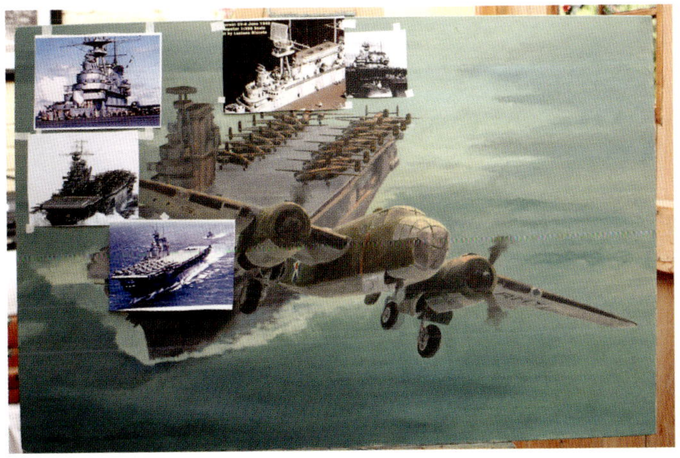

With the painting at the blocked-in stage I sometimes find it helpful to have photos of the subject stuck to the painting

foreshortening the subject, in other words making the after end of the carrier large enough for me to show all fifteen aircraft as I had wanted.

Although the Doolittle raid caused relatively little material damage the psychological impact upon the Japanese was immense, helping to destroy their conviction that they were invulnerable to attack from the air. The strategic impact of the raid was equally far-reaching with many Japanese military units being recalled for home defence instead of taking part in the major battles that raged throughout the Pacific. It also provoked Admiral Yamamoto into attempting a hastily-planned strike against the American outpost at Midway Island – an attack whose failure would be the turning point of the war in the Pacific.

During the research behind *Destination Tokyo* I came across a transcript of the official report submitted by Doolittle after the raid on 5 June. Something that struck me was the complete absence of the word 'I' in this remarkable document, and this from the man who had just been awarded the Congressional Medal of Honour – the highest US military honour awarded for personal acts of valour. I believe this highlights the type of selfless leader Doolittle was – a small detail I know, but one that impressed me.

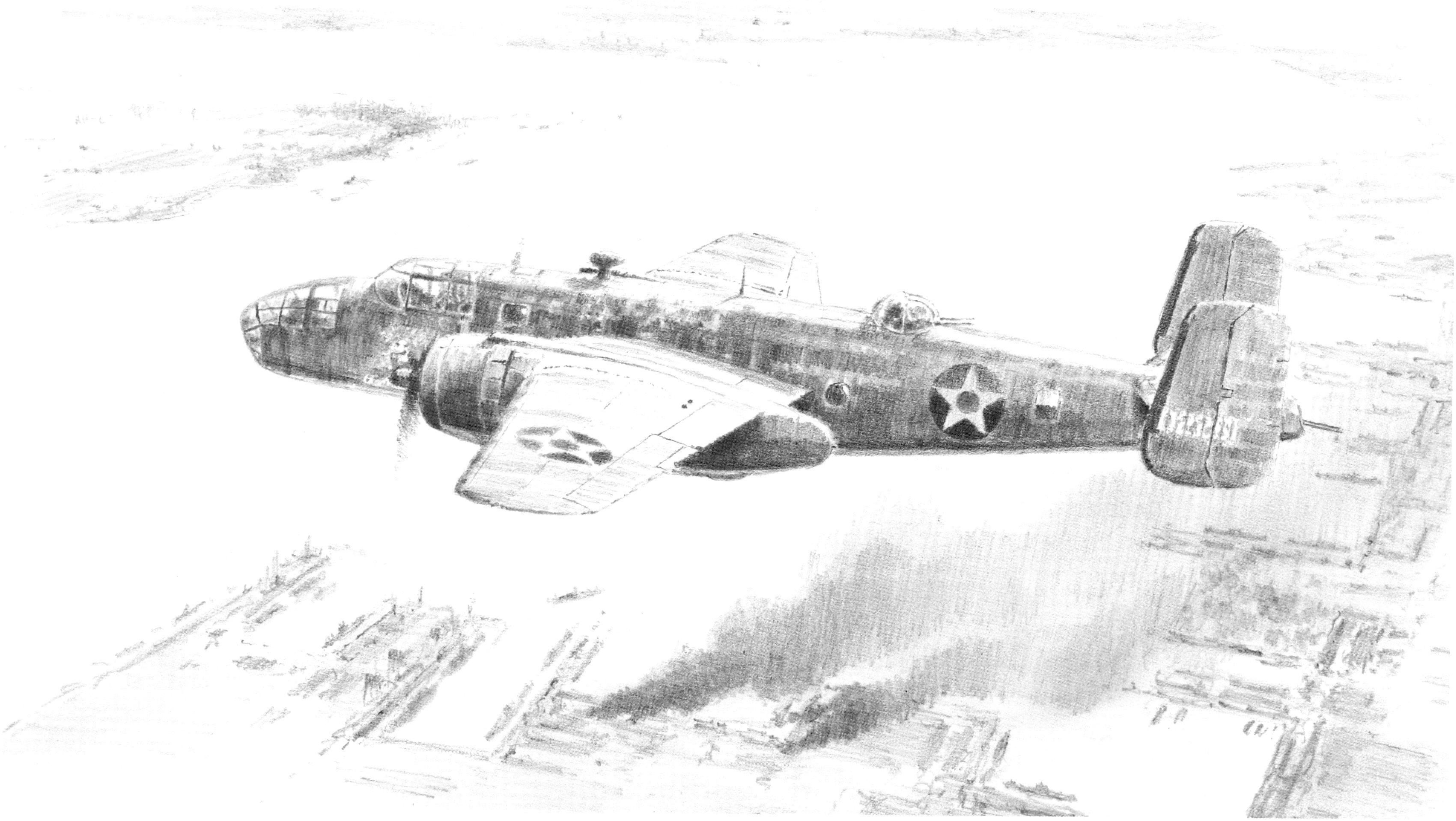

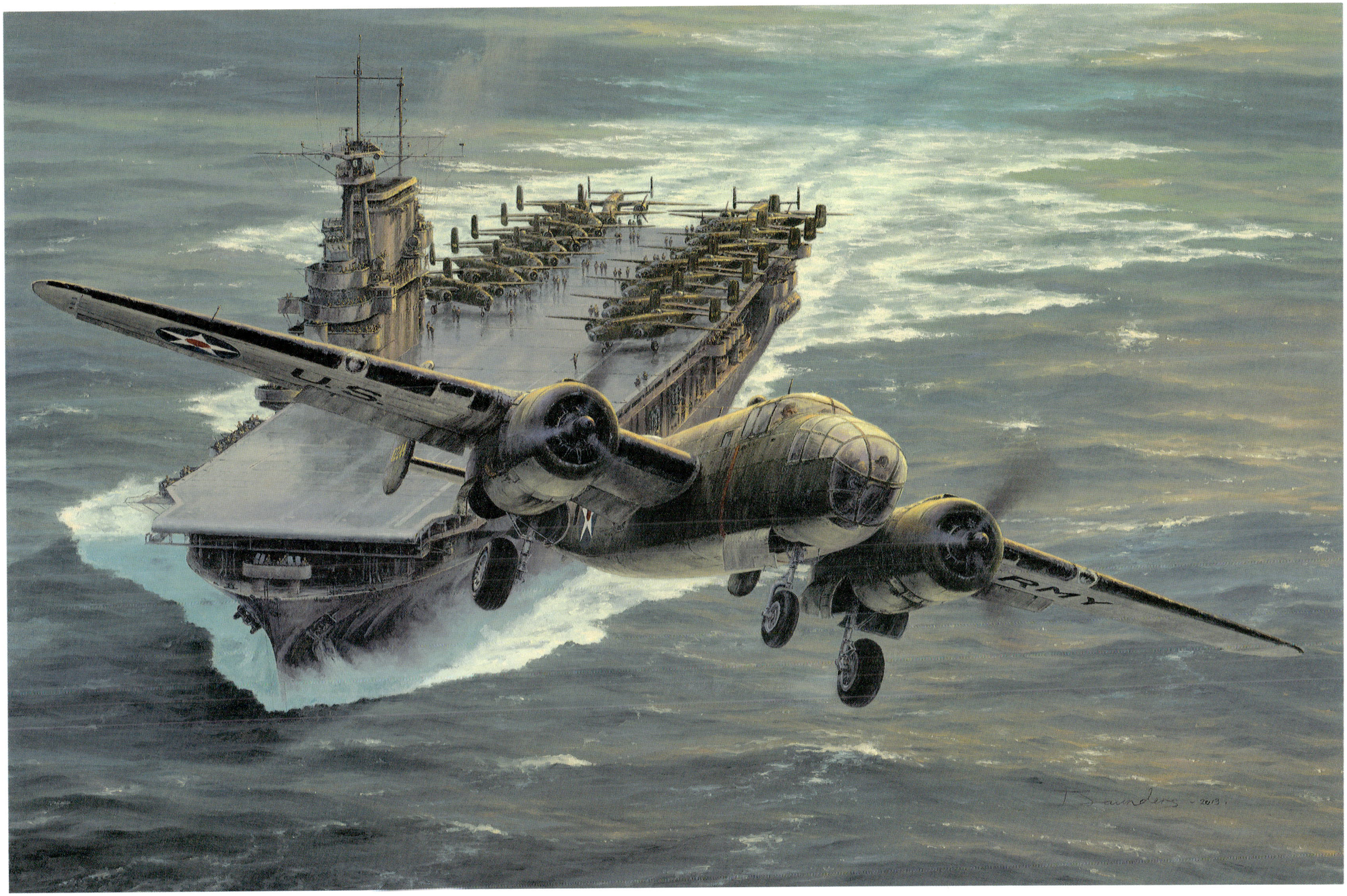

DESTINATION TOKYO IN THE COLLECTION OF MR & MRS M. HORSFIELD

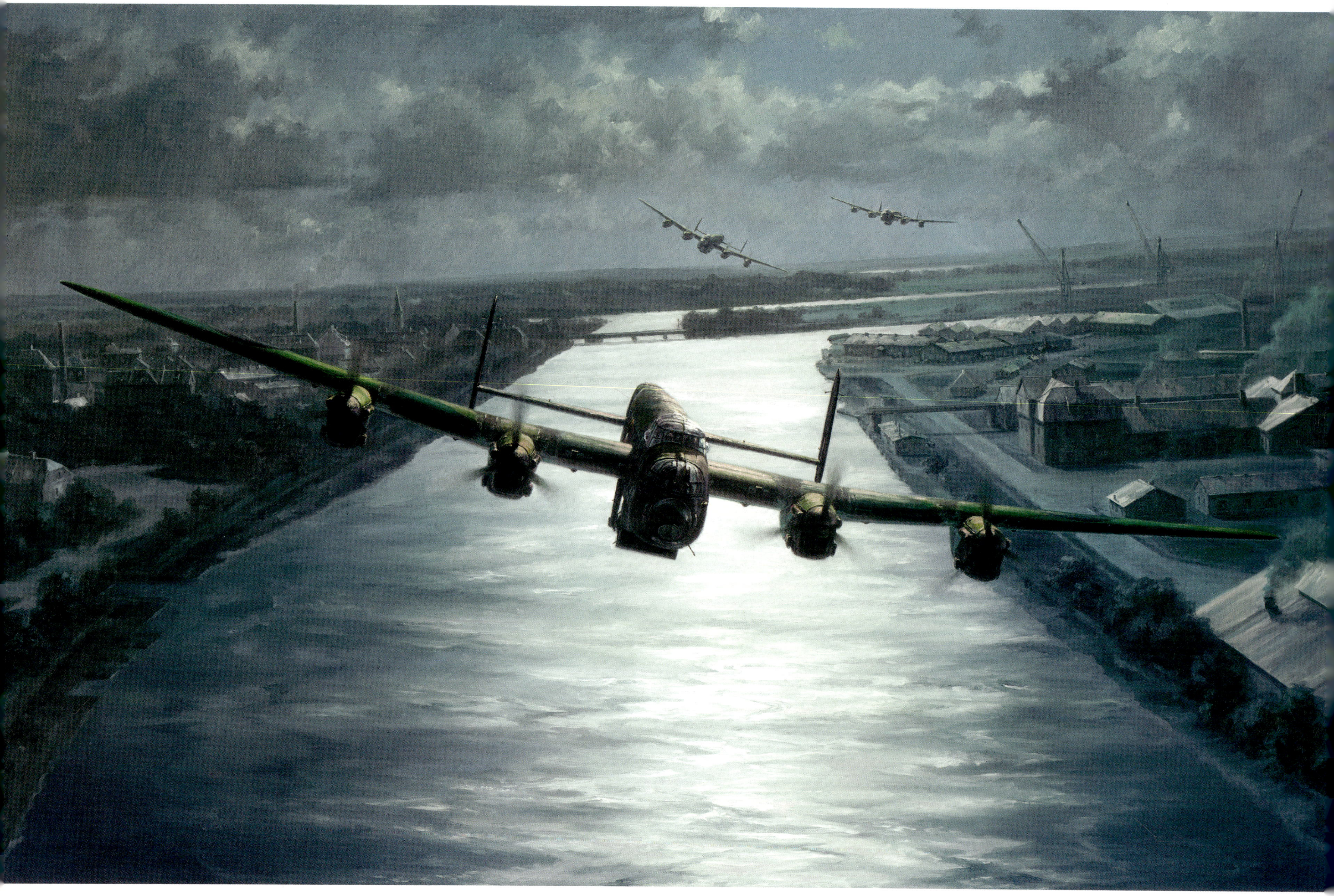

EN-ROUTE IN THE COLLECTION OF SIR PETER JACKSON

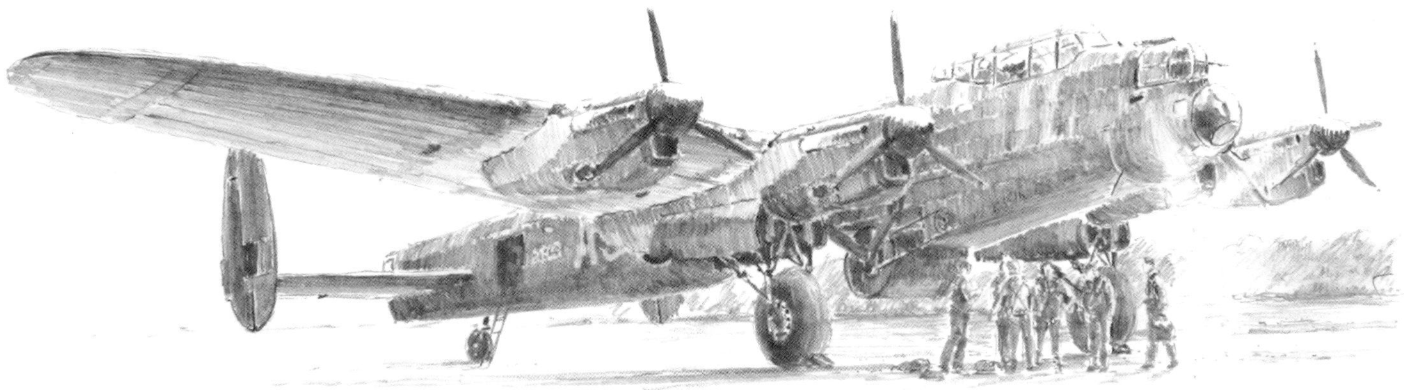

EN-ROUTE

At 21.10 hours on the evening of 16 May 1943, Flight Lieutenant Bob Hutchinson, Gibson's wireless operator, fired a red Very light from the cockpit of AJ-G. It was the signal for the first and second wave of Lancasters to start their engines: Operation Chastise was finally under way.

The mission's commander, Wing Commander Guy Gibson, led the first wave of nine Lancasters around the perimeter track at RAF Scampton and awaited clearance for take-off. With all final checks completed and the four ton *Upkeep* secure in the Lancaster's modified bomb bay, I wonder what thoughts must have gone through his mind in the few moments that he had to wait for the green Aldis signal for take-off? With so much responsibility resting on his shoulders there was probably little time for self-doubt or sentiment. I suspect the thought that was uppermost in his mind was getting his and the other two Lancasters in his flight to the Ruhr in one piece. Flying at night, at an altitude of just 100 ft for the two-and-a-half-hour journey to the Möhne Dam was only the first of many major challenges that night.

Because they were flying a longer route the second wave took off first. A few minutes later, at 21.39 hours the green flash from the Aldis lamp signalled it was Gibson's turn. With Flight Lieutenant John Hopgood to his right in *AJ-M* and Flight Lieutenant Harold Martin to his left in *AJ-P*, the three Lancasters of Gibson's flight thundered across the grass runway in close formation, the roar of the twelve Merlin engines reverberating through the still night air. Using up the length of nearly the entire runway due to their heavy load, the three Lancasters eventually lifted slowly into the air. Twenty minutes later, with the two other flights following at 10-minute intervals behind, they were coasting out over Southwold and heading towards Holland. The North Sea lay eerily calm beneath them, the only thing breaking the mesmerising monotony were the messages passed from time to time between the aircraft.

Gibson's flight crossed the enemy coast further south than anticipated, passing over the heavily defended island of Walcheron. Fortunately the enemy gunners stationed there were either asleep or caught off guard and the attackers were not punished. Hastily correcting his course towards Roosendale, Gibson was forced to climb to 300ft in an attempt to try and identify some expected landmarks and, once found, his navigator, Pilot Officer Taerum, quickly recalculated their course. Meanwhile Pilot Officer Spafford, in the bomb aimer's position, used a specially-drawn roller map to assist the navigator in pinpointing salient features and to try to avoid dangerous high tension cables. Interestingly, the RAF cartographers had become so adept at preparing these roller maps that they even provided the ones used by the USAAF in their famous raid on the Ploesti oil refineries a few months later.

Now back on course, Gibson took his three aircraft due east along the Wilhelmina Canal, conveniently running between the Luftwaffe's fighter airfields at Gilze-Rijen and Eindhoven. The route took them to Beek, near

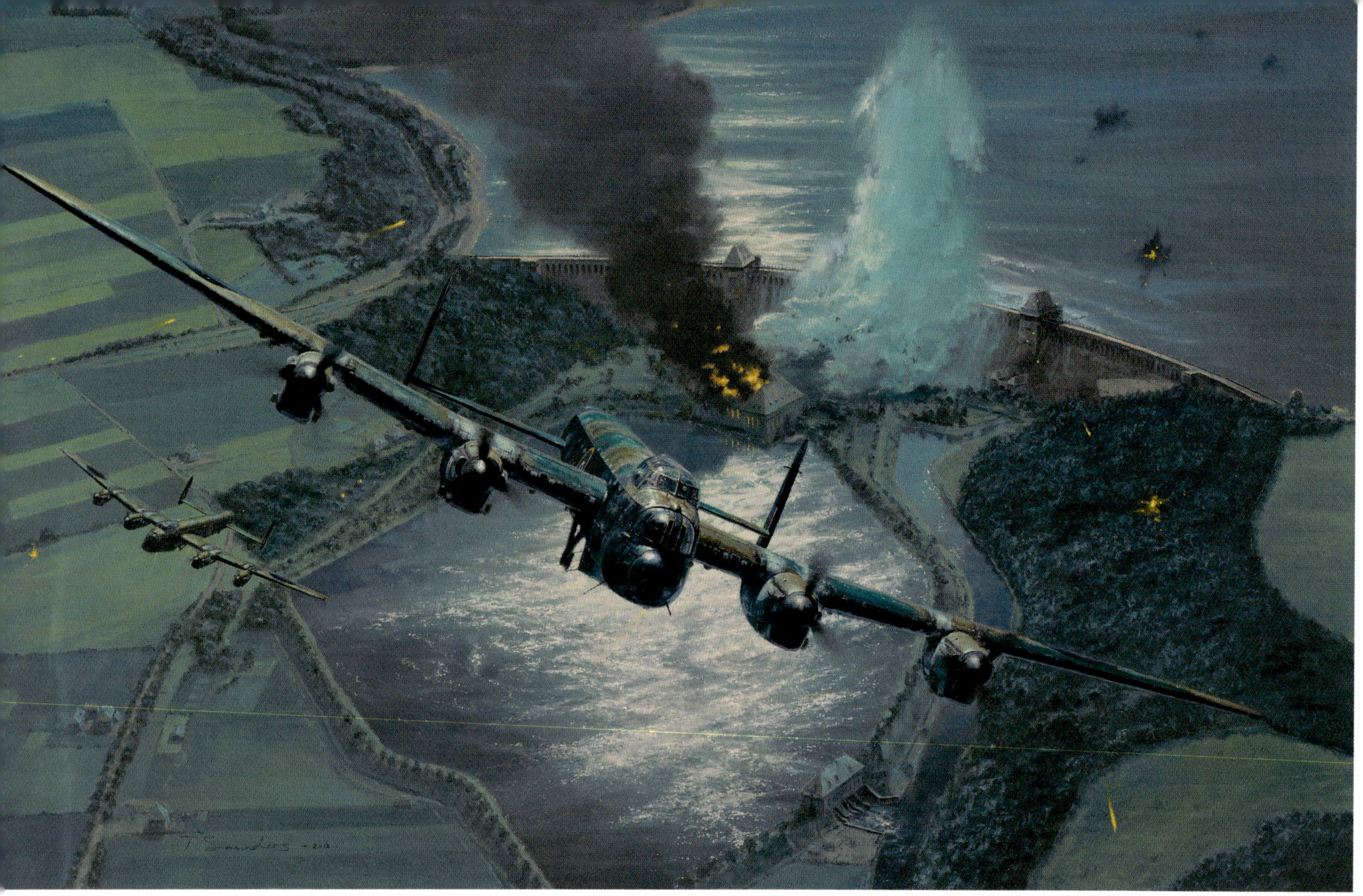

THE BREACH

IN THE COLLECTION OF MR JULIAN PARKER

the town of Helmond, where the Wilhelmina canal meets the South Willems Canal at a T-junction which would have been easy for the Lancaster pilots to identify in the bright moonlight.

I thought that depicting the three Lancasters as they veered around this T-junction would make an interesting and original concept for a painting but, despite a lot of research, finding a war-time photograph of the area proved impossible. There was, however, a modern aerial photo which showed that the banks were industrialised, and it also gave a good idea of the size of the two canals.

The makers of the legendary 1954 film *The Dam Busters* cleverly recreated the scene where Gibson's Lancaster flies over this Dutch canal junction; it's viewed from the bomb aimer's position. The location they used in the film, however, wasn't in Holland at all but in Yorkshire, at a place where the aptly named Dutch River meets the River Ouse at Goole and what particularly struck me were the tall cranes reaching up into the moonlit sky. They were definitely a feature I wanted to recreate in my painting. Although I replayed this brief part of the film over and over again, the actual shape of the buildings was very hard to make out with any precision, so I had to recreate most of them from scratch. It wasn't an easy task, especially when it came to working out which roof angles would reflect the moonlight and which wouldn't.

Eventually, when I was happy with the background, I set about placing the Lancasters in the picture. Although I'd done a preparatory sketch beforehand, I wasn't entirely pleased with it and once I had painted in all three aircraft, I realised it wasn't quite working. The two Lancasters following in the background, although quite small, are a key part of the composition and if the angle of one of them was wrong it would spoil the flow of the whole painting. I must have painted both of them two or three times before it worked properly and I was completely happy.

Painting a moonlit scene in oils is a tricky thing to get right. When there's a full moon I quite often go out into the garden and study the different effect its light has on various things, particularly on the trees and grass, but also on the house and the landscape in general. Capturing moonlight colours in a photograph is difficult as well. I have tried – frequently – but I find it far too subtle to capture accurately, whether on film or digitally, so I find the best way is to go outside and just spend some time observing the light, and then try to store those colours in my head. Nevertheless, when I do start painting, I usually have to start with a fair bit of experimenting in one corner of the canvas until I'm happy with the colour. And, despite trying to remember the exact mixture of colours I've used, I always seem to forget the formula!

It means, of course, that virtually every moonlit scene I paint will somehow always look a bit different to the next. But in the end that's probably a good thing.

THE BREACH

For years I'd been putting off painting the moment one of the bouncing bombs exploded, and the massive column of water it caused, because it's been done many times before.

So, as a compromise, when painting *The Breach* I decided to put the explosion further back than others have done and try to show a wider area around the dam. This included the equalising basin on the air side of the dam where the two power stations were located, an area little portrayed.

It was the main power station located close to the dam wall that 'Hoppy' Hopgood's *Upkeep* hit, with the explosion momentarily lighting up the entire valley and causing that thick plume of black smoke. The smaller power station was at the far end of the basin, nearest the viewer, and here the reflection of the moon provides the back light for the main Lancaster, which is that of Dave Maltby.

LOW PASS OVER THE MÖHNE DAM

'Now there was no doubt about it; there was a great breach 100 yards across and the water, looking like stirred porridge in the moonlight, was gushing out and rolling into the Ruhr Valley towards the industrial centres of Germany's Third Reich.'

So wrote Wing Commander Guy Gibson in his book *Enemy Coast Ahead*, the fascinating account of his wartime experiences, published posthumously in 1946. The book contains many vivid and often moving descriptions, especially about the Dambusters raid, and when I read these particular words again they conjured up a great image; a composition that I thought would not only make a great painting but one that I didn't think had been painted before – the aftermath of the breaching of the Möhne Dam.

Reading words written by someone who had not only taken part in the Dams raid but had led it, brings the events of that night in May 1943 to life like few others. At 00.15 hours on 17 May, Gibson and the aircraft of the first wave arrived over the Möhne reservoir. They'd already endured a gruelling, two-and-a-half hour journey at tree-top height, during which they'd had to weave and jink to escape the many searchlights and deadly flak defences on the way, the most prevalent of which had been in the Ruhr Valley, as well as having to avoid a great number of tall trees and pylons they'd encountered along the way. But, finally, they made it to the target. 'As we came over the hill,' Gibson wrote, 'we saw the Möhne Lake. Then we saw the dam itself. In that light it looked squat and heavy and unconquerable; it looked grey and solid in the moonlight, as though it were part of the countryside itself and just as immovable'.

As the bombers assembled in an anti-clockwise holding pattern over the Arnsberg forest to the south-east of the dam, Gibson called up Lancaster *AJ-B* for the first attack, but there was no answer: Flight Lieutenant Bill Astell and his crew were gone, their aircraft had hit a high-tension electricity pylon just after they'd crossed the German border near Marbeck, and was already a burning wreck. Gibson now decided to go in first, dropping Lancaster *AJ-G* down towards the flat, ominous water. Over the front turret he could see the great dam silhouetted against the haze of the valley beyond as Pilot Officer Fred 'Spam' Spafford, who could see everything from his bomb-aimer's position reported, 'Good show. This is wizard!'

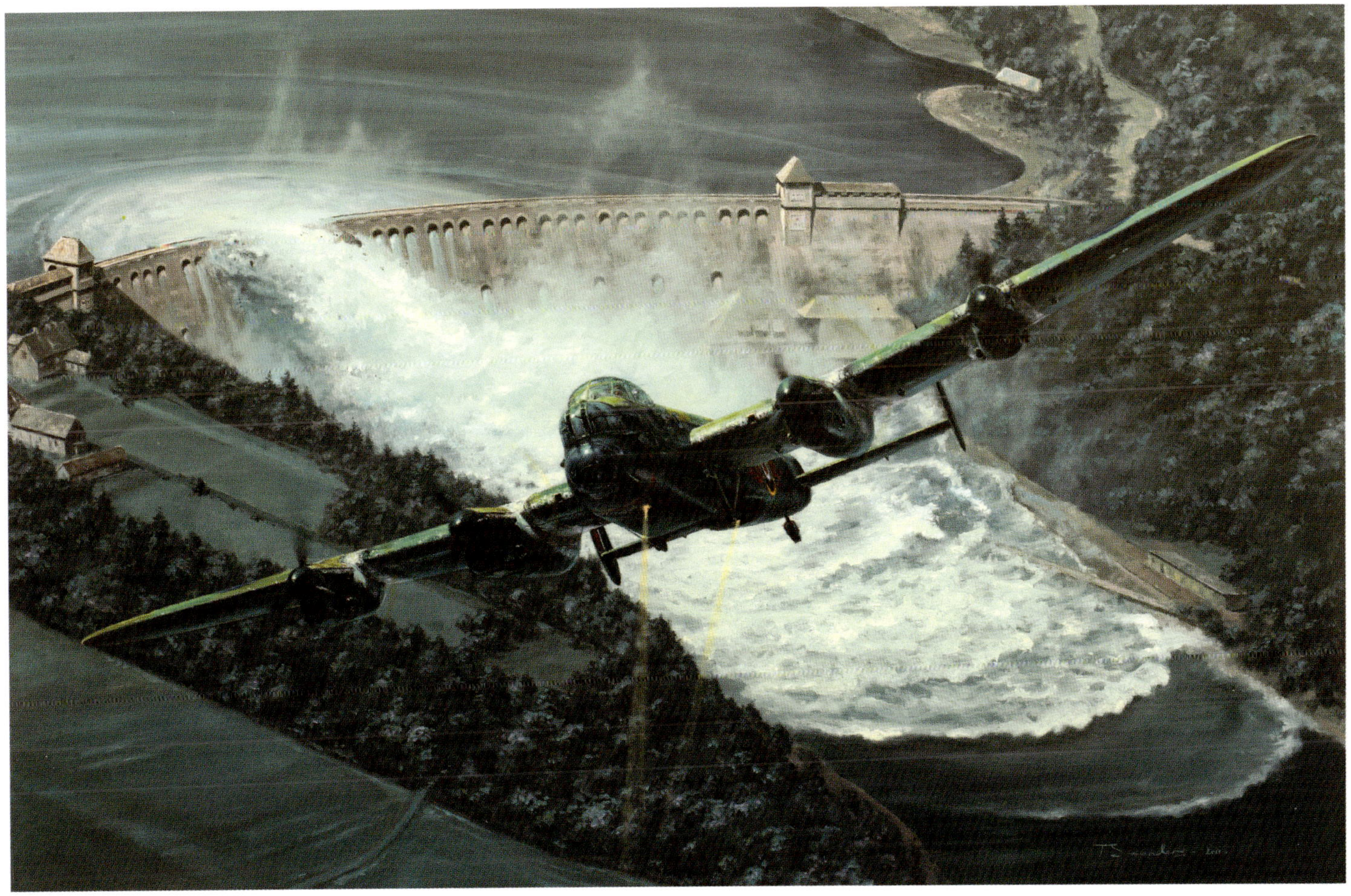

AFTER THE BREACH

IN THE COLLECTION OF MR JULIAN PARKER

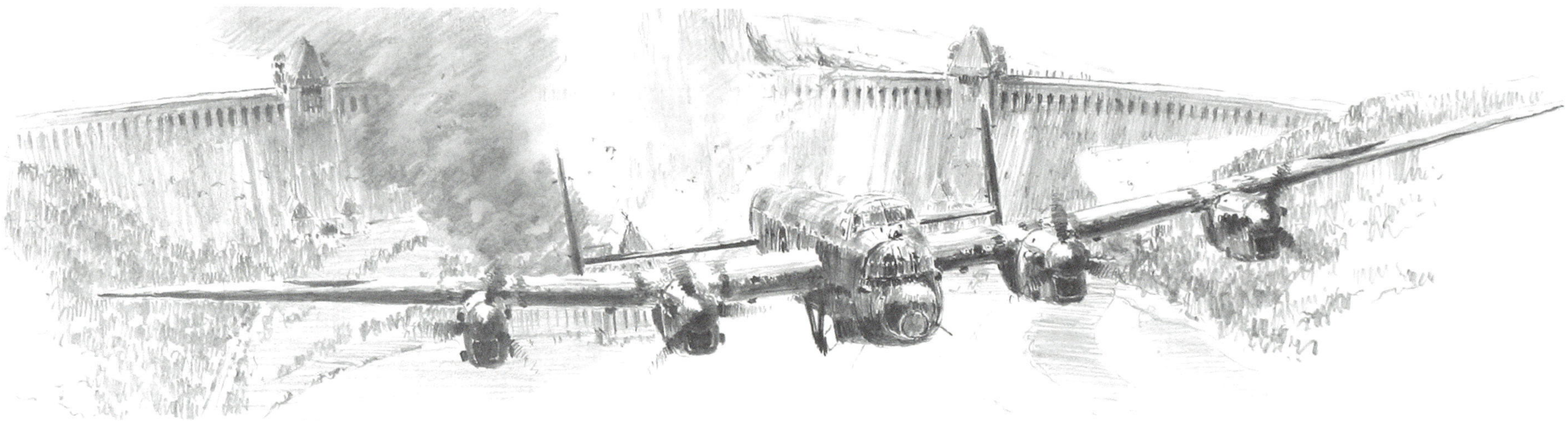

The navigator, Canadian Torger Taerum, now turned on the twin spotlights that would gauge their height and began giving Gibson directions, 'Down – Down – Down – Steady – Steady', and then they were at 60 feet. John Pulford, the Flight Engineer, quickly began working on the speed; first a little flap to slow the aircraft down, then opening the throttles to get the air speed indicator exactly right.

Spafford began lining up his improvised hand-held bomb sight with the towers of the dam. 'Left – little more left – steady – steady – steady – coming up.' The Lancaster was now doing exactly 223mph just above the surface of the lake and Gibson recalled that events seemed to kaleidoscope into one another – the chatter from the front guns, the smell of burnt cordite, the cold sweat underneath his oxygen mask, the tracer whisking

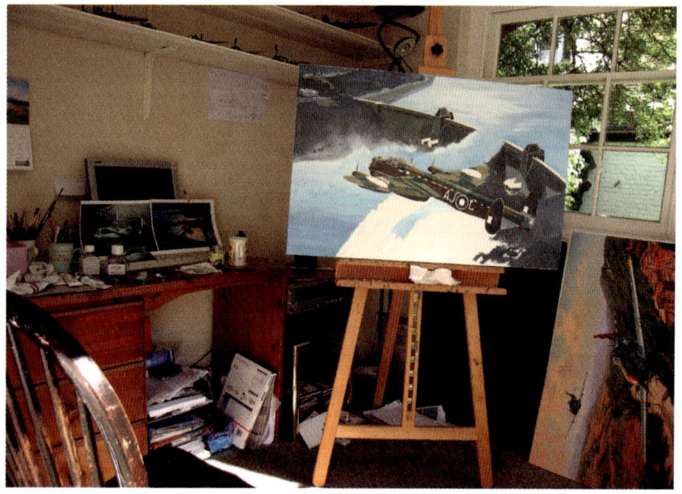

past the cockpit and then finally, an exultant 'Mine gone' from Spafford. Then it was suddenly over; they were out of range of the deadly flak and an enormous sense of relief engulfed them.

As they circled round they saw a great column of water shoot a thousand feet into the air. More water spilled over the dam and the surface of the lake looked as though it was 'being lashed by a gale'. But the dam held.

Gibson now had to wait 10 minutes for the waters to calm and be still enough for the next attack. For Flight Lieutenant Hopgood in *M-Mother*, the next in line to attack, the minutes must have seemed like hours before he, too, began his descent and approach to the dam. The German flak gunners now had a good idea from which direction the attacks were coming and all their fire was directed on Hopgood. They found their mark – 100 yards from the dam the Lancaster was hit.

One of the inboard fuel tanks erupted in flames, trailing a long jet of burning orange fire in its wake but, amidst the turmoil, Hopgood's *Upkeep* was dropped seconds too late – it bounced over the dam and hit the power station on the other side. Moments later it detonated in a huge fire-ball as Hopgood staggered on, frantically trying to gain altitude so his crew could bale out. But at 500 feet the blazing aircraft exploded – amazingly two crew still managed to bale out and survive.

The blazing wreck of *M-Mother* crashed three miles beyond the dam, where it burned 'gently and rather sinisterly' for the remainder of the raid.

Next followed attacks by Flight Lieutenant Mick Martin in *P-Popsie* and Squadron Leader 'Dinghy' Young in *A- Apple*. Both were on target, both detonating with the same huge eruption of water as Gibson's bomb, and both seemingly without success. Now Gibson ordered in Flight Lieutenant David Maltby in *AJ-J* for the fifth attack whilst he and Martin flew alongside to engage and draw some of the flak. A further Lancaster fired on the batteries from beyond the dam.

Maltby recorded that 'our load sent up water and mud to a height of a thousand feet. The spout of water was silhouetted against the moon. It rose with tremendous speed and then gently fell back.'

But, as his wireless operator incorrectly signalled another miss, the dam was already crumbling.

Gibson's view of the events unfolding below was temporarily obscured. 'It was rather hard to see anything' he wrote, 'for by now, the air was full of spray from these explosions, which had settled like mist on our wind screens.' Unsure whether the dam had been breached, he called in Flight Lieutenant Dave Shannon in *AJ-L* for the next attack but, as he swung round over the dam, it was clear that it had indeed been breached. Gibson ordered the other aircraft to: 'Standby until I make a recce.'

As he powered his Lancaster around the dam, Gibson got a perfect view of the breach. 'We began to shout and scream and act like madmen over the R.T., for this was a tremendous sight, a sight which probably no man will ever see again.'

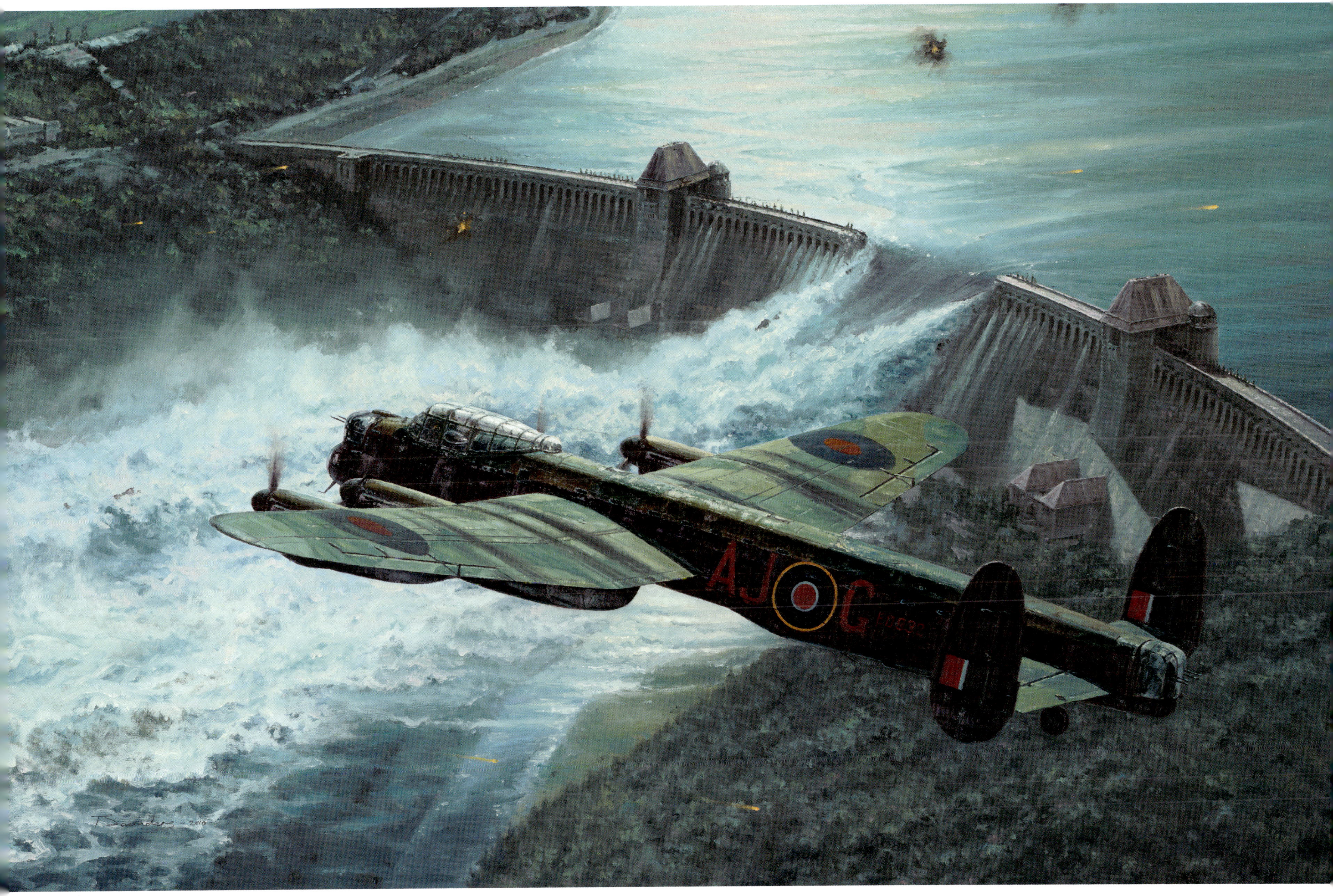

LOW PASS OVER THE MÖHNE DAM IN THE COLLECTION OF MR JULIAN PARKER

THE BIG PUSH

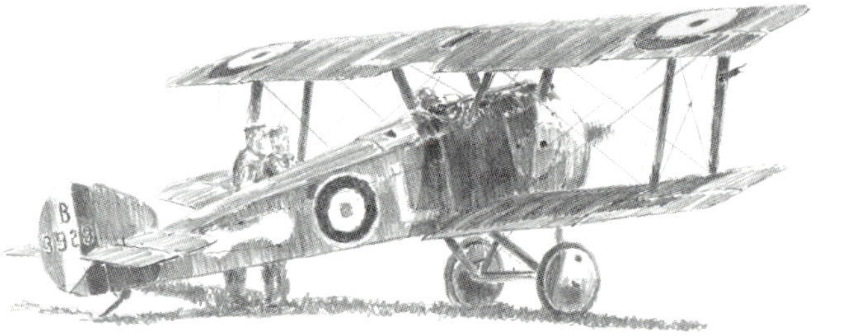

Quite often the idea for a painting takes shape long before the opportunity arises to put it into practice. Sometimes several years go past – but this one broke all records.

It's happened once or twice, when that period between thinking of a concept that would hopefully make a good painting, and the chance of actually carrying it out, has stretched to four of five years. I get an idea, prepare rudimentary drawings and embark on a little initial research, hoping the occasion to put it all into practice quickly crops up. But even I find it hard to believe that this particular idea took nearly thirty years before I finally got the chance to turn it into a painting.

It all dates back to 1988, the year that commemorated the 70th anniversary of the end of the First World War. Although little was made of the anniversary at the time, there were a few very good documentaries shown on television and it was while I was watching one of these that I started sketching out a few ideas for a painting, mainly of men and horses getting bogged down in the mud.

I think those original drawings are stored away somewhere in the loft but, when I eventually got the chance to paint *The Big Push*, I decided to leave them there – I remember they were all rather sombre affairs.

Nevertheless, the drawings had planted the seeds of an idea in my head which, from time to time, had kept popping up until, in the summer of 2013, I described them to my publishers for what I thought would make a great painting to commemorate the centenary of the outbreak of the First World War that was coming up the following year. I didn't tell them it was an idea I'd been dreaming of for years, nor that I was making the suggestion more in hope than any anticipation of their agreement. But I was wrong – they loved it, and, to my surprise told me to make it top priority!

This was music to my ears, but where to start? I was very pleased to have sold the idea, what I now needed to do was come up with a polished, well-researched and interesting scene, and then plan it out on a proper drawing that I could readily commit to canvas.

One thing that did stick in my mind about those early sketches was the mud, just one of the awful things that encapsulate the horrors of life in the trenches. And in

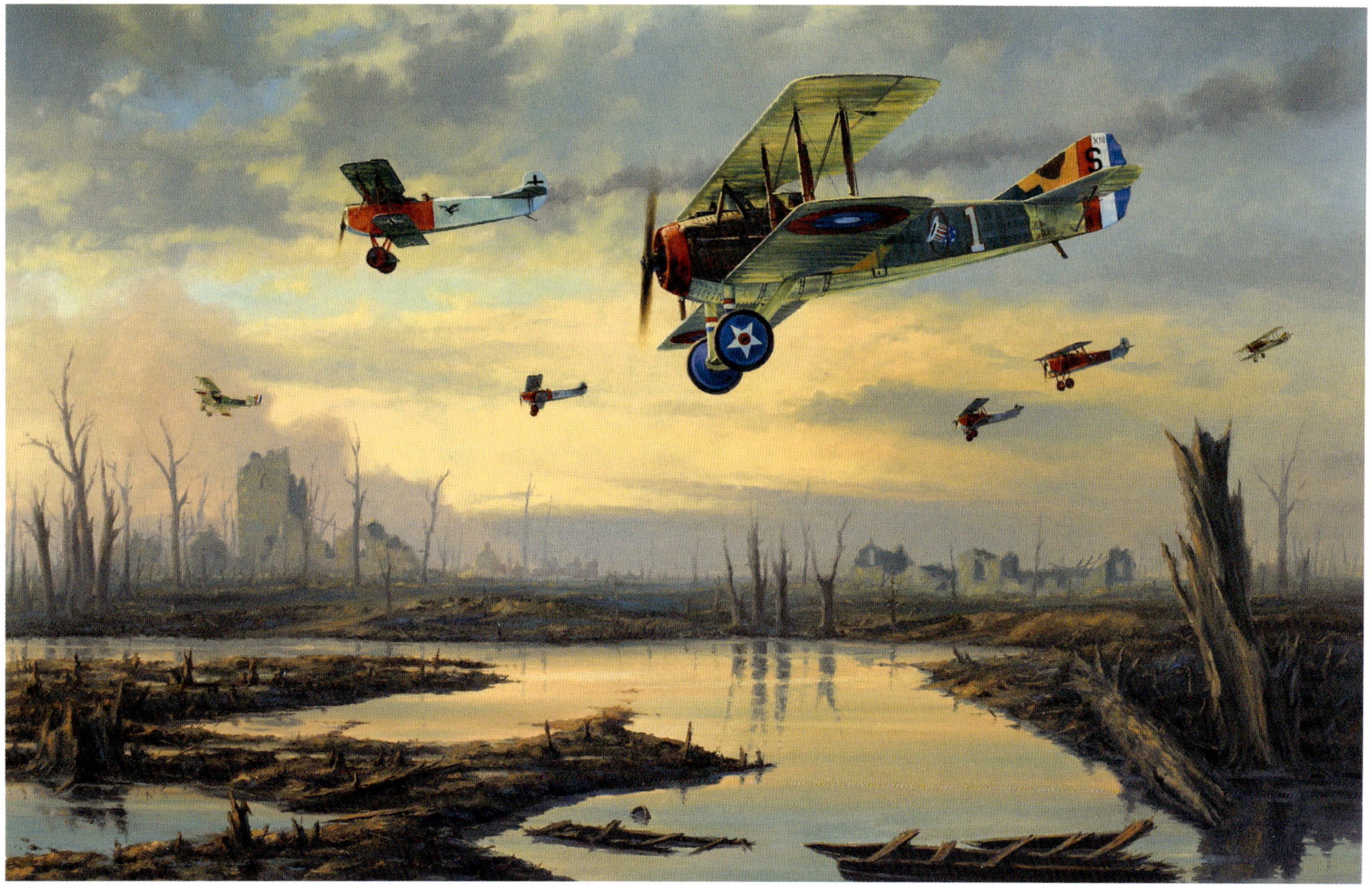

RICKENBACKER AND THE HAT IN THE RING SQUADRON
IN THE COLLECTION OF SIR PETER JACKSON

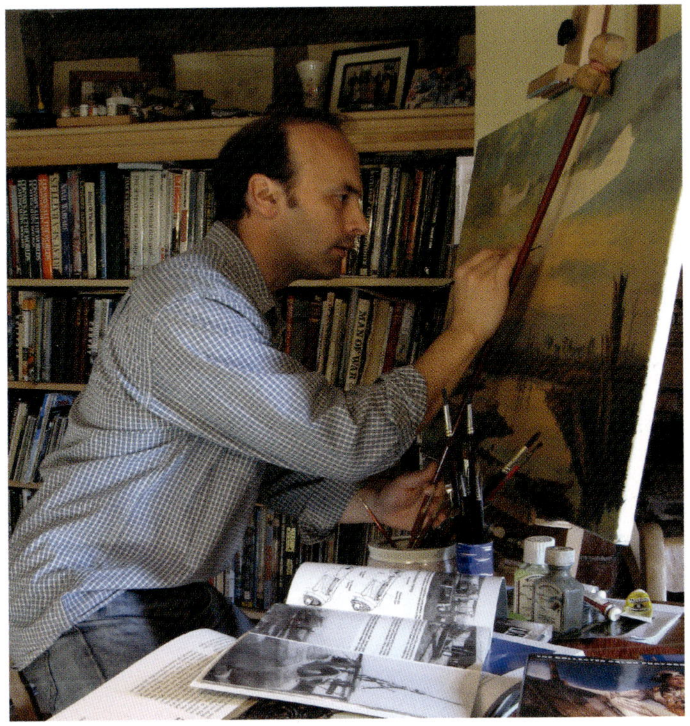

When I'm painting I usually surround myself with as many research books and photographs as I can find, often running out of space on my studio desk; the floor will frequently get covered too!

1917 a battle took place which, more than any other, was synonymous with mud. Its name was Passchendaele.

Passchendaele was part of a series of battles that took place around the Belgian town of Ypres, in an area which became known as the Ypres Salient – about twenty square miles where the Allied front line extended into German-held territory. The First Battle of Ypres in the autumn of 1914 had seen the Allied and German armies try to outflank each other in order to reach and secure the ports on the northern French coast. Offensives and counter offensives continued for the next three years, with both armies suffering heavy casualties. But neither side gained much ground until, in July 1917, Field Marshal Sir Douglas Haig launched a major offensive to capture the village of Passchendaele and the land to the north and east of Ypres.

Officially known as the Third Battle of Ypres, the muddy slaughter that followed became better known simply as Passchendaele.

Haig argued that his objective could be achieved in a fortnight and, if things had gone as planned, it might have ended the war a year earlier than it did. But, as happens in war, the unexpected often sends even the best-laid plans awry. At Passchendaele it was the weather.

The summer of 1917 had been one of the wettest in living memory and the ground in this part of Flanders was low and marshy. The water table was incredibly high, close to the surface, and streams meandered in full spate across the area. Unsurprisingly the heavily shelled battleground quickly deteriorated into a deep sea of oozing mud, a quagmire of flooded pits in which exhausted men floundered and were often swallowed alive.

The mud was now as lethal as the Germans. H. R. Brewer, serving with the Royal Field Artillery, wrote in his diary: 'For seven months our battery had been operational in front of Passchendaele. It is an exceedingly unhealthy spot and has been most viciously contended. Everything is aggravated by the awful conditions. Wherever man and beast have to go, special tracks must first of all be prepared or there are good chances of their being literally lost in the mud: no foundations of any kind can be found, dig as you may, not a stone or anything solid is discovered. Almost as soon as a spade is lifted its place is taken by water.'

In contrast to the soldier's war on the ground, the airman's war was very different, but no less hazardous. Usually based some miles behind the lines, pilots lived a 'relatively' comfortable life – relative, that is, to the trenches – until they took to the air. And then the odds

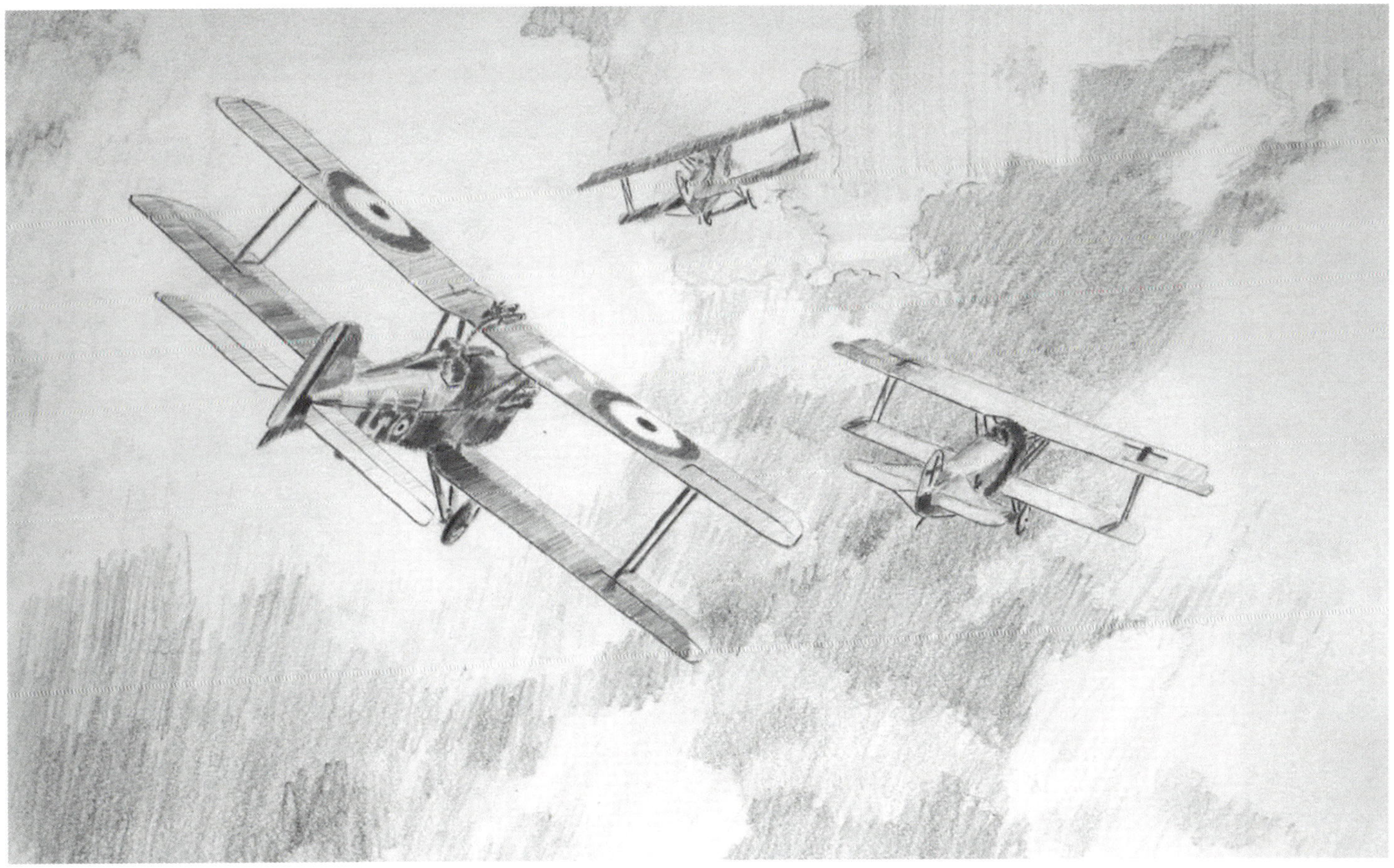

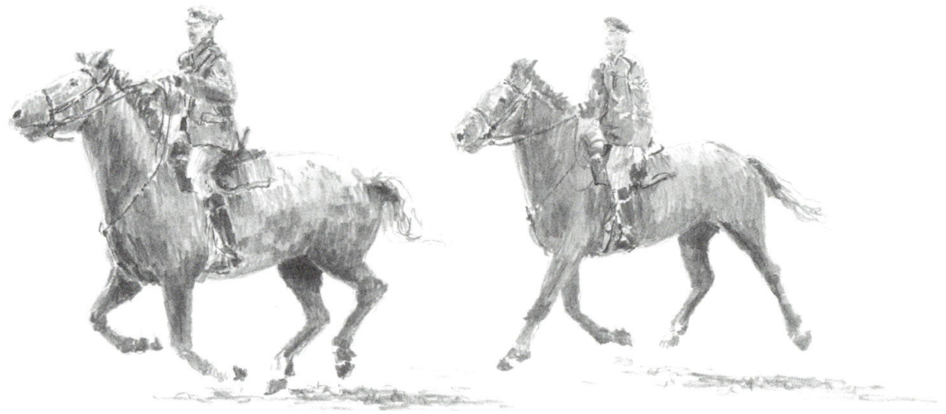

changed, especially for the inexperienced pilot whose life expectancy on front line service was often as little as two weeks. The longer he survived, the more combat experience he gained and, with experience, his chances of survival crept up.

For my painting I decided that I'd like to combine these two very different worlds – that of the soldier and that of the airman. Reading through various books I found a wonderful account of an aerial combat that had taken place over the Ypres Salient on 15 November 1917 involving Second Lieutenant Kenneth Montgomery, a Sopwith Camel pilot with 45 Squadron RFC who was already an Ace. The squadron had taken off on what was a cold, bleak morning to patrol the Ypres Salient for, although the British advance on the ground had halted for the winter five days beforehand, shortly after the capture of what remained of the village of Passchendaele, fighting had continued. The few miles of hard-won territory still had to be held until conditions improved in the spring and heavy artillery was being hauled across the muddy morass into new defensive positions.

Haig had estimated the battle would last a fortnight. In reality it turned out to be three months and, although Passchendaele had been taken, it had cost the lives of a quarter of a million Allied soldiers. It was over this scarred battlefield, near the village of Langemarcke, that 45 Squadron now encountered the Albatross D.V. fighters of Jasta 6.

In the skirmish that followed Montgomery claimed his tenth victory when he shot down and killed one of Germany's top Aces, Leutnant Hans Ritter von Adam, the CO of Jasta 6 and victor of 21 previous engagements. I chose to view the scene not from the air but as seen from the soldiers' perspective on the ground as men and horses of the Royal Field Artillery haul one of their 18-pounders through the mud.

I hope that I've managed to convey a glimpse of how hard those desperate struggles for Passchendaele must have been. It was also the painting, more than any others, that I was glad to see come to fruition – at long last!

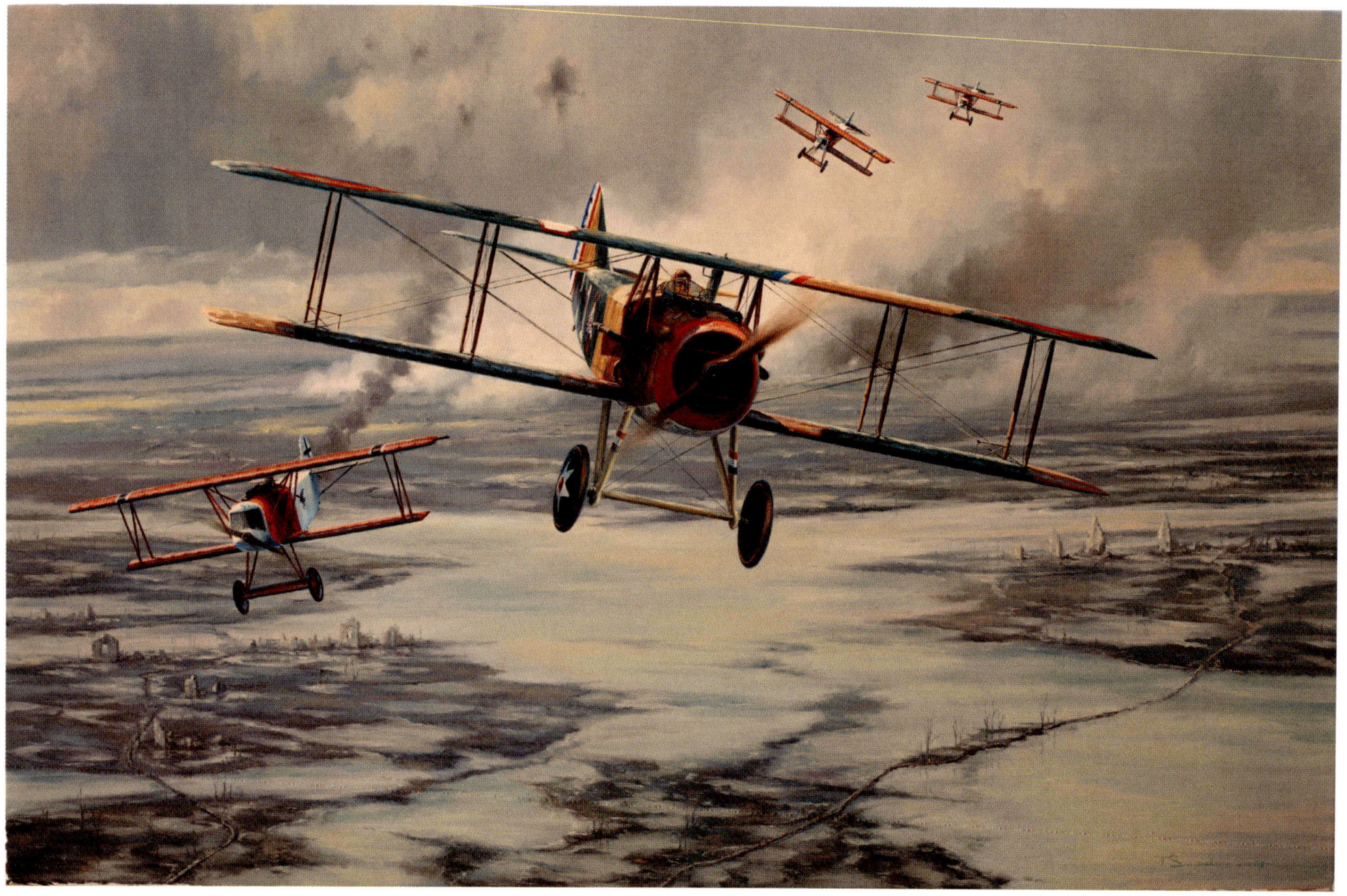

RICKENBACKER

IN THE COLLECTION OF SIR PETER JACKSON

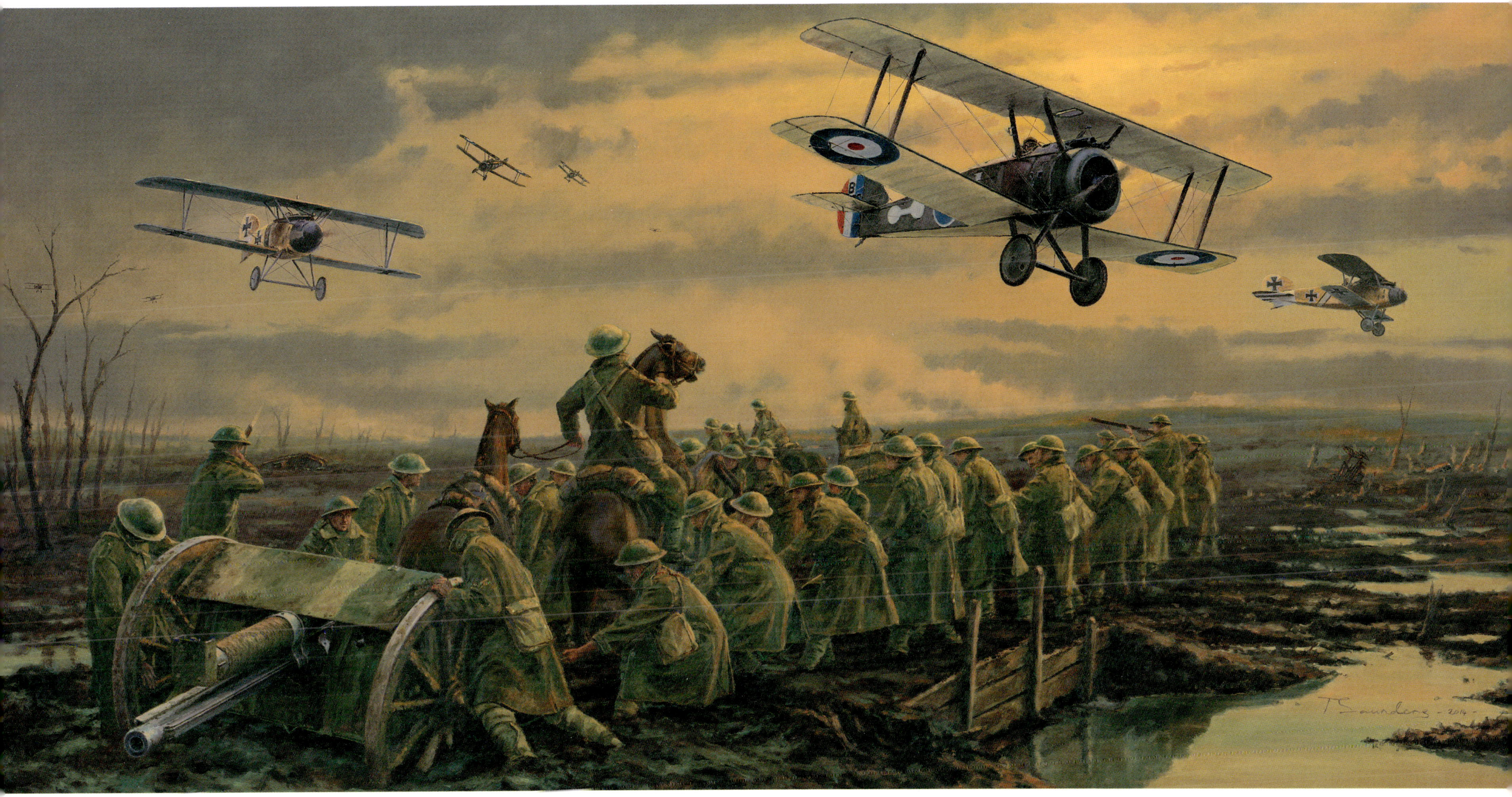

THE BIG PUSH IN THE COLLECTION OF SIR PETER JACKSON

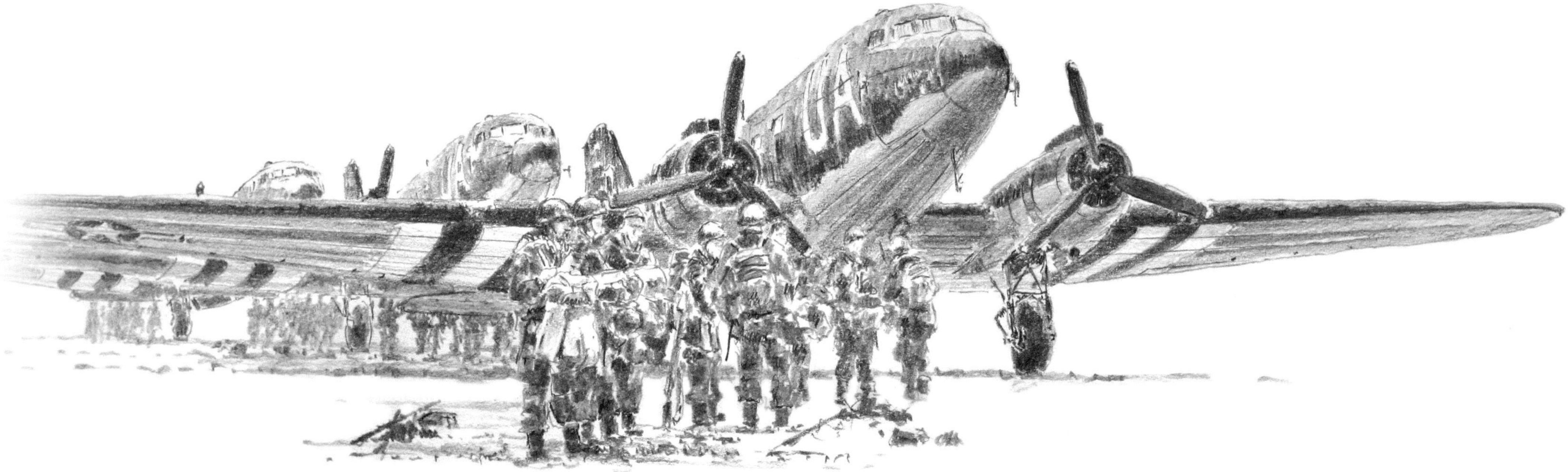

FINAL ROSTER

I have no idea of what it must be like to jump from a plane at night; especially when under heavy fire and knowing that you'll have to fight for your life when you land. That is, of course, if you make a clean landing, and that's something far from certain in pitch darkness.

Many years ago, when I was nineteen, I did make a one-off parachute jump. It was to help raise money for a local charity and the only similarity to the jump made by the paratroopers on D-Day was that it was with a static line from around 2,000 feet. Otherwise my experience was a world away from theirs and I can only imagine how different and unpleasant things must have been for the men of the Allied Airborne Divisions.

I was jumping in broad daylight, on a still, sunny, autumn morning in the peaceful skies over Suffolk. The ride was perfectly steady and the only time I remember feeling a bit scared was in those few moments just before leaving the plane when my main thought was 'why did I agree to this?' The airborne troops who jumped in the early hours of D-Day, however, had little time for such personal introspection; the stakes were far too high. As they stood and prepared to jump their aircraft was buffeted by exploding flak that lit up the darkness with flashes of blinding light. It must have been a terrifying experience.

The men of the 82nd and 101st US Airborne Divisions, some 13,000 men in total, dropped to secure the right flank of the invasion area where, on *Utah* and *Omaha* beaches, the US First Army commanded by General Omar Bradley would land. The two airborne divisions had three main objectives: to stop any German reserves attempting to reinforce the defending coastal units, to attack the coastal defences from the rear, and then block off the Cherbourg Peninsula. The strategically important port of Cherbourg would then fall to Bradley's forces. Failure to achieve these would have been a disaster for the invasion plans.

To carry such a large force of men across the Channel to Normandy was going to be a huge logistical operation, a task that primarily fell to the C-47 Troop Carrier units based all over southern England. Better known to the British forces as the Dakota, the American Douglas C-47 had already proved a valuable asset to the Allies during the invasions of North Africa, Sicily and southern Italy. Huge numbers of C-47s had rolled off the Douglas assembly lines and by the beginning of June 1944 most of those now sat waiting on English airfields ready for the invasion of Normandy.

The commanding officer of the 82nd Airborne Division later wrote about his experience on the evening of 5 June 1944 in his book *Soldier: The Memoirs of Matthew B. Ridgway:*

'In the last long light of the clear June day, weighted down with my battle gear, I climbed heavily up the little ladder of the plane that was to take me to France. In the doorway, I turned for one last look at the sweep of the English Midlands, now grown soft and green with spring. All around me, the dusty aircraft of the 52nd Troop Carrier Command were taking on their cargoes of fighting men – 6,000 booted, burdened paratroopers of my 82nd Division. For many of them this was an old story, for they had jumped to battle in Sicily and in Italy. For me it was a new adventure. I was no stranger to combat nor to jumping. I had jumped in training; and, in Sicily and Italy, seen battle on the ground; I had been with them when the fighting was the hottest. But I had never yet shared with them the very special dangers that are a combat paratrooper's particular lot – the quick leap out of the plane into the buffeting prop wash, the slow float down, hanging helpless in the harness, the drop into the darkness where armed enemies wait behind every bush and tree.'

Reading these words made me want to find out a little more about the 52nd Troop Carrier Wing to which Major General Ridgway had referred. I discovered that it

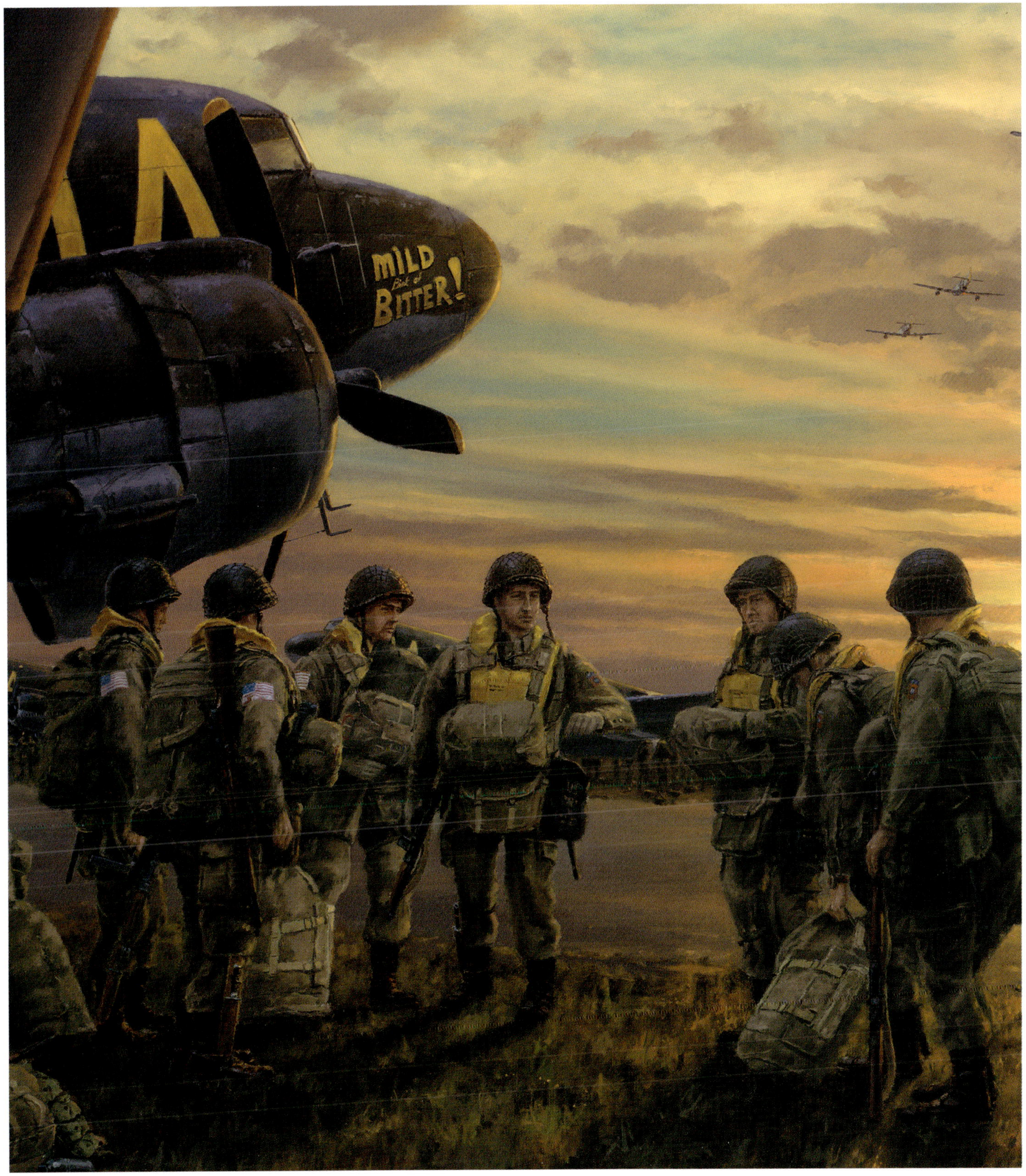

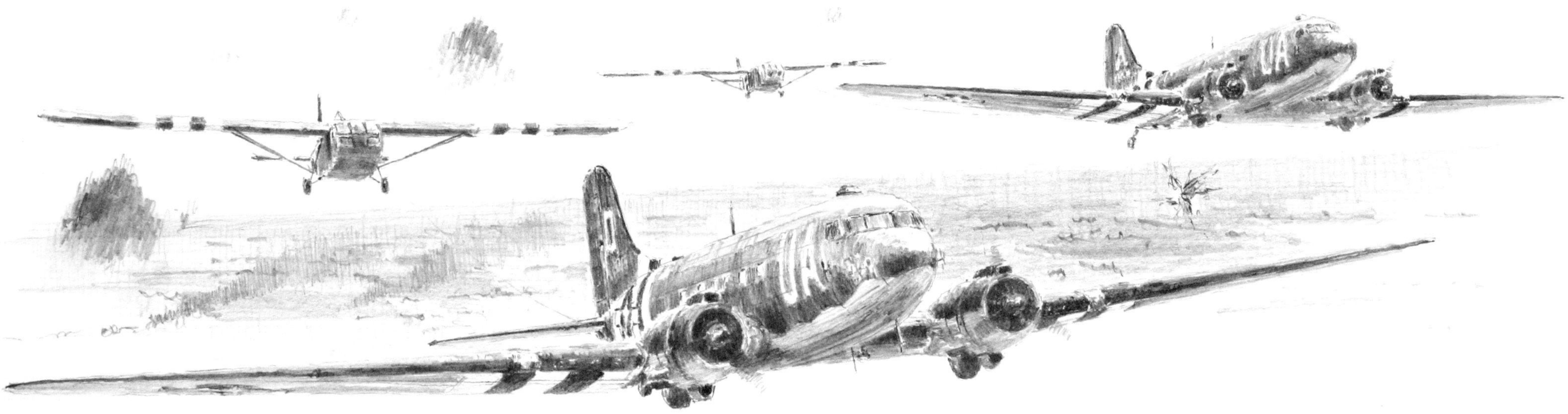

consisted of many separate Groups and after several days of research I found out that Ridgway flew into battle with the 315th Troop Carrier Group, which was based at Spanhoe in Northamptonshire. The 315th was made up of two squadrons, one of which was the 43rd Troop Carrier Squadron and carried the yellow identification letters 'UA'. It was one of their C-47s that Ridgway flew in.

Although I'd done a lot of research finding all this out, I decided that I didn't really want to portray Ridgway himself in the painting. I reasoned that being the commanding officer, he would have been surrounded by a lot of staff, and I was looking for a scene that would be a little more intimate. But, then again, as I'd found out so much about this particular squadron, including a lot of detail on the particular aircraft that were used in the D-Day operations, it seemed only right to feature them.

For me, as for many aviation artists, the trickiest part of any painting is always the human element but in this case I got a lucky break. Just before I started out on planning the painting I was fortunate enough to find, quite by chance, some re-enactors dressed as 82nd Airborne troops. They were taking part in a Second World War event held on the National Trust's Wimpole Estate at Royston near Cambridge where I'd taken my children for a day out. The re-enactors were more than willing models and I took a lot of photos that would soon come in very handy when planning the composition. It was a great bonus to a very enjoyable day.

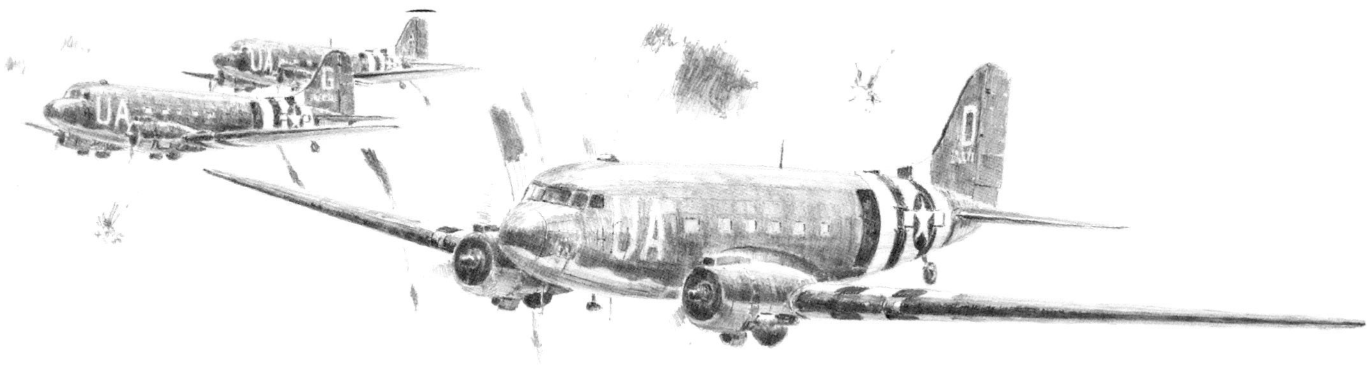

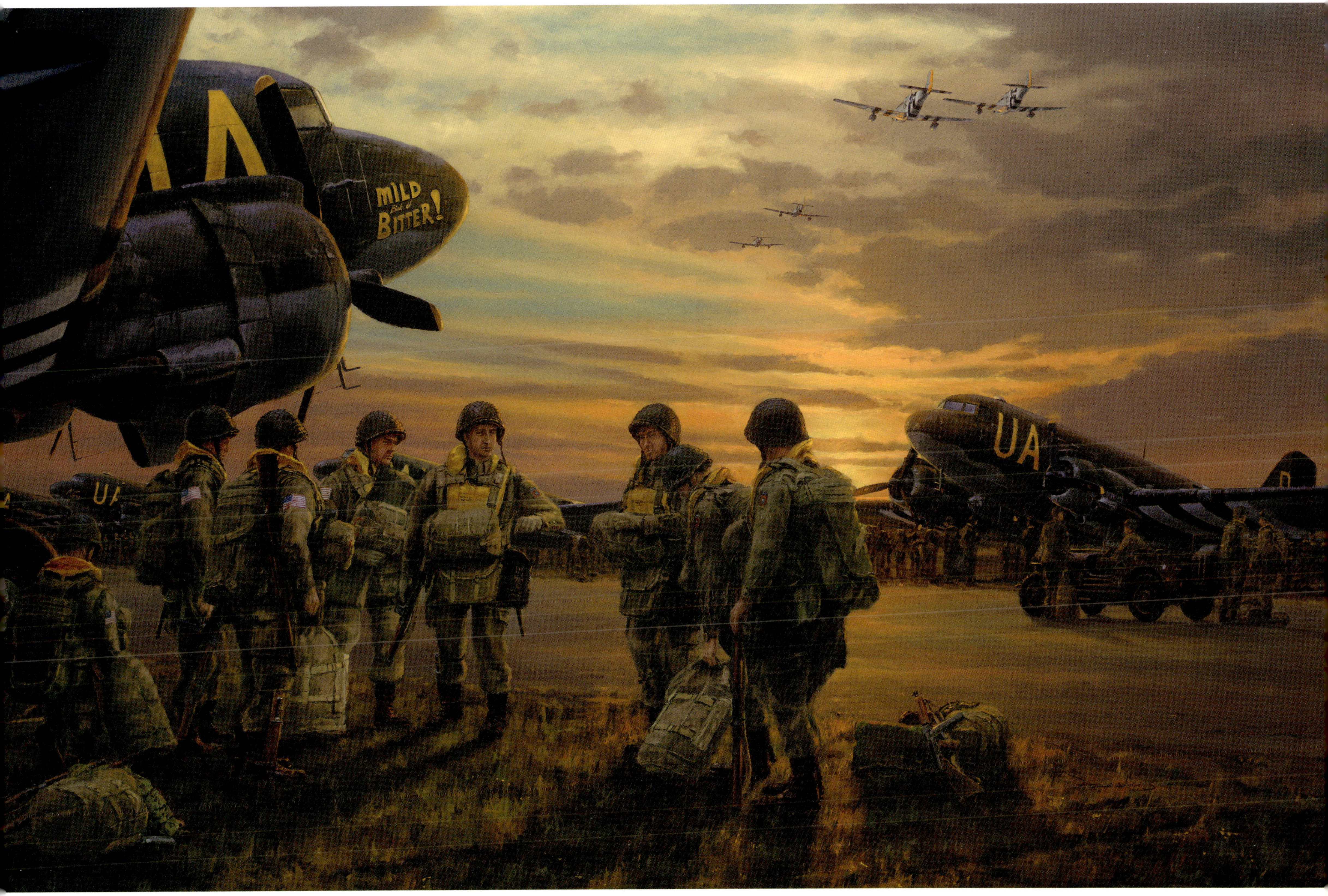

FINAL ROSTER PRIVATE COLLECTION

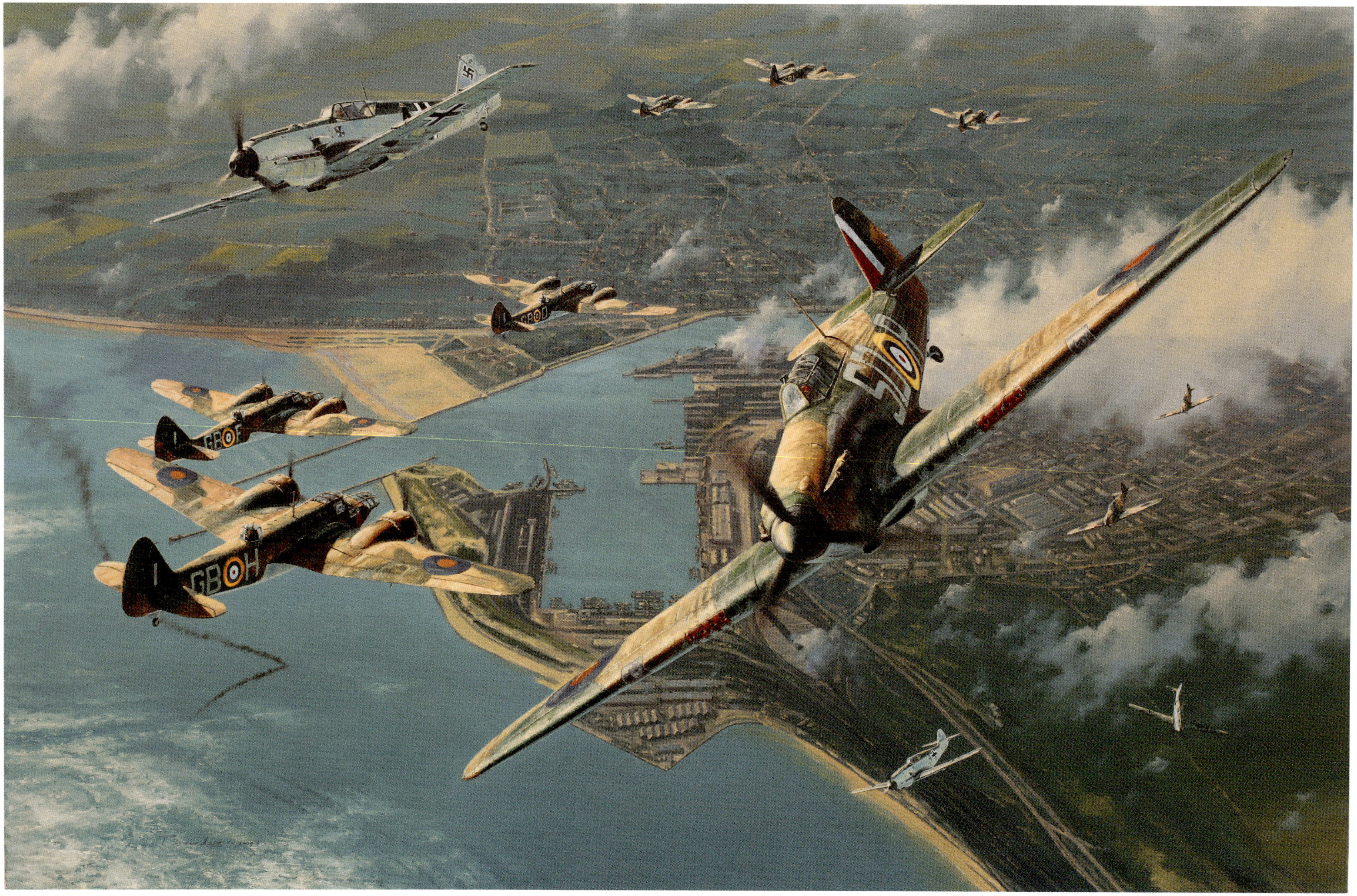

FEAR NOTHING PRIVATE COLLECTION

FEAR NOTHING

I, and I suspect many others, have always thought that the Battle of Britain was waged only by 'the few', the now legendary fighter pilots of Fighter Command, but it was only when I started to research the background for this painting that I realised this wasn't the whole truth.

The Battle of Britain Chapel in Westminster Abbey, dedicated in 1947, contains a roll of honour that lists 449 pilots and air crew from Fighter Command who paid with their lives in the struggle to repel the Luftwaffe and the threat of German invasion. What is perhaps more surprising is that this figure represents only 30 per cent of total RAF casualties for the period; the other 70 per cent was made up primarily of crews from Bomber Command and Coastal Command.

On 25 June 1940 the armistice between Germany and France came into effect, and it was now that German High Command began to make serious plans for Operation *Sealion*, the codename for their invasion of England. Pioneers from the German army joined navy and Luftwaffe personnel to work all-out on improvising the vast fleet of landing vessels needed for the invasion, using requisitioned freighters, fishing vessels and, in particular, tugs and barges from the great inland canals and waterways that criss-crossed north-west Europe.

By August some 3,000 of these vessels had been assembled in the Channel ports facing England, in a crescent that stretched from Rotterdam, Antwerp and Ostend in the east to Cherbourg in the west.

The job of preventing this invasion fleet ever leaving port fell to the Hampdens, Whitleys, Wellingtons and particularly the Blenheims of Bomber Command, a task carried out tirelessly by day and by night. It became a battle which was just as hard-fought and costly as the one being waged in the skies of southern England by the Spitfires and Hurricanes of Fighter Command.

By the end of August a heavy toll meant that only the Blenheims were still operating by day, and as well as the invasion ports, the hard-pressed bomber crews were now also targeting the Luftwaffe airfields that would provide the vital aerial support for the invasion fleet. Unsurprisingly these proved to be particularly costly targets.

But it wasn't only in the air that Bomber Command was losing aircraft; it was also losing them on the

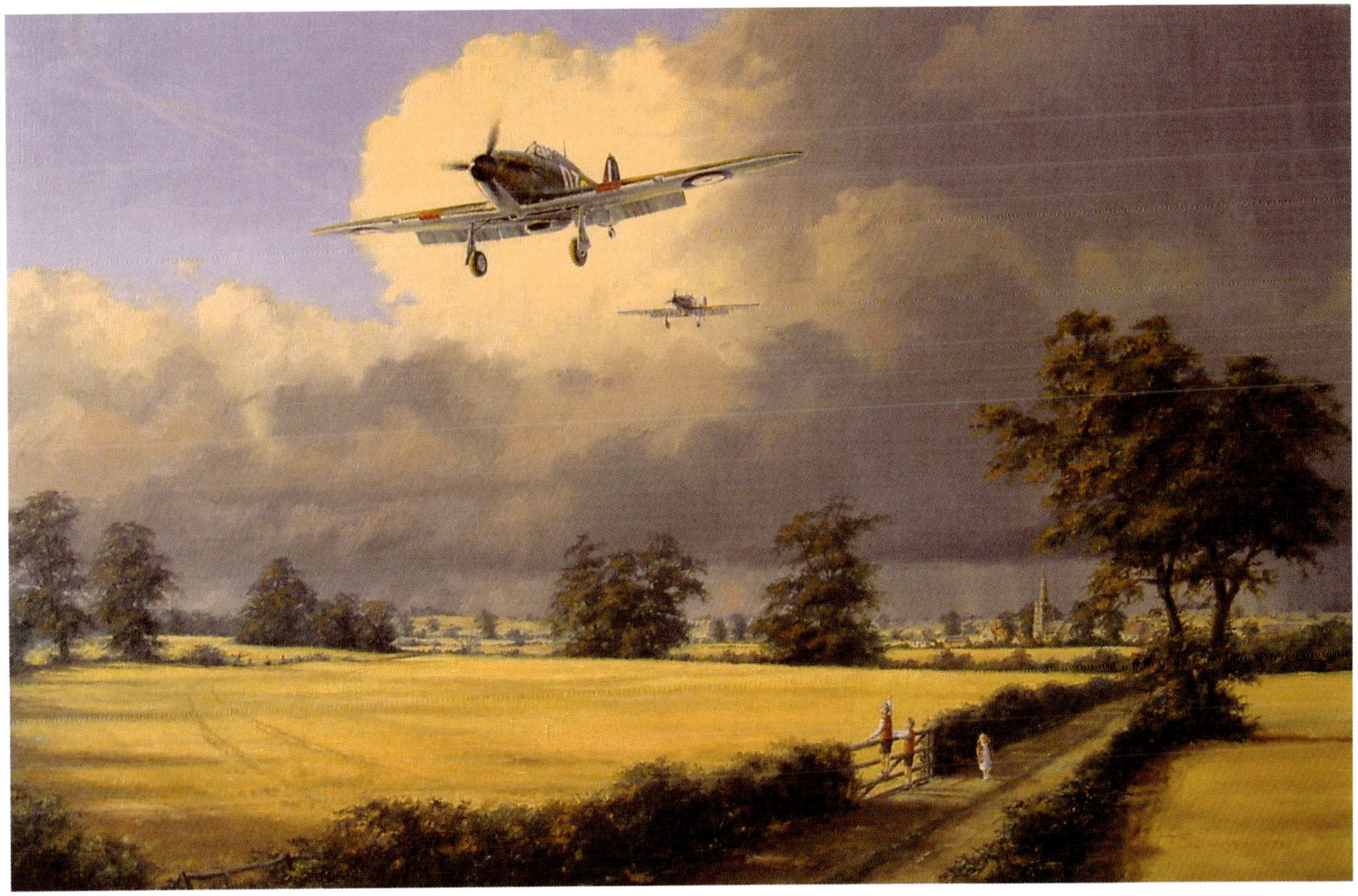

SALUTE TO THE FEW

PRIVATE COLLECTION

ground. Very early every morning, weather permitting, high-flying Luftwaffe reconnaissance aircraft were sent over the Channel to photograph the active RAF airfields and the information was quickly processed to decide which targets to attack that day. Being well aware that it was Blenheims that were raiding German airfields and targeting the invasion fleet gathering in the Channel ports, and knowing that if the invasion was launched it would be mostly Blenheims that would attack the landing craft and support ships, they frequently selected airfields that had many Blenheims.

In his speech made on 20 August 1940, Winston Churchill's immortal phrase – 'Never in the field of human conflict was so much owed by so many to so few' – perfectly encapsulates the Battle of Britain and has gained a rightful place in the nation's collective memory. But few remember that in the same speech he went on to also praise RAF Bomber Command: 'On no part of the Royal Air Force does the weight of the war fall more heavily than on the daylight bombers, who play an invaluable part in the case of an invasion and whose unflinching zeal it has been necessary in the meantime on numerous occasions to restrain.'

While I wanted to highlight the important role the Blenheim played in the Battle of Britain, the main focus for this painting was going to be reserved for another unsung hero of the battle, the Hawker Hurricane. It's true that the Spitfire was the undoubted thoroughbred of all RAF fighters, but the Hurricane was the sturdy workhorse that accounted for more victories during the battle than the Spitfire. I know it should be borne in mind that the Spitfires would normally go for the faster fighters, leaving the Hurricanes to concentrate on the slow bombers but, nevertheless, the Hurricane could more than hold its own in a dog fight with an Me109, the other aircraft I wanted to portray. To show Hurricanes, Blenheims and Me109s over one of the invasion ports was a tall order in terms of research but, after a lot of reading, luck eventually got the upper hand and I found a scenario that fitted.

The research led me to 501 (County of Gloucester) Squadron, part of the Auxiliary Air Force initially formed from a band of so called 'weekend flyers'. In the early days the auxiliaries attracted some degree of ridicule from the Regulars. But not for long – the 21 squadrons that made up the Auxiliary Air Force quickly developed a reputation for enthusiasm and efficiency and by the time of the Battle of Britain, 501 Squadron had developed into a potent fighting force and one that would produce some of the top-scoring aces of the battle.

I discovered that on 28 August 1940 the Hurricanes of 501 Squadron had escorted a force of Blenheims from 105 Squadron to attack the French port of Boulogne, one of the German invasion ports. They were intercepted by Me109s of JG3 as they approached the target and during the encounter three Me109s were shot down. It all fitted together perfectly, especially as there were no British losses.

On 17 September 1940, Hitler postponed Operation *Sealion*. RAF Fighter Command had been successful in denying the Luftwaffe air supremacy over the Channel and southern England but the constant attacks by Bomber Command on the enemy's ports and airfields, together with the ever-present threat from the Royal

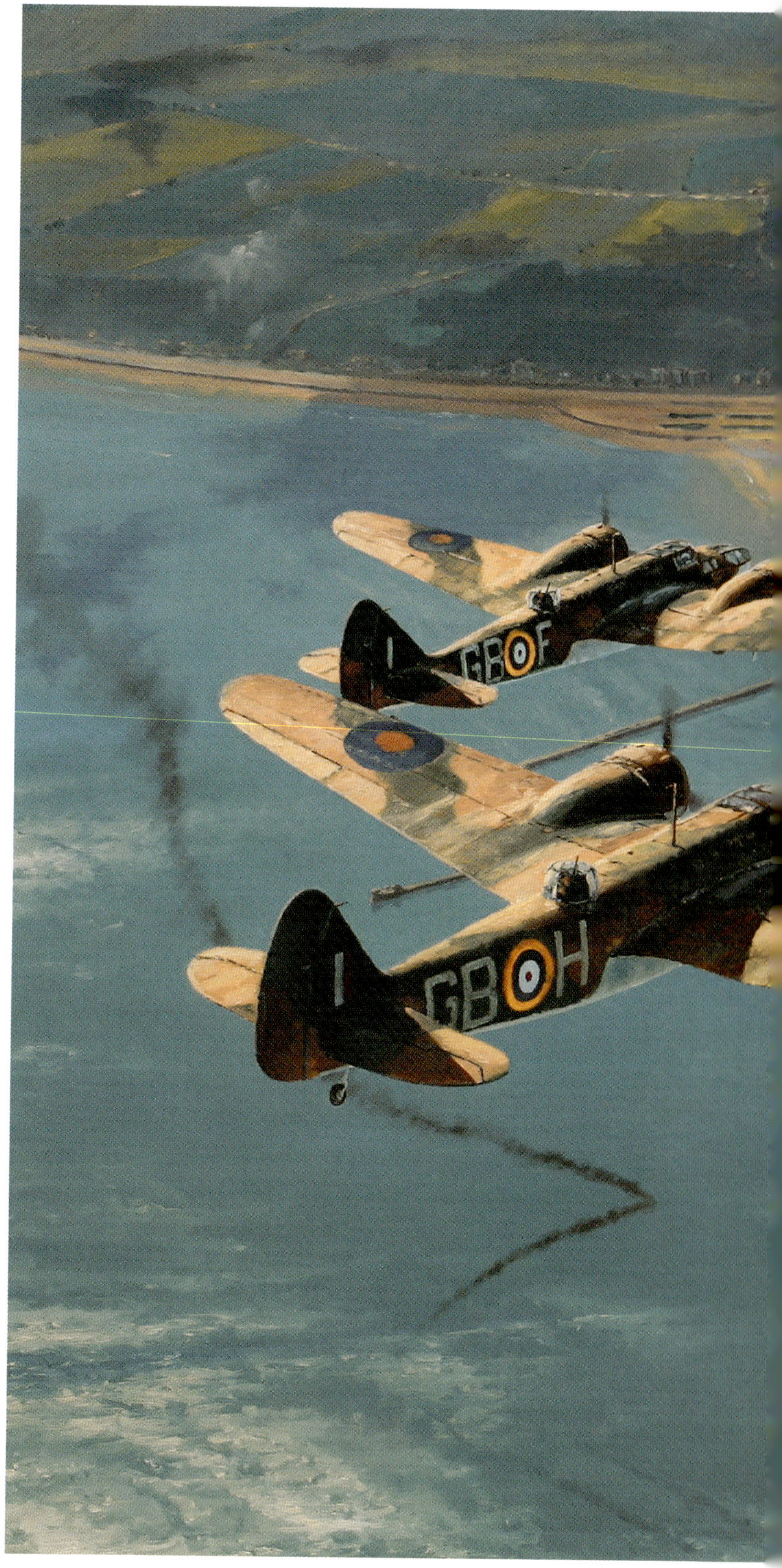

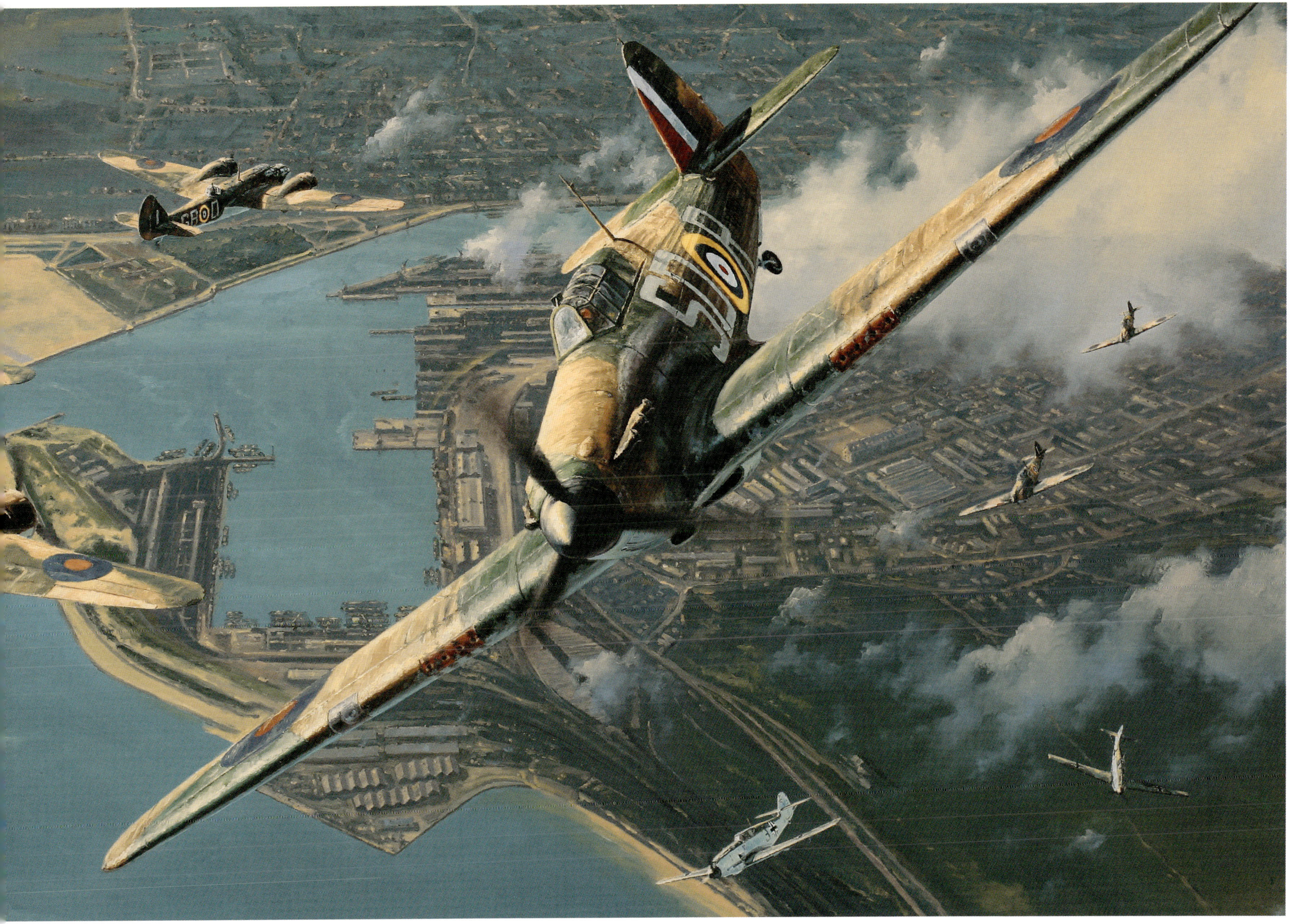

Navy, were also vital factors that had saved Britain from invasion.

It was therefore great to learn later that the two Battle of Britain veterans – Terry Clark, who had served as an air gunner on Blenheims, and Tony Pickering, a Hurricane pilot with 501 Squadron – who had signed the limited edition print of this painting, both commented on the authenticity of the painting and that Tony Pickering particularly liked the title: the 501 Squadron motto is *Fear Nothing*.

MERLIN CHORUS

Although much of the heaviest fighting took place in the south-east, around London and the shores of Kent, in reality the Battle of Britain was fought along the entire coastline of southern England.

Merlin Chorus portrays the Spitfires of 152 Squadron, who were based at Warmwell, a small village about three miles from the Dorset coast and ideally situated to protect the important naval base at Portland, one of the largest man-made harbours in the world, as well as the port facilities at nearby Weymouth.

The squadron was part of 10 Group and its duties included covering the Channel and south coast, and it was also drawn into some of the great air battles over London, although it was too far away to make a full contribution to these. Long after the battle was over, throughout the winter, they continued to repel Luftwaffe attacks.

Lulworth Cove is located a few miles east of Weymouth and is one of southern England's most famous beauty spots. I think that 152 Squadron must have passed over this idyllic place many times during the battle and they weren't the only ones. I found out from part of the research for the painting that on 7 October 1940 a force of more than 60 enemy aircraft had been intercepted by RAF fighters, including Warmwell's Spitfires, as they crossed over Lulworth on their way to attack targets at Yeovil further inland. The German intruders were met with such a determined and spirited response that they were forced to turn-tail and beat a hasty retreat back towards the sea. Two Ju88s of KG51 were shot down in the encounter, as were seven Me110s of ZG26, one of which crashed into the sea close to Lulworth Cove.

Initially I'd thought that this major air battle would make a great scene before remembering that limited edition prints from the painting would be released as one of a pair alongside *Fear Nothing*. As that was definitely going to be an aerial combat scene I thought it best to perhaps make the new one more of a contrast and a little more serene. So instead I decided to show the battle-weary Spitfires returning home after another of their many sorties that summer.

There were quite a few to choose from but I plumped for an action that had occurred quite early in the battle, on 13 August. 10 Group had sent up fighters, including those from 152 Squadron, to intercept a large force of Me110s and Me109s heading for the naval base at Portland and several of the attacking German aircraft were shot down in the mêlée that followed. All of Warmwell's Spitfires, however, returned home safely, and although Pilot Officer Inness was wounded, he too managed to get himself and his damaged Spitfire back to base.

In the painting Inness's damaged Spitfire can be seen in the background and you can imagine how relieved he must have felt as the squadron flew over Lulworth, this time heading home. Hopefully a well-earned pint was waiting in the Mess!

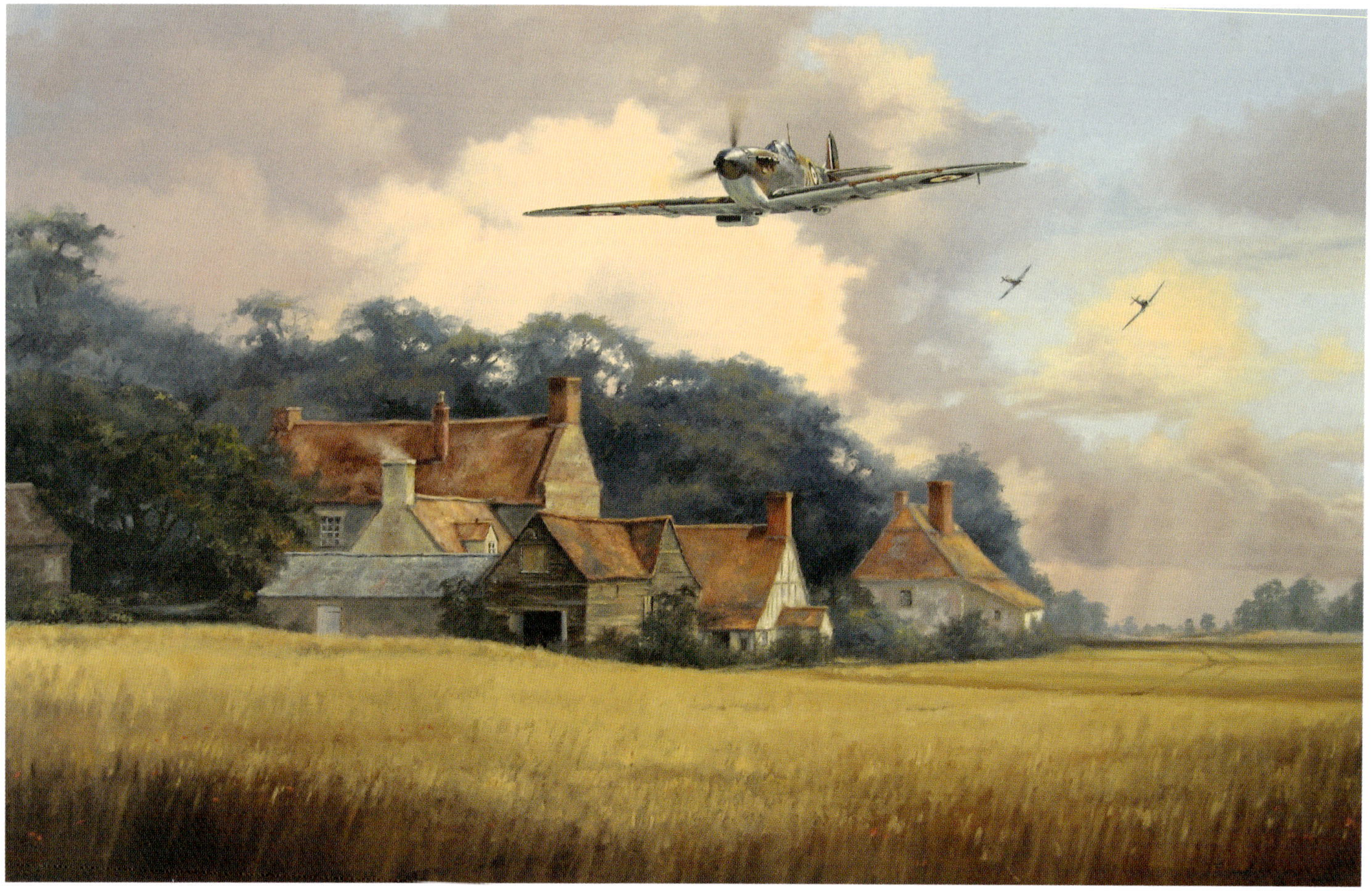

LOW PASS AT THE HOMESTEAD

IN THE COLLECTION OF MR & MRS P SHIPP

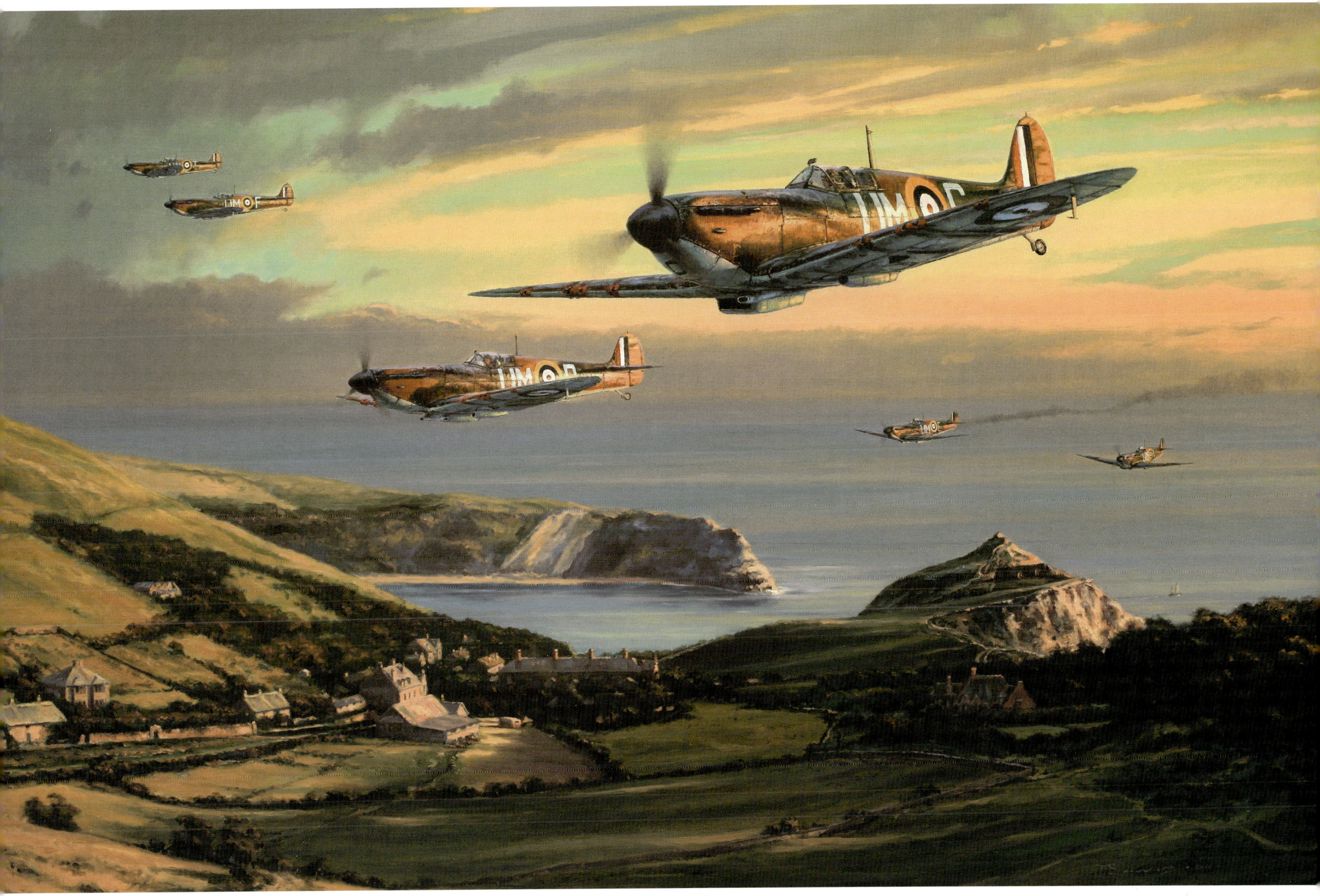

MERLIN CHORUS IN THE COLLECTION OF MR JULIAN PARKER

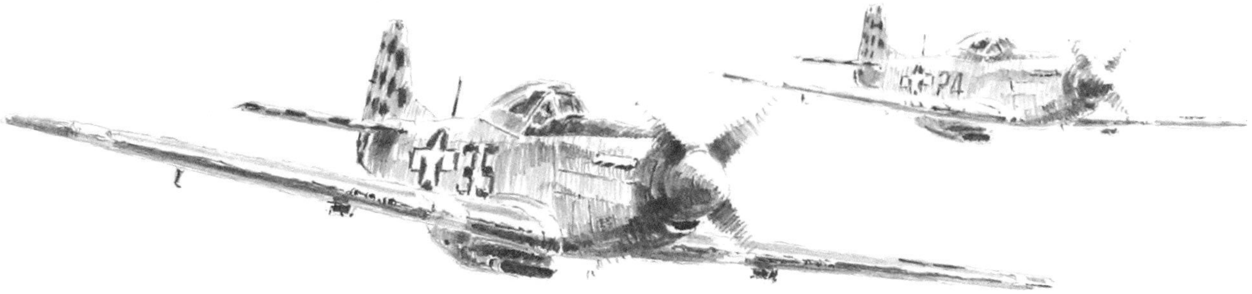

ROAM AT WILL

Once described by Churchill as Europe's soft underbelly, Italy became better known to the Allies as the 'Tough Gut'. Bogged down in the mud of the harsh winter of 1943, it took months of desperate fighting for them to finally push the Axis forces north and into retreat.

Castell'Arquato is a small medieval village in northern Italy about twenty miles west of Parma. Its ancient stone houses and narrow cobbled streets remain much the same as they did when they were built over five centuries ago. The village overlooks the Arda valley in the foot hills of the Apennine Mountains and my mother was born just a few miles from here. She came to England when she was 19 to work as a nurse and it was in a London hospital that she met my father and has remained here ever since. When I was growing up, however, we always returned to this part of Italy for our family holidays and I have many fond memories of the area.

A few years ago my great uncle Pierino was kind enough to sell me an old, but dilapidated, stone-built house in the village and, after spending several years making the place habitable, life has turned full circle. I now return each year with my own family. The surrounding countryside is stunningly beautiful and I have always wanted to somehow depict the place in a painting.

Pierino had been in the Italian Army at the beginning of the war, serving in North Africa, but in 1940 he was captured by the British and had spent the rest of the war in various POW camps in England and Scotland. I'd spent many warm summer evenings in his company, usually sitting on his veranda and drinking the wonderful wine he made from his own vineyard, as he and a few old friends quietly chatted about their various wartime experiences.

It was great to listen to, and one of them, knowing my interest in aviation, recalled the time he saw a plane fly very low and fast down through the valley. He didn't know if it was British or American but clearly remembered that it had lots of squares on the

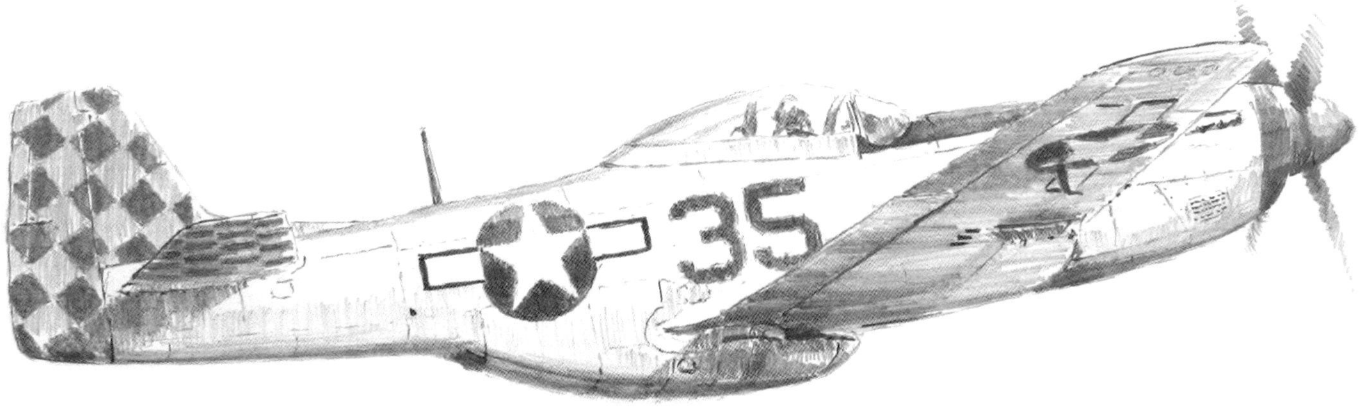

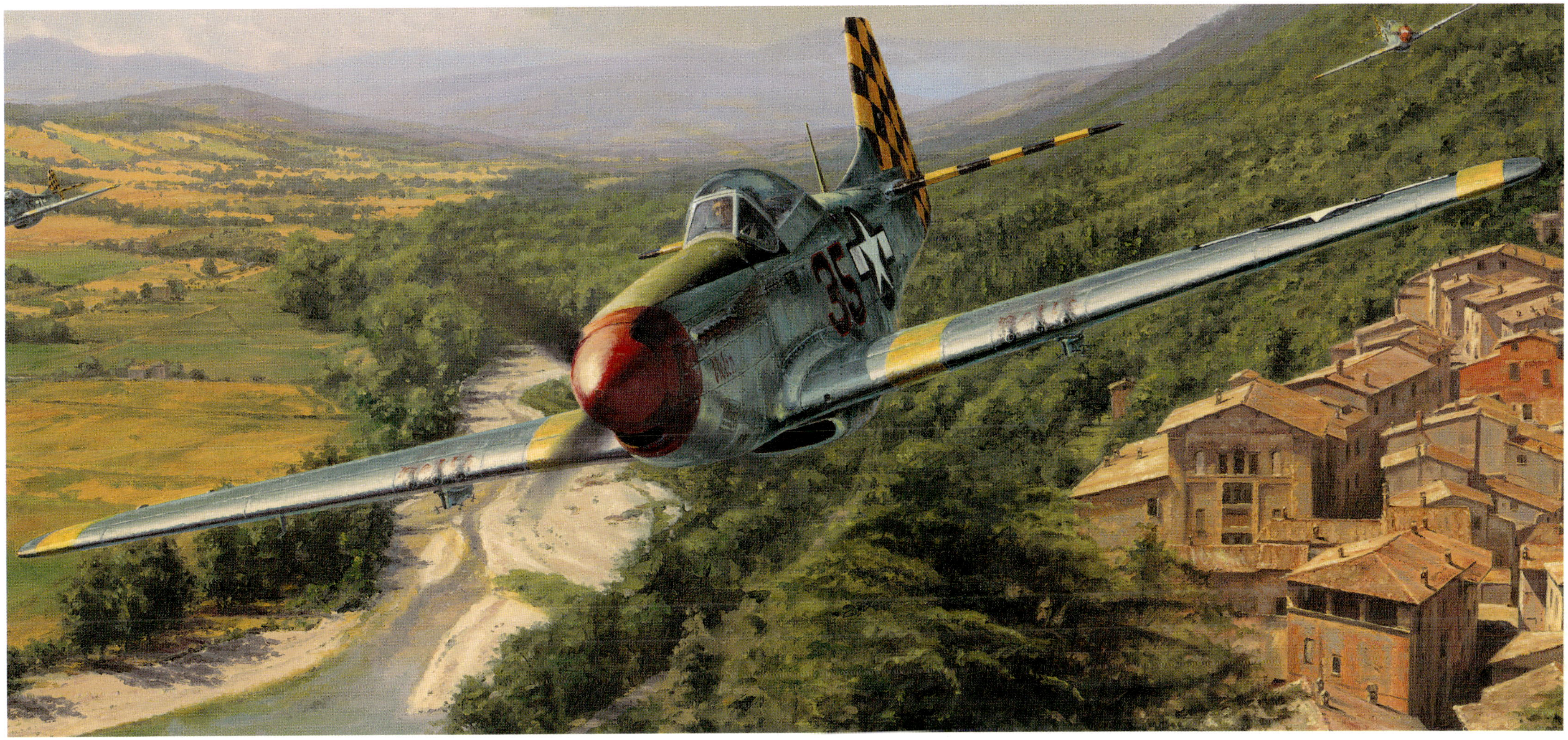

tail. Although I didn't give it much thought at the time the image must have struck a chord somewhere in my mind because a few years later when I got the chance to depict a P-51 Mustang of the U.S. Fifteenth Air Force, I immediately thought of that plane and the scene Pierino's friend had described.

Doing some research I discovered that there were only two units that the aircraft could have come from. The first was the 350th Fighter Group, known as the 'Checkerboard Squadron' but they flew P-47 Thunderbolts. The second, however, were the P-51's of the 325th Fighter Group, the famous 'Checkertail Clan' and, as much as I personally love the looks and character of the chunky P-47, it was a P-51 that I had been asked to portray. And I wasn't complaining – any P-51 is a joy to paint and none more so than the D model, the bubble-canopy version flown by the 'Checkertails' in the summer of 1944.

As luck would have it the research I'd done into the P-47 markings wasn't completely wasted. I was later commissioned to paint *Deadly Pass*, a combat scene over the Alps featuring the exact same 350th Fighter Group.

The 'Checkertail Clan' transitioned on to P-51s in 1944 whilst based at Foggia on the south-eastern coast of Italy. Despite enduring a winter of torrential rain, and the dreaded mud that had hindered the advance of the Allies' ground forces, they were soon escorting American bombers on a regular basis to targets across the length and breadth of enemy-occupied Europe, as well as the long-distance shuttle missions to Russia. In two years of combat the 'Checkertails' gained an impressive record, destroying 537 enemy aircraft in the air as well as many more on the ground.

The scene I had in my mind was of them roaming the Po valley on their way back to Foggia after a typical escort mission, looking for any retreating Axis forces to attack. The date would be around July 1944 and, as I had some excellent photographs of Captain Art Fiedler's P 51D *Helen*, I decided to show that as the main aircraft. Besides, Art Fiedler was one of the units most respected Aces who, before the end of the war, was to notch up eight air victories.

I'd almost finished the painting when I was lucky enough to be put in touch with Art, who was more than generous with both his time and information. He gave

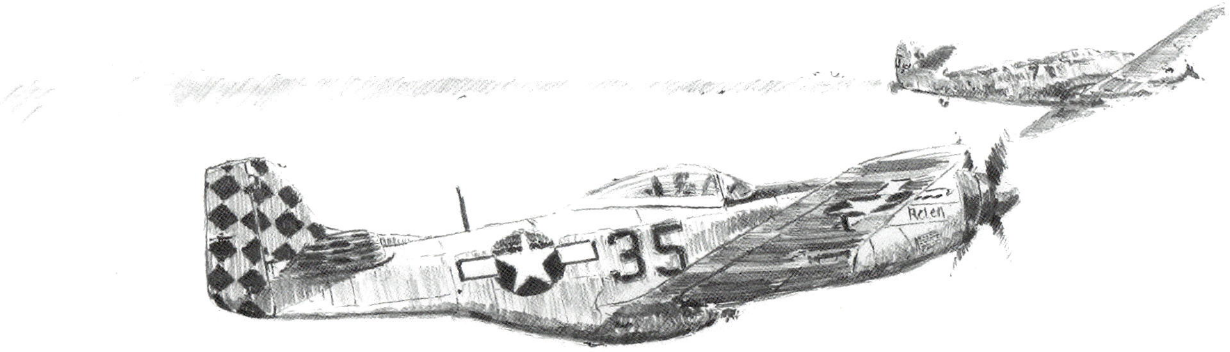

me lots of small, personal details, such as the diagram illustrating the words ‘Hell’s Bells’ that had been painted in red over the gun ports. He explained how the words had been removed one day and when he’d asked the ground crew why, they told him there had been a fatal accident involving an armourer after one of the guns had shorted out. Knowing that pilots didn’t like bad omens they’d thought it best to remove the words.

Art was also kind enough to point out that the red wing tips I’d painstakingly painted were in fact added at a later date, when the plane was reassigned to another pilot.

After the prints had been published, I sent him a copy as a thank-you for all his help. It was great to receive a long letter in return saying how thrilled he was, and going into lengthy detail describing the pilots of all the other aircraft that I’d included in the painting. It’s a letter I will long cherish.

Since finishing *Roam at Will* I’ve often walked up the steep narrow streets of Castell’Arquato but now I can’t help but look up and imagine those beautiful P-51’s roaring overhead, and hear the distinctive roar from their Merlin engines reverberating all around me.

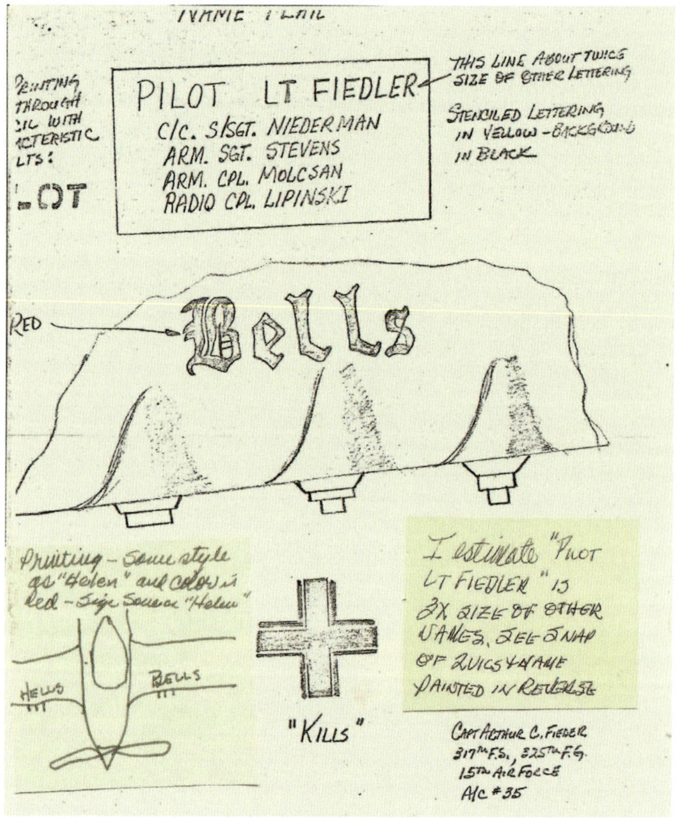

Straight from the horse’s mouth – one of the diagrams that Art Fiedler sent me, complete with hand-written notes.

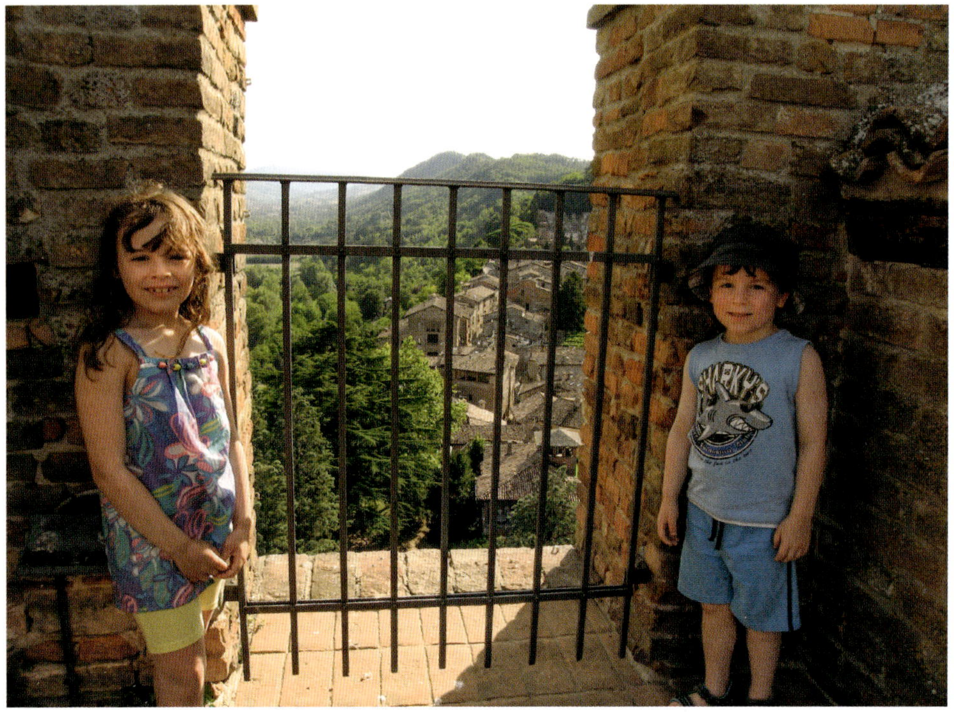

Amelia and James at the top of the old tower in Castell’Arquato. At some two hundred feet in height – note the nervous smiles, it’s a long way down! – there’s a fantastic panoramic view over the valley. It was perfect for the painting.

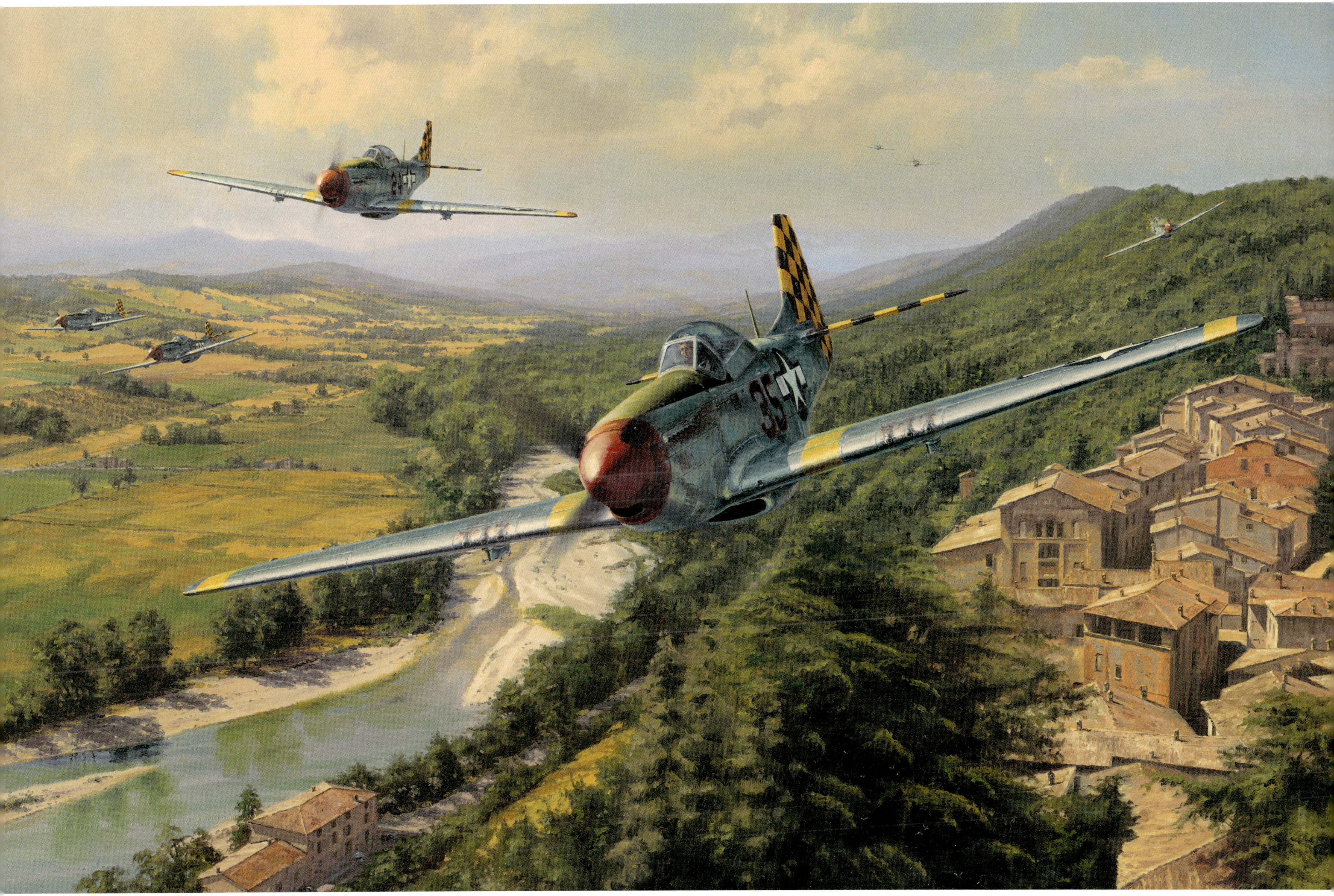

ROAM AT WILL PRIVATE COLLECTION

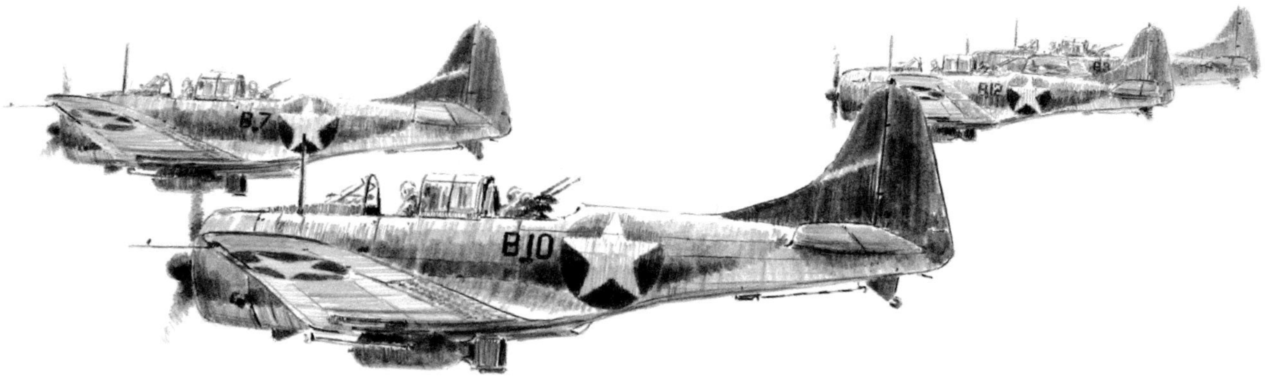

MIDWAY

THE ATTACK ON THE SŌRYŪ

Some historians hail it as 'the greatest naval battle since Trafalgar.' Before the Battle of Midway the forces of Imperial Japan seemed unstoppable. After Midway the Japanese would never again take the offensive.

Whilst doing the research for this painting one of the first things I wanted to do was to find out where the island of Midway actually is and what it looks like. I'd heard about it often enough but had no real idea about its appearance or size so it came as a bit of a surprise to discover that Midway is in fact two islands, about six square miles in size, and part of a small atoll. As the name suggests, it's roughly half way across the Pacific between North America and Asia.

The larger of the two islands – Sand Island – today has a large but seldom used runway that's part of the US Air Base, but in 1942 the place was simply called Naval Air Station Midway Islands and the only airfield was on the smaller Eastern Island. Now, more than seventy years after the battle, that island looks somewhat different.

Nature has largely reclaimed Eastern Island and it's now a wildlife refuge, the old runways are overgrown with vegetation and the only sounds that can be heard today are from the many different varieties of sea bird that make it their home. In the early morning light of 4 June 1942, however, those same runways had reverberated to the sound of US Navy aircraft preparing for battle.

Admiral Yamamoto, Commander-in-Chief of the Japanese Combined Fleet, had badly wanted to sink the American aircraft carriers that evaded him at Pearl Harbor. The Battle of the Coral Sea, just a month before Midway, had been fought entirely by aircraft, reinforcing his belief that the American carriers were his main threat and must be destroyed at all costs. To do so Yamamoto planned to invade and capture Midway, a

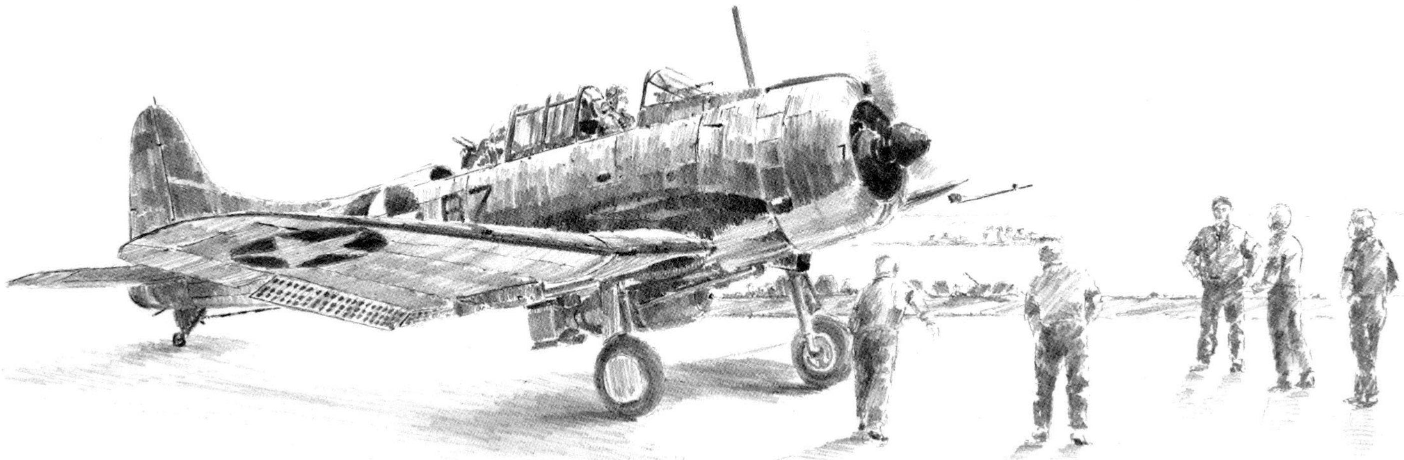

target relatively close to Pearl Harbor, in order to draw out the American fleet. He calculated that even though his fleet was exhausted and many of his best ships were in desperate need of a refit, the assembled might of his Combined Fleet had more than enough strength to crush the Americans.

But he was wrong. Unknown to the Japanese, American intelligence had broken most of their naval codes, enabling US Pacific Fleet commander, Admiral Chester Nimitz, to pre-empt and prepare for Yamamoto's forthcoming attack. At 05.30 hours, as the Japanese fleet approached Midway, it was quickly spotted by patrolling US Navy PBY Catalina flying-boats and American bombers were soon in the air, but not only were they severely mauled but the Japanese were able to inflict considerable damage on both Sand and Eastern islands. Completely unaware that American carrier aircraft were now fast approaching, the Japanese prepared to launch a second attack on Midway.

For Vice Admiral Nagumo, commander of the Japanese carrier force, it looked like things were going well: several uncoordinated attacks by enemy aircraft had been easily swept aside but, shortly before 10.00 hours, the Americans got the lucky break that can so often turn failure into success. Lieutenant Commander Wade McClusky leading a force of 33 SBD Dauntless dive-bombers from the American carrier *Enterprise* arrived over a vast empty ocean expecting to find the Japanese carriers, but there was nothing. After searching the area for some time and running low on fuel, McClusky spotted the wake of a ship moving at high speed – he decided to follow it. It was a wise decision, as the ship was the Japanese destroyer *Arashi*, and it unwittingly led the Americans straight to Nagumo's carriers.

McClusky's force reached the Japanese carriers to find that American torpedo bombers from the *Yorktown* were already pressing home an attack at low level but were taking heavy losses from Japanese fighters in the process. The mêlee below, however, left McClusky's dive-bombers completely unnoticed and unhampered. Then arriving hard on the heels of *Enterprise's* dive bombers another force of dive bombers arrived, this time from the *Yorktown*, and under the command of Lieutenant Commander Maxwell Leslie. By a miraculous coincidence

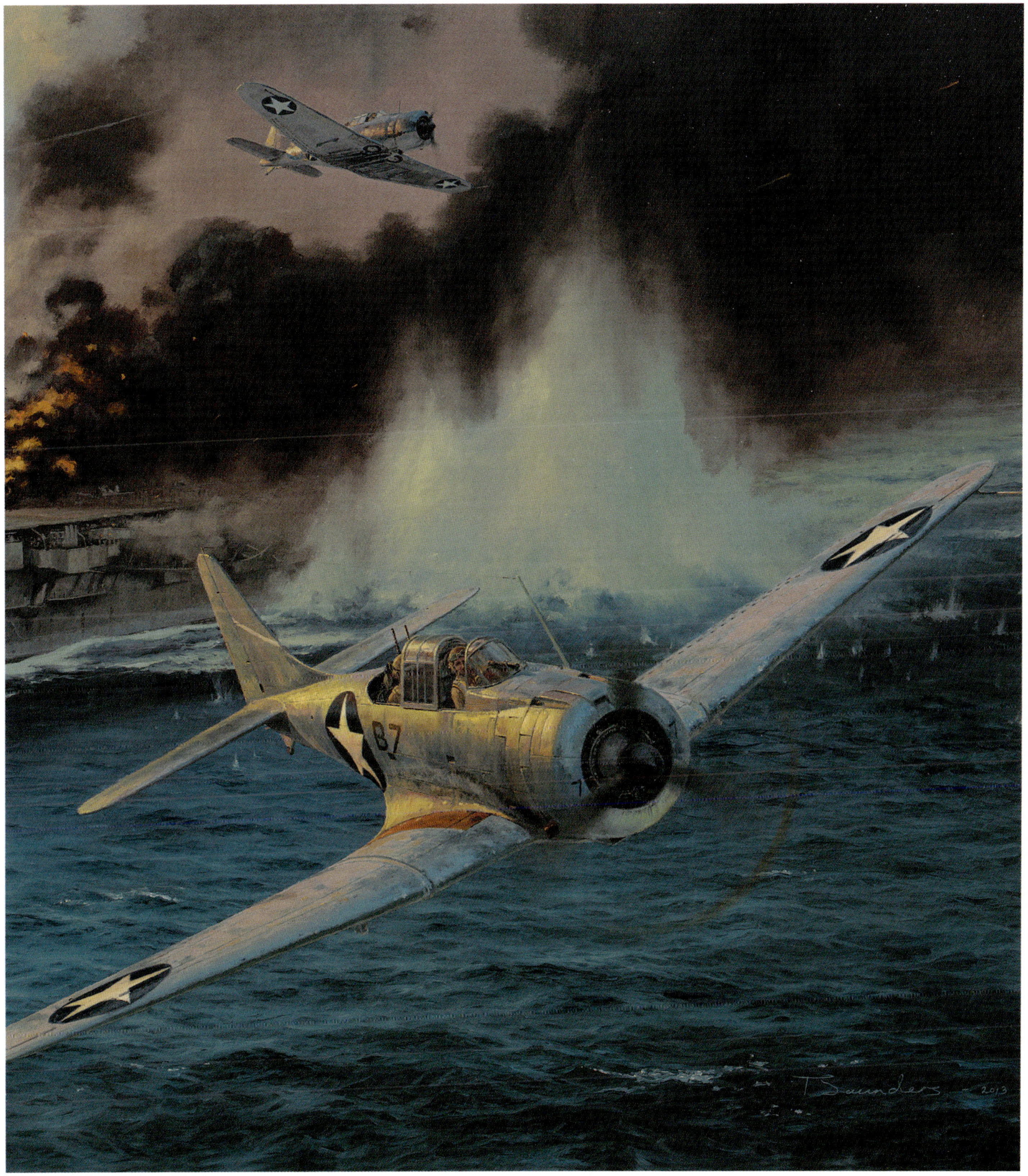

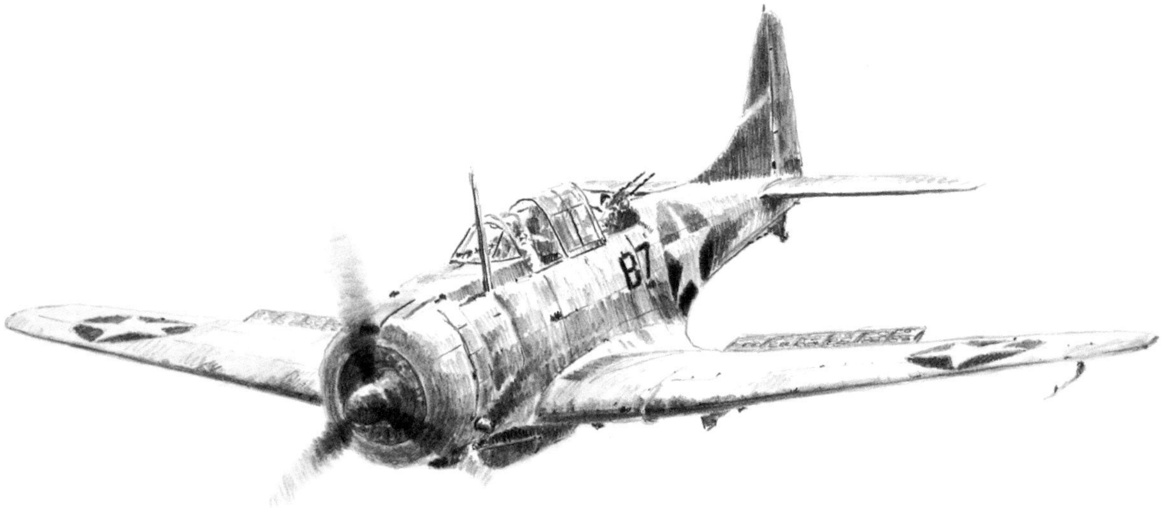

the two groups had taken off from the *Enterprise* and the *Yorktown* almost two hours apart, but both now arrived over the Japanese fleet at exactly the same moment, and just when all the enemy fighters were flying at low level and the Japanese carriers were in a state of maximum vulnerability, the American dive-bombers attacked.

What followed were six fateful minutes that changed the course of the war in the Pacific.

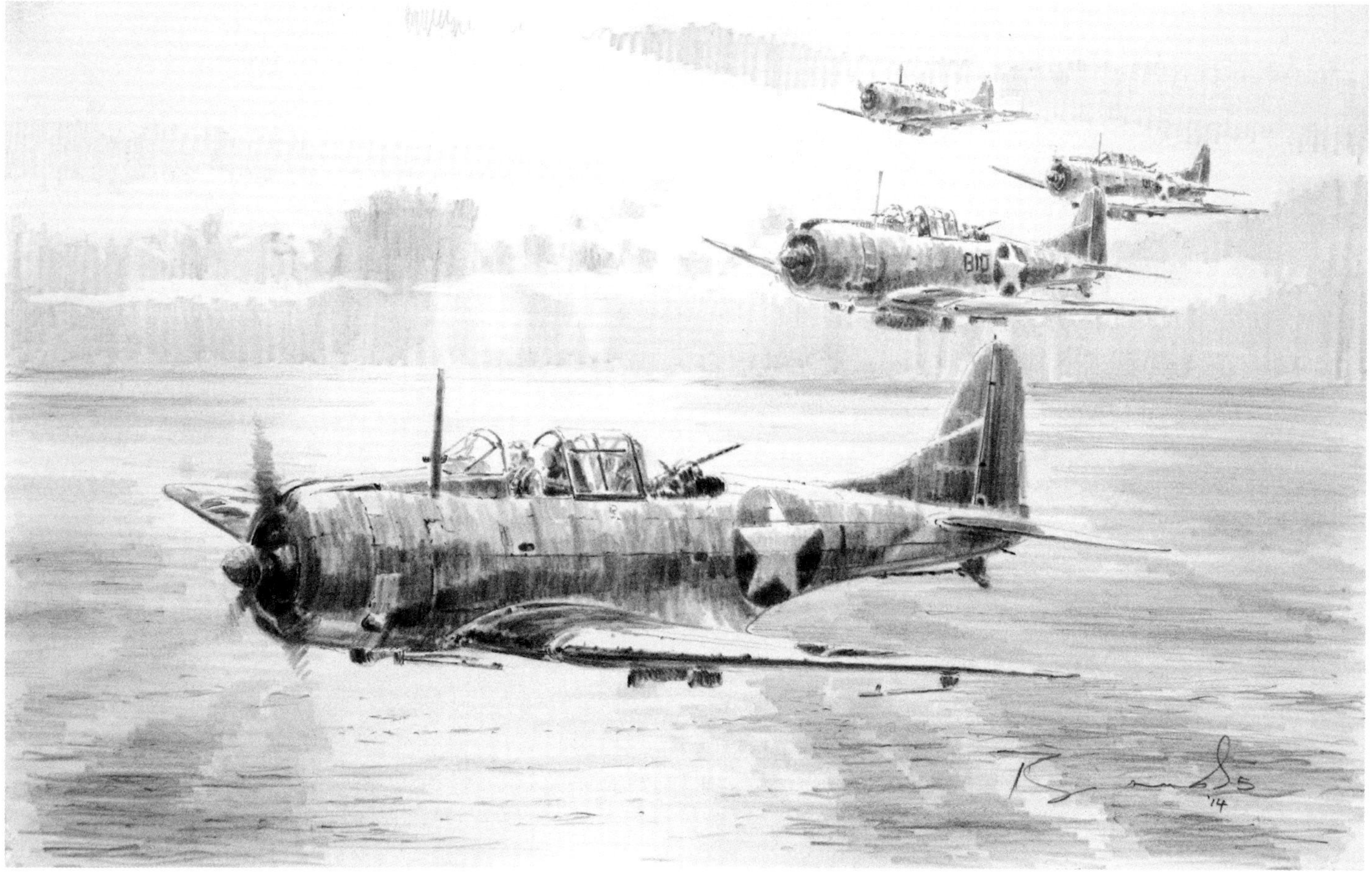

Almost simultaneously the Japanese carriers *Kaga*, the *Sōryū*, and the *Akagi* came under sustained dive bomber attack. Only the *Hiryu*, well to the north, escaped their attention, but she too, would later be sunk. The American dive-bombers attacked at 10.22 hours; by 10.28 hours the three Japanese carriers were nothing but burning wrecks, dead in the water.

The dive-bomber had been the only American aircraft that the Japanese feared and those six minutes showed why. Carrier-launched Dauntlesses sank all four Japanese carriers at Midway but it was the *Sōryū* that I chose for the painting. She took three direct hits, one of which was scored by Lieutenant Holmberg in Dauntless *B2* that had set the carrier alight with fires spreading from stem to stern. He later reported that the explosion had caused a Japanese fighter to fall back on the deck just as it was attempting take-off, and this was the moment I decided to capture in *Attack on the Sōryū.* Holmberg's aircraft is the one pulling up and away from the burning carrier whilst in the foreground another SBD Dauntless, that of Lieutenant G. A. Sherwood, in *B7*, is seen close up, leaving the scene of complete destruction behind him.

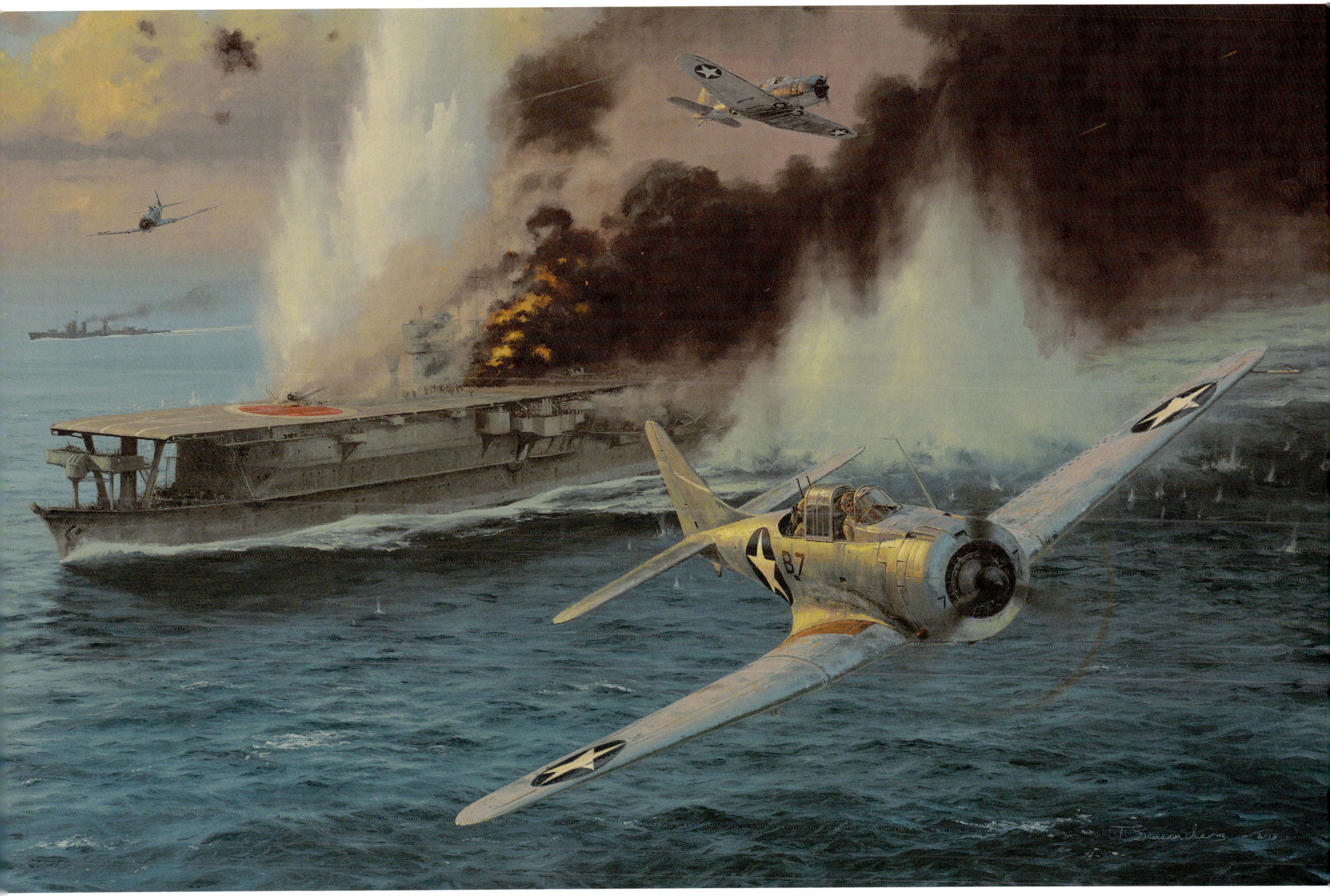

MIDWAY – THE ATTACK ON THE SŌRYŪ IN THE COLLECTION OF MR & MRS M. HORSFIELD

LONGEST SUMMER

Very occasionally I'm lucky to have a free hand and treat myself to a bit of self-indulgence in choosing what type of subject to paint, especially when it's a generic painting; that is to say one that's not constrained by a specific event or moment in history.

Longest Summer was just such a painting, one in which I was able to inject a little piece of theatre, thanks to my two children, Amelia and James. When Amelia was in her final year of primary school I'm pleased to say they spent several weeks teaching the children about what life was like on the Home Front during World War Two. This included a trip to one of my favourite museums – the Imperial War Museum at Duxford – a visit in which the whole class was able to go dressed-up as evacuees.

Amelia was really interested in the whole topic and, as she's something of a perfectionist, wanted her 'costume' to be as authentic as possible and although there were some outfits for sale on the internet, the materials looked a bit too modern. What she did find on eBay, however, was a wonderful old gas mask complete with the original box. She turned out to be the only bidder, got it for the bargain price of £12 and was over the moon when it finally arrived, especially when she discovered the original owner's name and address carefully written with an old-fashioned fountain pen on the lid of the box – Jean Newman, 38 Wiggenhall Road, Watford. It was a particularly nice touch.

After adapting one of her old school dresses into something that really looked like it had come from the 1940s, Amelia bought an old cardigan from our local Oxfam shop and made a little brown address label for her button hole: she had now become none other than Jean Newman of Watford. In fact she had so much fun creating the outfit that she then turned her hand into making gas mask boxes and address labels for the whole class. We also made a special trip to see my Dad, who was evacuated from Walthamstow in the war when he was only five, so that she could ask him lots of questions about his experiences as an evacuee, something that I, too, learnt a lot from.

The school trip to Duxford was a great success and for months afterwards Amelia enjoyed dressing up as Jean and playing at being an evacuee. Occasionally she even managed to coax her younger brother James to join in and once managed to convert our entire hallway into a

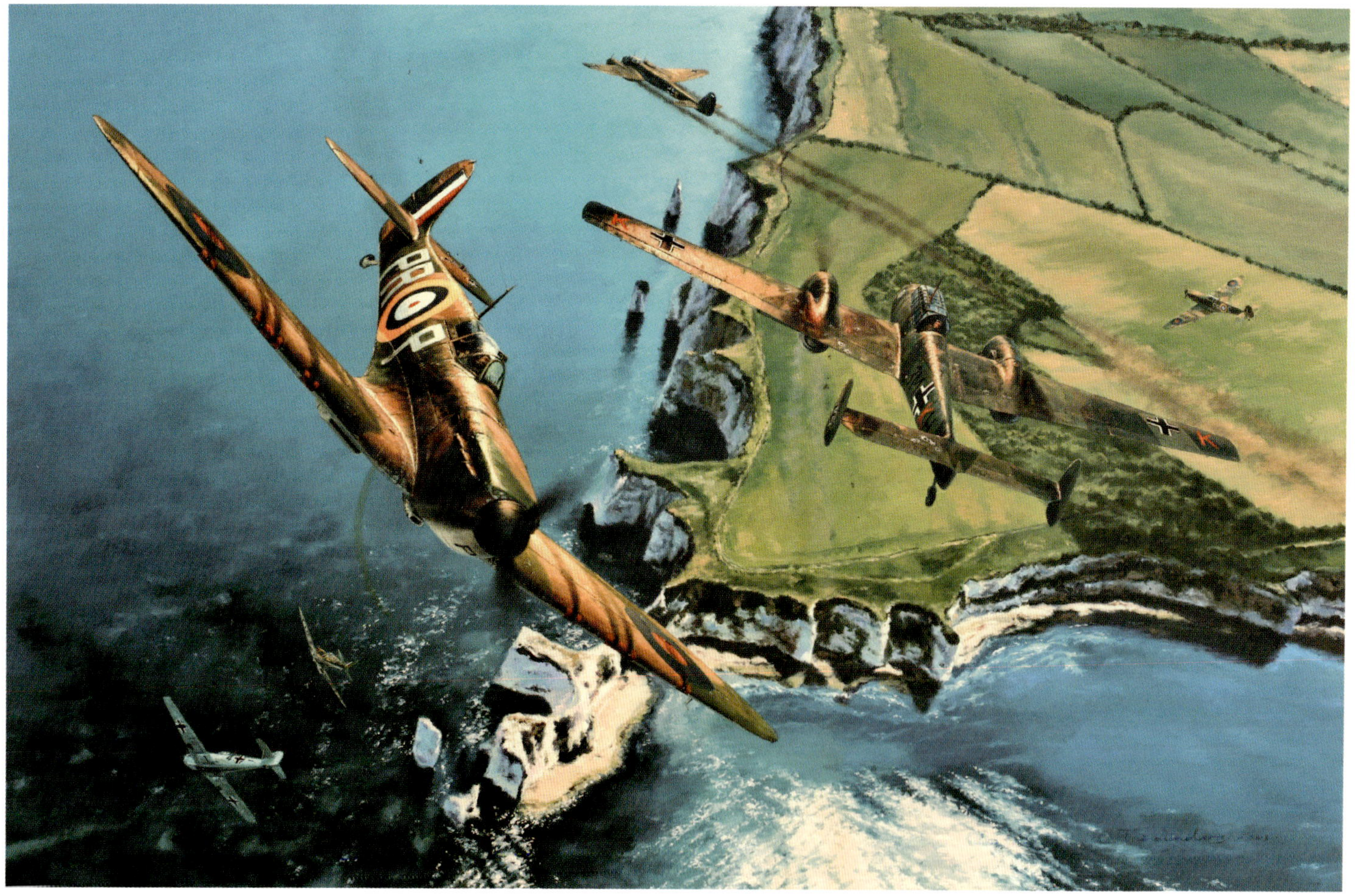

DOGFIGHT OVER FORELAND POINT

IN THE COLLECTION OF MR RICHARD HORN

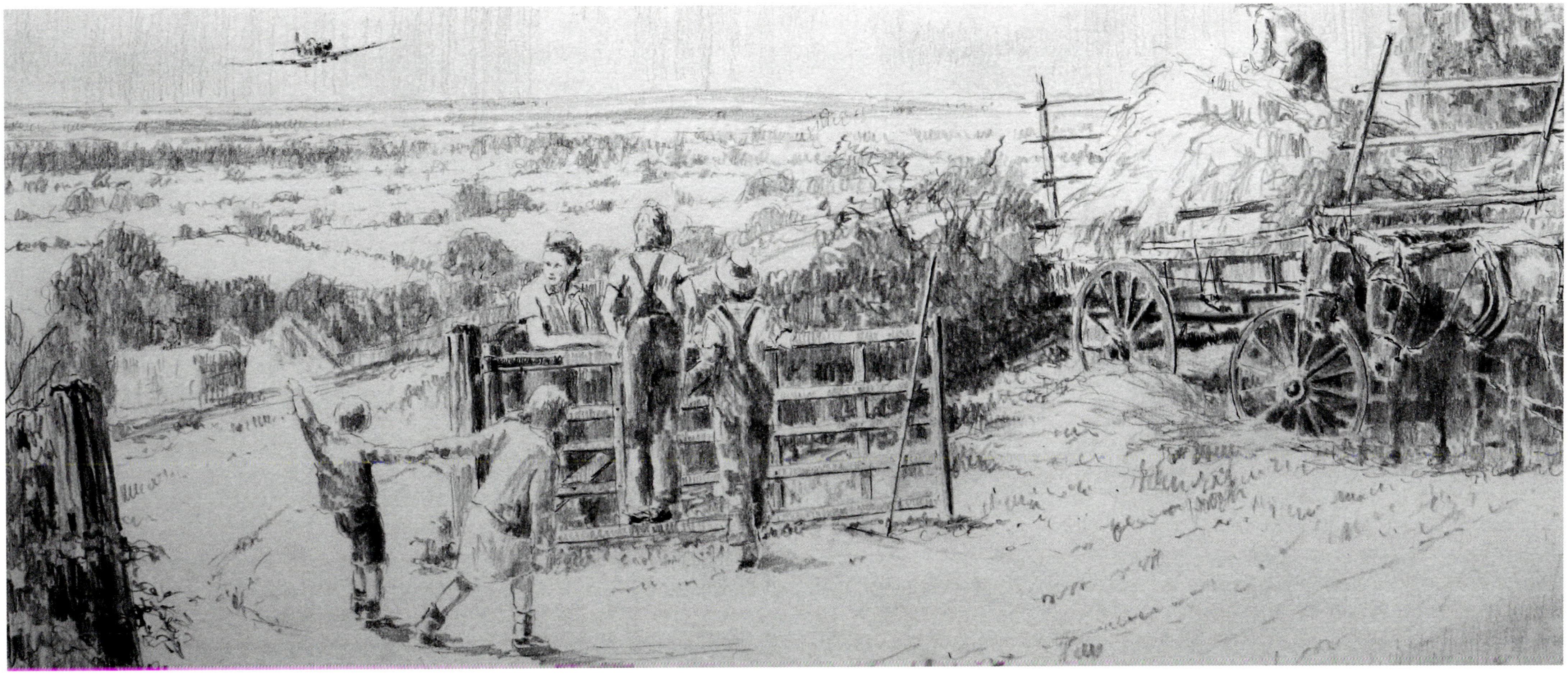

very convincing Anderson shelter, complete with air raid siren and bombing sound effects!

It was on one of these days whilst I was watching them, dressed up in their evacuee outfits, playing in the garden, that I thought I should take some photos as a record of all this happy childhood creativity; after all, I was pretty sure that the dressing-up phase wouldn't last for ever, especially as Amelia was due to go to senior school in a few months' time – something that no doubt would put an end to such playful tendencies. As I did so a composition was slowly forming in my mind.

One photo in particular that I thought could work well was one of Amelia dragging James in a typically 'older sister knows best' fashion in a direction that he clearly didn't want to go. It was a shot that an artist couldn't have recreated without the assistance of a life model, and I had two of them in front of me. All I needed was to come up with a suitable setting.

I know some artists have the ability to create a landscape on canvas from scratch, and it's something that I have sometimes done in the past, but I never quite convince myself by it even though others don't seem to notice. Perhaps it's just knowing that I've made everything up makes it seem contrived so now I always try to base my landscapes on something I've actually seen; I'm then quite happy to embellish or adapt it to fit the composition.

I had an idea of the sort of landscape I was after for the painting. I wanted the viewpoint to be from the top of a hill with a vast expanse of fields and hedgerows stretching away as far as the eye could see to the horizon. It wasn't the sort of thing I could easily find where I live in Cambridgeshire!

It was by pure luck, therefore, when I arrived for a meeting with my publishers at Wendover last summer, that I found exactly the landscape I was looking for. I'd arrived half an hour too early and decided to take a short trip down one of the small country lanes just outside the town. As the road started to go uphill through some woods, it began to get narrower and narrower and

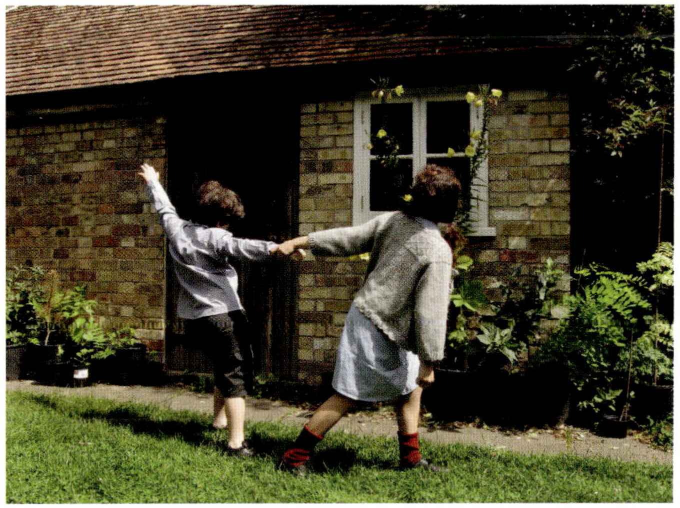

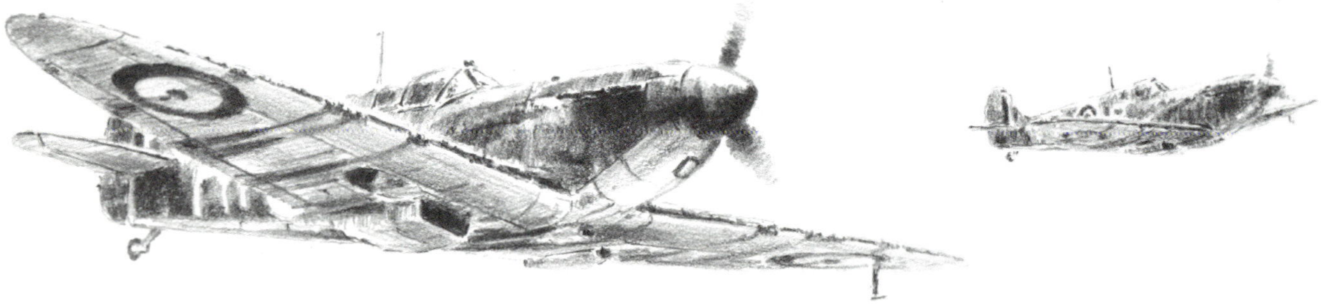

reminded me of the lane that William Beach rode his red bicycle down at the end of the wonderful ITV production *Goodnight Mr Tom*. Just as I was starting to wonder how on earth I was going to find somewhere to turn around and get back to the meeting, the lane came to a small clearing, and there it was – one of the most breathtaking landscapes that I've ever seen in England, or anywhere else for that matter.

It was perfect, but I still needed a focal point other than the two children and settled on introducing a few farmhands busily at work making a hayrick. I was going to include a group of Land Girls leaning on the open gate but decided that this not only made the scene a bit too busy but would have the effect of blocking the viewer from entering further into the picture. In the end I settled for just one Land Girl, modelled, of course, by Amelia, who is busy calming the cart horses and I placed the gate so that it opened the other way, and was not so noticeable. Incidentally, if you look closely you may just notice the children's two small gas mask boxes close to the picnic hamper.

Now all I had to do was introduce the Spitfires, but that's a story for another time.

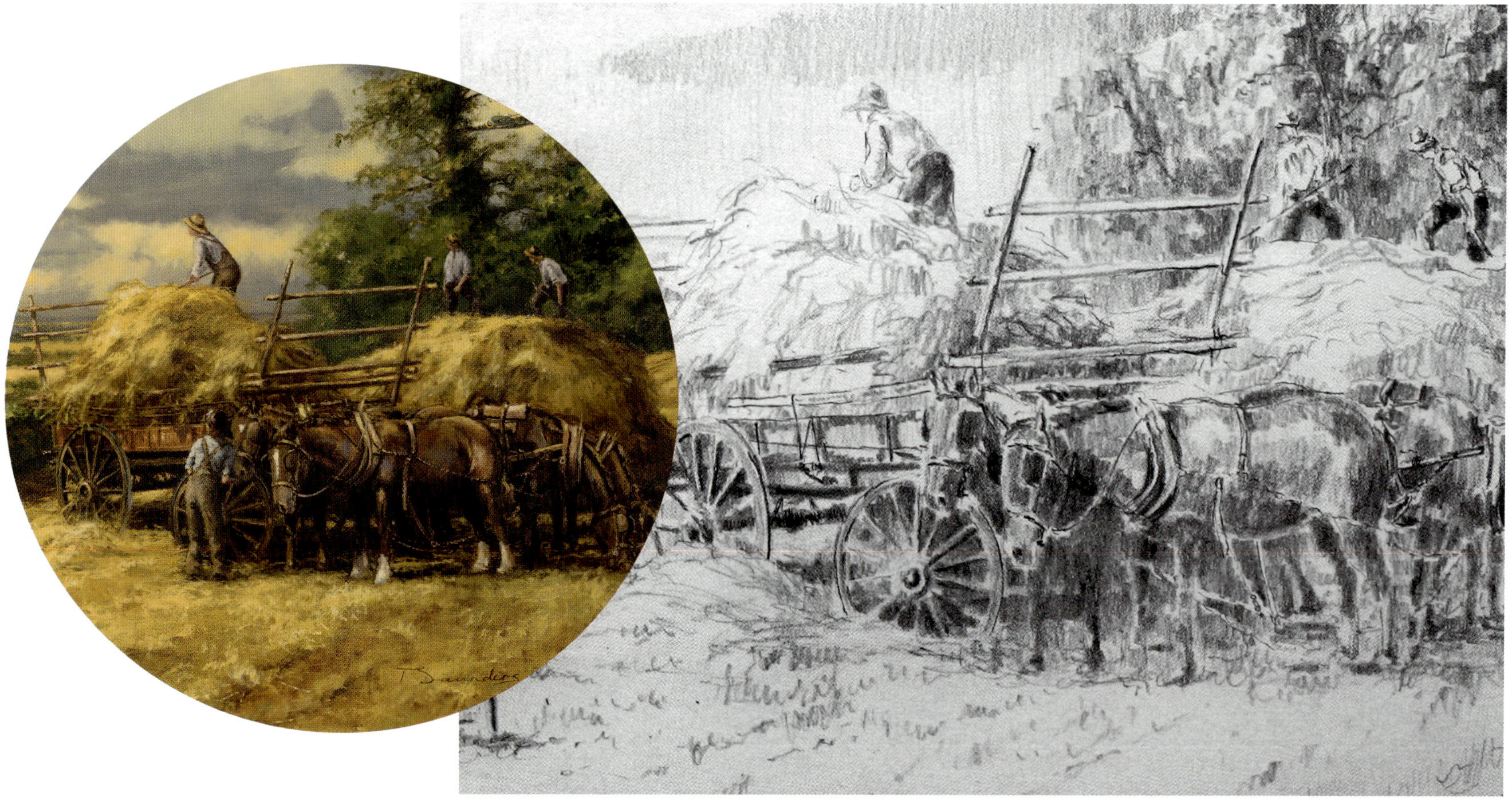

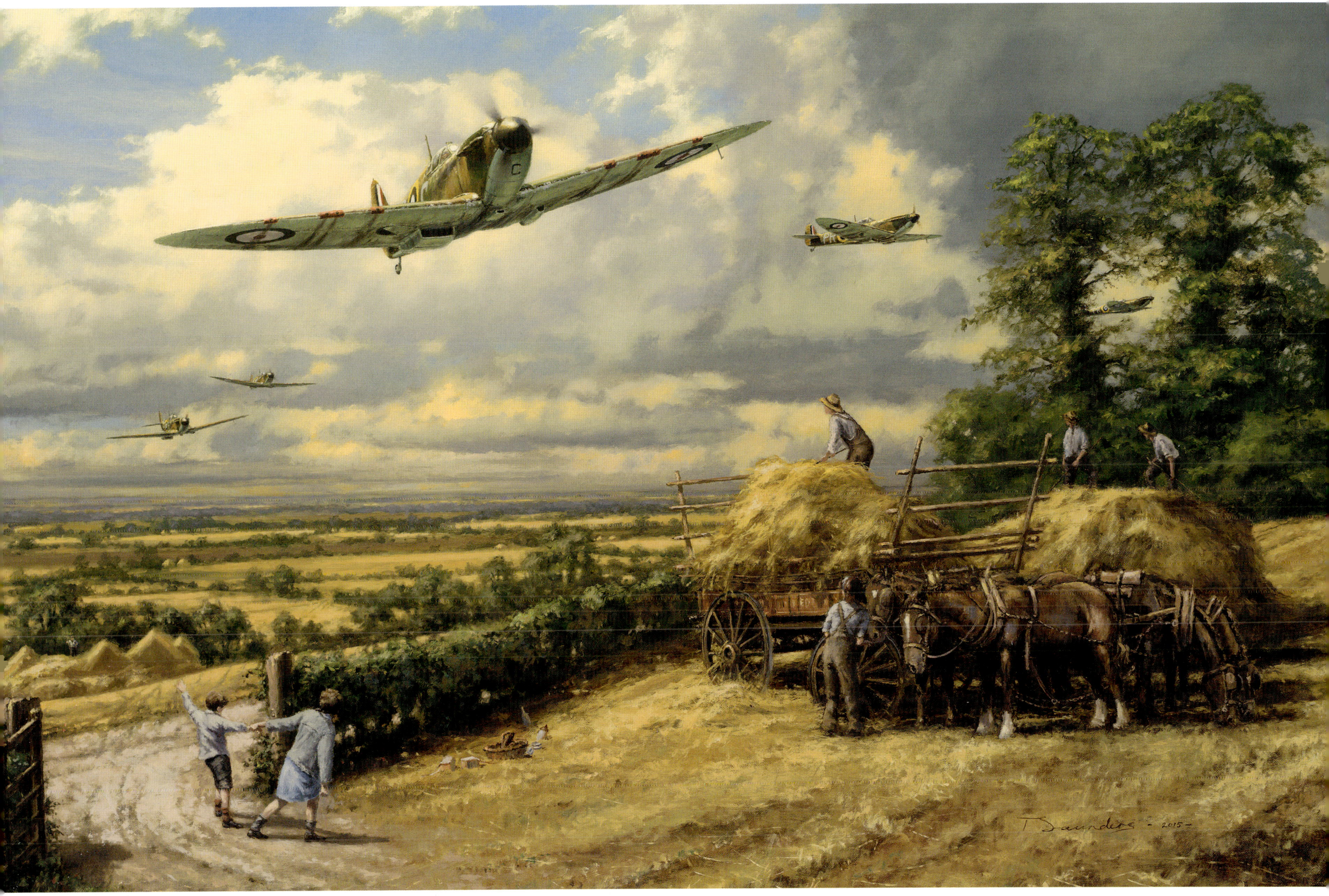

LONGEST SUMMER IN THE COLLECTION OF MR & MRS P. SHIPP

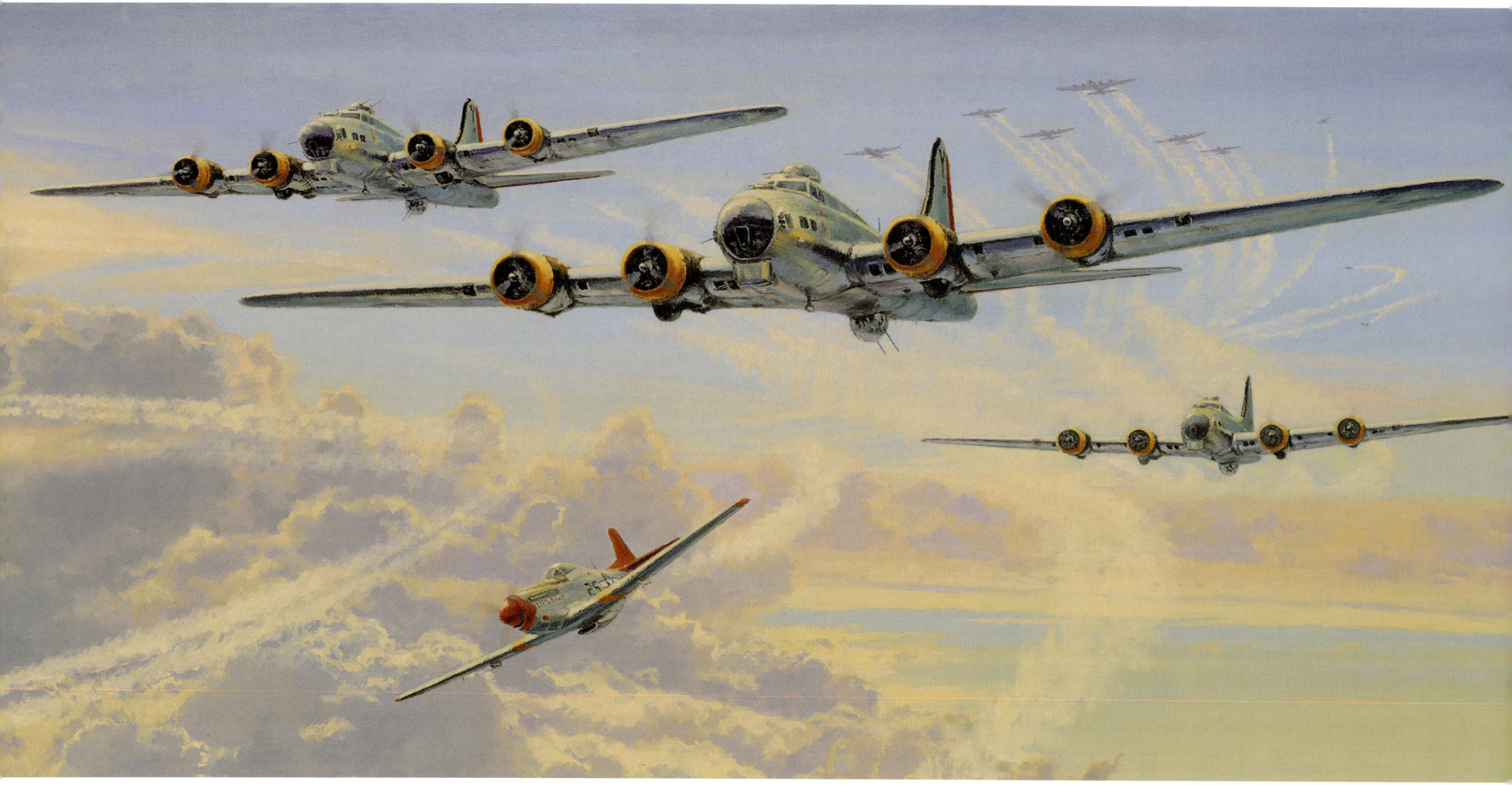

LONG HAUL TO BERLIN

By the spring of 1945 Luftwaffe interception of the Allied heavy bombers ranging over the German Reich had become a rarity. This was good news for the vulnerable bomber crews but, with the end of the war in sight, it was not always so welcomed by the escorting fighter pilots, many of whom still wanted 'a piece of the action'.

On 24 March 1945, however, the Tuskegee pilots of the 332nd Fighter Group – the *Redtails* – got more than their share of the action. They were escorting the heavy bombers of the 5th Bomb Wing, part of the Fifteenth Air Force, on their way to bomb the Daimler-Benz tank assembly plant on the outskirts of Berlin when, as they approached the city, they suddenly found themselves under attack by 25 Luftwaffe fighters.

From the razor-sharp contrails fast approaching above the bomber force, it soon became clear that these were not the usual Me109s or Fw190s they'd got used to: they were Me262s, the revolutionary jet-powered fighter that could not only fly over 100 mph faster than any Allied fighter, but also carried a deadlier punch in the shape of four nose-mounted 30mm cannons. But now, heavily outnumbered by over fifty P-51 Mustangs, not to mention hundreds of machine guns trained on them from the B-17 gunners, the Me262 pilots, predominantly from JG7, faced an impossible task.

It was now that First Lieutenant Earl Lane of the 100th Fighter Squadron finally got his chance to claim one of the new jets when the Me262 of Oberleutnant Alfred Ambs, a highly successful Luftwaffe Ace with seven victories, made a pass at the bombers. Lane wrote: 'He appeared as if he was peeling off from an attack on the bombers, I came in for a 30-degree deflection shot from 2000ft away. He didn't quite fill my sight. I fired three short bursts and saw the airplane emitting smoke. A piece of it, either the canopy or one of the jet orifices, then flew off.' Lane had managed to achieve complete surprise over the battle-hardened Ambs, whose canopy was shattered by one of the shells from Lane's guns. The German pilot took to his parachute, coming down in a tree near Wittenburg and sustaining injuries to his legs. It would be his last flight of the war.

In the same encounter the *Redtails* managed to shoot down three Me262s, an amazing achievement for which they were awarded a Distinguished Unit Citation, something that many of the often-maligned black Tuskegee aviators might have thought highly unlikely on their formation two years earlier. Dispensing with three jets in air-to-air combat, however, went a long way to silencing those critics that had doubted their abilities.

At nearly 1600 miles, this was the longest mission ever launched by the Fifteenth Air Force from their bases on the Foggia plain in southern Italy. For the bomber crews it meant a gruelling ten-hour mission and the knowledge that they would not have enough fuel to return to their bases. They would have to make it back to whatever Allied airfield they could find in northern Italy.

And when, or if, they eventually did get back to their home base the crews didn't have much to look forward to. The vast majority endured the most basic and meagre

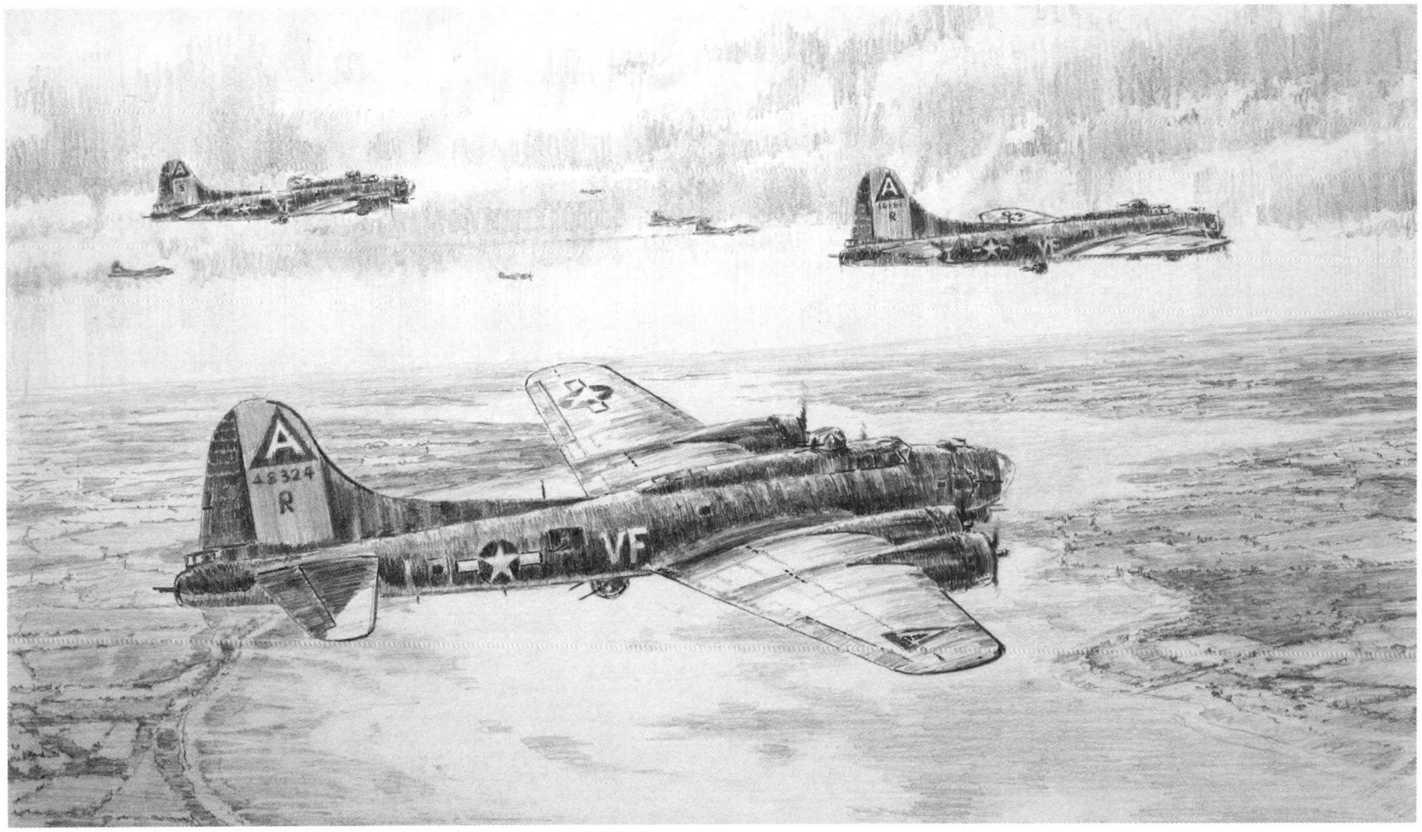

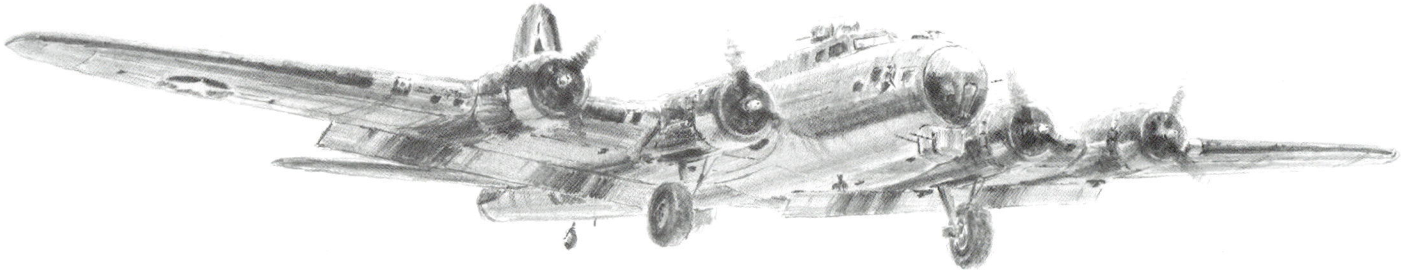

temporary accommodation – often just a tent on a vast barren field. In summer it would be stiflingly hot, the air warm and dusty; in winter surprisingly cold, often wet and muddy.

In living standards at least, their Eighth Air Force cousins in England had things a little more comfortable, even if they didn't realise it at the time. Some were fortunate to find their accommodation was in relatively plush brick buildings that had been built by the RAF before the war; the less lucky would have a Nissen hut which, although cold in winter, did at least have a warming stove to keep out the worst of a cold winter night – if they could find enough solid fuel.

Most of the Eighth Air Force crewmen, however, appreciated their surroundings and would write letters back home describing the 'quaintness' of the East Anglian countryside with its many historic buildings and, of course, its pubs! Surprisingly many took to the 'warm local beer', to eating fish and chips, and even a liking for the tea that the English loved so much.

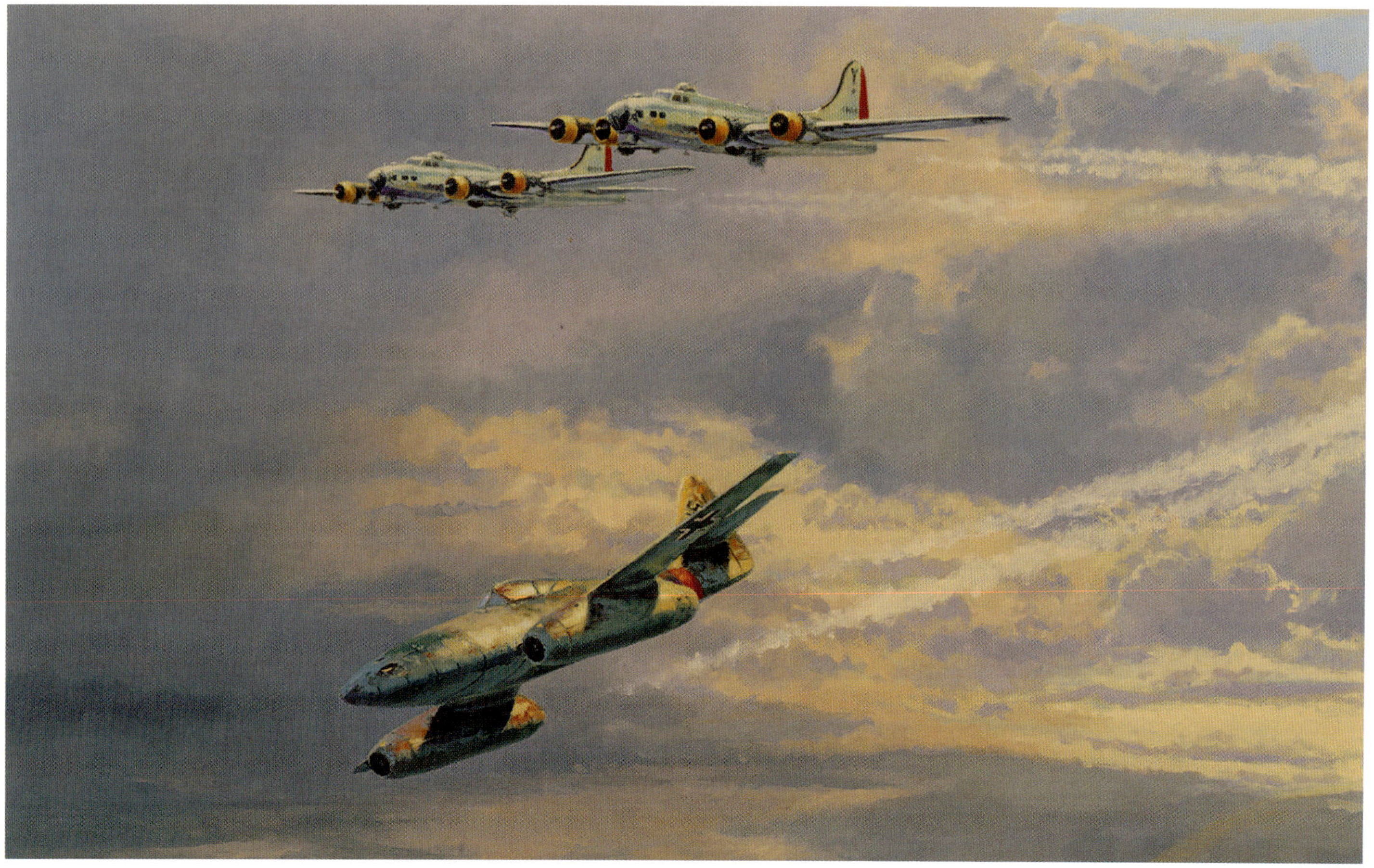

When the Fifteenth Air Force was formed in November 1943, a proportion of the new units were made up from some belonging to the 'Mighty Eighth' in England and what, at first, seemed like a pleasant secondment to the warmth of the sunny Mediterranean in fact turned out to be a rather unpleasant, and uncomfortable, surprise.

Strategically, however, the establishment of the Fifteenth Air Force in Italy in late 1943 meant that Germany and the occupied countries of Europe now faced a heavy bombing offensive on two fronts. From the north RAF Bomber Command attacked by night and the US Eighth Air Force by day, whilst the heavy bombers of the Fifteenth Air Force now began their assault from the south. No part of occupied Europe was now out of reach of the Allied 'heavies' and if bad weather prevented missions from one direction, they could usually be flown from the other.

For this painting I wanted to capture the moment that Lane had described when the Me262 of Alfred Ambs peeled away from the bombers in front of him, and was also keen to include an angle of the P-51 that clearly showed the simple but effective piece of 'Dearly Beloved' nose art that Lane had painted on his aircraft's engine cowl.

But, as the title of the painting suggests, the important thing was to show the unsung heroes of that day – the B-17s and crews of the Fifteenth Air Force on their long haul to Berlin.

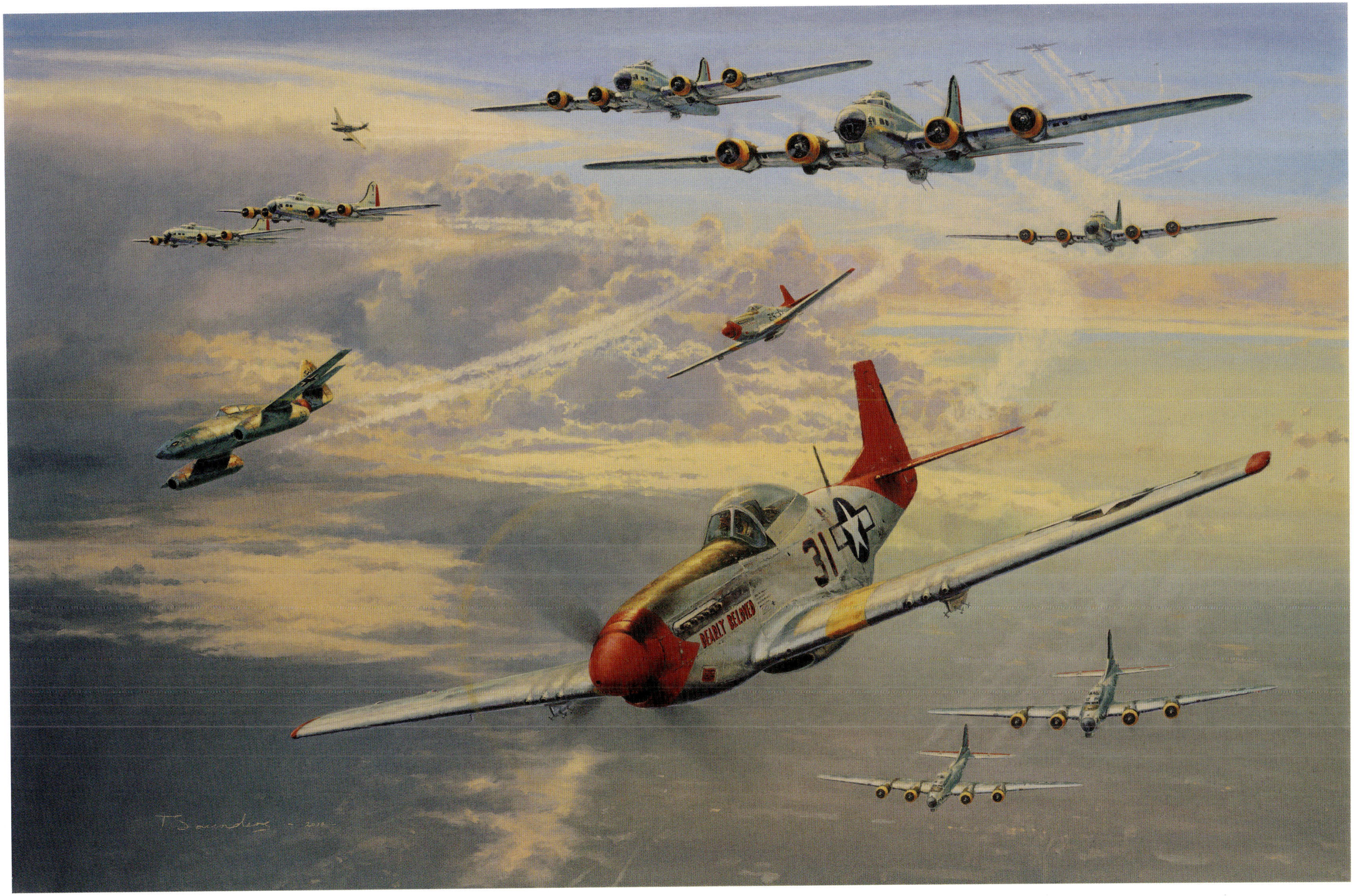

LONG HAUL TO BERLIN IN THE COLLECTION OF MR & MRS M. HORSFIELD

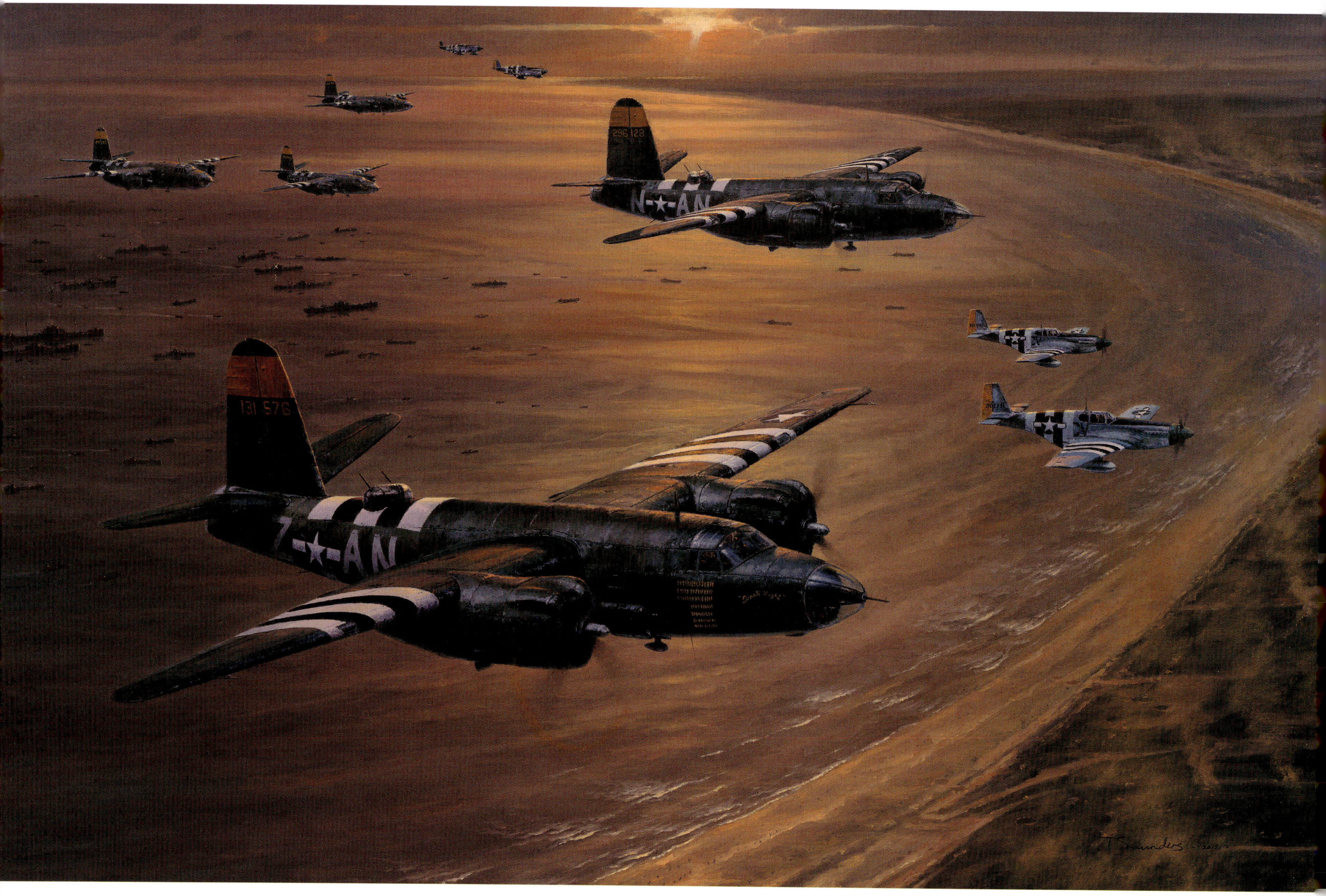

UTAH DAWN IN THE COLLECTION OF MR MICHAEL BURR

UTAH DAWN

In 2012 I was lucky enough to be invited by Aces High to attend their exhibition in Normandy, which was then located within the Utah Beach Museum. The museum had recently reopened after an extensive renovation and expansion project, and now included an impressive aviation hangar.

The centrepiece of this huge steel-framed glass hangar is a magnificently restored B-26 Marauder medium bomber and, for the re-opening exhibition, Aces High had been asked to showcase their work around this beautiful aeroplane. It formed an impressive site, and I was more than happy to discover that one section of the display was dedicated solely to my work, which included both prints and original paintings. It's not often that I get to see several of my originals displayed together, and in such a great setting, particularly as one of them was *Utah Dawn,* a painting of the same B-26 on display that I had just completed especially for the occasion. To see the two displayed alongside each other was a great thrill.

The event was also a good opportunity to hear what people thought about my work, without them knowing it was the artist who was standing close by. Many of the visitors, of course, were local and although I'd been brushing up my schoolboy French before the trip, it was still quite hard to follow the conversations. Nevertheless, French is a much more expressive language than English and I think I could tell, hopefully with a fair degree of certainty, that they liked my work.

That evening, after the museum had closed to the public, I was able to spend a little time on my own admiring the B-26, which was meticulously restored in the colours of the 386th Bomb Group, 553rd Bomb Squadron. Christened *Dinah Might* by her aircrew, the B-26 had been flown on D-Day by Major David H. Dewhurst, but at this particular moment it bathed in a warm glow from the setting sun that shone through the glass walls and made its olive drab paintwork come to life; in this setting it was anything but drab.

The 386th Bomb Group was based at Great Dunmow in Essex and *Dinah Might* was one of their original aircraft. Accordingly it had its fair share of battle repairs, including a new rudder and various patched holes from flak damage. The ground crew, apparently, had been too busy to get round to updating the wing insignia with white bars as they should have been after 1943, one of the things I found out from a wonderful, highly-detailed, colour photo of the same aircraft taken in flight contained in a book in my collection entitled *The Ninth Air Force in Colour* by Roger Freeman.

The original *Dinah Might* had been lost, with a different pilot, over Germany while bombing storage facilities at St Wendle on 18 November 1944 so, although beautifully restored in the colours of the 386th, the actual airframe now on display in the museum wasn't Dewhurst's original Marauder. This one had come from a museum near Paris and was previously painted in the colours of a Free French unit.

How the B-26 came to be painted in the colours of the 386th Bomb Group is an interesting story. In 2007, two brothers, David and Eugene Dewhurst, came over from America to visit *Utah Beach* on a family trip. Their father had died in a road accident when they were both young children, and they knew very little about his role on D-Day, other than that he was a B-26 pilot. When

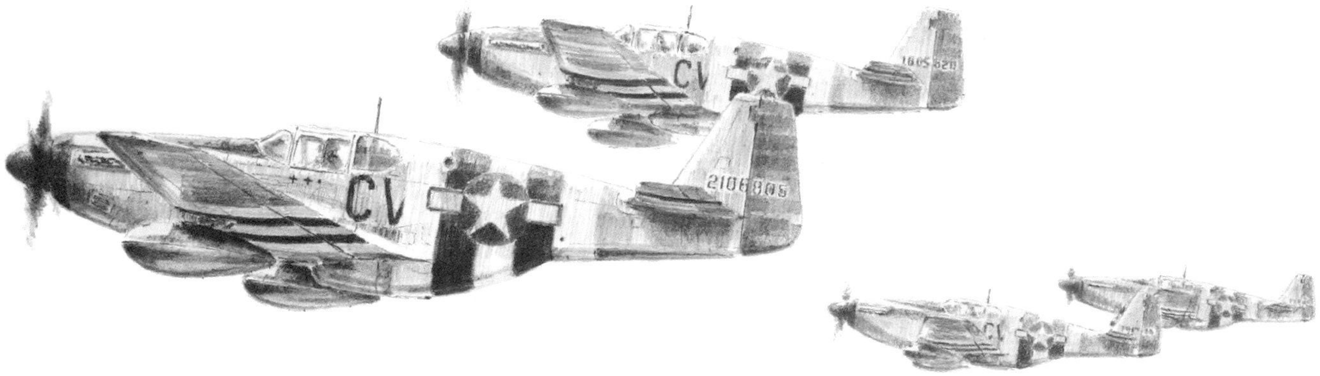

they visited the small museum on *Utah Beach*, however, they were astonished to find a photo on display of their father, Major David Dewhurst, and his crew posing underneath their B-26. They read that he was a decorated squadron commander and had led the final bombing run on German bunker *WN5* – the very building they were now standing in – moments before the Allied landing.

Inspired by their visit, the two brothers decided to give a substantial donation towards the renovation and extension of the museum. All they asked in return was that an exhibition area be reserved in memory of their father and the various other bomber crews that attacked *Utah Beach* on D-Day. As a thank-you for the brothers' generosity the museum re-painted their newly-acquired B-26 in the colours of their father's aircraft. I can only

DINAH MIGHT

IN THE COLLECTION OF DR HENRY GOODALL

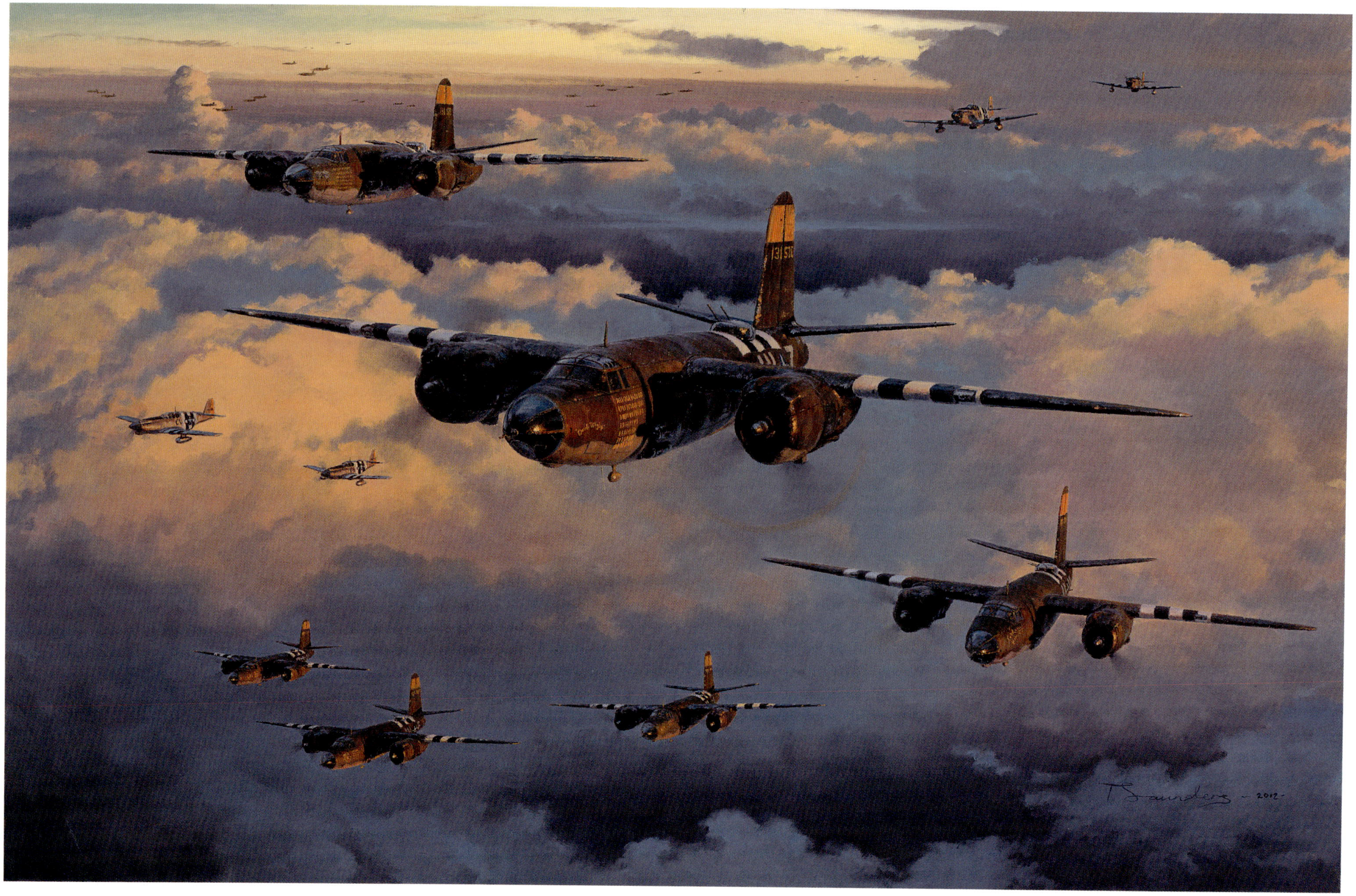

imagine how pleased and proud the two brothers must have been to see the finished result, perfect in every detail to how it appeared on D-Day, apart from the flak damage patches!

'H-Hour' at *Utah Beach*, the moment when the first wave of soldiers would go ashore, was 06.30 hours. Due to a navigational error the main landing force found themselves a mile further south than planned, which resulted in some confusion for those involved. But fortune was on their side that morning, due in no small part to the bombing accuracy of the Ninth Air Force, who, as well as pounding the German shore fortifications and gun positions, bombed the beach itself which provided badly needed shelter for the soon-to-be-landing infantry, cover that was sorely missing on the beach at *Omaha*.

In *Utah Dawn*, Dewhurst's B-26 is seen just before it crosses the beach where it will turn to port and head up the beach to its assigned target. They did this so that they wouldn't overfly the amphibious assault force below, with the obvious danger of being hit by friendly fire. This was the final bombing run over the beach before the landings and was timed to perfection – just moments before the landing craft hit the beach.

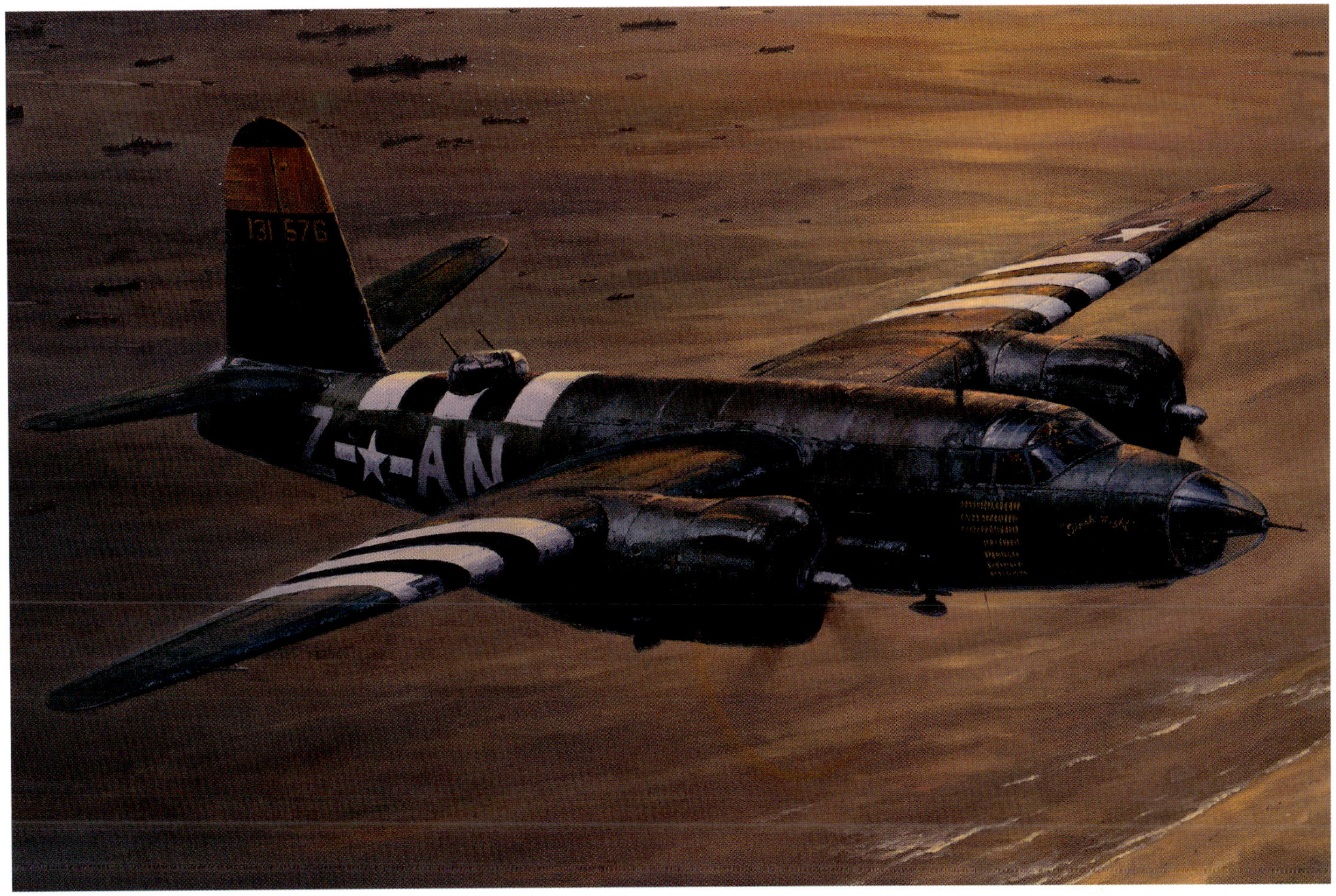

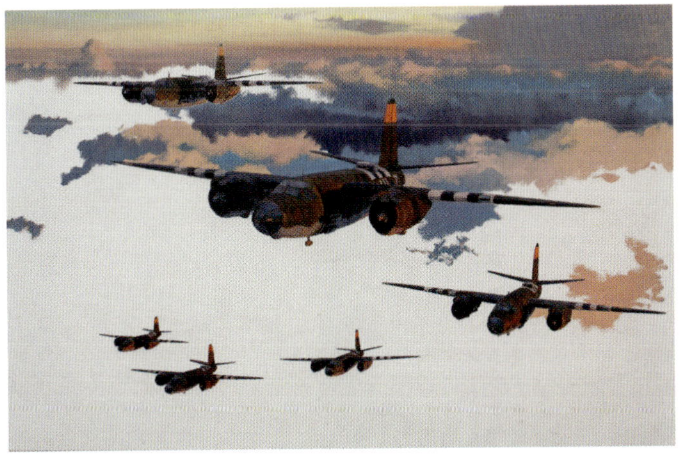

Once fully 'blocked-in' a painting could almost be considered as an oil sketch. I've often thought how nice it would be to sell some of my paintings at this stage, and how much easier that would make my life. But alas, with this genre of painting at least, one of the things collectors seem to demand is detail – and lots of it!

DINAH MIGHT

I painted Dinah Might, *the painting seen on the opposite page and to the left, shortly after* Utah Dawn.

I'd known that there was a lot of cloud around at sunrise on D-Day, but from reading some aircrew reports I found out there were significant breaks in the thick cloud which, in *Utah Dawn*, enabled them to accurately find their targets and get a good view of the impressive armada below. *Dinah Might*, however, depicts the same mission but slightly earlier, and from a different angle. This time I opted to go with the thicker cloud scenario.

Dinah Might is painted on a 30 x 20 inch canvas, slightly smaller than the 36 x 24 inch size I normally use, and on this occasion I didn't apply my usual base coat either. With my larger paintings I generally apply this base coat, which consists of a fairly thin grey-green oil paint, to the pre-primed canvas before I start 'blocking-in' – the process of quite quickly painting in the scene as it will appear when completed, but without any of the finer detail. This will be applied once the 'blocking-in' has fully dried, and usually takes about a month to complete.

When working on a painting I will, from time to time, stand back and view the painting from a distance, which in my case means having to step outside my studio, a small converted Victorian outbuilding, into the garden and look back through the open door. Sometimes I also look at the painting with a small hand-held mirror, which allows me to view it from a different perspective. It never ceases to amaze me how little change there is between a blocked-in and a completed canvas at this distance.

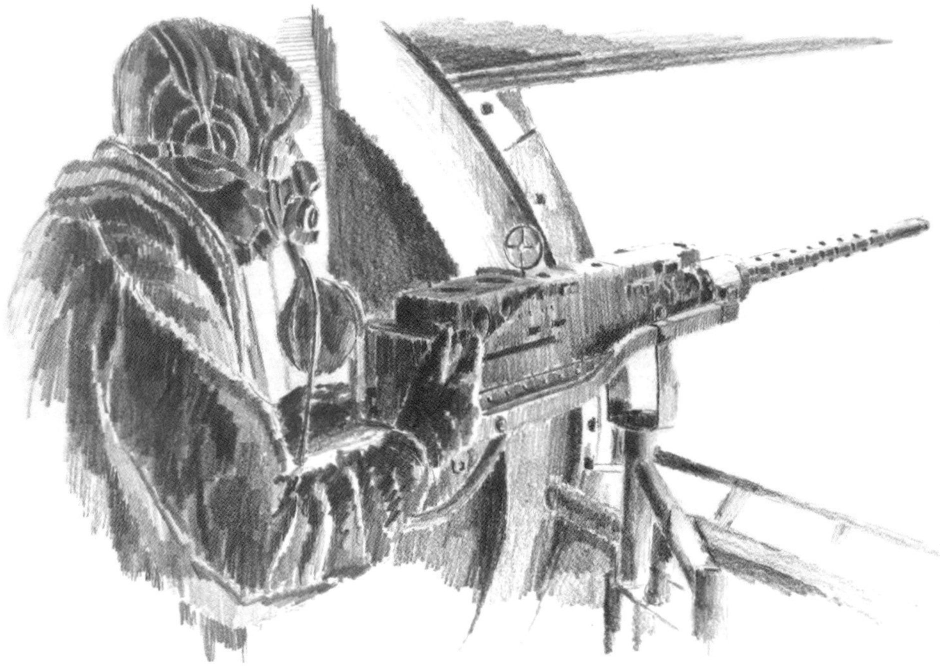

TO HELL AND BACK

OPERATION TIDAL WAVE

Jimmy Doolittle's daring raid on Tokyo in April 1942, following the Japanese surprise attack on Pearl Harbor, had galvanized American morale and shocked the enemy but, in strategic terms, the gains were minimal. When the Joint Chiefs of Staff met later in Washington they were looking to strike a much more decisive blow. Their chance came at Ploesti....

In January 1943, two months after the Anglo-American landings in North Africa, US President Franklin D. Roosevelt and British Prime Minister Winston Churchill met in Casablanca to decide on how best to co-ordinate their fight against the Axis Powers. One of the decisions they took was to launch a massive air attack on the oil refineries centred on the ancient city of Ploesti in southern Romania. It was here that the world's first oil refinery had opened in 1856 and the same oil fields now supplied about 40% of the fuel that powered Hitler's war machine. Destroy these refineries and it wouldn't be just the Wehrmacht's panzers that stopped in their tracks. The Luftwaffe would also be grounded.

The task of dealing such a crippling blow fell to Colonel Jacob Smart. He argued that although losses might be heavy, a single low-level surprise raid would ensure greater accuracy than high-level bombing. His plan was novel: to attack Ploesti from the nearest airfields available, in Libya, would involve a round-trip of over 2,000 miles. The raiding force would use B-24 Liberators, the only heavy bomber with the necessary range to carry out the task. But the colonel's plan was controversial: B-24s were large and relatively slow, designed for high altitude operations. Operating at low-level the Liberators would be highly vulnerable to enemy anti-aircraft fire. Surprise, therefore, would be vital.

Five B-24 Bomb Groups would be used for the operation, code-named *Tidalwave*: two from the Ninth Air Force, the 98th and 376th Bomb Groups, were already stationed in North Africa and three others, the 44th, 93rd and 389th Bomb Groups, would fly in, lent by the Eighth Air Force in England.

After several weeks of intensive low-level training from temporary airstrips near Benghazi, in the Libyan Desert, all five units were as ready as they would ever be. Much work had gone into the preparation of Operation *Tidalwave* and in planning the arduous route that would take the B-24s from Libya across the Mediterranean Sea, over Albania and Yugoslavia before crossing the Balkan Mountains into Romania. The success of the mission now depended on the ten men who crewed each of the 179 B-24s.

On Sunday, 1st August 1943, as dawn broke over the dusty makeshift airfields, the first of the heavily-laden Liberators lumbered into the air. One aircraft crashed soon after take-off, perhaps a bad omen of things to come because, over the Balkan Mountains, the plans started to unravel.

First, heavy cloud had caused the three trailing groups to lose contact with the leading two; strict radio silence meant that no contact could be made to rectify the problem. Then, when only 30 miles from Ploesti, the leading 376th Group aircraft made their scheduled turn to the south too early and the 93rd Group followed. It was only when the towering spires of Bucharest loomed into view that the navigational error was realised, and the formation doubled back to the target area to try and find their assigned targets. The 93rd decided to attack whatever installations could be found and, coming across target *White IV*, the Astra Romana refinery, and *White V*, the Colombia Aquila refinery, attacked with delayed-action bombs. They started exploding just as the 98th and 44th Bomb Groups, who had officially been assigned these targets, began to arrive.

What greeted Lieutenant James Merrick, pilot of B-24 *Lil' De-Icer*, as he approached the Astra Romana refinery, was the sight that inspired this painting – a vision of hell. Flames licked upward as he flew through pillars of seemingly impenetrable black smoke as shrapnel from the exploding, delayed-action bombs flashed past his cockpit. With any hope of surprise long gone, the anti-aircraft batteries surrounding the site added their flak to the chaos. Little wonder that the 98th were to lose more aircraft than any other group.

Dropping his bomb load as planned, Merrick now pushed the throttles wide open and powered *Lil' De-Icer*

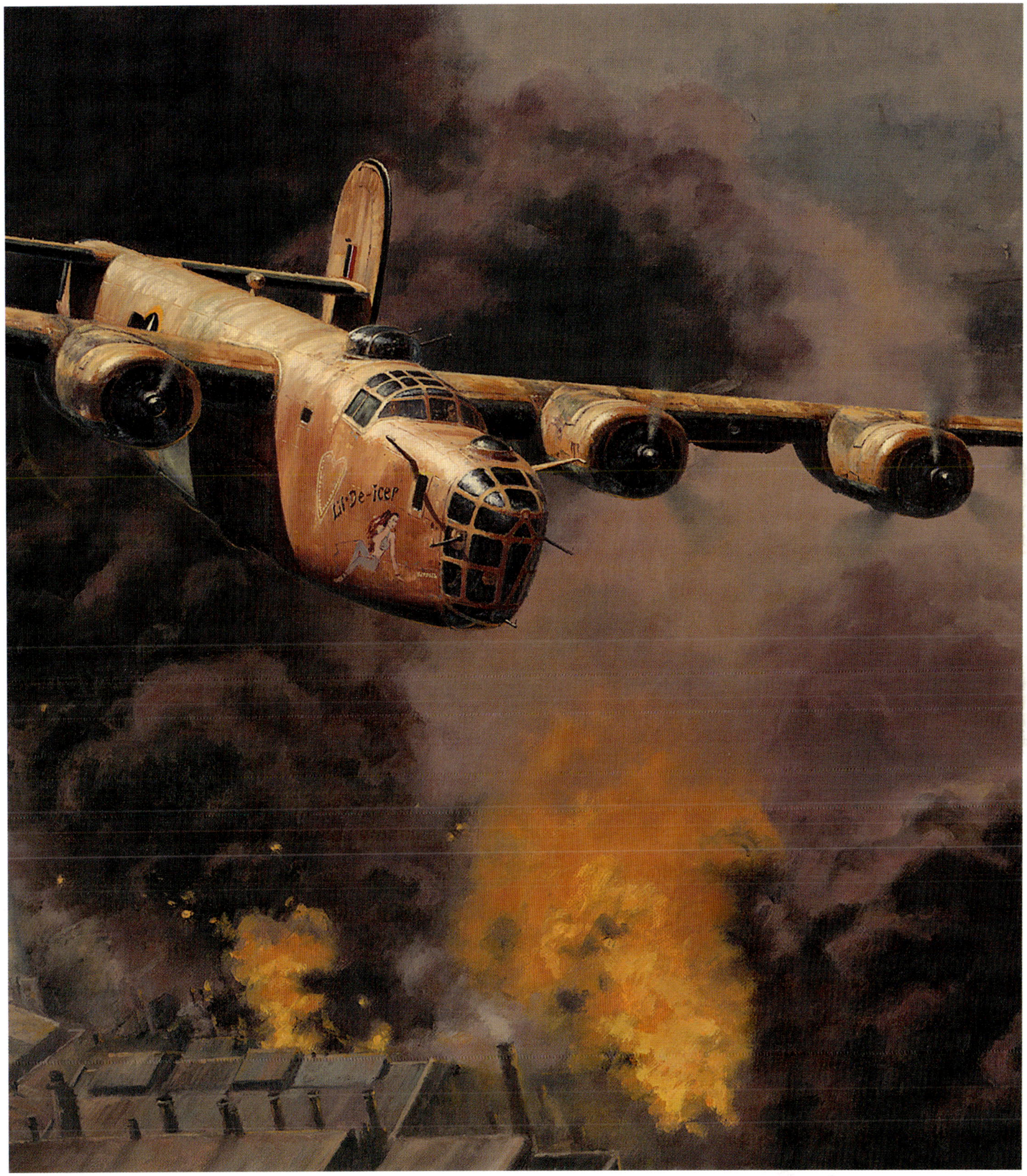

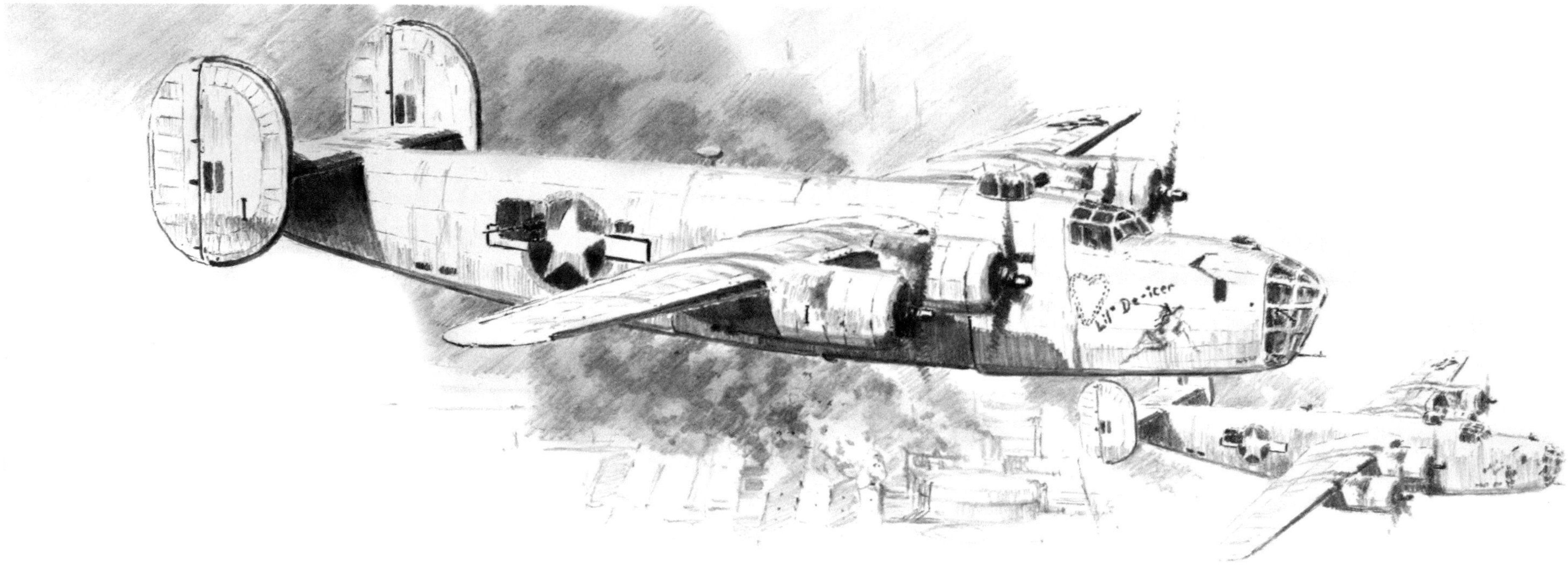

away from the target and turned for home. His troubles, however, were far from over; crack squadrons of enemy fighters were gathering and, as Merrick's B-24 emerged from the inferno, an Me109 struck.

Thankfully the gunners on-board *Lil' De-Icer* knew their business better than most and put up a wall of defensive fire. Coupled with the bomber's increased speed and low altitude, the enemy fighter was unable to bring the big bomber down and, after half an hour, broke off the attack to look for a less capable crew. But any sense of relief was short-lived. At 8,000ft over Bulgaria they were intercepted again by Me109s and, in a bitter firefight, the B-24's gunners once more fended off the attack. Just over an hour later, with the Liberator now over the Mediterranean on the final leg, enemy fighters struck yet again and, for the third time that day, *Lil' De-Icer* rode her luck. James Merrick finally touched down at 21.25 hours. He'd brought his aircraft safely home with no injuries or damage and his gunners could claim two Me109s destroyed.

With their 14-hour ordeal now over, I can only imagine the huge sense of relief that the crew must have felt as they set foot on hard ground again. The pounding drone of the Liberator's four engines would continue to ring in their ears for hours, but, although they'd survived, the memories would never leave them. They had been the fortunate ones; on a day when five Medals of Honor would be awarded – the most for any single American action – more than fifty B-24s had been lost and a similar number badly damaged.

For many paintings I sometimes struggle to come up with an apt or appropriate title, but this time there could only be one – *To Hell and Back*.

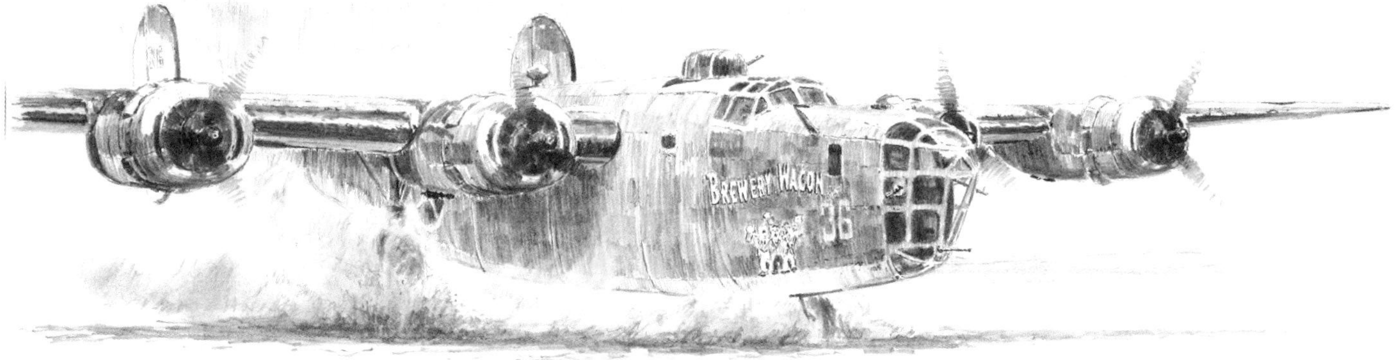

Brewery Wagon – one of more than 50 B-24s that failed to return from Ploesti. Piloted by First Lieutenant John Palm it took a direct hit from flak, killing the navigator and bombardier. With one engine destroyed and two on fire Palm struggled to keep his bomber flying but was then shot down by an enemy fighter to be taken prisoner with the survivors of his crew.

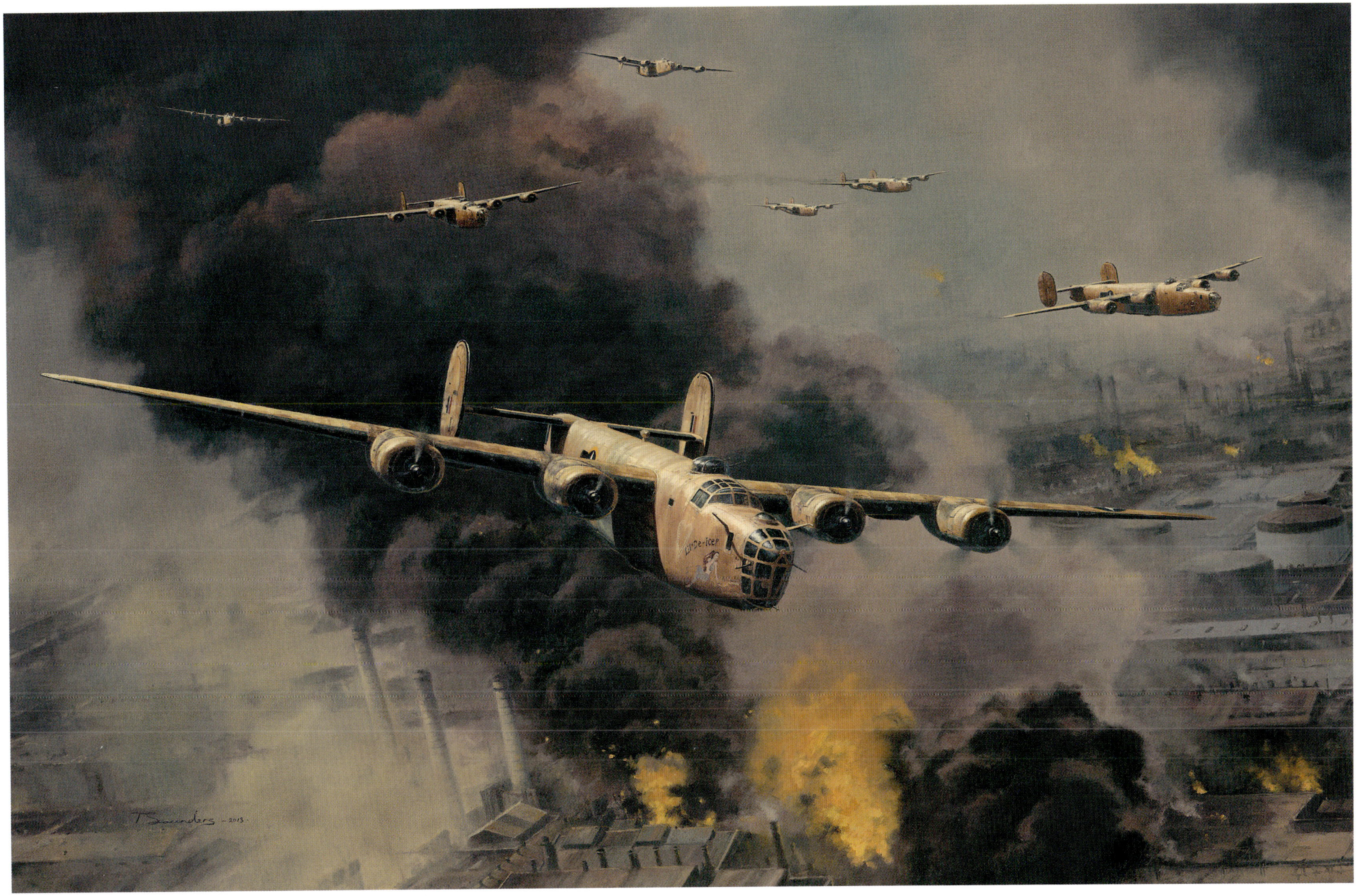

TO HELL AND BACK IN THE COLLECTION OF BILL WARD FINE ART SERVICES

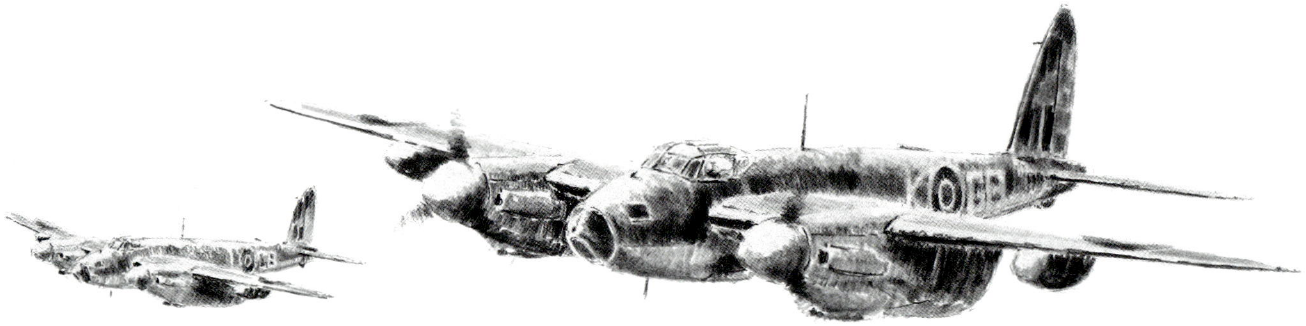

STRIKE ON BERLIN

"On the anniversary of your assumption of power, the Sixth Army sends greetings to the Führer. The swastika still flutters over Stalingrad. May our struggle stand as an example to generations yet unborn never to surrender, no matter how desperate the odds. Then Germany will be victorious. Heil, Mein Führer."

On 30 January 1943, with his beleaguered and starving army staring defeat in the face amongst the frozen ruins of Stalingrad, this was the message that General Friedrich von Paulus sent to Hitler on the tenth anniversary of the Nazi party coming to power. Hitler responded by promoting von Paulus to Generalfeldmarschall – a rank von Paulus would hold for barely a day before he was captured by the Russians.

Back in Berlin this wasn't the only anniversary greeting Hitler was to receive that day because the RAF were planning to deliver their own special message to help the Führer celebrate. And they were going to do it in such a way that the whole of Germany would hear it.

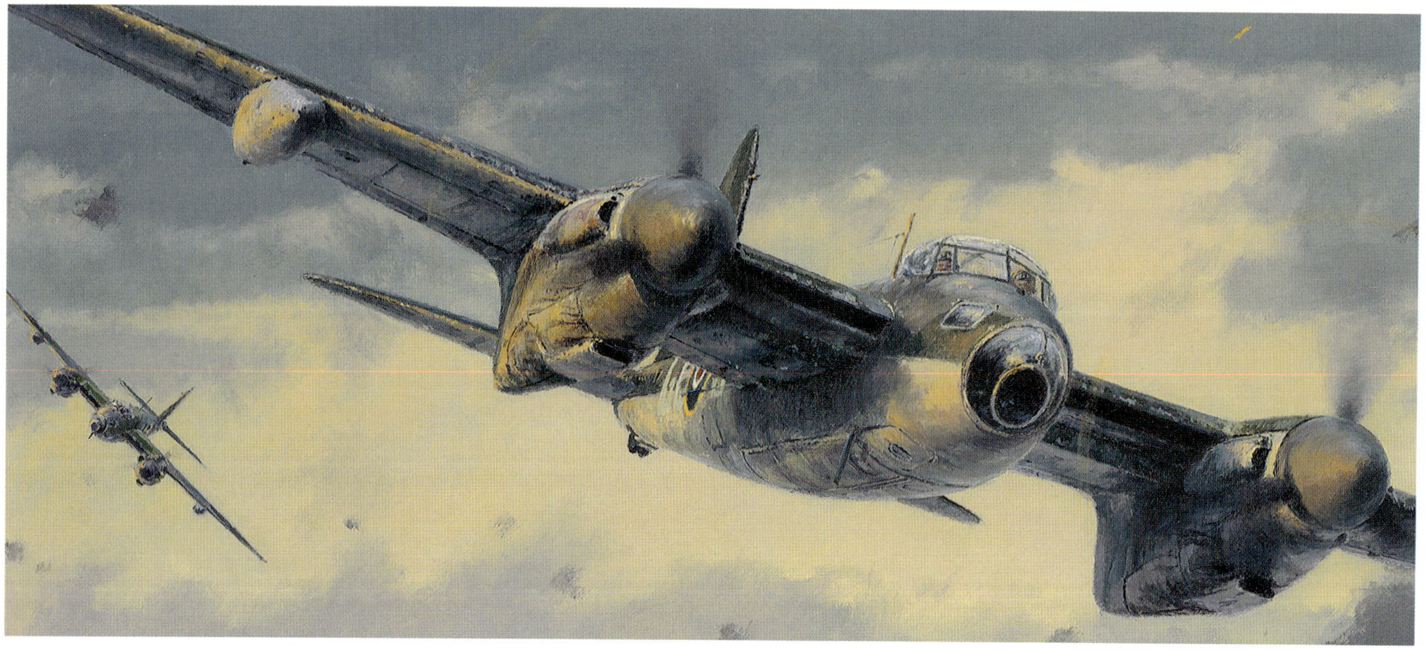

The *Haus des Rundfunks* – Broadcasting House – was a distinctive, almost triangular shaped building on Masurenallee in west Berlin, and headquarters of German State Radio. It was here, at 11.00am, that Deputy Führer Hermann Goering rose to deliver a glowing speech in tribute to the Party and its leader, Adolf Hitler. Propaganda minister, Josef Goebbels was to give another speech in the afternoon. With immaculate timing, just as both broadcasts went live, the RAF struck in the first daytime bombing raids on Berlin. Mosquitos of 105 Squadron and 139 Squadron swooped low over the city in a daring low-level attack on the building at the precise time of each speech. All of listening Germany heard the distant shouts and the unmistakable crump of an exploding bomb.

Goering, the man who had once promised that 'no enemy aircraft will fly over the Reich' was so enraged at the audacious attack, he later commented: 'It makes me furious when I see the Mosquito. I turn green and yellow with envy. The British, who can afford aluminium better

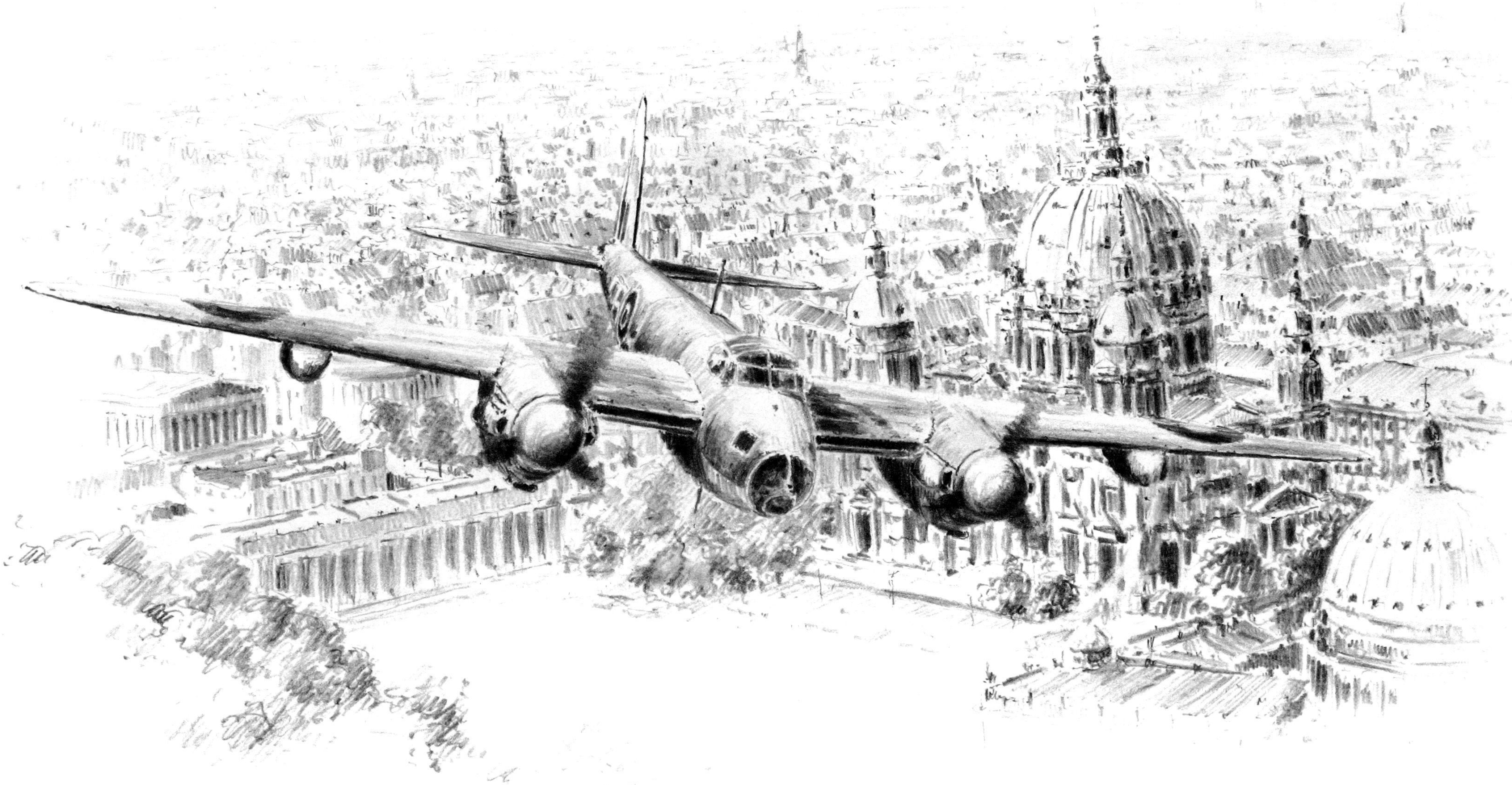

than we can, knock together a beautiful wooden aircraft that every piano factory over there is building, and they give it a speed that they have now increased yet again'.

The object of his vented spleen – the de Havilland Mosquito – was constructed almost wholly of wood and up until the introduction of the revolutionary Me262 jet, could outrun all enemy fighters. It was probably the most versatile aircraft of the entire war whose operational roles included day and night bomber, night-fighter, intruder, pathfinder, ship-buster, bomber support, photo reconnaissance – the list goes on. In short, it was an outstanding aircraft and highly regarded by the men who flew it, not least because it got them home. I can't think of any other war-time aircraft that had two affectionate nicknames, namely the 'Wooden Wonder' and the 'Mossie'.

There are many amazing stories about the Mosquito. For me, one that particularly encapsulates what the Mosquito was all about was when an American B-26 Marauder crew met a Mosquito over England. The word had 'gotten' round that there was a British bomber that was faster than most fighters, let alone bombers. But the B-26 crew knew their bird was no slouch and after some signalling between the two bombers a race was on. As the Marauder pounded along with all throttles through the firewall, the Mosquito flew over them, inverted and flying on one engine – *touché!*

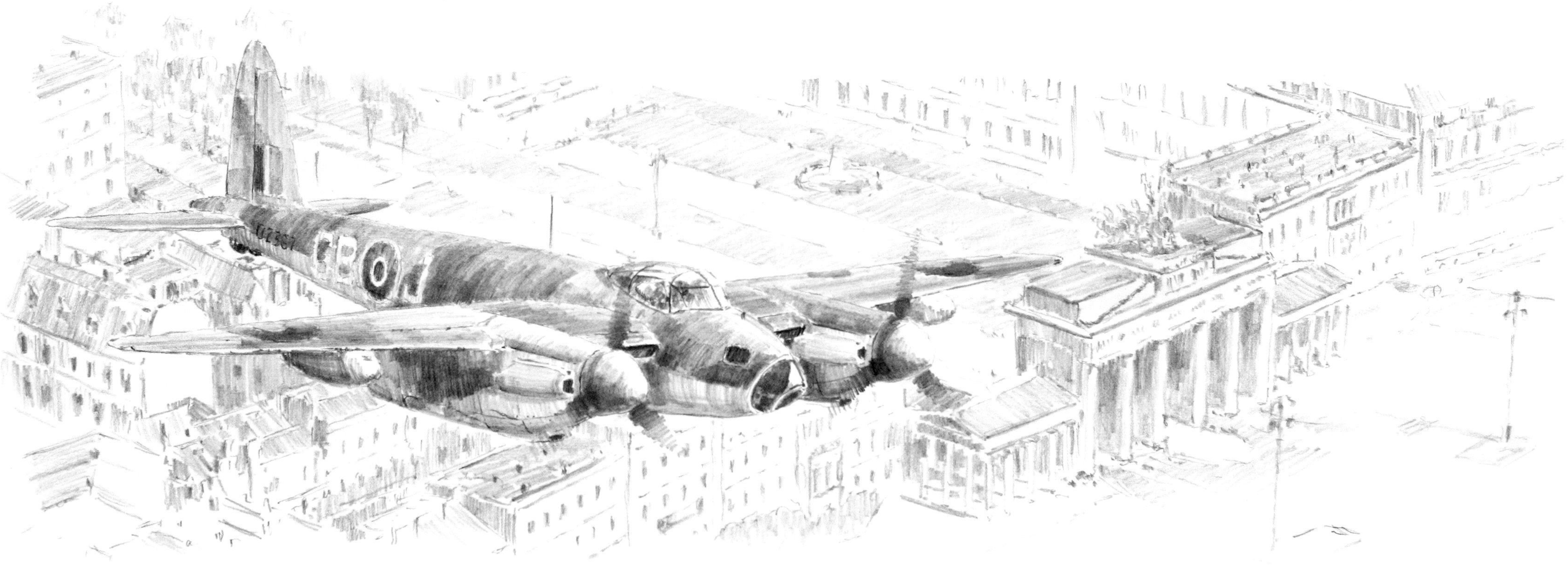

When I planned *Strike on Berlin*, my initial thought was to have the Mosquitos flying directly over the Broadcasting House at the moment of attack. But, when I finally found a decent picture of the place, I knew at first glance that it wasn't a building I wanted to spend the next few weeks painting. Opened in 1931 as the world's first dedicated broadcasting centre, the interior was technologically more advanced than any other, but the exterior had one of the most featureless looking, geometric facades you could imagine. So instead I chose to show the Mosquitos over the city centre as they made their rapid escape.

Before I started researching this subject, I had no idea what a beautiful city pre-war Berlin had been. It was full of handsome buildings, a mixture of neoclassical and Gothic architecture, and I could have chosen any one of them as a backdrop, but I settled on something that is not only visually dramatic but can still be seen today – the *Berliner Dom*, Berlin Cathedral. Much like St Paul's in London, Berlin Cathedral withstood much of the punishment inflicted on it by the aerial bombardment but, unlike its London counterpart, by the time the Russians entered the city at the end of the war, the cathedral was in a sorry, ruined state that would take decades to restore.

The large square building with the domed cupola to the left of the cathedral was the City Palace, a former royal palace and the building from which Kaiser Wilhelm II declared the First World War. A beautiful neoclassical building dating back to the 18th century, it too survived the war as a ruin, but was demolished by the Soviets in 1950. It is now being completely rebuilt.

I knew beforehand that by incorporating all these fine buildings I was making a rod for my own back but, even though it involved hours of painstaking and laborious hard work to get it right, these buildings were wonderful things to paint – and much more interesting than the *Haus des Rundfunks*.

I didn't want to make the painting too bright. Although the effects of sunlight can be seen, especially by highlighting the architectural features of the buildings, I wanted to give the painting an almost subdued greyness, to make it appear almost forbidding. That's how I imagine the RAF pilots would have felt approaching Berlin.

Another element I wanted to convey in the painting was the speed of the Mosquito. The narrow angle of the lead aircraft goes some way to achieving this, but I've arranged the clouds and the rising smoke in the background in such a way as to help the eye lead the aircraft out of the painting towards you.

Although *Strike on Berlin* took much longer to complete than usual – nearly seven weeks – it's one that, in the end, gave me an equal amount of satisfaction. But although I do like to set myself difficult challenges, I'm not so sure I'll be tackling a city centre again. At least not for a while!

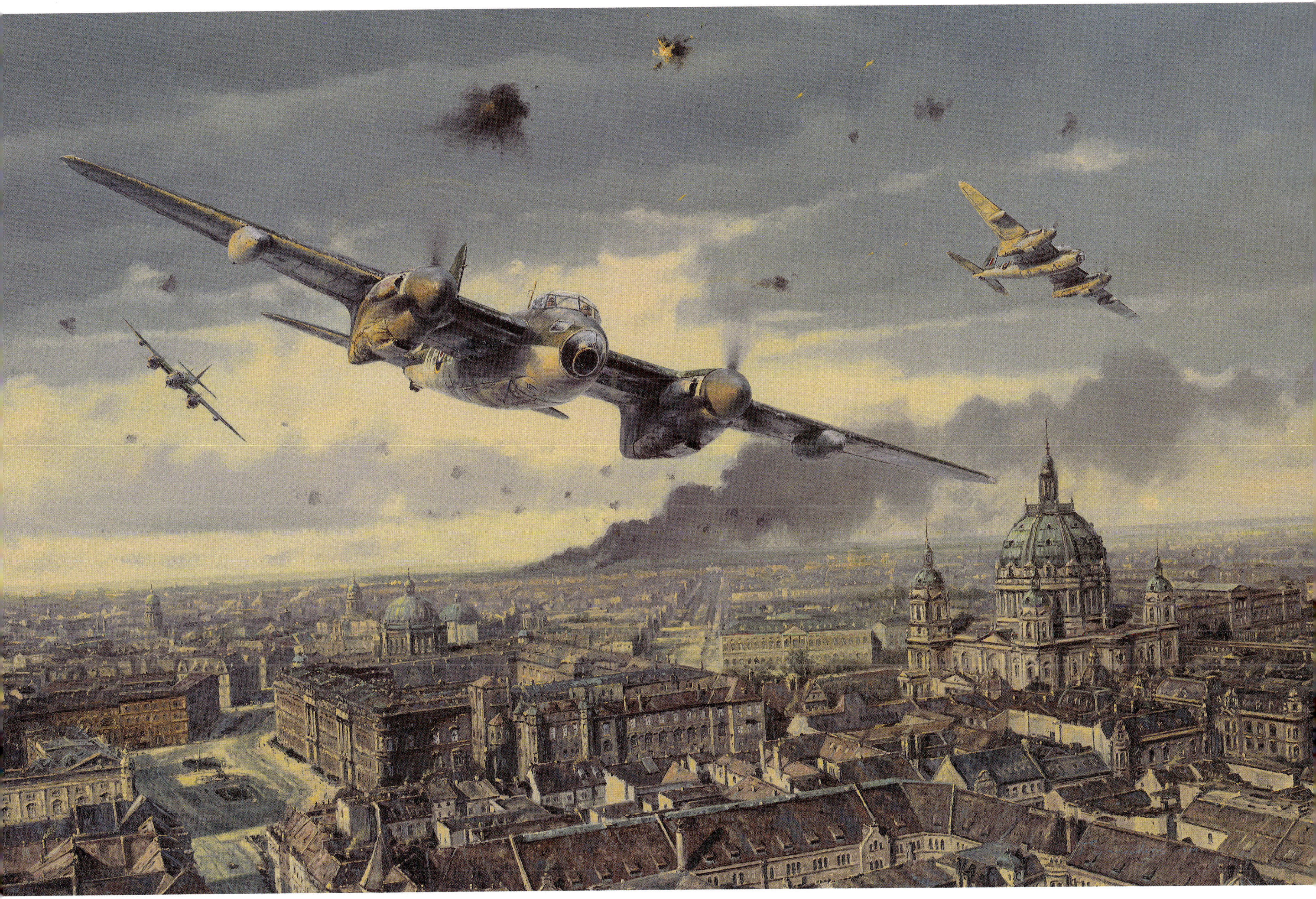

STRIKE ON BERLIN IN THE COLLECTION OF MR JULIAN PARKER

FINAL BRIEFING

The large briefing room in the Officers' Mess at Scampton was full. At 18.00 hours on Sunday 16 May 1943, aircrew of the newly formed 617 Squadron took their places – in front of them a huge map of Western Europe, on which three carefully-plotted routes had been marked out with red tape to destinations deep in the Ruhr Valley.

As Wing Commander Guy Gibson stood up, the buzz of excited chatter fell silent. Months of highly secretive and meticulous planning were finally shared as Gibson pronounced to the expectant aircrews – 'Tonight you will attack the great dams of Germany.'

Some of those present had suspected the intense training they'd been undergoing in the past weeks was leading up to an attack on the *Tirpitz*. That would have been bad enough, but everyone in the room knew that attacking the dams was going to be an even more difficult target. Letting the news sink in, Gibson introduced the Assistant Chief Designer at Vickers-Armstrong to them – the inventor of an innovative bouncing bomb that they were going to use that night. His name was Barnes Wallis.

Many of the audience had heard of Wallis through his pioneering design work on the Wellington bomber, in which many of them had flown, and they listened carefully as he described *Upkeep*, the new weapon, in detail, including all the difficulties that had been encountered in its development. Wallis painstakingly explained the characteristics of each dam, the method of destruction and why the dams were deemed such an important target. Sergeant James Clay, the bomb aimer in Les Munro's crew, reflected later how 'detailed and clear' his explanation was, but couldn't help feeling that 'it seemed incongruous that this kindly and quietly spoken white-haired man should be involved with devastation'.

When Wallis had finished speaking, Air Vice-Marshal Cochrane took to the floor, stressing the need for total secrecy and finished, ironically, with prophetic words about the forthcoming raid: 'It will become historic'.

After going over the operational details once more, Gibson finally called the briefing to a close at 19.30 hours.

After a supper of bacon and eggs the crew members went back to their quarters, some to undertake the sobering task of composing letters to next of kin – in case they failed to return – whilst others just sat for a few moments of quiet reflection. For one or two the confidence exuded at the briefing had begun to ebb: Pilot Officer Bill Townsend later confessed of feeling sick, convinced that they were 'all for the chop.'

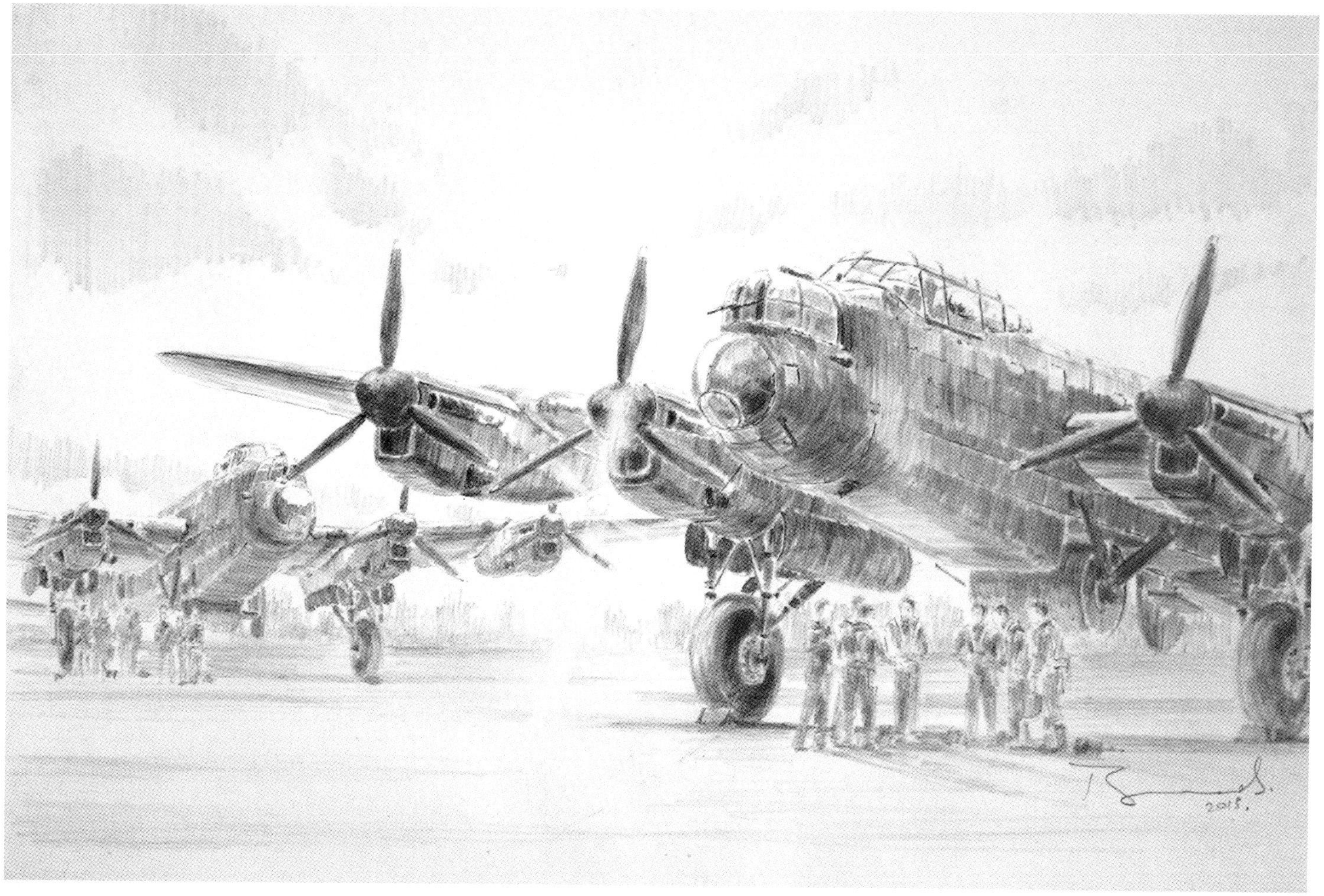

Gradually, as the clock crept towards 20.00 hours, the crews began to converge in small groups within the squadron hangar to collect their parachutes and other equipment. The 90 minutes before take-off was a tense time on any station, but the long prelude to this operation made it tougher than usual. Gibson, however, arrived with his entire crew packed into his car, exuding an air of complete confidence. One of them recalled that he seemed 'quite unperturbed,' a comment that Gibson later confided 'was a complete lie'. But, there again, the squadron commander managed to conceal his feelings better than most.

Outside the hangar some now lounged on the grass in the evening sun, while others sat in deckchairs, waiting. Then came the order to move: equipment was piled into buses, trucks and staff cars before the men clambered aboard to be driven to dispersal points scattered around the airfield. Here, waiting silently for them with cockpits pointed up towards the darkening sky, were the majestic Lancasters that would take them to the targets.

It was now that most of the crews saw *Upkeep* for the first time. Their surprise at the massive cylindrical object suspended from the modified bomb bay vindicated the obsession with security. This was also a time when many carried out little rituals for good luck. Pilot Officer Ivan Whittaker, for instance, the Flight Engineer aboard Lancaster *AJ-P*, watered the tail wheel of his aircraft as if it were a large pot plant, whilst the pilot, Flight Lieutenant 'Mick' Martin, wasn't immune from superstitious practices either as he quietly tucked a 'lucky' toy koala into his jacket pocket.

For this painting it was Gibson and his crew that I wanted to depict, assembling for one final briefing before

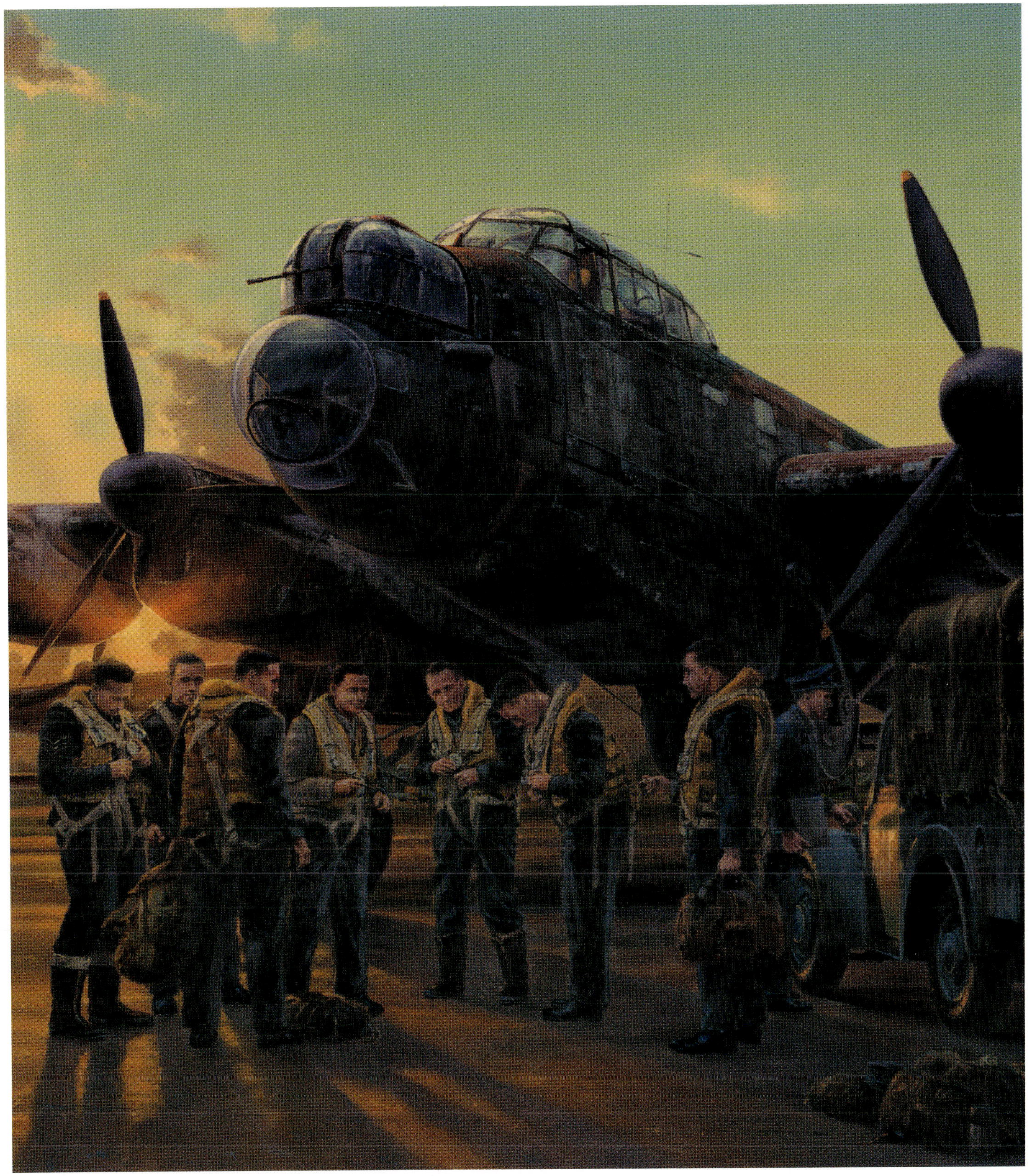

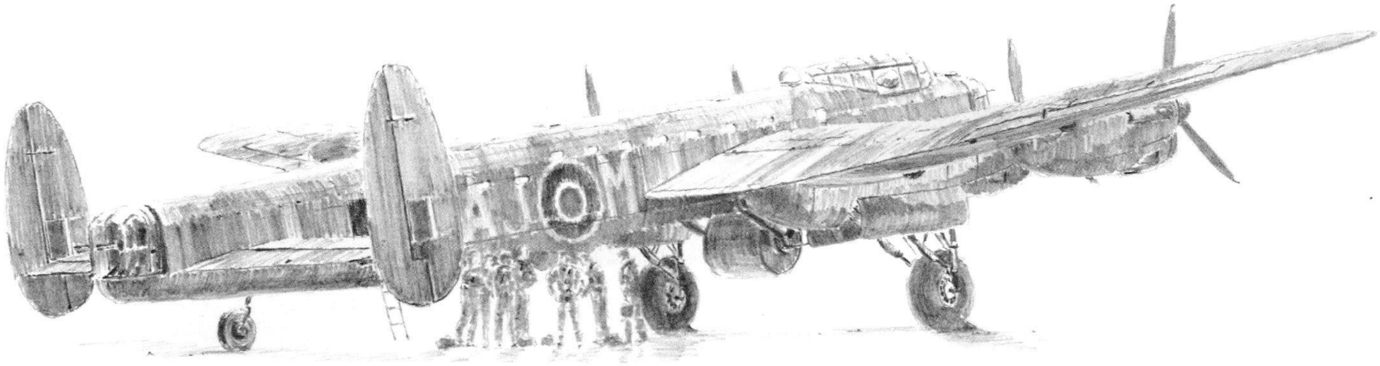

they board their Lancaster, *AJ-G* 'George'. Gibson holds his unlit pipe with which to gesture but, for others, this is a last opportunity to light up a cigarette. There won't be another until they get back – if they survive. Behind them the maintenance NCO, with the service log that Gibson has just signed off tucked under his arm, discusses something with the driver of the waiting staff car.

I had to spend quite a lot of time working out subtle ways with which to lead the viewer's eye into the centre of the picture, where Gibson stands. One of which was to use the shape of the clouds and the direction of the crews' shadows, and even the position and angle of that staff car was planned with this in mind.

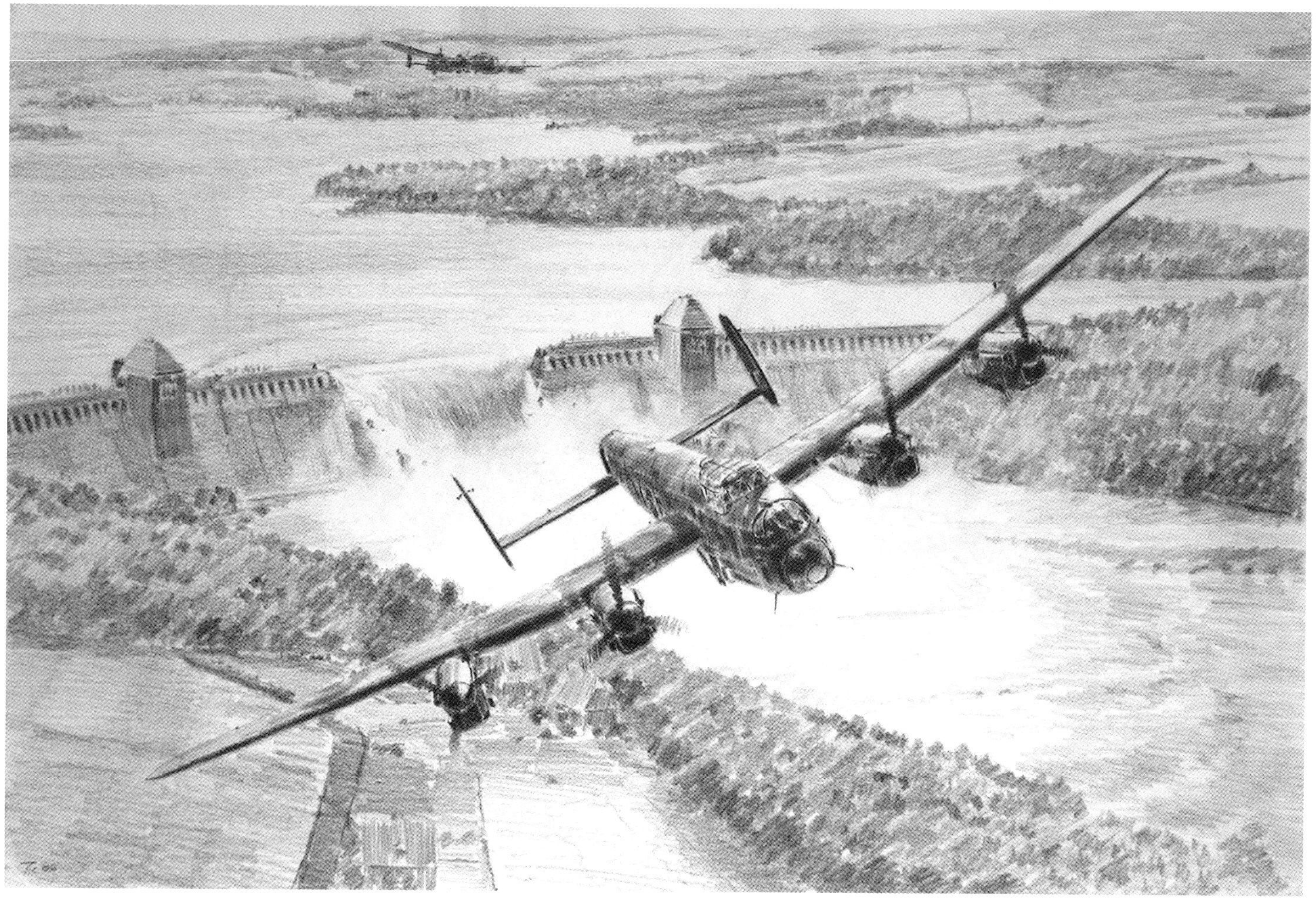

I found one of the trickiest things with painting *Final Briefing* was getting an accurate likeness of Guy Gibson. Most people with an interest in the Dambusters would easily recognise him so it was essential that I made his face as true to life as possible, which wasn't that easy considering the size of his face on the canvas only covered an area no bigger than that of the end of my index finger. The faces of the rest of Gibson's crew are not quite as well-known so I didn't have to be quite so meticulous with them although, fortunately, they were all captured by the RAF's official photographer at Scampton just as they boarded their Lancaster, so I had a good idea of what they all looked like, even down to their choice of footwear. They were certainly a lot less time-consuming to paint than their commander!

In the painting, from left to right, the seven crew members of *AJ-G* are: Sergeant John Pulford, flight engineer; Flight Sergeant George Deering, front gunner; Pilot Officer Fred Spafford, bomb aimer; Gibson; Flight Lieutenant Dick Trevor-Roper, rear gunner; Flight Lieutenant Bob Hutchinson, wireless operator, and finally, Pilot Officer Torger Taerum, navigator.

It's sobering to think that despite all their bravery and professionalism not one of these men would live to see the end of the war.

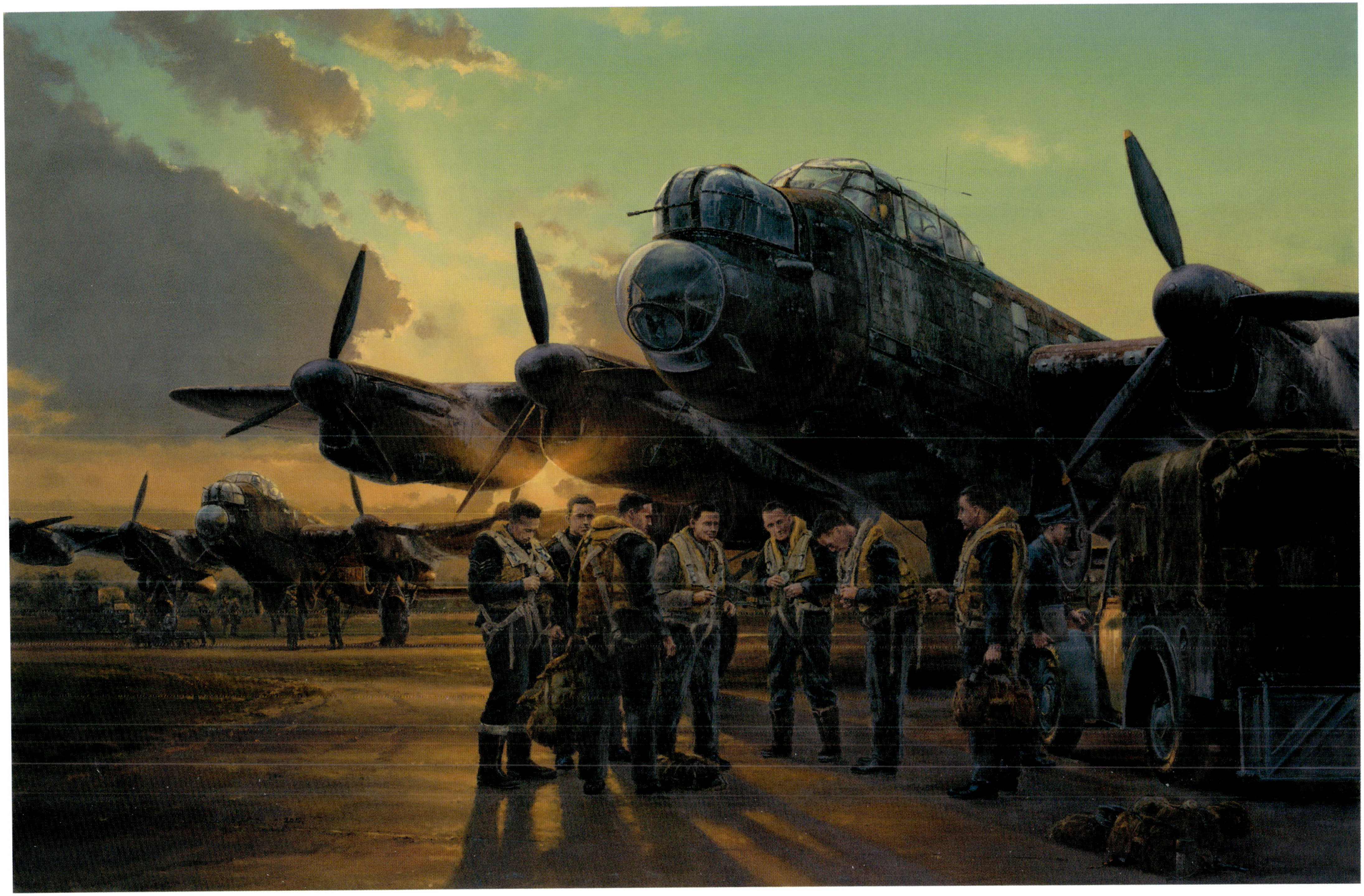

FINAL BRIEFING IN THE COLLECTION OF MR JULIAN PARKER

ACKNOWLEDGEMENTS

Firstly, I must thank my wife Bernadette who has always supported and encouraged me, especially after I made the great leap to leave my engineering profession and become a full time artist, and my two children, Amelia and James, who are always eager and happy to help me whenever I need it.

I was thrilled and honoured that Dambuster 'Johnny' Johnson agreed to write the Foreword and I would also like to thank all the other veterans that I have been lucky enough to meet over the years, and who have helped me immensely – particularly with some of the paintings in this book. They are, without doubt, the greatest generation and I always value and cherish their company.

I gratefully acknowledge the support of Colin Hudson and Rick Taylor, the Directors of my publishers the Military Gallery, in particular for their commitment to publish this, my first book. They have given me the rare opportunity of having so many of my paintings published as limited editions, for which I am exceedingly grateful.

A big thank you to Mike Craig for his expertise in writing this book and making sense of all my ramblings. Mike has been part of the Military Gallery for almost thirty years and his experience has been invaluable.

The sheer amount of work that is involved in creating a book like this is astonishing and I am indebted to the commitment of the whole publishing team, but a special thank you must go to Ingrid Freeman whose expertise in designing this book has been exceptional.

As an artist, spending hours alone in a studio comes with the territory but without great back up and support few people would ever see my work. So I must take this opportunity to thank the Military Gallery team, in particular Rod Tepesano and Mike Kentosh in the USA office and Penny Stratton and Craig Smith in the UK, for their tremendous support. Likewise John Foley does an outstanding job overseeing the reproduction of my paintings as prints and Mark Copeland has been a great help with research on a number of projects.

The worldwide dealership network of the Military Gallery is extensive and this section would not be complete without thanking all those who promote and distribute my limited editions. It is impossible to mention everyone individually but my particular thanks go to Bill Ward in Texas who has been an enthusiastic and passionate supporter along with Virginia Bader, Stuart at Brooks Aviation Art, Ross at Aviation Art Hangar, Carolyn at Sierra Aviation Art, and Bob at Alamo in the USA along with Mike Johnson of Wings Fine Art and John Skobeig at Johnies GB in Canada. In the UK I have had great support from a number of Aviation Art specialists including CCB, Oliver's Art, Summer Reflections and Gallery 18 along with Peter Dupre in Germany. Plus of course the wonderful staff at Aces High in the USA, UK and France who have staged numerous Gallery events showcasing my work and who extensively advertise my editions around the world.

Finally, over the years I have been lucky enough to meet many enthusiasts who have supported me by collecting my work – to you all I am extremely grateful. My career would not have had any kind of success without the patronage of those who purchase my original paintings, in particular Alain Mardle, Paul Shipp, Martin Horsfield and Julian Parker. It is also very satisfying to know that my work is considered of a high enough standard to be included the collections of Sir Peter Jackson, Bill Ward, and Eugene Eisenberg.

A big thank you to you all.

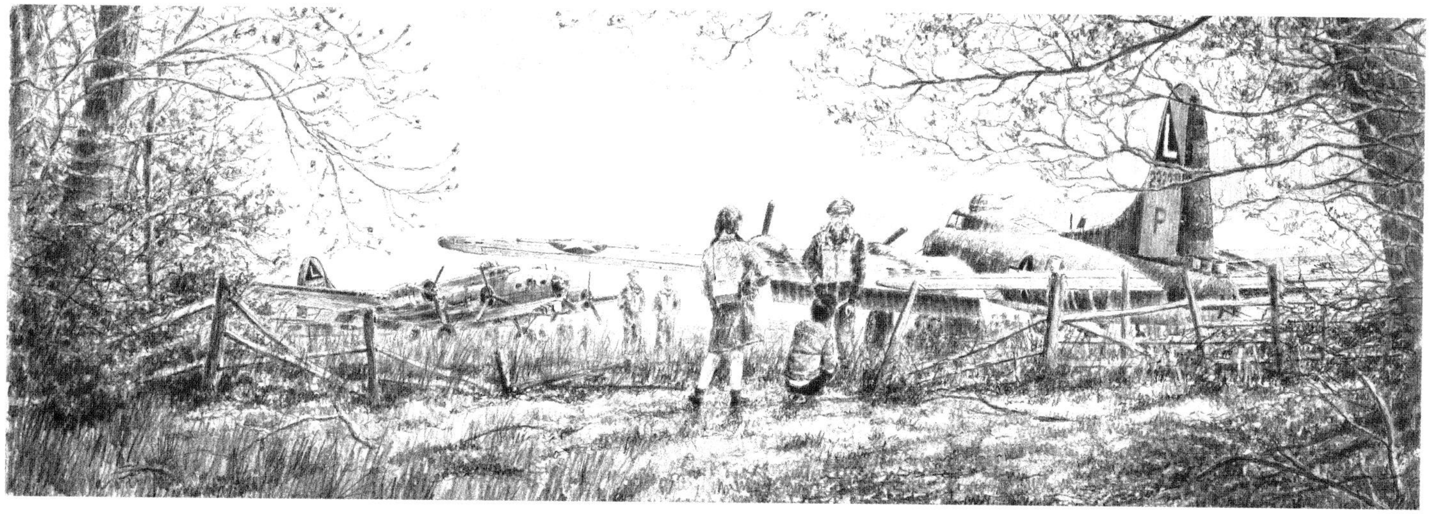

CREATED BY THE MILITARY GALLERY

With special thanks to our production team:

Written by Michael Craig
Production Manager: Craig Smith
Typesetting and Design: Ingrid Freeman
Coordinators: Penny Stratton & Rod Tepesano

Published by Griffon International Ltd

Printed in China

Many of the images featured in this book have been reproduced as limited edition prints by the Military Gallery.

www.militarygallery.com